Bluebeard

Blue Beard: Adorned with Cuts. London: Printed for N. Hailes, Juvenile Library 1817. Courtesy of The Lilly Library, Indiana University, Bloomington.

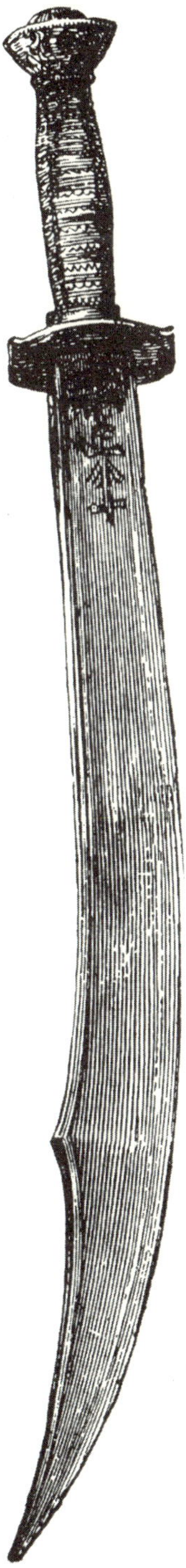

BLUEBEARD

A Reader's Guide to the English Tradition

Casie E. Hermansson

UNIVERSITY PRESS OF MISSISSIPPI
JACKSON

www.upress.state.ms.us

Designed by Peter D. Halverson

The University Press of Mississippi is a member of the Association of American University Presses.

Manufactured in the United States of America

First printing 2009
∞
Library of Congress Cataloging-in-Publication Data

Hermansson, Casie.
Bluebeard : a reader's guide to the English tradition / Casie E. Hermansson.
p. cm.
Includes bibliographical references and index.
ISBN 978-1-60473-230-6 (cloth : alk. paper) — ISBN 978-1-60473-231-3 (pbk. : alk. paper) 1. Bluebeard (Legendary character) in literature. 2. English literature—History and criticism. 3. American literature—History and criticism. 4. Fairy tales—History and criticism. 5. Fairy tales in literature. 6. Perrault, Charles, 1628–1703. Barbe-bleue. 7. Perrault, Charles, 1628–1703—Adaptations. 8. Perrault, Charles, 1628–1703—Translations into English—History and criticism. I. Title.
PR153.B58H47 2009
820'.9351—dc22 2008049949

British Library Cataloging-in-Publication Data available

To Gil

Contents

Preface
Three Hundred Years of "Bluebeard" in English ix

Acknowledgments xxi

PART 1. VARIANTS AND VARIATIONS
1. Principal Variants 3
2. Pirates and True Bluebeards 21

PART 2. BLUEBEARD IN THE ENGLISH EIGHTEENTH CENTURY
3. Found in Translation
Charles Perrault's "Bluebeard" in English 37
4. A "Three Tail'd Bashaw"
Bluebeard Takes a Turkish Turn 51

PART 3. BLUEBEARD IN THE ENGLISH NINETEENTH CENTURY
5. Cheap Thrills
Bluebeard in Chapbooks and Juveniles 69
6. "You Outrageous Man!"
Bluebeard on the Comic Stage 89
7. Bluebeard in Victorian Arts and Letters 108

PART 4. BLUEBEARD IN THE ENGLISH TWENTIETH CENTURY
8. Bluebeard in Crisis 129
9. Modernist Bluebeard 144
10. Contemporary Bluebeard 159

Epilogue
Bluebeard Today 177

Notes 179

Bibliographies
Bluebeard Variants 223
Bluebeard Chapbooks and Juveniles 228
Primary Sources 233
Bluebeard Filmography 250
Secondary Sources 251

Index 276

Preface

Three Hundred Years of "Bluebeard" in English

This gallimaufry of stuff insists that traditional forms and ideas arise, thrive, and fall away over time, taking shape in the tangible, traceable materials, circumstances, and ideologies of history. –DIANNE DUGAW (1995, 10)

Looking for Bluebeard in the contemporary landscape produces a riot of examples that appear to have very little in common. Peering through the colorful fog of blue-bearded lilies and dog breeds, he is revealed as a glorious pirate. He is in fact the first pirate to spring to the mind of Bart Simpson when Bart tries to fake a homework report on Treasure Island ("Bart Gets an F," October 11, 1990). But the story told of the numerous pirates and their paraphernalia is as disingenuous as Bart's homework report. Bluebeard has only recently become a pirate and only through the force of popular contemporary belief in his existence. Elsewhere, he appears in his older form as a blue-bearded murderer of many wives. Here, he is the stereotypical Turkish tyrant: beturbaned, wielding a scimitar, about to strike off Fatima's head for her disobedience. The art deco razor stroppers that illustrate Bluebeard cutting his beard with his own scimitar suggest the widespread phenomenon of Bluebeard of Baghdad (or Constantinople). Although this story is closer to Bluebeard's fairy tale origins, he has only become Turkish since an enormously popular English melodrama of 1798, *Blue Beard; or, Female Curiosity!* made him so.

Outside the English tradition, Bluebeard is neither a pirate nor a Turk. Instead, he derives from the French fairy tale of Charles Perrault, one of the *Mother Goose* set first published in 1697, who married several wives, telling each not to venture into a certain forbidden room, supplying each with the keys and the time to transgress, and beheading each in turn when they did so. The last wife is rescued in the nick of time by her military brothers, hastened by her sister Anne signaling them from the tower. This Bluebeard is also present in the contemporary landscape, as in the episode of the HBO television series *Six Feet Under* in "Terror Starts at Home" (Kate 2004). Ruth has married George, a man she knows little about, who has a past. When she confronts him about it, he is enraged and says he left his previous wives because they asked too many questions. The next episode begins with Ruth dusting his fossil collection, only to have them turn into six women's heads in jars, and they tell her she is being too snoopy. When she asks these women—his previous six wives—to tell her about George, they only laugh until they begin to cry. This version of Bluebeard romps through New York in the pages of the Vertigo comic book series *Fables*, the dangerous arch enemy of Prince Charming. He is sung about in three songs titled "Bluebeard," by Troubadours of Divine Bliss, Gravenhurst, and the Cocteau Twins, and he cuts off women's heads in shadow play in Jane Campion's celebrated film *The Piano* (1993). Although this Bluebeard is pervasive in popular culture, most Anglophones are not on a first-name basis with him as they once were.[1] Indeed, Charles Dickens' prophecy for Bluebeard has come true: "With seven Blue Beards in the field, each coming at a gallop from his own platform mounted on a foaming hobby, a generation or two hence would not know which was which, and the great original Blue Beard would be confounded with the counterfeits" (1853, 58).

In the eighteenth and early nineteenth centuries, Bluebeard was a staple story in juvenile reading materials in England and the colonies, whether in chapbook form alone or in expensive colored editions of fairy tales. In either case, the forbidden chamber was depicted in word and image, bathed in blood. He terrified generations of children from James Boswell to Charles Dickens. Passing references to Bluebeard can be found in the writings of numerous authors, such as this by Thomas Carlyle: "A dark tragedy of Sophie's this; the Blue-beard chamber of her mind, into which no eye but her own must ever look" (Wheeler 1866, 49); or this by Herman Melville in the poem *Clarel*: "She comes, the bride; but ah, how pale: / Her groom that Blue-Beard, cruel Death, / Wedding his millionth maid to-day; / She, stretched on that Armenian bier, / Leaves home and each familiar way— / Quits all for him" (1876, 130). In these allusions the symbolic function of Bluebeard is presupposed; he is widely known as an emblem for the dangerous husband, the unknown secrets of the spouse, the retribution for transgressive female curiosity. The name and the story continue to be used by famous writers as well as lesser-known artists to the present day, but even as "Bluebeard" has become a relative stranger and an exile from the nursery (unless prefaced with a "warning" label, such as in *The Headless Horseman and other Ghoulish Tales*[2]), the intertextual use of the story has become ever more complex and self-conscious. The accretions of three centuries come into play at the mention of Bluebeard's name.

At the same time, the Bluebeard story did not spring fully-formed from the head of Charles Perrault. Instead, the fairy tale is one expression of enduring archetypes: the marriage to death, the animal groom, fatal curiosity. Within the folk and fairy tale realm, there are global variants of these archetypes in cultures around the world. Close European cousins to Bluebeard are plentiful, including the English folktale "Mr. Fox," which was referenced by Edmund Spenser in Book III of *The Faerie Queene* (1590) a full century before Perrault published his *Contes*. In Shakespeare's play *Much Ado About Nothing* (1600) it is already called "the old story."

Despite the arrival and success of the Grimm versions in English ("Fitcher's Bird" and "The Robber Bridegroom," both kindred to "Mr. Fox") in the mid-nineteenth century, the French version—with oriental twists—is the one that continued to dominate late Victorian culture. Only relatively recently have the Grimm versions come into their own and, with the necessary exceptions such as Eudora Welty's 1942 novella *The Robber Bridegroom*, works like the two *Fitcher's Bird* (one a book of Cindy Sherman's photographs, the other a novel by Gregory Frost) or *The Robber Bride* (novel by Margaret Atwood), have only lately contributed to the popular conception of the story.

This book attempts to trace with some thoroughness the story of the Bluebeard fairy tale in the English tradition of arts and letters from those early named allusions to "Mr. Fox" to the present. I have aimed to capture some of the comprehensive nature of a survey, while focusing particular attention on seminal influential works (such as George Colman and Michael Kelly's 1798 melodrama, or Béla Bartók's 1912 opera) and trends (such as the cross-dressed comedies of the nineteenth-century stage). My focus is on English expressions, which must frequently take into account influential European works. For all that Bluebeard was a French fairy tale, and likely because of it, the untold history of Bluebeard in the English tradition is one of wresting ownership of it. By referring to Henry VIII as or "our old Harry Bluebeard," the English claim a precursor figure with evident fondness.

Finally, I have a fascination for the "gallimaufry of stuff" that Bluebeard has strewn through history. No doubt a study of any such enduringly popular fairy tale would occasion a similar list, but filtering three hundred years through the lens of Bluebeard reveals some interesting "stuff." The child riding the elephant as Abomelique (Bluebeard) in the first production of the Colman and Kelly spectacle (1798) is the future-famous actor Edmund Kean (Kelly 1826, 2:130). Charlotte Cushman, the androgynous Romeo of the Victorian stage, played

Selim (the male rival) as a child in her mother's attic "theater." All the costumes for *Bluebeard* (and the animals) burned in the fire that ended the New York Hippotheatron, Christmas Eve, 1872.[3] The Grand Opera House and Cirque (Belfast) opened to *Bluebeard* in 1895. Eddie Foy was playing Sister Anne in the 1903 pantomime *Mr. Bluebeard* when the newly opened Iroquois Theatre in Chicago burned, killing more than six hundred people at a matinee performance. Beatrix Potter's grim 1932 novella *Sister Anne* was the last publication in her lifetime, and Boris Karloff had been cast to play Bluebeard in the film *Bluebeard* that John Carradine made famous in 1944. The New York Ballet Theatre opened its first international engagement at Covent Garden in 1946 with four arrangements, including *Bluebeard*.[4] Such footnotes to history have been indulgently recorded here as well.

INTERPRETING BLUEBEARD

As should by now be clear: no single or global interpretation of the fairy tale exists, and none is offered here. Nevertheless, attempts to explain and interpret the tale have been made. Over the past three hundred years, folklore scholars and artists using the Bluebeard story alike have made statements about the meaning and importance of the fairy tale and have tried to account for its endurance. At the same time, the *Mother Goose* and Grimms' tales have remained in print, and every new edition and translation offers its own interpretation or bias. While the tale can be read through the perspectives of curiosity, taboo, secret spaces, the gothic and representation of women (dead or alive) and of spectatorship, the dominant strains of criticism on the tale briefly surveyed here derive from historical anthropology, universal folklore classification, psychology, feminism, and postmodernism.

Historical Anthropology

Criticism of this type insists that "folktales are historical documents" (Darnton 1984, 13), and as such represent national and historical specifics reflecting authorship and society of origin. French criticism of "Bluebeard" dominates the field, although it is often in comparison to other European variants. Here, a number of scholars focus specifically on the relative social stations of Bluebeard and his wife, his "blue beard" as either a marker of nobility or the desire to attain it through marriage, and on the caked (sullied) blood on the floor of the bloody chamber as a commentary on the blood purity of the nobility. In such readings, "Bluebeard" is a fable of the French *ancien régime* (see Apostolidès 1991; Cashdan 1999; Hannon 2001; Lewis 1987). Barchilon and Flinders (1981) and Zipes (2001) discussed Charles Perrault's biography in detail to interpret the tale as the product of a lawyer, engaged in a debate over the Ancient and the Moderns with Nicholas Boileau; "Bluebeard" thereby contains a number of specific ripostes. Marina Warner (1989) also returned to seventeenth-century France but to argue for Perrault's parable of "the right of women to administer their own wealth" and of the story's allusion to the dangers to women of death in childbirth (Bluebeard has had a number of wives, but remains childless).

In French scholarship the search for borrowed sources features large. As proposed historical precursors, Comôr the Accursed and Gilles de Rais were both French, and almost all French nationalist criticism of the tale discusses them (see in particular Van Raamsdonk 1976; Odio 1986). Elsewhere, Jean-Louis Pichérit (1988) studied a little-known French term *barbeu* to designate werewolf (*loup-garou*). He thus attributed the beard of Bluebeard, his one sign of terrifying abnormality, to an association with this man-beast, and dated it "well before Charles Perrault" (377, my translation). Further in the search for origins, Catherine Velay-Vallantin focused on French regional variants of the "Bluebeard cycle" (1992, 68), be they folklore variants, ballads (*Renaud, le Tueur de femmes*), or local legends of Triphine (from the Comôr story) or Gilles de Rais. Earlier, Paul Delarue (1952) also analyzed French regional variants to determine that a particularly French subcategory of AT 312 exists, which he termed 312B: a Christianized variant.

Robert Darnton commented on European national variants of the tale: "Although each story adheres to the same structure, the versions in the different traditions produce entirely different effects—comic in the Italian versions, horrific in the German, dramatic in the French, and droll in the English" (1984, 46).[5] Fabienne Raphoz concurred with him that the French variants of Bluebeard, compared to those of other European nationalities, are less horrific (1995, 46–47).

German scholars of the Bluebeard tale and variants must contend with the legacy of Perrault, which loomed large in the successive editions of the Grimm brothers' tales. One scholar went so far as to argue that all German *Märchen* were in fact modeled on French salon precursors: "evidence of such *Volksmärchen* in Germany before the eighteenth century is meagre."[6] With regard to the Bluebeard tale, another German scholar "interpreted all versions of Bluebeard to be emanations from Perrault."[7] Grimm scholars also point out that while "Blaubart" was deliberately omitted from the second and subsequent editions of the *Kinder- und Hausmärchen* as a French derivative, in fact the

Grimms' contributors were Huguenot French and the "German-ness" of the tales was constructed after the fact, in large part through the deliberate efforts of the Grimms themselves.

In a full-length study of the Bluebeard story in the German tradition, Meredid Puw Davies studied the "cultural ambivalence" toward the Bluebeard story that dates to the Grimms. She argued (with support from German and Grimm scholarship[8]) that the tale "breaches a series of specifically German *Märchen* taboos as codified in the *Kinder- und Hausmärchen*" (2001, 59): first, acquisition of knowledge by a female character; second, "taboo on the acquisition of riches by a woman"; and third, breaking a *Kinder- und Hausmärchen* taboo on "depicting irrational, human, male evil" (66–67). She noted that the German literary versions that have followed "blunt the tale's pro-feminist or subversive potential in one of three ways": they reinterpret the moral as a warning against female curiosity, transpose the tale into a distant context, especially the Middle Ages, and/or they exculpate Bluebeard explicitly (69–70). Her own conclusions make the civilizing process a major theme.

English studies of the Bluebeard tale as a national phenomenon are essentially nonexistent. However, Juliet McMaster (1976) noted the existence of an English tradition, citing Henry Tudor and George Smith as English examples of historical Bluebeards, the English variant "Mr. Fox" and its presence in Spenser and Shakespeare, and then focused on the Romantic and Victorian examples, referring to them as "explorations of the Fatima-Bluebeard syndrome" (17). In *Secrets Beyond the Door: The Story of Bluebeard and His Wives*, Maria Tatar (2004) broadened the scope of her earlier discussions of "Bluebeard" (1987, 1988, 1992), which largely focused on the historical prejudice against female curiosity demonstrated by it. In *Secrets* she revisited the tale, asking specifically why it has been so enduring a phenomenon in Western culture.

Universal Folklore Classifications

Scholars focusing on international variants with common motifs collect the forbidden chamber examples together (see Hartland 1885; Yearsley 1924). *The Types of the Folktale* by Anthi Aarne and Stith Thompson (1961), as well as Vladimir Propp's folktale morphology (1958) in which he identified thirty-one common functions in folklore, are useful categorization tools and continue to be widely used. For instance, Fabienne Raphoz (1995) collected in one place several regional French variants of "Bluebeard" in addition to other major international variants. With fifty or so variants in place, the second part of the work analyzes these while relying heavily on Propp's formulations and on the anthropological reading of initiation rites that result (107). However, Allison Tuthill's study "Forbidden Curiosity: Episodic Repetition in 'Bluebeard' Tales from France, Germany, and the West Indies" (1999) critically examined the prevailing classification systems (Aarne's types classification, Thomson's motif index, and Propp's morphology) and their limitations, especially their Euro-centrism. She examined the Bluebeard tales of the French Antilles (Guadeloupe, Martinique) and demonstrated how they do not "fit" the models (and are therefore marginalized by it, frequently as "fragments"). Tuthill also redefined the essential element of the tale as "forbidden curiosity," a paired motif, to broaden the variant set.

For many scholars, the story represents an initiation, with a central problem of overcoming Death.[9] P. Saintyves' 1923 study built on the anthropological school of folktale readings and argued that: "the various incidents of the tale, in its various variants, correspond to various aspects of the ritual temptation of the initiate" (393, my translation). He was also concerned to discredit the "solar theory" reading, whereby the sun kills the dawn each morning, arguing that in no folkloric examples where the sun has keys are they ever given away or made to form part of a temptation ritual or test (363).[10] After surveying three tales (the "Story of the Third Calendar" of the *Thousand and One Nights*, "Maria Morévna," and "Marienkind") Saintyves concluded: "The forbidden chamber, or its equivalent . . . is always connected with a sort of formation and serves precisely to test the hero or heroine" (374, my translation).[11] He went on to show evidence that in many cases, women are excluded from male huts of initiation, in many initiation rituals there is a test, magical obstacles are frequently described, and in many, the simulation of death and resurrection form an integral part.[12]

Psychological Archetypes

In Freudian analyses of the Bluebeard tale, the focus is on sexuality. The key is phallic, while the lock into which it is inserted and the forbidden chamber are both vaginal. Kay Stone's feminist reading stated the lesson: "There are many symbolic hints that women should not become too familiar with their own bodies. Bluebeard's wives are murdered for looking into forbidden rooms" (1975, 47). Freudian readings of "Bluebeard" frequently draw on the biblical story of Eve to indicate that transgressive knowledge has sexual connotations, played out explicitly in God's punishment of Adam and Eve: shame of nakedness, pain in childbirth.

In *The Uses of Enchantment* (1976), Bruno Bettelheim offered the well-known Freudian reading of the tale in which sexual infidelity is Bluebeard's wife's transgression: "The nature of the betrayal may be guessed by the punishment: execution. In certain parts of the world in times past, only one form of deception on the female's part was punishable by death inflicted by her husband: sexual infidelity" (300). The cautionary tale is therefore: "Women, don't give in to your sexual curiosity; men, don't permit yourself to be carried away by your anger at being sexually betrayed" (302). Bettelheim's reading has been criticized on several grounds. First, by ignoring the gender of the reader, his interpretation essentially conflicts with his arguments about the acculturation of children through a fairy tale education. Second, the blood on the key would indicate that Bluebeard's wife was a virgin when she transgressed ("defloration is an irreversible event," 301). Third, Bettelheim must misread Perrault's French in order to insist on mixed company at Bluebeard's house (the site of her adultery) when only feminine company is present.

Still, the concept of female infidelity in the Bluebeard tale existed long before Bettelheim. Ludwig Tieck's play (1797) associates the transgression with sexuality (Davies 1997, 122 n.). It was a staple of the stage, particularly after the English tradition supplied a preexisting rival to Bluebeard, Selim, from whom his wife was unwillingly parted to marry Bluebeard himself. A popular song from 1932 made the connection explicit, as eight of the eleven wives were caught by Bluebeard having an affair: "Wife ten was a flighty Spanish Do nah, / Bluebeard came home one fine night— / Found here with a 'Knut' from Barcelona! / Chop! Chop! Chop! And her head came off! / That left nine" (Ewing 1932).[13]

Freudian concepts such as the uncanny (*das unheimlich*), the return of the repressed, repetition compulsion, penis envy, and castration have been applied to the tale. Winfried Kudszus analyzed repetition compulsion as a feature of the tale's own enduring repetition (1990, 117), an approach more thoroughly and recently taken by Shuli Barzilai (2009).[14]

In Jungian analysis the conflict between Bluebeard and his wife is between two warring aspects of the psyche, reconciliation of which is necessary to individuation. Verena Kast argued in "Bluebeard: On the Problem of the Destructive Animus" that the pattern is identifiably sadomasochistic and operates on both the personal and societal levels: "an enthrallment with the animus is constellated that murders the feminine principle in oneself" (1978, 94). In the more recent article "'Fitcher's Bird': Illustrations of the Negative Animus and Shadow in Persons with Narcissistic Disturbances" (1991), Kathrin Asper applied Jungian frameworks to the Grimm fairy tale to illustrate the struggle of the anima to "depotentiate" the "chopping" negative animus. The negative animus problem (and the corresponding negative shadow problem in men) is a form of narcissistic disturbance acquired through childhood development and exacerbated as a condition of living in a patriarchally biased collective consciousness that mirrors the animus rather than the anima. The anima does not possess self-identity strong enough to contain the dominant negative animus, which manifests as a destructive self-fragmenting nihilism. As read through "Fitcher's Bird," the animus is the wizard while the three sisters symbolize a series of attempts to overcome him. The egg is the true identity, the blood the sign of the inability of the first two sisters to delimit their inner self from the negative animus. The third sister has developed the ego strength required to delimit her true self; she acquires autonomy over the animus within her own psyche. Setting the skull in the window and transforming herself into a bird, Asper read as showing the negative animus what he finds alluring (Death); the sister makes her shadow manifest in order to delimit his power. She has overcome the enemy to her individuation.[15]

Philip Lewis offered a Lacanian/Irigarayan reading of "Bluebeard," focusing on the doubling in the narrative: the similarities between frame and embedded narratives, the role reversals of Bluebeard and his wife. Similarly, a mirror double is the blood creating a speculum.[16] Lewis compared the traditional mirrors in the tale with the vital blood mirror. The key offered to the wife is double: both the sign of her lack and as such the sign of Bluebeard's masculine difference, one based on "a superiority that depends on knowledge from which others are expressly excluded" (1996, 221). Her blood symbolically claims the key for her female sex (even as she is unable to keep hold of it), and what she reflects to Bluebeard now is her knowledge; she has erased the difference between them. Her refusal to recognize identity constituted for her by Bluebeard triggers crisis, one borne of "recognition of an alarming resemblance" (223). The two-sided key simultaneously reveals parallel crimes (murder; discovery of murder), further conflating the difference in their identities into sameness. To return the wife to the state that marks her difference from him (that of not knowing), Bluebeard must quickly kill her. His "repetition compulsion" manifests the death instinct.

In an article studying two German texts using the Bluebeard story, Meredid Puw Davies commented that in Lacanian terms the compulsion repetition is inherent in narrative: "the act of narrative itself is a compulsive repetition of the traumatic fantasy of the fragmented body which represents and repeats the painful separation of the Symbolic and the Imaginary" (1997, 127). Thus, the double repetition (within the tale and of the tale) is both a thematic and formal (generic) repetition: "the 'Bluebeard' tale itself and its use in these texts, in its generically ordained repetition of patriarchal prohibition, transgression, punishment and compulsive, serial dismemberment fantasies, makes manifest the latent content of all narrative. Bluebeard's repressed and bloody chamber becomes a metaphor for writing itself" (127).

Feminist and Postmodern Approaches

As the quotation above implies, a number of studies look at the Bluebeard story as not just an apt expression of several themes but as self-reflexive "meta-tale." Its particular doubled structure and Bluebeard's embedded serial murders indicates a generic predisposition to narrative self-reflexivity even within the tale, suggesting another possible reason for its popularity as an intertextual mirror.[17] In almost all cases, this generic and postmodern ability of the Bluebeard tale has been adopted into scholarship and criticism with a feminist focus. Cheryl Walker examined "why women have relished the telling of this barbed and grisly story" (1996, 13). Walker concluded that the room represents different things: for the wife, it is History: "the history of violence against women and the complicity of culture" with it; for Bluebeard it is Psyche: "a creative potential locked in a dark cocoon," so that for the woman writer "the predator is there and knowledge of that self that we have tried to avoid." The "scene of writing" then is "a chamber littered with corpses" (23).

In *Reading Feminist Intertextuality through Bluebeard Stories* (Hermansson 2001), I also argued for the tale's inherent metatextual status. The tale illustrates intertextual processes of two kinds: Bluebeard's (monologic repetition) and his wife's (dialogic engagement). The tale illustrates monologic intertextuality and the wife's escape artistry at the end (often featuring a tale-telling component in variants of the tale) offers both a dialogic alternative and simultaneous criticism of Bluebeard's closed and foregone reiterations. This reading offered a way of examining all later works using the Bluebeard intertext as privileging either the monologic or dialogic variety of intertextual relationship and of thereby distinguishing a form of feminist intertextual engagement that privileged the latter.

Looking specifically at the roles of the helper figure, Rose Lovell-Smith in "Anti-Housewives and Ogres' Housekeepers: The Roles of Bluebeard's Female Helper" (2002) built on earlier work by Daniela Hempen (1977) on the neglected female helper in the "Bluebeard" stories (Sister Anne in Perrault, the old woman in Grimms' "The Murder Castle" and "The Robber Bridegroom"). She also studied the "alternative tradition" of revisions by women writers: "Within English-language traditions, oral and literary, in the past two centuries, women have re-told 'Bluebeard' in ways that run counter to the contemporary scholarly moralistic silencing of the uneasiness generated by this tale type" (199).

She agreed with Hempen that the character exhibits inherent ambiguity and instability, giving rise to the diversity of representations in story retellings. She determined that in most cases, "they are more properly defined as the heroine's helpers than Bluebeard's" (199).

In "The Evolution of Bluebeard," Patricia Burris applied a recent disability studies approach to the Bluebeard story and three rewritings by women. With changes in women's status in Western society a successful choice of life partner now involves different criteria: "The 'modern' Bluebeard tale suggests empowerment for the disabled male character and the woman who chooses him" (2003, 2).

Finally, in a more global feminist reading, Emily Ruth Moore (2002) discussed women's use of the Bluebeard tale to demystify patriarchy's powerful encoding. Outlining several useful contexts in addition to the Bluebeard tale itself—domestic violence and corporal punishment of wives, female orality, biographical conditions of select women writers—Moore argued that women writers use focalization (visual and cognitive) as a way to privilege a voice that is traditionally silenced in the story, that of the wife. Moore contended that reader response is essential to this strategy, as focalizations converge in the reader.

The criticism surveyed above sketches the major themes of analysis. However, it is assumed that all "Bluebeard" works discussed in this book, whether film, visual art, music, literature, or popular culture artifacts, also offer their implicit comment on the fairy tale through their manner of its use. Just as there is no single tale of origin for all of these works, there is no single, unifying interpretation of what the Bluebeard story means: to the English or anyone else. Rather, that idea is continually evolving, reshaping, and creating new stories from the old. The Bluebeard story is a particularly engaging conversation, begun some time ago and still thriving. I aim to trace from the present perspective the evolutions of a many-headed fairy tale from its manifestations in many genres, high and low, to tell the story of an English preoccupation.

Acknowledgments

Portions of this book have appeared in print and are published here with permission. Some of the material on historical precursors and true crime Bluebeard, *Caleb Williams*, and work by Kurt Vonnegut, Angela Carter, and Margaret Atwood in particular was adapted from my earlier book, *Reading Feminist Intertextuality through Bluebeard Stories* (Edwin Mellen Press, 2001). The section on piracy from chapter 2 was first published as "'Whatever color the beard may be . . .': Bluebeard's Journey from Charles Perrault to Pirate," in *International Journal of the Humanities* 3.7: 35–41, 2005/2006. "Found in Translation: Charles Perrault's 'Blue Beard' in the English Eighteenth Century" appeared in *University of Toronto Quarterly* 76.2: 796–807, 2007. Some of the chapbook research for chapter 5 was presented at the International Conference on the Book, Emerson College, Boston, October 2006.

Pittsburg State University funded my sabbatical leave in Fall 2005 and provided additional support for visits to the British Library (London); the Lilly and Wells Libraries of Indiana University (Bloomington); the Houghton, Lamont, and Widener Libraries of Harvard University (Boston); and the Toronto Public Library (Toronto), in particular the Lillian H. Smith branch. The Eichhorn Fellowship from Pittsburg State University's English Department also funded partial teaching release time for this project, and Eichhorn stipends assisted in funding library costs.

This book would have taken years longer to research and would have suffered greatly if not for the efforts and talents of Lorean Hartness, my research assistant. A great many thanks to you.

The assistance of staff at all libraries was invaluable, but in particular that of Linda and Alexis at Indiana University's Wells Library; Kris McCusker at University of Colorado, Boulder; and Lori McCleod at the Toronto Public Library. Thanks are also due to the Pittsburg State University interlibrary loan department, and Richard Samford in particular, without whom this project would have been literally impossible, and to my colleagues at Pittsburg State

University in French (Dr. Myriam Krepps, for her laborious transcription of the Grétry manuscript libretto) and in Theater (Dr. Cynthia Allan and her assistant Chelsea Smith, who pored through decades of American Stage annals on my behalf). Thanks also to my friends Daniela and Gabriel Leroy in Dourlers, France, who pursued Bluebeard in the bookstores of Paris on my behalf. Thanks to the many people who drew my attention to a Bluebeard reference they found; I am grateful for all of them.

Finally, thanks to Gil, Griffin, and Corin for your support, patience, and humor with blue napkins.

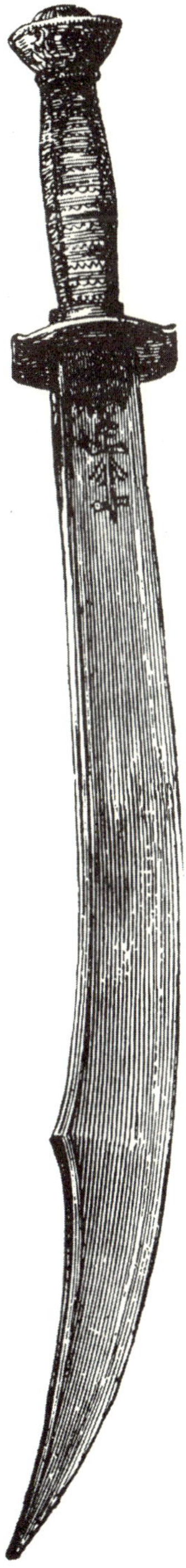

Part 1

Variants and Variations

Chapter 1

Principal Variants

The French fairy tale of Charles Perrault, "La Barbe bleue" ("Bluebeard"), was penned in 1695 and published in 1697. The figure Perrault named, however, had dominated international folklore and myth for centuries before Perrault gave him the particulars of a blue beard and a sumptuous castle with one forbidden room with which to tempt and test his wives. Whether for its ever-popular depiction of female curiosity or for serial wife murder, the story in Perrault's form took prompt and lasting hold over the English imagination.

This fairy tale is one of the grisliest in the canon. But one of the first issues to address is that while there is a French fairy tale named "Bluebeard" by Charles Perrault, translated into English in 1729, the "Bluebeard story" that is referred to throughout this book does not exist. In more necessarily general terms, the Bluebeard fairy tale is a nexus of variants related by themes: curiosity, forbidden chambers, punishment, wife murder. The smallest core of tale variants that have influenced the English tradition consists of Perrault's "La Barbe bleue," Grimms' "Fichters [*sic*] Vogel" ("Fitcher's Bird") and "Der Räuberbräutigam" ("The Robber Bridegroom"), and the main English variant itself (predating Perrault), "Mr. Fox." The next ring out includes primarily other Grimm tales, such as "Marienkind" ("Mary's Child"), in which the Virgin Mary punishes a young girl for disobedience, specifically for looking into a forbidden chamber. Beyond them are hundreds of variants interconnected by shared themes and story elements. Variations between regional French versions of "Bluebeard," for instance, are usually slight, while the details of comparative tales from different nationalities may be greatly different. But, at its most elemental, the fairy tale concerns a prohibition and its transgression. Tales most closely approximating "Bluebeard" feature a secret kept by a male suitor and discovered by his wife or betrothed. The secret is the source of the prohibition, often manifested as a prohibited room. Discovering the secret means death for the woman, and typically the revelation is that the groom has murdered his previous wives or betrotheds. Nonetheless, transgression by the final wife enables her to be saved from such death in time. The useful German term *Blaubartmärchen* groups these related folk and fairy tale variants and ballads, but has no equivalent in English; reference to the generic "Bluebeard tale" or "Bluebeard story" (as opposed to Perrault's "Bluebeard"), presumes a deliberate imprecision.[1]

In categorizing international fairy tales, the Aarne and Thompson classification (1961, 101–04) groups examples by type, assigning each type a number. The principal variants of Bluebeard discussed so far fall into the three groups of variants: AT 311: "The Heroine Rescues Herself and Her Sisters" (for "Fitcher's Bird"), AT 312: "Bluebeard," and AT 955: "The Robber Bridegroom."[2]

Bluebeard

The earliest of the three principal recorded variants, and the only one to use the name "Bluebeard," is Perrault's literary fairy tale "La Barbe bleue" ("Bluebeard," AT 312). If there is such a thing as "the real Bluebeard," this tale is it. The name itself does not appear to have been applied to any real or fictional personage prior to Perrault's version. Perrault's tale appeared quickly in England in chapbook form and was translated in 1729 by Robert Samber.

In Perrault's "Bluebeard," a wealthy nobleman with an unfortunate blue beard courts and marries one of two sisters, who overcomes her trepidation at the beard in order, it seems, to enjoy the wealth. Bluebeard gives her the keys to all the rooms of his extensive castle, but forbids her to use one of them, threatening her with extreme punishment should she disobey him. He leaves, and quickly she opens the forbidden chamber, discovering there the bodies of his murdered former wives. She drops the key in the blood on the floor, and because the blood is magically indelible, it betrays her guilt when Bluebeard suddenly arrives home and asks for it. He says she is to die. The wife asks for time to pray and uses it to call repeatedly to her sister to tell whether she sees their brothers coming.[3] One of the hallmarks of Perrault's tale is the haunting and desperate repetition as the wife hopes to be rescued by her avenging brothers: "Sister Anne, Sister Anne, do you see anyone coming?" The keys, the forbidden chamber, the trespass, and the murdered women are the essential elements of the tale. After Perrault, Bluebeard is firmly a figure of fairy tale, despite the fact that the story really only has a couple of *fée* (fairy, or magical) elements: strictly speaking, only the magic indelible blood on the key, but perhaps also the blue beard.

Helpers such as talking animals or crones who serve as housekeepers and cooks to the murderer are frequent in these tale groups. In Perrault's version,

Sister Anne signals from the turret and the brothers dispatch Bluebeard. With the exception of the ruse to gain time to pray, the heroine is passive in her rescue. Rescue of a sister by her brothers is a common folkloric formula: "Don Firriulieddu" is able to rescue his sister when he is only three days old. In "Mr. Bluebeard," one of the brothers is "an old-witch" like Bluebeard himself, and by seeing water turn to blood he knows something is wrong with his sister. Often, the bride or family members set up a warning system in advance, already uneasy with the bridegroom. The bride is given messenger doves or dogs to send in an emergency.[4]

Fitcher's Bird

The Grimms' *Die Kinder- und Hausmärchen* (first edition 1812–1815, second 1819), selectively translated into English in the early nineteenth century (1823–1826), contributed two more principal variants in addition to "Blaubart", the German version of Charles Perrault's tale.[5] "Bluebeard" was in fact omitted from editions following 1812 for the very reason that it was considered to be Perrault's and not an "authentic" older tale. The two principal variants of the Bluebeard tale group deriving from Grimm are "Fitcher's Bird" ("Fichters [*sic*] Vogel") and "The Robber Bridegroom" ("Der Räuberbräutigam"). The English translations of Grimm in *German Popular Stories* were the first in any country to be fully illustrated (Darton 1932, 216), and by the already-famous English illustrator George Cruikshank. Whereas *German Popular Stories* featured "The Robber Bridegroom," the other major German variant, "Fitcher's Bird," was not published in English until decades later.

In Jacob and Wilhelm Grimm's "Fitcher's Bird,"[6] Bluebeard is a wizard who magically kidnaps two of three sisters in turn, giving each a bunch of keys to his castle and an egg, telling them not to open the locked chamber door and to carry the egg everywhere as great harm would result from its loss. In turn each sister opens the door, dropping the egg into the basin of blood and dismembered body parts she finds there. She is betrayed by the stained egg and murdered. But the youngest (third) sister is "clever" and immediately places the egg out of harm's way. When she opens the door to the chamber and finds her two sisters there, she is able to resurrect them. The wizard, believing that he has found a woman who can master her curiosity (or who has none), announces that she has passed the premarital test. Because she is to be his bride he no longer has power over her, so she is able to command Bluebeard to carry a basket of gold home to her family, hiding her sisters in the basket. She decorates a

Maurice Sendak, "Fitcher's Bird."
Courtesy of Maurice Sendak.

skull in bridal ornaments and places it in the tower window so that Bluebeard will believe she is watching him and he will not pause on his way. She bedecks herself in honey and feathers to disguise herself as a bird, whereby she tricks the wedding guests arriving at the castle and escapes. Even Bluebeard does not recognize her after this metamorphosis, and she is able to gather her kinfolk together to burn the castle, the wedding guests, and Bluebeard himself.

The "three sisters" motif that "Fitcher's Bird" presents is common in folklore. The story is told in detail for the first (usually eldest) sister, the second sister briefly succumbs to the same fate as the first, and the third telling of the sequence presents the difference that in some way the murderer is outwitted by the (usually youngest) sister.

The Bluebeard stories all revolve around seeing: the wife sees what she is not allowed to see, and what she sees in the bloody chamber is her own end at her husband's hands.[7] Bluebeard himself sees that she has disobeyed him. In "Fitcher's Bird," the ability to see is alluded to by the bridal skull decorated and set in the window to watch the sorcerer on his way. In many kindred variants, the outwitting of the Bluebeard figure involves this turning of tables. It is now the wife who makes the injunction that Bluebeard must not stop on his way (back to her house with the hidden sisters and, often, with his own treasure).

Further, he must not look in the bag, basket, or chest he is carrying. The wife tells him she can see a very long way and tells her sisters that should he set them down, they are immediately to cry out "I see you! I see you!" and thus prevent him from looking where he is forbidden. Ironically, Bluebeard attempts to be as disobedient as his wife had been. And each time he tries, after believing his wife can still see him, even around corners and behind trees, he expresses his amazement at her ability to see so far.

In stories of this type, it is a common motif to have the wife or captured woman make an effigy of herself in some form: to use a rag or straw doll ("Devil Gets Tricked," "The Fair Young Bride"[8]), to dress her pillow ("Jurma") or stuff her clothes ("How the Devil Married Three Sisters," "Silver Nose," "Ímarasugssuaq, Who Ate His Wives"), or to put her clothes on a well pole ("The Robber's Bride") and hold a broom ("Hen Is Tripping in the Mountain") or cooking spoon ("The Hare's Bride"). In all these versions, when attempts to get her attention fail, the man (or animal) becomes violent, and only by decapitating or hitting the effigy does he realize that he has been tricked.

An important feature of "Fitcher's Bird" is that, by contrast to Perrault's tale, the heroine rescues herself and her sisters and without assistance. Also, the stained egg, instead of the stained (or sometimes broken) key, is the magical tale-teller in "Fitcher's Bird." In the Italian "Silver Nose" (and variant "Devil Gets Tricked"), the devil sneaks flowers into the three sisters' hair during the night before they open the forbidden door leading to the Inferno. In turn the rose and the carnation are singed by the heat and flames of the abyss, giving away the disobedient women. The third sister puts her jasmine in water to keep it fresh, thus escaping detection. In the Spanish "Merchant and His Three Daughters," an apple falls and is bruised until the third sister wraps it in cloth before opening the door.

The Robber Bridegroom

The first English translation of Grimms', *German Popular Tales*, features "The Robber Bridegroom," ("Der Räuberbräutigam," AT 955) with a footnote giving the tale "a general affinity to that of *Bluebeard*."[9] Notably the list of variants of this tale type is predominantly British. One of the variants, "Mr. Fox," is the form of the Bluebeard tale type earliest known in English, predating Perrault's "Bluebeard" in writing by a century.

In Grimms' "The Robber Bridegroom" (1857 version), a miller's daughter is betrothed to a suitor she does not quite trust. She goes out on Sunday as

Corinna Sargood, "Old Foster" ("Mr. Fox"). We see at once the brutal dismemberment of the woman Foster has captured and the proof the woman will use to denounce him later landing in her lap: "and here I have the hand to show." Courtesy of Corinna Sargood.

appointed, following the trail of ashes he laid for her. But because she doubts him, she fills her pockets with peas and lentils and makes her own trail also. The house is empty, but a bird calls out: "Turn back, turn back, you young bride. / You are in a murderer's house." It repeats the warning. She goes through the house, finally coming to the cellar, where an old woman tells her she is in danger from the robbers who eat women. She hides behind a large barrel just as the band return dragging a woman. They kill that woman by giving her three glasses of different colored wines (white, red, yellow), which cause her heart to break. They chop her up and salt her. They cut off her finger to get her ring, but the finger bounces into the betrothed's lap. The old woman diverts the bandits from searching behind the barrel and puts a sleeping potion in their wine. That night both women escape. On the wedding day the fiancée tells her story, interjecting the reassuring refrain, "Darling, it was only a dream," until she produces the finger as proof. The robber and his gang are killed.

The motifs of this variant type, recognizable in other variants, are the secret visit to the man's house after he has laid a trail to follow (often ashes; sometimes of flour or red silk thread or even a trail of pig's blood).[10] The woman is warned at the house by writing over the gate and doors or frequently by a bird who speaks or a crone helper-figure (a housekeeper or the bandit's mother). She is able to take a token of the murderer's crime away with her: a hand, finger, or ring, which usually falls to where she is hidden. In all stories of this type, there is a public event in which the murderer is denounced as the heroine tells her story disguised as a "dream" story or a riddle, over the man's repeated interruptions and objections. In some cases, it is the wedding feast itself. In others, a story-telling event is either already planned or created specifically to entrap the criminal (the heroine dresses as a boy to tell her story on more than one such occasion, and constables are planted or a regiment surrounds the house or inn where the event is taking place). In a last grisly detail, the dead hand is sometimes recognized by someone in the crowd.

The other motif present in "The Robber Bridegroom" and in many Bluebeard tales is the cannibalism of the bandit-groom.[11] In one version of "Pretty Polly" the woman is invited to help herself to food and does so; the meat is delicious, until she finds a hand in it. In others, there is a cook or a boy boiling meat over a fire. In "The Robber's Bride," the woman is told to decide her own method of being cooked: boiled in water, or in oil. In Charles Dickens' literary variant "Captain Murderer," the ogre requires his wife to bake a pie. She makes the crust, but when she asks him where she is to get the meat that goes in the pie, he takes her to a mirror to see her own reflection as she is murdered.

Mr. Fox

The English variant "Mr. Fox" belongs to the same tale type as "The Robber Bridegroom" and has a plentiful set of variants of its own. There are two main types of "Mr. Fox" tales. One is typified by the motif of "the girl who sees her own grave dug."[12] In this, a slick man named Fox (sometimes, an actual fox) invites the girl he is courting to visit him at a prearranged place. She is suspicious but does so, or even goes early, and hides herself up a tree to wait and watch. What she sees is Mr. Fox digging a grave, which she understands only too well to be her own. In some instances, as in "Mary, the Maid of the Inn," he has an accomplice, and in these the pair may be killing and/or burying another woman's body. These variants share another motif: that of a riddle told at the end to publicly denounce Mr. Fox, akin to the following from "The Oxford Student": "One moonshiny night, as I sat high, / Waiting for one to come by, / The boughs did bend; my heart did break, / To see what hole the fox did make."

The second variant set of "Mr. Fox" tales ("Mr. Foster," "Old Foster") bear a closer resemblance to the plot elements of "The Robber Bridegroom," with a specific formula used for the warnings given the curious betrothed and a parallel formulaic series used by the betrothed to allay the bridegroom's fears as she tells the tale publicly and denounces the groom. Lady Mary is suspicious of her fiancé and decides to visit him at his home unannounced. The warnings are sequential: "Be Bold, Be Bold"; then "Be bold, be Bold, But not too bold"; and finally: "Be Bold, Be Bold, but not too Bold, Lest that your heart's blood should run cold." She nevertheless goes upstairs and finds a "bloody chamber," in which are the bodies of many murdered women. On her way out, she must hide to avoid Mr. Fox, who is dragging another woman. He cuts off that woman's hand to get a diamond ring, which is then taken up by the hidden betrothed. In many variants, the victim grabs at a stair rail or door frame in an effort to save herself, and the hand is severed to prevent further resistance. Lady Mary denounces him at the wedding breakfast by telling of her dream. At each sequential warning, he interjects: "It is not so, nor was not so, And God forbid it should be so." When she produces "hand and ring . . . to show," she points the hand at him to denounce him.

"Mr. Fox" was earliest recorded in Edmund Spenser's English epic romance *The Faerie Queene* (1590). When Britomart the (female) knight of chastity enters the castle of the wizard Busyrane to rescue Amoret, who has been kidnapped, she is warned by inscriptions over inner doors to "Be Bold, Be Bold" and then "But Not Too Bold":

Tho as she backward cast her busie eye,
To search each secret of that goodly sted,
Ouer the dore thus written she did spye
Be bold: she oft and oft it ouer-red,
Yet could not find what sence it figured:
But what so were therein or writ or ment,
She was no whit thereby discouraged
From prosecuting of her first intent,
But forward with bold steps into the next roome went.
. . . .
And as she lookt about, she did behold,
How ouer that same dore was likewise writ,
Be bold, be bold, and euery where Be bold,
That much she muz'd, yet could not construe it
By any riddling skill, or commune wit.
At last she spyde at that rooms upper end,
Another yron dore, on which was writ,
Be not too bold; whereto though she did bend
Her earnest mind, yet wist not what it might intend.
(3:11, 50, 54, my emphasis)

Shakespeare's play *Much Ado About Nothing* also refers to it: "Like the old tale, my lord—'it is not so, nor 'twas not so, but indeed, God forbid it should be so!'" (1.1: 203–04). Although the tale is not named, the refrain is precise and by 1600 it is already referred to as "the *old* tale."

Appalachian Mr. Fox

One Appalachian variant furnishes another interesting hybrid, containing several motifs: Pretty Polly sees her own grave dug, then follows the trail to the man's house to discover what has happened to three other women. In a prearranged play-telling, she tells both the riddle (common to the grave-digging motif) and also denounces using the dream-story formula. In this particular Southern "Mr. Fox," Pretty Polly first spies Mr. Fox digging a grave for her in the woods. As she does not appear that night, he stops coming to see her, but three other women disappear. Although he is suspected, there is no evidence and no one knows where he lives. When he begins courting Polly again, the story includes the "Mr. Fox" story that is more commonly told, except that Polly is deliberately on his trail to discover what happened to the three missing women. She follows a flour trail to his house and there spies a woman being dragged along. She keeps a severed hand as dramatic proof that the story she later tells is true. The common animal helper warning, given here by a parrot ("Don't go in, pretty lady! / You'll lose your heart's blood"), fails as it must. Before Mr. Fox returns dragging another woman, Polly has entered his house and seen a chamber containing women's beheaded bodies: "But she opened the door anyhow and looked in. It was like a slaughter room in there: women hung up all around the walls with their heads cut off. Polly shut the door right quick" ("Mr. Fox" 1993, 97). This story adds an extra exchange in that she asks the bird to promise to lie when it is asked if anyone has been there, which it does. During the subsequent "play-party in the settlement," Polly tells a riddle: "Riddle to my riddle to my right! / Where was I that Saturday night? / All that time in a lonesome pine, / I was high, and he was low. / The cock did crow, the wind did blow. / The tree did shake, and my heart did ache / To see what a hole that fox did make (1993, 99)."[13] She delays the answer until after she has completed the sequence of dream descriptions (with the ritual protests from Mr. Fox). Somewhat clumsily, the riddle wraps up at the end: "After they took Mr. Fox out [for trial], everybody recollected Pretty Polly's riddle and asked her about it, and she told 'em about the grave and all" (101).

The "Mr. Fox"/"Old Foster"/"Pretty Polly" tales of Appalachia have also generated a set of ballad variants named "Pretty Polly" or "Pretty Molly." Unfortunately, the end for the ballad heroines is rarely a happy one, as Polly (or Molly) is killed by her lover, who throws some dirt over her and leaves nothing behind but the birds to mourn. Other ballads share the theme: Annie Miller, Lady Isabel, and May Colven and even another Pretty Polly are related ballad heroines[14] who manage to turn the tables on their murdering spouse. Invariably, the groom says: "I have drowned seven young ladies, / The eighth one you shall be." In some variants, the heroine must convince a parrot not to betray her.

In contrast to the other Appalachian variants that adapt "Mr. Fox" in a fairly straightforward fashion, there is another contribution to the Bluebeard story nexus that is a "Jack Tale." In these tall tales, Jack is always the hero: quick witted and a trickster figure, he always comes out on top. In "Old Bluebeard," the focus is on Jack outwitting a Bluebeard who gets away with eating the brothers' dinners (Tom and Will are unable to prevent him); when it is Jack's turn, he changes the pattern by offering Bluebeard food instead of trying to prevent him from having any. Until this point, Bluebeard is referred to as "old indigo beard," but there is no evidence of woman-collecting tendencies. But once Jack follows him to his hole in the ground and determines to go after him, his women-collecting propensity is revealed. Jack finds, by turns, three women sitting down the hole in three houses and rescues each one. The last one becomes Jack's own wife.[15]

Animal Grooms

Just as the marriage to death is archetypal, most if not all cultures offer versions of the marriage to an animal groom: a snake, a bull, a fierce tiger; some include human transformations. When these marriages are cruel or linked with curiosity and disobedience, they fall within the realm of the Bluebeard story, although they have never gone by that name.

The bestial nature of the murderer is often expressed by representing him as an actual animal like "Mr. Fox"; examples abound internationally. One American variant, "The Secret Room," collects in one place obvious threads from Perrault's "Bluebeard," "Fitcher's Bird," and the animal helper variants, as well as the betrothal to a nonhuman (who is transformed into the marriageable prince by her trickery). In this tale, a mother and her three daughters are spinning outside their cottage when they see a bull in the cabbage patch (in "The Hare's Bride" it is a hare stealing cabbages who then steals the girl away;

in "Peerifool" it is a giant, and in "The Widow and Her Daughters" it is a gray horse). The oldest daughter runs after it, chasing it to a house on the edge of a wood. Here, the bull gives her a bunch of keys, "and told her that she could go anywhere in the house she liked except one room" ("The Secret Room" 1960, 149). The story follows Perrault's "Bluebeard." As the bull leaves her, she succumbs to curiosity and opens the forbidden room. The room contains headless bodies of other women. There is blood now on the key, on her hand, and on her shoes. A cat offers to tell her the secret to cleaning the blood off in exchange for a dish of bread and milk, but the daughter shoos the cat away and is killed when the bull returns.[16] The same happens to the second sister, as in Grimms' "Fitcher's Bird." The youngest daughter does everything the same, including getting blood stains on the key, her hand and shoes, but she does give what the cat requests and is given the secret spell to clean away the blood. This releases the bull from his spell, and he transforms into a prince: "'I was bewitched,' he said, 'by a girl who first loved me and then hated me because I wouldn't marry her. I killed many a girl while I was a bull, but now we will have the bodies taken care of, and then we will be married'" (1960, 152). They marry and live happily ever after.

The Thousand and One Arabian Nights

The Turkish Bluebeard, a common English depiction of the French noble tyrant, is often ascribed to the influence of the *Thousand and One Arabian Nights*, itself illustrating a Bluebeard tale in the frame story of King Schahriar and Scheherezade. The Arabian Nights stories were recorded around 1545 in Arabia, but are much older.[17] Within the collection, "Story of the Third Calendar" is another example. Scheherezade's own father is the grand vizir commanded to procure the Sultan's brides. After his first wife betrayed him (sexually, it is implied) and was executed, Schahriar resolved to have a bride a night and to kill her in the morning. Scheherezade implores her father to bring her to the Sultan as his next bride so she can end the practice once and for all. She asks her sister Dinarzade to attend her. She relies on her sister to keep watch in the night and to wake her an hour before dawn and beg a story of her. She tells the stories to keep his interest, and thus to stay alive.

The embedded tale "The Story of the Third Calendar" is set within another internal frame: it is the story of one of three men who are blinded in one eye and who have come to see the Caliph of Bagdad. Prince Agrib, the third calendar, tells that it was not fate, but rather his own curiosity that cost him his eye. He tells of meeting ten men all blind in the right eye and asking how they came that way. Like them, he too elects to be whisked away by a giant bird to a palace with beautiful women. After many days of rich living, they leave him alone for forty days and ask him not to open the golden door or he will have to leave forever. On the last day before their return he gives in to temptation and opens the door, falling across the threshold. He finds and mounts a black horse that carries him immediately to the place he began, knocking out his eye with its tail.

As with *Mother Goose*, the *Arabian Nights* arrived in English via France. Antoine Galland translated and adapted into French the *Mille et une Nuits* (1705–1717). The English translations began to be published in 1705–1708, even before Samber's *Mother Goose* translation, and launched a trend for orientalism that was reflected in myriad forms throughout the eighteenth century.

The Pentamerone

The Italian collection of tales of Giambattista Basile, *Lo Cunto deli Cunti overo Lo Trattenemiento de' Peccerille* (1634), modeled after Boccaccio's *Decameron*, contains a "Bluebeard" incident within Day 4, Tale 6. Marchetta, a wandering princess, is forbidden by an ogress (ghula) to open a certain door: "here are the keys of all the chambers, and be thou mistress, and faculty, and most arbitrary power; only one thing I reserve for myself, and that is, that on no account must thou open the door of the last chamber, which this key fitteth, because then thou wouldst make mustard rise to my nose; . . . Now when the ghula went forth, great curiosity got hold of Marchetta to see what was within that forbidden chamber, and she opened the door, and found therein three damsels arrayed in golden raiments, seated upon three imperial seats, and seemingly fast asleep" (Burton 1893, 293).[18] She wakes the three sisters (who are daughters of the ogress), which angers the girls' mother and launches Marchetta on to her next adventure.

Bluebeard in Myth and Bible

While Perrault's tale was an original composition, the story of Bluebeard is archetypal. Andrew Lang wrote in his scholarly preface to *Perrault's Popular Tales* (1888): "Blue Beard is essentially popular and traditional. . . . The leading idea, of curiosity punished, of the box or door which may not be opened, and of the prohibition infringed with evil results, is of world-wide distribution" (188, lxi).[19] Bluebeard's wife disobeys a strict injunction (specifically, not to look), and when she transgresses she sees something horrific and punitive: her own fate for looking. Traditionally, she disobeys because she cannot contain her curiosity. She is a fairy tale representation of the archetype of female transgressive curiosity, which has expression in the Western canon through Greek mythology (Psyche, Pandora) and the Bible (Eve, Lot's wife, Judith of Holofernes).

Forbidden Curiosity in Greek Mythology

The myth of Psyche is a lengthy narrative, recorded by Apuleius in *The Golden Ass* (second century) from oral tradition. It concerns the path of the mortal woman, through many trials at the hands of Venus (Aphrodite), to immortality and her marriage to the god of love, Cupid (Eros). The pertinent part of her story is when she betrays an injunction by her husband not to look upon his face. She is betrayed in the act of doing so by hot wax falling from the candle onto his shoulder while he sleeps. Frightened of the jealousy of his mother Venus toward Psyche, Cupid forbids Psyche to see him; she has been told he is a monster. As Apuleius described the transgression, Psyche becomes bold and takes a razor as well as a lamp; but when she sees the beauty of her sleeping husband she falls to embracing him. The lamp—perhaps, suggests Apuleius, out of jealousy or a desire to embrace Cupid also—spills its hot wax and burns him. Cupid immediately flees, but later tells Psyche she is to be punished by his abandonment of her. After severe trials set by Venus, she is rescued by Cupid, and her punishment ends with immortality.

If Psyche was rendered miserable by her breach of a husband's taboo, Pandora's transgression is famous for the ills others suffered as a result of her curiosity. Pandora was a revenge on man for Prometheus' act of stealing fire from Zeus. In Hesiod's *Works and Days* (ca. 700), he related the myth that Zeus ordered her to be made by the gods as a bait. Hephaestus formed her, and the gods contributed both beauty and deceit for her nature. Hermes took her to Epimetheus, Prometheus' brother, who immediately forgot the warning his brother had given and took Pandora. Pandora is now best known for her transgressive curiosity; she opens the box sent by Zeus containing the evils of the world, sending them out among mankind and leaving only hope behind.

Although the templates here firmly establish transgressive curiosity as a female trait, the example of Orpheus offers an exception. Orpheus was famed for his musical prowess. He fell in love with Eurydice, and they were married in splendor. But at the wedding procession, Eurydice was bitten by a snake and died. Heartbroken, Orpheus descended to the underworld to beg for her back. By playing his lyre and singing his tragedy, he won the right to take Eurydice back to the world: on the condition that he not look back during the arduous journey out of the underworld to check that she is behind him. Despite managing to keep the injunction for most of the journey, with the end in sight Orpheus looks back and, in that instant, loses Eurydice again to the underworld, this time forever. The remainder of his life was unhappy, and his death was violent.

Forbidden Curiosity in the Bible

The archetype of female transgressive curiosity takes its most castigating form for the Christian tradition in the Biblical story of Eve. Like Pandora, Eve's transgression resulted not only in her own unhappiness and that of her husband, but in the eviction from Eden, the attendant curses of mortality, shame in nakedness, and pain in childbearing. Thus, by eating the fruit of the tree of Knowledge, expressly forbidden to Adam and Eve by God, and by offering the fruit to Adam as well, Eve's curiosity is deemed responsible for the fall of man. That the punishment entails consequences for human sexuality implies a connection between cognitive and carnal knowledge, and this taint of illicit sex frequently underpins the archetype of female curiosity, as stated by one late-Victorian commentator: "It symbolizes the eternal curiosity of the eternal Eve concerning that which has been forbidden" (Saltus [1880–1899], 177).

Because of Eve's transgression, she is among several women in the Bible who transgress through curiosity. Lot's wife is another well-known example. Lot's family is assisted by the angels in fleeing from Sodom before its destruction by God, but they tell the family not to look back or to stop or they too will die. As God destroys Sodom and Gomorrah, Lot's wife disobeys the injunction and looks back; instantly she is transformed into a pillar of salt.

Of the Biblical women who form the Western context for Bluebeard's wife, Judith of Holofernes, from the Apocrypha, is perhaps less self-evident as she does not breach any injunction. Indeed, she functions as God's agent in successfully ending the siege of Bethulia and thereby rescuing her people. Yet she does so by beheading a man (Holofernes) in his sleep. She has become part of the tradition of representing Bluebeard's wife, most recognizably after Balázs-Bartók's early twentieth-century opera *Duke Bluebeard's Castle* named

Bluebeard's wife Judith, drawing on turn-of-the-century depictions of both Judith and Salome as sexualized mankillers.

Historical Precursors

Although there is no known specific source for Perrault's tale, much work has explored possible precursor figures. The main two are French, from two millennia. Comôr the Accursed was a sixth-century Breton chieftain, said to have killed his wives when they became pregnant. Gilles de Rais was a noble marshal of France from the Nantes region and was executed in 1440 for killing many children. The third precursor figure is England's Henry Tudor. In many ways his story is closer to Perrault's plot than the other two.

Comôr the Accursed

Although Comôr predates the next possible historical precursor for the role by centuries, he is a lesser-known contender and not the star of his own story, but the tyrant who occasions a Christian resurrection miracle. Comôr was a sixth-century Breton chieftain, who supposedly killed his wives when they became pregnant because his death by a child's hand had been foretold. In legend he beheaded Triphine, the daughter of the count of Vannes, who had tried to escape when she became pregnant. She was then resurrected by St. Gildas de Rhuys, a British historian and monk and the author of *De excidio et conquestu Brittanicae*. One story has it that her murdered infant miraculously walked to Comôr and killed him. In fact, it is reputed that he was killed in battle by Judwal, a stepson from a previous marriage whose own life Comôr had attempted.

The legend of Comôr appears as early as 1514 in the *Grands Cronicques du Bretagne* of Alain Bouchard and had the status of a *conte populaire*.[20] In the serial murder of wives who became pregnant, the story is actually closer to the Perrault tale (and closer yet to the German "Fitcher's Bird") than that of Gilles de Rais, who is ironically the most popularly ascribed historical precursor to Bluebeard, reflective perhaps of "the pranks of oral tradition." But in another account closer to Perrault's time, the *Vie de Saint Gildas* (1636) by Albert le Grand, the context for the account is given more fully, as is the future of her son, Saint Trémur, and an interesting iconographic moment occurs in this telling: Comôr catches up with her, tracks her down, and, unmoved by the tears of poor Triphine, now kneeling before her slayer, grabs her by the hair and beheads her with one swipe of his sword.[21]

Gilles de Rais

After sending the Duc d'Aumale a copy of his *Fairy Tales*, which included his translation of Perrault's "Bluebeard" ascribing the role of Bluebeard to Gilles de Rais, nineteenth-century English writer James Robinson Planché recorded his irritation that the Duc corrected him: "His Royal Highness's information respecting the Maréchal de Raix [*sic*] is extremely interesting, and very important, inasmuch that it contradicts on official authority a report which had been circulated for centuries, and quoted without suspicion by French antiquaries" (1872, 360).[22] It is no legend but historical fact that the fifteenth-century nobleman Seigneur Gilles de Laval Rais (1404–1440), a lieutenant of Joan of Arc and a Maréchal of France, murdered more than a hundred children of both sexes at his castle, Tiffauges, in Nantes, France.[23] The transcript of his trial survives and records his confession to a number of macabre sexual crimes that were linked to his alchemical pursuits. As an already-famous nobleman, his trial was unusual, as was the overwhelming number of peasant witnesses and victims' family members. The fact of his execution was also therefore very public.

However, although he was married to Catherine de Thouars and had been previously betrothed, he did not murder wives but rather children.[24] Yet Gilles de Rais, "*dit Barbe Bleue*,"[25] is now widely known as Bluebeard. While it is worth noting that "Rais was never called a Bluebeard in contemporary documents" (Mowshowitz 1970, 65), nevertheless the association is now so strong that critics may allude to such a thing as the "Bluebeard-Rais complex" (183). Even Rais' castle advertizes itself as: "Tiffauges: Château de Barbe-Bleue."[26] As one critic remarks, Rais is "now virtually synonymous with Bluebeard whereas less than two hundred years ago, only Perrault's tale bore that name" (Odio 1986, 286), and it is perhaps for this reason that the historical figure may be called by this same critic, "an international leitmotif in the Western world."[27] Gilles de Rais continues to be infamously connected with Bluebeard, even in contemporary mysteries such as the novel *Thief of Souls* by Ann Benson (2002).

Henry VIII, "Our Old Harry Bluebeard"

In *A Dictionary of the Noted Names of Fiction*, William Wheeler stated: "Bluebeard is also the name by which King Henry VIII lives in the popular superstitions of England" (1866, 49).[28] Henry Tudor married six wives in all, and he had more than one of them executed in order to make way for the next. His first marriage to Katharine of Aragon (daughter of Isabella of Spain and widow to Henry's older brother Arthur) lasted twenty-two years (1509–1526). When the marriage produced no living male heir in addition to their daughter, Mary, Henry set Katharine aside, annulling the marriage with the claim that Katharine had consummated the marriage to Arthur. The second wife, Anne Boleyn, was decapitated at the Tower of London after three years of marriage (1533–1536), having borne Elizabeth and no living male heir. The marriage was annulled, as Anne was found guilty of treason for sexual infidelity. Henry's third wife was Jane Seymour, one of Anne's ladies in waiting. Jane died eighteen months later, two weeks after giving birth to Henry's only legitimate male heir, Edward, in 1537. Henry's fourth marriage to Anne of Cleves was made to form a Protestant alliance, but the marriage was again annulled in the same year (1540). The fifth wife, Catherine Howard, was married for only two years (1540–1542) before she was also beheaded on the Tower Green for sexual infidelity to her husband. The sixth wife, Catherine Parr, married him in mid-1543 and survived three and a half years of marriage to Henry by outliving him (he died in January 1547).

Obviously, Henry Tudor predates Charles Perrault's Bluebeard by a century and a half. But the story of the English king and his six wives was popular and just as well-known in France as in England. It is possible that Henry Tudor's marriages contributed to the fairy tale of Perrault. Regardless, once Perrault had created a name for the figure of the wife murderer in fairy tale, the English used it to label the safely long-dead Tudor king.[29] One theory states that it was a Catholic plot to discredit Henry.[30] It is an interesting example of ownership or adoption of the French fairy tale, another way in which these "fashionably dressed French invaders" became "naturalized" English (Darton 1932, 94). At the same time, having married "only" six times, and thus being "a wife or two in arrears of the Turk" (D. G. [1837?]),[31] the English maintain a genteel view of Henry compared to his continental counterparts.

As a pirate, Bluebeard has gained broader criminal notoriety, and his connection with serial wife murder seems at first glance to have become obscured by this new reputation. But even as a pirate confused with Blackbeard (Edward Teach), this salient feature of his fairy tale history remains intact and the graft of the two stories has been further generative of a variant tradition. In true crime, the "Bluebeard" label has become a useful noun for the male serial killer whether of wives or, more recently, simply of women. The "female Bluebeard" borrows the label and, through it, is depicted as taking on the male properties of the serial killer; she is labeled a perversion of the female. What is clear for serial killers of either sex is the public needs to ally them with folklore. They both derive from folklore, and they generate it.

Chapter 2

Pirates and True Bluebeards

The one thing that has been relatively clear, from the fairy tale side of things anyway, is that Bluebeard was never a pirate. How then to explain the common confusion between Bluebeard and piracy—even the specific identity confusion between Bluebeard and Blackbeard, the very real Captain Edward Teach of Bristol, who was contemporaneous with Charles Perrault's tale? It is tempting to assume that the beards have simply created the confusion, and thus it exists merely in name. Blackbeard's beard was one of the most powerful weapons of fear he had, and he apparently made good theatrical use of it. Several commentators mention that his beard was unusual because at the time most men were clean-shaven (Roberts 1924, 5). Furthermore, his beard covered his whole face, up to the eyes, and so was not merely a beard but evidence of barbarity. To enhance it, Blackbeard braided it into pigtails, some say he tied them with brightly colored ribbons as well, and then he used lighted slow-burning fuse cords, tucked under his hat, to wreathe his bearded face in smoke and create a terrifying effect. Captain Charles Johnson published an account of Blackbeard that is thought to have been researched, appearing just six years after Teach's death: *A General History of the Pirates* in 1724. For much of the twentieth century, Johnson was thought to be Daniel Defoe, although that remains in question.[1] In his illustrated chapter on Teach, Johnson wrote:

> Now that we have given some account of Teach's life and actions, it will not be amiss that we speak of his beard, since it did not a little contribute towards making his name so terrible in those parts.
>
> Plutarch, and other grave historians, have taken notice that several great men amongst the Romans took their surnames from certain odd marks in their countenances: as Cicero, from a mark or vetch on his nose, so our hero, Captain Teach, assumed the cognomen of Blackbeard from that large quantity of hair which, like a frightful meteor, covered

> his whole face and frightened America more than any comet that has appeared there a long time.
>
> This beard was black, which he suffered to grow of an extravagant length; as to breadth it came up to his eyes. He was accustomed to twist it with ribbons, in small tails, after the manner of our ramilies [*sic*] wigs,[2] and turn them about his ears (Johnson 1724, 60).

Beyond the beard, a closer look at the pirate known as Blackbeard, who went "on account" off the American Atlantic Coast and into the Caribbean in the early 1700s, reveals another powerful possible cause for the confusion between Bluebeard and Blackbeard. Edward Teach married his fourteenth bride, reputed to be Mary Ormond,[3] a 16-year-old planter's daughter, just months before his death in 1718. This detail of his multiple marriages is mentioned by Captain Johnson and repeated widely in later accounts that draw on Johnson's, such as the *Pirate's Own Book*, a product of the Marine Research Society in 1837; and in an authoritative biography of Teach by Robert Lee. Johnson wrote: "Before he sailed upon his adventures, he married a young creature of about sixteen years of age, the governor [of South Carolina, Charles Eden] performing the ceremony. As it is a custom to marry here by a priest, so it is there by a magistrate, and this I have been informed made Teach's fourteenth wife, whereof a dozen might be still living" (Johnson 1724, 50).

Johnson's source is unknown, and most commentators since 1724 quote variations on Johnson. By the time of the Marine Research Society's publication a century later, which drew heavily on Johnson's and used his own phrases, with slight deviations, the report is as follows: "Before he entered upon his new adventures, he married a young woman of about sixteen years of age, the governor himself attending the ceremony. It was reported that this was only his fourteenth wife, about twelve of whom were yet alive; and though this woman was young and amiable, he behaved towards her in a manner so brutal, that it was shocking to all decency and propriety, even among his abandoned crew of pirates" (Ellms 1837, 338).

Governor Charles Eden's reputation had suffered at the hands of his contemporaries and through Johnson's account, and popular belief has been that Eden's dealings with Blackbeard were far too favorable altogether, indicating that the two were in league for mutual profit. Retractions of Johnson's comments were not as widely read as the initial imputations, of course, but it is interesting that the 1837 account has Eden attending, but not performing the ceremony, even where it would have been one of the governor's normal duties to have done so (Lee 1974, 74).[4] Also interesting is that the details of Blackbeard's treatment of his wife were omitted in favor of editorializing on the "manner so brutal" it shocked even his fellow pirate crew. Johnson had gone on to provide the following detail, which has been omitted from just about every account since: "His behaviour in this state was something extraordinary, for while his sloop lay in Ocracoke Inlet, and he ashore at a plantation where his wife lived, with whom after he had lain all night, it was his custom to invite five or six of his brutal companions to come ashore, and he would force her to prostitute herself to them all, one after another, before his face" (1724, 50–51). It is less clear how this treatment of his wife shocked the pirate crew than the sensibilities of the readers of 1837. The Marine Research Society also omitted Johnson's comment that Teach and his crew were reputed to take liberties "with the wives and daughters of the planters" (52), so there seems to be a deliberate attempt to edit out such salubrious statements. It is also interesting that without them, Teach is altogether a much more gallant figure. With the exception of threatening to murder all the captured Charles Town citizens during his blockade of their harbor unless certain medicines were provided to him within a stipulated time (which was several times extended), Teach appears to have been a fairer and less bloodthirsty character than many other of the Brethren of the Coast. His list of exploits include taking a number of ships but releasing crews and taking provisions but allowing ships to proceed.

There are no reliable reports and little apparent interest in Teach's previous thirteen wives,[5] although there have been a few brief discussion on the topic. Ironically, the entire blockade of Charles Town, with the threatened loss of so many hostages' lives and threats to fire upon the town itself, may have had its cause with one of Blackbeard's wives. According to Lee: "Another writer has speculated that Blackbeard 'wanted the mercurial preparations in the chest because his most recent girl friend had not only married him but also left him with venereal disease to remember her by'" (Whipple 1957, 185). The number (fourteen) is consistent, a point of reference that remains stable through all accounts of Teach's piratical years. Johnson's comments about Teach's brutality toward his last young wife paint altogether a different picture from the many accounts that depict Blackbeard, almost comically, as a man briefly attempting to live a reputable life amid the high society of Bath Town before giving up and going back to sea with a royal pardon and a ship courtesy of Governor Eden.

In his biography of Blackbeard, Robert Lee commented that "Few pirates treated women or girls with greater respect than he" (24); he went on to say that Blackbeard was "as successful in love as he was in the scuttling of ships" (24). But Lee's rhetoric is suspect when discussing Blackbeard and women:

Teach had no power of resistance to the charms of an attractive trollop. Having grown fond of her, he was so much putty in her hands, until the girl became convinced that she had found the Achilles' heel in this outwardly invulnerable pirate. The great Blackbeard, terror of the seas, was temporarily at the mercy of his new-found love, and often actually proposed marriage. Such was Blackbeard's nature, infatuated with every harbor-town girl who caught his fancy.

As a consequence, he more than once found the girl and himself aboard the Queen Anne's Revenge, standing before his first mate, who solemnly conducted a marriage ceremony and pronounced them husband and wife. It is doubtful if any of these brides actually considered themselves married to Captain Teach. To them it was an adventure in port with the notorious Blackbeard, carried through to the finish as a lark. In any event it helped them financially in their business dealings with other men of the sea. To be known as "Blackbeard's wife" accorded them prestige and enhanced the value of their services. [Quoting Whipple:] "To Blackbeard's crew, especially the mate who performed all the marriage ceremonies, it was a running joke. To Blackbeard it was apparently a source of annoyance when he got to sea and realized he had been taken again by a doxy whom he could have had for a few doubloons. But he never learned" (Lee 1974, 24–25).

Despite painting Blackbeard thusly as a victim of the women he could not resist, with suspiciously symmetrical rhetoric such as: "On the high seas a ruthless pursuer, on land he was the pursued" (25), Lee did reveal in a footnote that his extended account of Blackbeard's manner with women can only be traced to one source, and it proved to be the same one who speculated on the venereal disease theory behind the Charles Town blockade. Lee's footnote read: "There is a paucity of materials dealing with Blackbeard's relations with women. The statements in this book have been based upon accounts found in Whipple, pp. 180–81" (1974, 182 n.).[6] The accounts must be unsubstantiated, because Lee elsewhere exhaustively cross-references all sources for his information. B. C. Addison Whipple was the author of *Pirate Rascals of the Spanish Main* (1957), dated less than twenty years before Lee's own book.

Robert Lee also went on to say that there is no evidence of further Bluebeard-like behavior from Blackbeard: "There is no record or any historical intimation that Blackbeard ever caused the termination of a marriage by bringing about the death of one of his so-called wives. He is not to be confused with the fictitious Bluebeard, the monster of Charles Perrault's tale *Barbe Bleue*, who murdered his wives and hid their bodies in a locked room" (1974, 26). Usually, it is Bluebeard who is mistaken for the pirate and not the other way around. But it is interesting that there is such a striking parallel that here, in a biography of the pirate, Dr. Lee needed to remind the reader early on that the two figures are not one and the same.

Johnson is in most cases the primary source for Blackbeard's story, supplemented with documents from the period. But Johnson's account is not infallible; he said that governor Eden's secretary died "within a few days" of Blackbeard, which was apparently not the case. Even the official London newspaper reports of Blackbeard's death just weeks after the event itself contain rampant inaccuracies, such as that he and another crewmember were taken alive and executed after; no eyewitness account supports it. Rather, all eyewitness accounts and documentary evidence say that Blackbeard was decisively killed on board Lt. Maynard's ship, during hand-to-hand combat with Maynard himself, and with the assistance of others of Maynard's men, and that Maynard sailed from the encounter with Teach's head hung from the bowsprit of his ship, where it remained for weeks. Blackbeard featured among the original thirteen pirates discussed in Johnson's first edition (1724),[7] and the book was sensational and a hot seller. Nonetheless, Johnson asserted repeatedly that his accounts were researched, and editors of his work up to the present day have commented that "the majority of the facts in Johnson's *History* have been proved to be accurate" (Cordingly 1998, ix–x) and that his history of Blackbeard accords with contemporary records.

It may be tempting to think that all pirates were fond of serial matrimony, for any one of several reasons, and that it would therefore be a widespread phenomenon in pirate biographies. But this does not appear to have been the case either. Some pirates had families on shore—respectable men who began as privateers, for instance, and had established families before going to sea. There were communities of pirate families in Cuba and elsewhere. At least one pirate, Jack Rackham, nicknamed "Calico Jack," had his "wife" Anne Bonny on board as an accomplice. But, for the most part, pirates do not seem to have been the marrying kind, and it is an unusual feature of Blackbeard's biography that he did so, let alone fourteen times. It is also perhaps a feature remembered and repeated because of Governor Eden's involvement. His last marriage is also connected to one of the collection of fairly stable quoted anecdotes that have not changed much since Johnson's rendition: "The night before he was killed, he sat up and drank 'till the morning, with some of his own men and the master of a merchantman, and having had intelligence of the two sloops coming to attack him, as has been before observed, one of his men asked him, in case anything should happen to him in the engagement with the sloops, whether his wife knew where he had buried his money? He answered that nobody but himself and the Devil knew where it was and the longest liver should take all" (Johnson 1724, 61).

As early as 1822, in the juvenile drama *Black Beard, the Pirate; or, the Captive Princess*, Blackbeard is depicted as a domestic villain. The play features Blackbeard married, at home with his wife Orrah, but having designs on the princess Ismaen (the captive of the play's title). It is Orrah who threatens Blackbeard: "Beware how you trifle with the feelings of your faithful Orrah, or you both may have reason to repent it" (17). Blackbeard reveals that he does indeed plan adultery: "It shall be as Orrah suspects—Ismaen shall be mine! Then my name will increase in terror, and the world will have more cause to dread the name of Black Beard!" (17). When Orrah tries to help Ismaen escape, in order to rid herself of the rival, Blackbeard threatens her death for betraying him: "More treachery! —die base woman!" He finally stabs Orrah: "Fear not; you shall never more exist, if Black Beard has a will. Die, traitress!" (23). While Ismaen is rescued and reunited with Abdullah, Orrah apparently remains dead; thus we have an unusual literary example of Blackbeard the pirate killing a wife (specifically for betraying him) and pursuing another.

Aside from his wives, Blackbeard and other pirates had treasure reputedly hidden,[8] and so perhaps their stories are conducive to intertextual connection with Bluebeard, who forbade his wife to examine his affairs too closely. The Blackbeard figure is associated with other stories, such as the following: "It is said that over the years Blackbeard buried his enormous treasure in many places. Of one these was Smutty Nose Island among the Isles of Shoals. Natives of the area tell a story that he once returned from England with a beautiful girl, and while he buried the treasure, she explored the island. Surprised by a man-of-war, he hurriedly sailed away and left her. In vain she waited for his return until her death. Natives of Portsmouth, New Hampshire, say her ghost haunted the island for nearly a century" (Roberts 1924, 16–17). Stories that feature Blackbeard leaving a trail of women behind, presumably to their death, and the fact that the woman was exploring the island when she was marooned there, strengthen the connection between Blackbeard and Bluebeard.

Bluebeard Becomes a Pirate

In many cases, the name Bluebeard is used where Blackbeard might or must have been intended, such as beneath a description of Teach's pirate flag. There is one popular American printing of Charles Perrault's "Bluebeard", the *ur-text* of Bluebeard, that circulated in the early 1800s, printed in New York and Vermont, authored under the jocular parental pseudonym "Gaffer Blackbeard." Perhaps that has contributed to the confusion that exists today, particularly in the United States, where the pirate has all but eclipsed the serial wife killer of fairy tale. But at times they both appear together, so there can be no charge of simple mistaken identity. In the children's book version of *Puff the Magic Dragon*, by Romeo Muller (1979), there is a pirate character comically known as Very Long John Black and Bluebeard Kidd. In a comic book called *Scurvy Dogs* (issue no. 4), Blackbeard's crew are forced to look for help from the only man who can: "that's Blackbeard's one-time co-captain and brother, Bluebeard" (Macpherson 2005, n.p.). In the town of Charlotte Amalie on the island of St. Thomas, in the U.S. Virgin Islands, there is Blackbeard's Castle, said to have been used by Edward Teach and now a U.S. National Historic Landmark. On the other side of town is Bluebeard's Castle. It is a stone watchtower which, according to island lore, was "the castle build by the pirate Bluebeard for his lady love" (Varadan n.d.). The castle is now, ironically, a resort hotel. And it is one of the first examples of a demonstrable hybridity that has occurred between the pirate tradition and the actual fairy tale of Perrault. The hotel's self-description includes this legend: "It is believed that Bluebeard built this castle for his love, Mercedita. When he found out she had cheated on him, he killed her and left her never to return" ("Welcome" n.d.).[9] Here we have the pirate connected to recognizable elements from the fairy tale; not simply the murder of women, but in the supposed transgression of Mercedita.

In another interesting example from popular culture, the Marvel Comic Book *Moon Knight* (Hobson 1985) features Bluebeard as the alter ego of a crazed reporter, Arnold Perril. In a nice twist, his base of operation is the Bluebeard's Castle at an abandoned amusement park in New Jersey. He wields an axe and a set of huge keys that emit neuron rays. Furthermore, his anger is misogynist. Angered at being fired from his job by a woman, he adopts the guise of Bluebeard. He captures four women, and threatens in print (thanks to his reporter alter ego) that once he has five they will all be killed. His editor, the woman who first fired him, is captured as his fifth "wife." The women are rescued by the eponymous Moon Knight, hero of the comic book's title. So far, so Bluebeard. Except the axe-wielding madman is depicted artistically, even on the cover, in pirate garb; instead of a cutlass at his waist, the all-important oversized keys are clearly visible. The tall boots, tailored and frilled coat, buccaneer hat, and ribbon around his shirt all suggest a pirate costume.

Finally, the most clearly hybrid version is the striking example from the 1930s *Good Housekeeping* series of stories about pirates written by Emma-

Lindsay Squier. The series was called Pirate-Plunder, and the first episode, from a December 1932 issue, was titled "Bluebeard and the Spanish Witch." Squier knew that Bluebeard was not Blackbeard, because Pirate-Plunder number 8 (March 1935) featured Captain James Thatch (formerly Edward Teach) and was called "Blackbeard vs. Blue Eyes." In this latter episode, Blackbeard is described as he should be: "Under the wide brim of the felt hat his shaggy black hair hung shoulder length. An unkempt, matted growth of beard all but covered his swarthy face. The beard had been braided into small strands and tied with red and yellow ribbons" (1935, 46). Also, the story is set in the town of Charlotte Amalie, St. Thomas, and after the events narrated he allegedly "took up his lawless existence in North Carolina and continued his depredations among merchant vessels," and is "slain in a terrific battle on the decks of his own pinnace by a young Virginia lieutenant" (203). It is evident both that Squier had done her Blackbeard homework and that she was supplying a narrative that goes with the tower in the town of Charlotte Amalie bearing the pirate's name. The magazine announced the series with this notice: "Since early last spring Miss Squier has been in the West Indies gathering and verifying stories about some of the most romantic figures that ever sailed the seas—the pirates of the Spanish Main" (59).

In "Bluebeard and the Spanish Witch," the story concerns "the young pirate captain known as Bluebeard, and his sweetheart, who, in the almost forgotten annals of the year 1697, was called 'the Spanish Witch'" (Squier 1932, 59). (Is it a coincidence that the story references 1697, the date of Perrault's fairy tale Bluebeard?) This man, Edouard de la Barbe Bleue, was "a Frenchman born" and "rumored . . . of gentle birth." His home is the other castle in St. Thomas, on the Eastern Hill, the one that now has a resort hotel in it. The story's "Spanish Witch" is named Mercedes, a version of the "Mercedita" that Bluebeard built his castle for, but in Squier's story he did not build the castle for her, nor was she unfaithful. Instead, Squier's story has all the high-blown style of a Harlequin romance; Mercedes' ship is overcome while she is on her way to Spain, an unwilling fiancée. Bluebeard is gallant, literally disarms Mercedes, and offers her the choice to continue on her way or go with him. He is genuinely taken with her fierce independence and refusal to be cowed by him. As in the Bluebeard fairy tale, Bluebeard goes away; in contrast to the tale, and echoing the injunction that Perrault's Bluebeard issues to his wife, it is Mercedes who threatens him: "I ask naught of thee except faithfulness! Go where thou wilt, do what thou wilt, for good or ill, I will share thy fate. But deceive me or love another woman, and my hatred will be more consuming than fire, blacker than death itself!" (165). There is no forbidden chamber as she is given full run of his castle, but what she discovers among his treasures is a locked box to which she has the key, and the rhetoric is recognizably Bluebeard-like: "Then yielding suddenly to curiosity, she selected from the clanking bunch the key that fitted and thrust it into the lock" (168). It opens to reveal love letters from other scorned women, the same who have been sending her dangerous gifts. It is not merely the secret of the other women that has been kept from her that she finds in this box but, in a continuation of the reverse of Perrault's dynamic, it is evidence of Bluebeard's breach of faith. Mercedes' revenge is to bring the women to the castle to divide up his treasures. In an ironic twist, Bluebeard's return rescues her from the stake where she has been sentenced to burn as a witch. After riding out a hurricane together in his ship, Mon Désir, they are reputed to have made it to Cuba where they were married, never again returning to St. Thomas.

Not only does it appear that the omission of the story as a nursery story lessened our familiarity with the fairy tale, but that an encounter with the pirate tradition waylaid the character (and, in the case of American popular consciousness, at least, has completely usurped Perrault's "Bluebeard"), later borrowing some of his own details back from the fairy tale. Blackbeard and Bluebeard have always had more in common than at first may appear, and thanks to the new tradition of Bluebeard-as-pirate they will continue to have dealings with one another in the English tradition.

True Crime Bluebeards

Although the term "serial killer" is a twentieth-century coinage, of course the phenomenon itself is not. While numerous men have murdered wives, several prominent murderers were labeled in the contemporary media as "Bluebeard" or "lady Bluebeard."

H. H. Holmes

Perhaps the earliest example is that of Herman Mudgett, a.k.a. H. H. Holmes, a "Bluebeard" for whom the press coined the term "multimurderer." He has also been called America's first serial killer.[10] Holmes was convicted in 1896 of killing one man that led to his hanging, but he confessed after his conviction to killing twenty-seven men, women, and children.[11] He married bigamously (proving this point was important for his prosecution, as one of his "wives" could then testify against him) and murdered mistresses. His confession also says that a housekeeper and her niece opened a door on him with a victim: "It was a time for quick action, rather than for words of explanation on my part, and before they had recovered from the horror of the sight, they were within the fatal vault, so lately tenanted by the dead body" (Schechter 1994, 348). But Holmes became "Bluebeard" in the popular imagination immediately upon the discovery of his specially designed "murder castle" in postfire Chicago. Ostensibly a hotel and nicknamed "the Castle," Holmes designed two massive floors above a shopping arcade that he fitted with labyrinthine corridors, chutes to the cellar, a vault disguised as a room, trapdoors, and dead ends. Rooms were linked to gas lines so that sleeping tenants could be murdered quietly. Bodies were disposed of on the premises using a crematorium, acid vats, and lime, but Holmes also sold skeletons and buried several in other cities in rented premises. The floor plans appeared in *The New York World*, captioned "Blue-Beard's Chamber of Horror."[12]

Henri Landru, "The Bluebeard of Gambais"

The Frenchman Henri Désiré Landru (1860–1922; the irony of his middle name is unfortunate), nicknamed *"l'assassin bien aimé"* (the well-loved assassin), earned the title "Bluebeard" for his series of bigamous marriages and alleged murders for money during World War I. Landru is one of a number of contemporary "Bluebeards" of both sexes who exploited the newspaper classifieds to seek out spouses. Landru went under several aliases, but his assumption of the title "Bluebeard" is confirmed in the film directed by Claude Chabrol, entitled simply *Bluebeard* (1963; French title: *Landru*). In fact, though, Landru was being labeled "Bluebeard" within two days of his arrest in both the French and international press, while no hard evidence of murder was ever produced. Landru was convicted on circumstantial evidence alone, and the widely circulated characterization of him as the Bluebeard of Gambais no doubt contributed.[13] Further resonating with the Bluebeard story was the theory held by police for his murder of Andrée Babelay, who had no money. The police surmised that she had opened his locked upper room and discovered artifacts known to belong to missing women.[14]

The trial and execution of Landru draw inevitable comparison with his compatriot and forbear, Gilles de Rais. The French claim to Bluebeard as a national figure is perhaps exemplified by the choice of title for Rayner Heppenstall's study of twentieth-century murderers, *Bluebeard and After: Three Decades of Murder in France* (1972).

After Landru

Landru also makes highly public a form of Bluebeardism whereby monetary gain is the motive for serial seduction and murder of women or wives (or, in the case of the "Lady Bluebeards," men or husbands). Charles Sterling is an early example, by comparison. Henry Fay's heartfelt account is dated 1835 and subtitled: "who is now a prisoner in the City of New York"; it is catalogued with nineteenth-century legal treatises (no. 36632). Johann Otto Hoch was another so-termed in a 2006 account by Troy Taylor, "Chicago's 'Bluebeard'" (Taylor alluded to a contemporary *Chicago Sun* segment on Hoch that called him "Bluebeard"). Hoch, a German immigrant, married at least 44 women across the United States and murdered many of them,[15] sometimes within days of the wedding, using arsenic. He was hanged in 1906. George Sims wrote in 1915 of George Joseph Smith, calling him "the Bluebeard of the bath." Smith was charged with marrying five women bigamously, for insurance money willed to him. In all cases, his wives were persuaded to take a bath in a public lodging house and to leave the door open in order to admit him. Mr. James "Bluebeard" Watson was likewise so designated throughout the account of his capture by Detective Nick Harris and Helene Rico in "The Modern Bluebeard" (1923), and in Craig Rice, "Bluebeard's Buried Treasure" (1952). Watson confessed to killing seven women between 1915 and 1919; the suspected number of his victims is much higher. Like several other "modern Bluebeards," Watson used matrimonial advertisements to lure his victims.

According to the lurid account by his lawyer Evan Bartlett, *Love Murders of Harry F. Powers: Beware Such Bluebeards* (1931), Henry Powers nodded when asked by one of the officers if he had read about "Desire Dandru" [*sic*]. Powers was called a Bluebeard repeatedly by this author and shared with Landru the use of correspondence and bigamous marriage for money. His proven murders of two women and three of one of the women's children at a purpose-built garage in West Virginia were clearly motivated by monetary gain, and his letters illustrate that he was adept at luring women this way. Landru's trial predated Powers' by only a decade. Like Landru, the Austrian Max Gufler used "matrimonial advertisements" to his financial gain, but he answered rather than initiated them. The bodies of three of his victims were pulled from the River Danube.[16] As late as 1993, the Bluebeard label served in Ann Rule's book *A Rose for Her Grave* (1993), an account of American Randy Roth's serial wife murders for monetary gain.

Later twentieth-century serial killers generally do not have the label for multiple marriages, but rather for "collecting," and frequently dismembering, women. This is the case with Ed Gein, the American whose murders inspired both *Psycho* and *The Texas Chainsaw Massacre*. Ed Gein was arrested in 1957, and among the many horrors of his house he had the "trophy heads" of nine women.[17] In this way, the Bluebeard label has lost much of its specificity.

"Lady" Bluebeards

One critic commented recently, "Interestingly, there is no term for the killing of a husband by a wife" (Frigon 2006, 5). Instead, the Bluebeard term is feminized, although the rhetoric of monstrosity and freakishness intensifies, as the label "Bluebeard in Skirts" indicates.[18] There is an entire book devoted to *Women Bluebeards* (O' Donnell 1928) in which the author groups anecdotal discussions of many women alleged to have murdered their spouses and sometimes their dependents.

The early-twentieth-century American serial murderer Belle Gunness has, thanks both to headlines of the time and to her critical biographer Janet Langlois (1985a), a claim to the counterpart title, "The Lady Bluebeard." But in first according this title to Gunness in print, even the journalist Stewart H. Holbrook gestured to the multiplicity of American Bluebeard contenders: "Of all the many Bluebeards of both sexes the United States has produced, none I believe has been the subject of more comment, or the source of more folklore than Mrs. Gunness" (1941, 240).[19]

Again, however, the label appears infinitely regenerative, as evinced by the title of a recent work by William Anderson on Lyda Dooley-McHaffie-Lewis-Meyer-Southard-Whitlock-Shaw (née Anna Eliza Trueblood) of Idaho: *Lady Bluebeard: The True Story of Love and Marriage, Death and Flypaper* (1994). Lyda Trueblood married and dispatched a series of husbands before her sensational capture in and extradition from Hawaii, trial, and imprisonment in 1921 (contemporaneous with Landru). She boiled the arsenic from flypaper after her husbands had been persuaded to take out large life insurance policies and to will their estates to her. The narrative of her escape from prison after a decade and recapture from another marriage in the interim continues the sensationalist aspect, as does her later pardon at age 49 when considered "no longer a threat to society." She died of natural causes in 1958, ironically enough after another marriage and while holding a position as a cook in a home for wealthy bachelors.[20]

Whether as a crossover from pirate lore or in true crime descriptions of serial killers, the "Bluebeard" label has been borrowed from fairy tale and lent to a host of others, imagined and real, male and female. In the course of doing so, it has acquired the status of noundom—a Bluebeard—trading its specificity in favor of general allusions to monstrosity and seriality. In the case of serial murderers, their borrowed name reflects their status as folkloric figures and generative of folklore themselves.

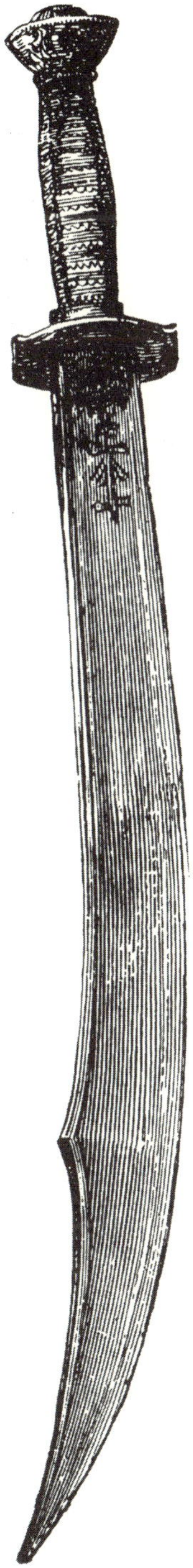

Part 2

Bluebeard in the English Eighteenth Century

Chapter 3

Found in Translation

Charles Perrault's "Bluebeard" in English

Robert Samber was the first, in 1729, to provide an English translation of Perrault's French fairy tale. His edition not only launched a series of reprints, new editions, and bilingual versions into the English publishing scene throughout the eighteenth century, but it also strongly impressed itself on the "Bluebeard tradition" that continued to thrive exponentially throughout the Victorian years. Versions based on Perrault's "Bluebeard" continued to be the norm even after the tale was joined by Grimm stories from *Kinder- und Hausmärchen* (Grimm 1812–1815, 1819), which were translated (without any "Bluebeard" variant) into English as *German Popular Stories* in 1823–1826 (Grimm). But the eighteenth century (and, as far as "Bluebeard" is concerned, the first half of the nineteenth) belonged to Perrault. It is Perrault's "Bluebeard" after all that was translated in editions of *Mother Goose* and that almost immediately broke out and headlined chapbooks on its own, or sometimes with one other tale, traveling to villages, markets, fairs, and many a funeral throughout Great Britain in the chapman's bags (or, in America, the peddler's pack). It is Perrault's "Bluebeard" on which are based the late-eighteenth-century examples of *Blue Beard, or, The Flight of Harlequin*, a musical pantomime by William Reeve (1791); *Caleb Williams* (1794), the novel by William Godwin; *The Iron Chest* (1796), by George Colman the Younger (a play apparently based on Godwin's novel); and the huge hit *Blue Beard, or Female Curiosity!* (1798), also by George Colman, with music by Michael Kelly.

Samber's 1729 edition, *Histories, or Tales of past Times . . . with morals, by M. Perrault, Translated into English*, was a critical moment in the English tradition of Bluebeard. In *The Folktale* (1946), Stith Thompson wrote: "To the literary world the story has become known through Perrault's famous collection of 1697, and wherever that version has exerted great influence it has determined the form of the story" (35). By "exert[ing] great influence" for 120 years or more

17

THE

BLUE BEARD.

TALE III.

THERE was once upon a time a man who had ſeveral fine houſes both in town and country, a good deal of ſilver and gold plate, embroider'd furniture, and coaches gilt all over with

Headpiece for Robert Samber's English translation (1729). The use of multiple sites of action viewed simultaneously is a visual technique for suspense frequently replicated as a "set piece" of Bluebeard illustration. From Samber, Robert. 1729. *Histories, or Tales of Past Times*. London: Printed for R. Montagu at the Book Ware-House, 1741. Courtesy of The Lilly Library, Indiana University, Bloomington.

prior to the Grimm versions entering the English lexicon, it effectively "determined the form of the story" for the English language.

The "Bluebeard" fairy tale was one of the "fashionably dressed French invaders" that became "naturalized" into English (Darton 1932, 94). Charles Perrault authored the "master text" of Bluebeard in a 1695 manuscript of tales (*contes*), dedicated to "Mademoiselle" (Elisabeth Charlotte d'Orléans, niece of Louis XIV and daughter of his brother Philippe, future grandmother of Marie Antoinette) that also served as a mock-up for publication: *Contes de Ma Mère l'Oye* (*Mother Goose Tales*).[1] Expanded by three prose tales from the manuscript's five, it became in 1697 *Histoires, ou Contes du Temps Passe*, with a "subtitle" on a sign on the door in the frontispiece illustration: *Contes de Ma Mère l'Oye*. While in French the stories are still known as Perrault's *Contes*, it was as "Mother Goose" that the tales were anglicized; first as fairy tales, later as unrelated collections of nursery rhymes. Samber's 1729 edition reflected a change in the original order of Perrault's tales[2] and translated the titles of the eight prose tales as follows: "The Little Red Riding-hood," "The Fairy," "The Blue Beard," "The Sleeping Beauty in the Wood,"[3] "The Master Cat, or Puss in Boots," "Cinderilla [*sic*], or the Little Glass Slipper," "Riquet a la Houpe" ["Riquet with the Tuft"], and "Little Poucet [Thumb] and his Brothers." The Samber edition also followed the example of French editions by including a novel, "The Discreet Princess," by Mademoiselle Marie Jeanne L'Héritier de Villandon, one of the fashionable fairy tale salon hosts contemporary with (and related to) Perrault. The novel continued to be reprinted as part of this collection throughout the next two centuries.[4]

Perrault's "La Barbe bleue" is the *ur*-text for what followed. Morna Daniels, writing about "Puss in Boots," noted the impact of Perrault's tales north of the Channel: "In Britain the individual stories were quickly pirated for chapbook versions, and other illustrated little books for children. . . . The illustrations were hand-coloured for those who could afford the more expensive version" (2002, 8). As the tales were not even credited with translation into English until 1729, the English chapbooks do not seem to follow as "quickly" on Perrault's heels as it may sound. After all, a pirated version of the entire *Contes* appeared from the publisher Moetjens, in the Hague, the very same year as the original Parisian publication (1697).[5] Harry Stone, in *Dickens and the Invisible World*, said: "Soon after they were translated into English, Perrault's tales . . . appeared in chapbook form, and in that guise became immensely popular and made their way into every village and hamlet in the British Isles. When Dickens was a boy, *Cinderella* and *Bluebeard*, and *Sleeping Beauty* were as well known and as 'English' as *Jack the Giant Killer, Tom Thumb*, and *Jack and the Beanstalk*" (1979, 24). Dickens was born in 1812, so he was not a boy so very "soon" after Samber's translation of 1729. But the prevalence and enduring popularity of the tale in chapbook form is undisputed.

In Margaret Spufford's book on English chapbooks, her very first quotation from a chapbook reader includes a testimony to "Bluebeard" (1981, 2): "My Father and Mother had to get me a new Halfpenney or Penney Book before those Leeches went on, nor do I think it was Money spent in waste, for when I got a little better I read those Books and I shall never forget the Impressions one of them left upon my mind the title of the Book was Blue Beard. . . . (Bowd [1889] 1955)" (original ellipsis). The author of this diary was writing in his sixty-sixth year, recollecting here his boyhood age of seven (1830), at the time of the bout with scarlet fever. It is perhaps coincidental that "Bluebeard" is the first chapbook referenced by Spufford, but surely not coincidentally so memorable to a childhood reader. In addition to such anecdotal evidence are the many extant copies of chapbooks in library and private collections, contemporary publishers' lists on the covers of these, and booksellers' catalogues.

It took over thirty years to translate such a popular work into English, if indeed Robert Samber's 1729 edition (London: Pote and Montagu, including a dedication by Samber to the Countess of Granville) is the first. A major debate over the chronology of the first translation was occasioned by several editions through the latter half of the 1700s that ascribe their translation to "G. M.

Gent." Most problematically, one now-notorious "G. M." edition was dated (in Roman numerals) 1719, apparently predating Samber's translation by a decade. Older reputable work on fairy tales, even a 1905 Harvard libraries publication, referenced "Gent's English version of Perrault." J. Saxon Childers, in his 1925 edition of Perrault's *Histories*, commented gleefully on the mistaken surname: "A really amusing mistake is made in the *Library of Harvard University Bibliographical Contributions*, No. 56, Cambridge, 1905; and, of course, the mistake is doubly amusing, because it is so seldom an error is able to avoid the searching eyes of the Harvard librarians."[6] However, Saxon Childers himself mistakenly credits the 1719 date with its face value (127–28).[7] It was the folklorists Iona and Peter Opie who demonstrated that the date was the result of a misprint of roman numerals for 1799 and that this edition was therefore not a first (1974, 30 n.), although they in turn mistakenly assert that Samber had not translated Perrault's two "*moralités*."[8]

It may well have been as a result of the erroneous "1719" text that Guy Miège was considered the likely translator, G. M. He was certainly qualified for the role. Guy Miège was born in 1644 and educated in Lausanne, coming to London in 1661 where he served as undersecretary to the ambassador to Russia, Sweden, and Denmark, the Earl of Carlisle. In addition to surveys such as *The New State of England under Their Majesties K. William and Q. Mary in Three Parts* (1693), *The New State of England under Our Present Monarch, K. William III* . . . (1701), *The New State of England under Our Sovereign Queen Anne* (1703), and *The Present State of Great Britain and Ireland in Three Parts . . . also The Present State of His Majesty's Dominions in Germany* (1723), and others besides, his list of writings on language are most impressive. In short, Miège wrote grammar handbooks *in* both French and English, *about* both French and English, and for both native and nonnative readers. His credentials for translating Perrault's *Contes* are sound. Further, titles such as *Miscellanea, or, A Choice Collection of Wise and Ingenious Sayings, &C. of Princes, Philosophers, Statesmen, Courtiers, and Others, out of Several Ancient and Modern Authors, for the Pleasurable Entertainment of the Nobility and Gentry of Both Sexes* seem to demonstrate that Miège was well-read and writing with a view to entertaining the "nobility and gentry of both sexes," in other words: the original audience for Perrault's *Contes de Ma Mère l'Oye*.

However, to date, the earliest edition ascribed to G. M. is the Collins edition of 1763, so while many libraries continue to reference Guy Miège as the translator G. M., it is perhaps unlikely to be him. Nevertheless, what is incontrovertible is that these two translations, that by Samber and that by G. M., dominate the English editions, and once attribution is correctly made, surprisingly the number of G. M. editions outnumber those by "R. S."[9] For instance, the first American edition (1794) is G. M.'s. More notably, it is widely but incorrectly assumed that Andrew Lang used Samber's translation for his *Blue Fairy Book* (1888). For "Cinderilla" [*sic*], he did so; but in fact, for "Bluebeard" he did not. This correction has further ramifications for sourcing twentieth-century "re-translations" of Lang's text.[10] Thus, both Samber and G. M. are equally important in "determining the form" of the story in English.

Distinguishing the G. M. and Samber translations is therefore not only possible, but extremely useful. The two translations are very close. As G. M.'s translation is more compact his is used as the base text in the following, while Samber's elaborations appear after within square brackets. Where relevant the text from which it deviates is then bolded. Quoted here are the first two paragraphs of the tale to illustrate the translations representatively:

> [The] Blue Beard.
>
> There was [*R. S.*: once upon a time] a man who had [several] fine houses, both in town and country, a [good] deal of silver and gold plate, embroidered furniture, and coaches **gilded** [gilt] all over with gold. But this [same] man had the misfortune to have a *Blue Beard*, which made him so frightfully ugly, that all the women and girls ran away from him.
>
> One of his neighbours, a lady of quality, had two daughters who were perfect beauties. He desired of her one of them in marriage, leaving to her the choice of **which of the two** [which of them] she would bestow upon him. They would neither of them have him, and sent him backwards and forwards from one another, **being not able to bear the thoughts of marrying** [being resolved never to marry] a man **who** [that] had a *Blue Beard*. **And what besides** [That which moreover] gave them [the greater] disgust and aversion, was **his having** [that he had] already been married to several wives, and no-body ever knew **what became** [were become] of them.[11]

Leaving aside for a moment the issue of whose name appears on the title page of these editions, there is a short list of hallmarks that distinguish the G. M. translation from Samber's translation, and generally the title is the first indicator: G. M. versions use "Blue Beard," while Samber translated the French article, "*The* Blue Beard," consistently from the title through to the end of the translation. Samber also wrote "a full eight days" instead of "a whole week," again choosing a more Gallic and literal translation over idiomatic English. Elsewhere, the reverse seems to be true, however, and Samber used more idiomatic English than G. M., such as "the floor was **covered over** [R. S.: all covered] with clotted blood."[12]

The translation is G. M.'s rather than Samber's if the text states: "a *deal* of silver and gold plate," "*the* lady their mother," "mirth and feasting" (instead of "feasts and collations"), "two great *wardrobes*" (instead of "rooms"); if she promises to observe "very exactly" Bluebeard's injunction, she runs down "a little back staircase" (instead of "a back pair of stairs"), she nearly "twice or thrice" breaks her neck running down these stairs (Samber prefers "two or three times"); if at the door "she made a stop" (instead of "she stopt"); and if Bluebeard castigates her "you was resolved to go into the closet, was you not?" (instead of "were"), and gives her "half a quarter of an hour" (instead of "quarter of an hour"). Bluebeards that "bawl" for their wife to come downstairs derive from G. M.; if they wield a "scimitar" they follow G. M., while Samber chooses "cutlass." A full list and a detailed interpretation of Samber's choices must keep for another time. But as the majority of the translations are identical, as are the verse morals at the end (inspired by, rather than translated from, Perrault's),[13] discussion below features the most striking examples of departure between them in the course of comparing these English translations to Perrault's French.

Having established the sources of the translation choices, it is now possible to look at the substantive highlights of the English translations in relation to the French original. Ideally, the French and English would be (re)published side by side. The eighteenth century produced several bilingual versions of the *Mother Goose* tales, as listed above, and "presumably for pedagogical purposes" (Daniels 2002, 6). For clarity in discussing the English translations in relation to the French, the translation will only be ascribed to either Samber or G. M. when there is a substantive deviation.

While the English translation of "Bluebeard" follows Perrault's French very closely indeed, the nature of translation necessitates shifts in meaning, connotations, and so on. Claire Lise Malarte-Feldman noted: "Perrault's style is deceptively simple: stripped of any superfluous ornaments, every word counts. Conscientious translators find themselves at a cross-roads at the moment of the definite choice for a word. Neil Philip [Philip and Simborowski 128] commented: 'It is hard to convey in English translation the splendid brevity of Perrault's prose. His distinctive wit and elegance are based on succinctness and economy'" (1999, 193).

The *Concordance* to the *Mother Goose* tales bears this out, noting an entire vocabulary of 2676 words, including different forms of the same verb. The concordance notes that this is half the vocabulary of either Corneille or Racine, other French classicists (Barchilon 1977, viii).[14] Does it matter that in translation the prospective bride goes to visit Bluebeard's house with "ladies of her acquaintance" as opposed to her "*meilleures amies*" (best friends)? Probably not, although arguments could be made: best friends exert more influence over the bride; they are therefore arguably implicated in her decision to marry him; the phrase needs to be compared later in the story with the young women who arrive at the house as soon as Bluebeard vacates it. But in most cases, even subtle differences in translation do make a palpable difference. A sentence such as the following, early in the story when Bluebeard is requesting a bride from one of the two daughters of a local lady of quality, illustrates this process: "He desired of her one of them in marriage, leaving to her the choice of which of them she would bestow upon him." In Perrault's 1697 text, "desired" was "*demanda*" (asked/demanded) and "bestow" was "*donner*" (give). While the literal meaning is similar, Bluebeard's early characterization is at issue. We already know that Bluebeard has a blue beard and that it frightens everyone; we know he is rich, having "several fine houses both in town and country" and so on. To "desire" and have a wife "bestowed" connotes a courtly process, in a sense wooing the mother as much as the daughters and characterizes a gracious man. Tellingly, it characterizes Bluebeard as a man who has desires, but his desire is not specific to one woman. If instead he had "asked" to be "given," it suggests rather a proprietary sense, a transaction, with an expectation of compliance. To illustrate further, he might "demand" that she "render" a daughter, characterizing him this early in the story as a domineering brute. Finally, are we to read in Perrault's original a balance between the verb "*donner*" used here and that used later, for example, when Bluebeard deigns to "give" his wife some time to prepare for death (*Je vous donne*)?

In another and rather more critical example, is Bluebeard a "civil" man or an "honest" one (*fort honnête*)? Both G. M. and Samber translate "*honnête*" here as "civil" following the term's specific currency at the time. Accordingly, the wife is "uncivil" when leaving her guests (*malhonnête*). But at the end where Perrault describes her new husband as also "*fort honnête*," G. M. chooses "worthy," while Samber chooses "very honest." Both translators thereby lose Perrault's irony of having the same epithet to describe the wife's initial opinion of *both* husbands she weds.[15]

We pick up the story at the early party in Bluebeard's house, where all the women have so much fun and see the wealth he has that the youngest daughter decides to accept Bluebeard in marriage. The English translation reads: "In short, everything so well succeeded, that the youngest daughter began to think." Perrault's version says "everything went so well" (*tout alla si bien*). Given what will follow, and that Bluebeard is commonly understood to have set up the test or trap for his bride, the concept of "success" underscores the sense of a script, or at least a plan. He not only succeeds in "engag[ing] their affection," but also in drawing in the youngest daughter. But in English, Bluebeard's subsequent absence is a more haphazard event: "About a month afterwards [the] *Blue Beard* told his wife, that he was obliged to take a [journey]." Perrault's French reads "*Au bout d'un mois*" (at the end of one month), which sounds more intentional on Bluebeard's part. Samber translates "*en Province*" as travel to a "distant country" rather than "take a country-journey," further enhancing the subtext of a premeditated trap.

The injunction is one-half of the most essential elements of this tale, the breach of it being the other. The English translation renders the first part of Bluebeard's instructions as follows: "desiring her to divert herself in his absence, send for her friends and acquaintance, carry them into the country, if she pleased, and make good cheer wherever she was." The notion of "desire" recurs, with the stronger endorsement of the verb "*prier*," as opposed to the earlier "*demander*." But the original for "wherever she was" is "*partout*" (everywhere). Again, the difference is subtle, but giving the bride a "*passe-partout*" in effect and then belying that with the injunction not to go into the little room is not the same. In other words, "have fun wherever you go, but do not go in there" is not the same as "go everywhere, but not there." Perrault's Bluebeard simply defines his good china as that which is not used daily (*qui ne sert pas tous les jours*), and so does G. M. (which is not every day in use), while Samber's Bluebeard appears to give instructions as to their use: "which is not to be made use of every day." Samber thus hints that already Bluebeard's generosity has limits and that he concerns himself with even the smallest of details of his housekeeping. The injunction itself is worth quoting in full: "Open them all, go into all and every one except that little closet, which I forbid you, and forbid it [you] in such a manner, that if you happen to open it, there is nothing but what you may expect from my just anger and resentment." The English translations follow Perrault very closely here,[16] except that "resentment" is an interesting and spontaneous addition to mere "*colère*" (anger). In English, Bluebeard promises both "anger *and* resentment"; the connotations of resentment are quite different from those of anger and characterize a different set of emotions and reactions in the man and in his relations with his wife.

When the bride's friends arrive, without even "stay[ing] to be sent for," they "ran thro' all the rooms, closets, wardrobes" and so on; Perrault emphasizes that they did so "*aussitôt*" (immediately), emphasizing their "great . . . impatience" to see the riches of the house. This emphasis on impatience and immediacy both generalizes the trait to the female sex, and not simply Bluebeard's wife alone, and foreshadows the nearly break-neck speed with which she will descend to the forbidden closet. But it also contrasts what she will do when she gets there. While the ladies rush about the house "immediately" upon arrival, she will hesitate at the door, thinking of the injunction and pondering its consequences. This pause on the threshold heightens suspense, but also characterizes the breach as a conscious decision to act. The English translations describe her curiosity as "press[ing]" her, as if an affliction, taking their cue directly from the French, which also contains this notion of pressure: "*elle fut si pressée de sa curiosité.*"[17] The translations also editorialize on her rush to get downstairs simply by translating "*tant de precipitation*" (so much speed) as "excessive haste" and commenting with narrative objectivity that "she had like to have broken her neck" as opposed to reflecting the character's own thoughts, as in Perrault: "she thought (*elle pensa*) she would break her neck."

Again, the moment of transgression is the iconic moment and the turning point of the tale, and I will quote the English translations in full (differences between the two separated by a backslash), noting on several occasions a more literal translation of Perrault's French in square brackets for comparative purposes:

> Being come to the closet door, she made a stop / stopt for some time, thinking upon her husband's orders [*defense*, prohibition], and considering what unhappiness might attend her if she was / were she [*d'avoir été*, to have been] disobedient; but the temptation was so strong she could not overcome it: She took then the little key and opened it tremblingly / in a very great trembling; [*D'abord*, At first] but could not at first see any thing plainly / see nothing distinctly, because the windows were shut; after some moments she began to perceive / observe that the floor was covered over / all covered with clotted blood, on which lay [*se miraient*, were mirrored] the bodies of several dead women ranged against the walls. (These were all the wives whom / that the *Blue Beard* had married and murder'd [*égorgée*, slit the throats of] one after another.)[18] She thought / that / she should have died [would die] for fear, and the key that / which she pulled out of the lock fell out of her hand.
>
> After having somewhat recover'd her surprise, she took up the key, locked the door and went up stairs into her chamber to recover herself, but she could not, so much was she frightened [*émue*, moved].[19] Having observed that the key of the closet was stain'd with blood, she tried two or three times to wipe it off, but the blood would not come out; in vain did she wash it and even rub it with soap and sand, the blood still

> remained, for the key was a Fairy [*Fée*, enchanted], and she could never quite [*il n'y avait pas moyen*, there was no way to] make it clean; when the blood was gone off from one side, it came again on the other.

Interestingly, Perrault's wife foreshadows her actual transgression by imagining it having already happened before she has even opened the door: "*d'avoir été*" is literally "to have been" and renders the transgression in the past of some as-yet-not-done act. Next, the English translators seem to dwell slightly less than Perrault on the grisly details. Perrault's dead women are displayed, their throats slit. The English translation states more clinically that they lay on blood and that they had been murdered. But in their brief section "Perrault in English" in their biography of Charles Perrault, Jacques Barchilon and Peter Flinders noted this translation as one example of Samber mistranslating from Perrault:

> Most mistranslations are not worth signaling, but an extraordinary one occurs in "Bluebeard" and refers to the terrifying moment when the unfortunate woman discovers the bodies of the previous wives. The passage in Samber's text read: "after some moments she began to observe that the floor was all covered over with clotted blood, on *which lay the bodies of several dead women ranged against the walls*" (our italics). Obviously the dead women could not at the same time "lay" on the floor and be "ranged" against the wall. This logical impossibility is the result of a careless translation. What the French text says is that the floor was covered with clotted blood in which were reflected (*se miraient*) the bodies of several women attached (or hanging) along the walls (1981, 111–12).

In fact, Perrault's original, in both manuscript and published edition, used "*se miroient*" (reflected, mirrored), making the mistranslation even more obvious. G. M.'s version is the same as Samber's on this point.[20]

The translation of the key as "*a* fairy", supplying the article to the adjective "*fée*" itself (enchanted), occasioned a number of later English translations to elaborate on this Fairy who gave the key to Bluebeard, and even to make another allusion to the scene in *Othello* in which Othello gives the handkerchief to Desdemona and tells her it has magical properties (that will specifically reveal a betrayal of trust within marriage). It supplies a literal fairy to the borderline "fairy" tale; the key (as is often mentioned) is the only literally enchanted element of the tale. Perrault made it clear that because the key is enchanted, there is no possibility of cleaning it. The revision between the 1695 manuscript and

1697 publication reinforces this notion of desperate futility; instead of merely wiping the key, she now wipes it two or three times (*Elle l'essuya* becomes *l'essuia deux ou trois fois*), and at the same time Perrault added that the blood had the magical ability to switch from one side of the key to the other (*quand on ôtoit le sang d'un costé, il revenoit de l'autre*). In later translations, the wife will use a variety of contemporary cleaning products, such as brick dust, in addition to soap (often referred to by brand) and sand.

In the Samber/G. M. English translations the wife pretends to be "extremely glad" of her husband's sudden and unexpected return home. It is not from either of them, then, that the phrase "in a transport of joy" derives, although it is used frequently thereafter in chapbooks. But their Bluebeard is almost casual about when he will get the key. It is true that in the original, also, he waits until the next morning to ask for the keys to be returned to him, and very little has ever been made by any commentator on the night the wife must pass in waiting for this inevitable moment. But when he does ask, they translate "*tantot*" (right away) as "presently," which sounds coyly casual. Similarly, the question he asks on seeing the indelible blood is not "*pour quoi*" (why), as in Perrault, but is translated as "How comes" it there. The difference is both subtle and important. Both Bluebeard and his wife know "how" the blood got on the key; the question of "why" it is there is a more general one: Why did you disobey me? Why did you open the door? Samber's Bluebeard accuses his wife of being "resolv'd" to go into the forbidden closet, but Perrault's Bluebeard shows a better understanding of his wife's nature when he accuses her instead of wanting to go in (*voulu*); this emphasizes the idea of temptation, rather than mere disobedience (resolve). Furthermore, it was only "*vouloir*" that could overcome the lack of resolve she demonstrates on the threshold. In English the wife shows "all the signs of a true repentance, and that she would never more be disobedient," which is not that same as repenting of not having been obedient, without future promises: "*toutes les marques d'un vrai repentir de n'avoir pas été obéissant*" [all the signs of a true penitent for not having been obedient]. Because she has already "witnessed" (*témoigner*) her happiness at his sudden return home, Bluebeard perhaps accurately reads these signs as meaningless. Already, the scene is reminiscent of Shakespeare's *Othello*, when Bluebeard tells his wife she must die, and she begs for time to pray, stalling the execution. But the English translations bring *Othello* even closer when Bluebeard states: "You must die, Madam, said he, and that presently." Perrault's French is "*tout à l'heure*," so the English "presently" is accurate, but had Samber or G. M. translated it as "soon" or "shortly" or "imminently" then we would not have the echo of Othello telling Desdemona that she is to die "presently":

Othello: Thou art on thy deathbed.
Desdemona: Ay, but not yet to die.
Othello: Yes, *presently*:
  Therefore confess thee freely of thy sin . . .
  Thou art to die (5.2, emphasis added).

While Othello goes on to tell Desdemona to pray before he kills her, he says only: "do it, and be brief." Bluebeard, however, gives (*Je vous donne*) his wife precisely "*un demi quart-d'heure . . . mais pas un moment d'avantage*" (half a quarter of an hour, but not one moment more). This is one of the few important substantive departures between Samber's and G. M.'s translations. Samber translates this as "a quarter of an hour," doubling the length of time given in Perrault, while G. M. translates the literal "half a quarter of an hour." A survey of other translations of this phrase demonstrate either how much creative license is given to conceiving this scene, or how much trouble the lack of a colloquial equivalent for seven and a half minutes has given English translators; the time given can be five, ten, or fifteen minutes, and even, from some more generous Bluebeards, half an hour or more.[21]

Another more notable departure between the Samber and G. M. translations occurs here, in the calls of the wife to her sister Anne, in the tower keeping desperate watch for the arriving horsemen, their brothers.[22] G. M. has the wife speak quite plainly: "I beg you . . . if you see them . . . do you see anyone . . . ?" Instead, in Samber the wife speaks with heightened diction, preparing the way for her evolution into a stage heroine: "I desire thee . . . if thou seest them . . . dost thou see nothing . . .?" Otherwise, this well-known prevarication sequence where Sister Anne is three times begged to look out the window and make signs of haste to the brothers if she sees them, and the maddening refrain that she sees "nothing but" dust, grass, and a flock of sheep, before finally the brothers are spotted, is closely translated.[23] In fact, Samber's translation "Anne, sister Anne, does thou see nothing coming?" is more faithful to the negatives of the wife in the French text (*ne vois tu rien venir?*) than G. M.'s or than will often be the case afterward. The required double negative in the French ("*ne . . . rien*"; do you *not* see *nothing* coming?) is reduced to the more colloquial English equivalent, "dost thou see nothing," but is still a question in the negative, rather than G. M.'s "do you see anything coming?" which would be the hopeful alternative. The focus, as it has been all throughout the tale, is on the act of seeing. Sister Anne is iconically pictured on the lookout by many illustrators of the tale. Perrault gets in another reference to seeing with mention of the brothers, who "*me viendraient voir*" (were coming to see me). The English translators lose this one reference by translating the brothers' expected arrival as: "they promised me that they would come to day."

Samber's Bluebeard repeats "presently" once when he calls to his wife to descend and be killed, before switching to "quickly" in a more literal translation of Perrault's "*vite*," used twice in the original (G. M. uses "instantly" from the beginning): "Come down, presently, or I'll come up to you. . . . Come down quickly, cried the *Blue Beard*, or I'll come up to you." The third time he calls up he asks, in both English translations: "Will you not come down?" which does not have the same possibilities for ironic nuances as the French: "*ne veux-tu pas descendre?*" While it can mean "won't you," as the English translators choose, it can also mean "don't you *want* to." If we return to the issue of "*vouloir*" that arose when Perrault's Bluebeard charges the wife with "wanting" to go into the forbidden chamber, we can read "don't you want to come down?" as a viciously ironic echo of the "wanting" that got the wife into this predicament in the first place, according to Bluebeard. Again, though, the English focus is on resolution: she "resolv'd" to go into the forbidden chamber and now she must resolve herself, or *will* herself, to descend: "*will* you not come down?"

Another iconic moment from the story, most often illustrated, is the moment of threatened death, and it is another major deviation in diction between the G. M. and Samber translations. Bluebeard stands over his wife, "cutlass" raised, and seems about to accomplish the murder. This was in fact the tale's first illustration, as seen in the Barchilon facsimile of the 1695 manuscript. It is rare that Perrault's "*coutelas*" will be translated as faithfully as Samber's "cutlass"; G. M.'s translation of the blade as a "scimitar" is most often followed in later decades, more in keeping with the images of the orientalization of the tale. The brothers, by contrast, have "swords" (*épeé*).[24] When the wife comes downstairs she supplicates in tears, hair disheveled. In Perrault's version, Bluebeard tells her that these signs of distress, just as the signs of repentance she showed a while earlier, are useless: "*ça ne sert à rien*" (that serves no purpose). But Samber's Bluebeard focuses on the signs themselves, choosing now to draw out the reference to seeing by focusing on signs: "This signifies nothing, says the *Blue Beard*." But immediately Samber loses yet another reference to vision when the brothers rush in. Perrault's French shifts to the third person neutral: "*on vit entrer*" (one saw enter) but Samber simply states the fact of their arrival: "immediately enter'd two horsemen."

Finally, the conclusion of the tale in Perrault's version begins to introduce the tone of levity and practicality that will be evinced by the two "*moralités*" at the end of the tale. In a return to the materialist focus of the beginning of the tale, the subject of this last paragraph is the wife's inheritance of all Bluebeard's estate and how she chooses to disburse it.[25] Anne is married to a long-time suitor, the brothers are advanced with purchased commissions, and Bluebeard's surviving wife dowers herself to marry another man. Perhaps in a move to grant more propriety to her remarriage, the Victorians often used the oriental story version's invention of the character of Selim, a lover from whom Fatima (Bluebeard's wife) has been parted by her marriage to Blue Beard. Thus, there is a preexisting character for her to marry at the end.[26] Otherwise, in further efforts to sanctify her inheritance, she remains single for the rest of her life, and for her charity is beloved by all.

Perrault's *moralités*, added between the 1695 and 1697 versions, have been the subject of many studies, usually commenting on their doubleness (their supplementarity, their ironic self-contradictions, and so on). Whether for their anachronism or for their problematic duplicity, they are often omitted from translations. Ségolène Le Men alluded to the shift in audience from adult to child when she noted in her study of the illustration history of *Mother Goose*: "By the nineteenth century, however, children's editions of Perrault's tales had begun to be published without the morals, which, supposedly, were not intended for children" (1992, 23). But Samber and G. M. both use the same translation, in verse, further demonstrating that one of them used the translation of the other as their template.[27]

Thus were launched the English versions of Charles Perrault's "Bluebeard," and they dominated the eighteenth century through multiple editions of *Mother Goose* alone. The eighteenth-century "prehistory" of Bluebeard in English and American culture established the inheritance for those who followed.

Chapter 4

A "Three Tail'd Bashaw"

Bluebeard Takes a Turkish Turn

When not mistaken for a pirate, Bluebeard is often characterized as a beturbaned Turkish tyrant. But Bluebeard did not become a "three tail'd Bashaw"[1] until the eighteenth century, perhaps beginning around the time that G. M. translated the "*coutelas*" in Perrault's story as "scimitar" (instead of Samber's "cutlass").[2] Bluebeard certainly did not get any of his eastern cast from Charles Perrault. Most crucially, for the English Bluebeard tradition, in 1790 the Irish composer and tenor Michael Kelly was in Paris and saw André Modeste Grétry's opera *Raoul Barbe Bleue* (1789, libretto by Paul Sedaine). He returned with a program and commissioned George Colman the Younger, then manager of the summer theater the Haymarket in London, to write a libretto inspired by Grétry's opera.[3] The resulting collaboration, *Blue Beard, or Female Curiosity!* (1798), was influenced by the French opera, largely in its secondary cast of characters and subplots. But despite the presence of a servant named Osman, there is no further intimation in the French libretto that the opera is set anywhere other than France. By firmly orientalizing Bluebeard as Abomelique, naming his wife Fatima, in love with Selim, and setting the drama in Turkey, the Colman-Kelly production indelibly stamped the Bluebeard story with an oriental countenance. Following from the popularity of Kelly and Coleman's gothic melodrama, in chapbooks all over the British Isles and on the nineteenth-century stage in just about every form, one is more likely to find a Turkish Bluebeard in England than a French one. One nineteenth-century play has a character refer to Bluebeard as "a Gaul" (French); but by this point Bluebeard was so removed from his French origins that the editor of the play was obliged to add a footnote: "Fact" (Millward 1869, 21). Why did Colman and Kelly make this critical choice, and why was it so popular with the English public?

An interesting series of linked literary and dramatic events seem to have carried the French tale in this new and fascinating direction, as an oriental story on the English stage. To begin with, the oriental fad of the eighteenth century built upon previous stock types (the figure of the Turkish despot was already a dramatic staple in England, and the "*Othello* dynamic" which makes use of this very type is frequently quoted in later Bluebeard plays). There was also a general fusion in the latter half of the eighteenth century with the gothic phenomenon that drew heavily on orientalism and for which the inherently gothic Bluebeard story was already primed.[4] Sedaine and Grétry's opera was influential and provided the sympathetic servant Osman. By renaming Fatima's sister Irene, the Colman-Kelly allusion would have evoked for a contemporary audience the then-well-known story of "The Sultan and the Slave Girl (Irene)". The pantomime called *Blue Beard, or, The Flight of Harlequin* in 1791 had also been inspired by the success of Grétry's opera, and its success as a Christmas pantomime money-maker for Covent Garden helped to inspire Colman and Kelly in turn. Meanwhile, the discovery in 1792 of Louis XVI's secret vault (*armoire de fer*) at the Tuileries palace and the role it played in the public imagination further contributed, no doubt as did the desire to distance and make France the "other" at a time of war with that country. William Godwin used the Bluebeard story (and the motif of the *armoire de fer*) for his political gothic novel *Caleb Williams* in 1794; and Colman himself adapted it for the stage as *The Iron Chest* (1796). In 1797 Ludwig Tieck's influential drama *Ritter Blaubart* appeared in Germany. And finally, the success of Lewis' gothic melodrama *Castle Spectre* (1797) influenced the creation of Colman and Kelly's drama.

A grand spectacle with lavish sets and extravagant special effects machinery, Colman and Kelly's melodrama was an immediate smash hit. It crossed the Atlantic in 1799 with equal success and, through reprintings and individual musical pieces for sale, enjoyed a very long afterlife, including celebrated revivals (notably that of 1811 with its use of live horses). The success of *Blue Beard, or Female Curiosity!* cemented an enduring parallel English tradition in which Bluebeard is a Turkish tyrant.

The Turkish Tyrant as Dramatic Stock Type

While Colman and Kelly's choice of Turkish characterization for Bluebeard was a surprising turn of events, there was already a persistent tradition of the Turkish tyrant as a stock figure. "Bluebeard" arrived in England not long after *The Thousand and One Arabian Nights* did; and both "Bluebeard" and the *Arabian Nights* came to England from the same source: France. Charles Perrault published "Bluebeard" in Paris in 1697, and it was translated into English by Robert Samber in 1729. *The Thousand and One Arabian Nights* was first translated into English from the French translations as early as 1705–1708.[5] Like Perrault's tales, these stories were immediately disseminated throughout the British reading public in chapbook form, as well as in more expensive editions, although, as one critic noted: "selection was much narrower than from Perrault: 'Ali Baba' seems to have been easily first in favour, with 'Aladdin' and 'Sinbad' some distance behind, and the rest nowhere" (Muir 1954, 40). How aware the same reading public would have been that the frame story of *The Thousand and One Nights* itself contained a Bluebeard motif in King Schahriar and his wife Scheherezade, and that "The Third Calendar" is also Bluebeard tale, is unclear. But a century later, chapbook illustrations for *Bluebeard* and for *Arabian Nights* were literally interchangeable.[6]

Bluebeard's connections with Shakespeare's *Othello* bolster this stereotypical portrayal. While Othello himself was not Turkish, he metaphorically aligns himself with the type of unruly and cruel Turkish despot in his breach of social and moral codes.[7] In his wife murder, if not in his fears of being cuckolded, there are echoes of the Bluebeard story. The sexual nature of Othello's fears is also not accidental: "Given the conventional association made by European Christians between Islam and promiscuity, it is not surprising that the English expression 'to turn Turk' carried a sexual connotation" (Vitkus 2003, 88).[8] These parallels with *Othello* are made much more overt by Robert Samber's diction in translating the tale in 1729, as has been noted. In later Victorian stage versions of Bluebeard, *Othello* is quoted frequently and with the persistency of a running joke: "He's like the black man in the play" (Planché and Dance 1839). The result is that Colman's choice appears, to a contemporary audience, obvious: "Mr. Colman has made him a bashaw of three tails; presuming, we may suppose, that the murderer of seven wives must have been a very Turk indeed" (Jones 1811, 2:62).

The Sultan and Irene

The Arab name Fatima for Bluebeard's wife has emphatically stuck, likely because she had no name from Perrault to usurp, although the name is often anglicized to Fanny. Her father Ibrahim (in the Colman-Kelly drama) invokes the prophet Mahomet, whose favorite daughter was Fatima (Colman 1983, 183 n.). There is a clear ironic contrast with this Fatima, who as the play opens is being berated by her father for betraying him in attempting to elope with Selim. However, the choice of the name Irene by Colman for Fatima's sister is mysterious. Grétry's opera used the names Isaure and Anne.[9] In no other version is Irene used for either character; even in burlesques of the Colman-Kelly melodrama immediately following 1798 Fatima remains but the name Irene reverts to Anne. But to contemporary audiences, the name Irene must have resonated with the well-known and frequently dramatized story of "The Sultan and the Greek Slave Girl, Irene."[10] In this story, the Sultan (Mahomet II) falls in love with a captured slave girl. In most versions of the story, he is so infatuated with her that he neglects his government. Howsoever he comes to this realization (the spirit of a dead father, his counselors, an epiphany), he demonstrates mastery over his passion by decapitating Irene.[11] The titles of most versions use variations on the name, and other contemporary plays reference variations as well: Hyrin, Hiren, Siren, and finally Irene (as in Gilbert Swinhoe's *The Tragedy of the Unhappy Fair Irene*, 1658). In this play, Irene plays along with the Emperor Mahomet to give her lover time to return from Hungary with enough men to overthrow the conqueror of the Greeks. While Mahomet falls in love with Irene, his people insist that she be killed to release him from her charms. She is decapitated a day before her lover's arrival. After Swinhoe's play the anglicized name Irene becomes more stable. There were also *Irena, a Tragedy* (1664); Charles Goring's *Irene, or the Fair Greek* (1708); and Dr. Johnson's *Irene*, produced by Garrick in 1749 (Chew 1937, 490 n.).[12] The use of the name Irene for Fatima's sister, in lieu of "Anne" a name already firmly associated with the Bluebeard story for a century at this point, is an interesting allusive gesture to this nexus of tales about the slave girl.

Further, there is both an Irene and a Selim in the play of another Turkish tyrant with a noteworthy beard: *Barbarossa* (Brown 1754).[13] Irene is Barbarossa's daughter. The play was well known; Garrick had performed in it, and it was widely written about. *Barbarossa* appears in the records of the New York stage as late as the 1803–1804 season (Ireland 1968, 222).

Through this story and others the Turkish despot had long been a stock figure for the English. When Edmund Burke in contemporary writings referred to Warren Hastings, the first Governor General, as "a Bashaw of three tails" (Burke 1786–1788, 267),[14] he was drawing on a long and rich English tradition of using this type as shorthand for a barbaric tyrant, and so the English audience of Colman and Kelly's drama would readily have recognized it.

Fatal Curiosity (1739, 1782)

George Colman the Younger appears to be a key author in bringing Bluebeard to such notoriety on stage. Among his many librettos are two dealing with similar subject matter, *The Iron Chest* (1796) and *Blue Beard, or Female Curiosity!* (1798). His father, George Colman the Elder, wrote *Fatal Curiosity* (1782), an adaptation of an earlier play of the same title by George Lillo (1739).[15] *Fatal Curiosity* is perhaps based on a "true story," and was possibly taken to be such by the contemporary audience.[16] The title alludes to the theme pronounced in the Bluebeard fairy tale, although there is no specific prohibition transgressed. Lillo's full title reads: *Guilt Its Own Punishment; or, Fatal Curiosity*.[17] Young Wilmot, long thought dead, returns incognito after many years' absence. After reuniting with his lover, he decides to visit his parents in the guise of a stranger, before revealing himself to be their long-lost son. He refers several times to his own curiosity to see them. He gives his poverty-stricken mother, Agnes, a coffer full of jewels to hold for him while he sleeps; she exhibits curiosity in opening the coffer, but the story then takes a Macbeth-like turn, as she convinces her husband, Old Wilmot, to murder the sleeping man. The identity of the murdered man is belatedly revealed. In despair the husband kills his wife, and then himself. In one version, the lover also dies after discovering the carnage. Evidently, and some of the play's tenuous connections with *Othello* aside,[18] this is not a Bluebeard story; there is no wife murder, no prohibition and transgression. However, the play contains elements of "Bluebeard": curiosity as an overt theme, Agnes opening a closed coffer that does not belong to her, and the use of gothic elements. It creates a strong precursor drama about the theme of "fatal curiosity" for George Colman the Younger by his own father.

Raoul Barbe Bleue (1789)

Michael Kelly, an Irishman, English tenor singer, and prolific composer, was responsible for the inclusion of André Grétry and Paul Sedaine's opera *Raoul Barbe Bleue* (1789)[19] in the Anglophone tradition, but the Colman-Kelly production, although inspired by the opera and borrowing its overture orchestration, otherwise bears little resemblance to it. In Grétry's opera, Raoul is a feudal tyrant who marries Isaure against her will. Isaure's family is noble but recently impoverished; she is in love with the valiant Vergi whom her brothers will not allow her to wed. Raoul has married three women, vassals, and each has failed the test of their curiosity. He has been told three times that a curious woman will be his downfall, and so attempts to make his next experiment with a woman who has the privileges of noble birth. Isaure has a sister Anne whom she loved but who was lost; Vergi tells her to call him Sister Anne. Later, he appears dressed as a woman at Raoul's castle, and is therefore with Isaure when Raoul departs, drawing up the bridge and imprisoning them during his absence. In a foreshadowing of the many male Sister Anne's of the nineteenth-century stage, there is some comic business when Raoul comments on what a large and handsome woman she is, but otherwise the opera was not comic. Osman is enlisted to help them get a message shot across the moat to Isaure's page, and after Raoul has given Isaure time to prepare for her death, "Sister Anne" reports from the turret until the brothers arrive.

Kelly noted in the final pages of the first volume of his *Reminiscences* seeing the opera in Paris in 1790 on his way home to England from a European tour. He wrote, some three decades after the first production of *Blue Beard, or Female Curiosity!*:

> We saw also the opera of "Blue Beard." "Racule [*sic*] Barbe Bleue," is the French title of it: the fine bass singer, Chenard, was famous in "Barbe Bleue;" and Madame Dubazzon, in Fatima, and Mademoiselle Cretue, in Irene [Isaure], were both excellent: the music, by Grétry, was very good; but so different are the tastes of a French and English audience, that when I produced my "Blue Beard" at Drury Lane, I did not introduce a single bar from Grétry. Mrs. C[rouch] was struck with the subject, and wrote down the programme of the drama, with a view to get it dramatized for Drury Lane; Johnstone got the music copied to bring to Mr. Harris, at Covent Garden, and it was got up at that theatre as a pantomime [*Blue Beard, or, the Flight of Harlequin* in 1791], I believe by Delpini; I never [saw] it in that shape, but have heard that it was not successful (1826, 347–48).[20]

This paragraph typifies the influence of French theater on London theater of the period. The influence results in two productions: the Covent Garden pantomime *Blue Beard, or, the Flight of Harlequin* in 1791, and eight years later in the Colman and Kelly *Blue Beard* intended to supply the place of a pantomime for a Christmas audience.

Blue Beard, or, The Flight of Harlequin (1791)

Covent Garden's pantomime *Blue Beard, or, the Flight of Harlequin* was a relatively popular pantomime, Michael Kelly's memory notwithstanding. By 1792, Covent Garden announced it was staging the production "for the 19th time." But in this pantomime by William Reeve there does not appear to be any oriental influence.[21] The characters are named Blue Beard, Harlequin, Haggard, Clown, and so on—at least two of these common to pantomime and Harlequinades—but also McCarney, Bounce, Swagger, Sligo, and Bobby Lobby. Bobby Lobby's song about being a lady's man comes straight from a British musical entertainment: "As I walk thro' the lobby, / The girls cry out "Bobby! / Here, Bobby! My Bibbidy Bob!" / Then pulling and hawling! / So smirking and pleasing! / So coaxing and teizing! / I can't get them out of my knob!" (*Airs, Glees* 1791). What is interesting about the pantomime is that it introduces "hellish legions" in the cast list (Daemons) and in Blue Beard's recitative. Act I, Air 1 references "a blessed crew / Of Spirits" obedient to his "wand." The "*fée*" key in "Bluebeard" opens the way for such magical characters and is often translated as an actual "fairy" in English rather than merely "enchanted." Here the inclusion of demonic characters also illustrates a move to incorporate more gothic machinery, one that will be fully exploited in the Colman and Kelly grand musical romance, with lively skeletons, devils, and puffs of smoke shown emanating from Bluebeard's secret chamber and the conclusion whereby Abomelique (Bluebeard) is killed by a Skeleton and sinks "beneath the earth—a volume of flame arises" (Colman, seventh edition [1837?]).[22]

Caleb Williams (1794) and *The Iron Chest* (1796)

One contemporary gothic novel in particular alludes to the Bluebeard tale relatively overtly, through the use of the preface. In the political gothic novel *Caleb Williams, or Things as They Are*, William Godwin had the servant Caleb Williams discover a murderous truth about his master, Ferdinand Falkland, by opening a trunk containing papers confessing the crime. Falkland spends the remainder of the novel demonstrating how power and wealth can be used abusively to persecute others; wherever Caleb flees, Falkland's power reaches him. In his preface, Godwin wrote:

I rather amused myself with tracing a certain similitude between the story of Caleb Williams and the tale of Bluebeard, than derived any hints from that admirable specimen of the terrific. *Falkland was my Bluebeard*, who had perpetrated atrocious crimes, which if discovered, he might expect to have all the world roused to revenge against him. *Caleb Williams was the wife*, who in spite of warning, persisted in his attempts to discover the forbidden secret; and, when he had succeeded, struggled as fruitlessly to escape the consequences, as the wife of Bluebeard in washing the key of the ensanguined chamber, who, as often as she cleared the stain of blood from the one side, found it showing itself with frightful distinctness on the other (Godwin 1794, 352–53; emphasis added).

Godwin's political gothic was itself quite successful, but it also proved to be a very popular dramatic encounter in the adaptation by George Colman the Younger.[23] In 1796, Colman wrote *The Iron Chest*, later included in the same influential drama collection as his father's version of *Fatal Curiosity*: Mrs. Inchbald's *British Theatre* (1808). It opened at Drury Lane, with music by Storace, and Kemble as Sir Edward Mortimer (the Falkland role). The play had an inauspicious opening run, a more successful run later that year, and according to at least one biographer of George Colman, it "held the stage 'for longer than forty years.'"[24] Michael Kelly also played a role in this production (Kelly 1826, 2:77–78). In viewing this play as another important precursor to the phenomenon that *Blue Beard* would become in 1798, it is necessary to note not only that *The Iron Chest* is a step closer to the Bluebeard story, but also that it too was "embryonic melodrama" (Cox 2000, 33).[25]

The title of *The Iron Chest* also brings more overtly another of *Caleb Williams*' (and thus Bluebeard's) many intertexts into play: the infamous *armoire de fer* that entered into popular legend with the execution of Louis XVI just three months after its discovery in November 1792. A locksmith informed the minister of the interior that he had installed in the Tuileries an *armoire de fer* (iron cupboard, or safe). Damian Davies wrote: "Roland [the minister], Gamain [the locksmith], and the inspector general of national buildings, Heurtier, hurried to the palace (foolishly and fatally for Roland, with no independent witnesses), where Gamain opened the *armoire*, hidden behind a wooden panel and iron plate in the wall, to disclose a cache of papers. The contents of this royal archive documenting the king's perception of the revolution proved to be rather innocuous and did not provide evidence, as many suspected it would, of the king's having conspired with French émigrés and with the Austrian court against the nation, though it did discredit high-profile figures such as Dumouriez, Lafayette, and Mirabeau" (Davies 2002, 526–27).

Roland corresponds to Godwin's Caleb, in this scenario, as he was accused of having altered the contents and could not prove otherwise: the use of the trunk of documents in Godwin's novel is thus "no mere Gothic prop" (Davies 2002, 529).[26] In popular contemporary representations, the iconography of its discovery echoes the discovery of the hidden closet in Bluebeard quite closely. Damian Davies reproduced a satirical print of the opening of the *armoire de fer* and footnoted another like it: the closet doors are flung open; one man (the locksmith) stands on the right, large key still in his hand; the closet reveals a skeleton (Mirabeau) arranged to look as if it is "dancing" in the closet (right arm and right leg up, knee and elbow bent); the picture on the wall above shows a serpent with a king's head (the serpent is frequently rendered in the iconography of the Bluebeard story); another male (Roland) is seated to the left of the closet, reacting to the vision: both his arms are raised, which is the standard configuration for Bluebeard's wife; finally, there is an axe on the floor in the foreground of the picture (528).[27] Bluebeard is a story from the *ancien régime*: it is therefore fitting that the fall of the *ancien régime* be represented using the iconography of this well-known French tale (Gorilovics 2000, 21).[28] It is perhaps another reason why the French fairy tale needed to be set farther afield than France; just as English gothic was doing, France and the Catholic continent were made to be the "other." Post-Reformation, "English Protestant texts associated both the pope and the Ottoman sultan with Satan or the Antichrist" (Vitkus 2003, 83).[29] By rendering Bluebeard as a Turk the parallels are drawn while at the same time the fairy tale is neatly cast further off than England's front doorstep.

Ritter Blaubart (1797)

In 1797 Ludwig Tieck's five-act drama *Ritter Blaubart*, closely based on the fairy tale of "Bluebeard," followed from his 1796 short fairy tale "arabesque," "Die Sieben Weiber des Blaubart" ("Bluebeard's Seven Wives," *Volksmärchen* 1797). In the fairy tale, there is nothing in the forbidden chamber.[30] The play, translated by John Lathrop Motley, was first published in English in 1838–1839. Hugo von Wolfsbrunn proposes to Agnes von Friedheim, and she takes her sister Anna to live with her. Von Wolfsbrunn's worst fear is to be cuckolded by his wife: "'Woe, says he,'to the deceived man who trusts to the false charms of women. . . . Deceit is a woman's trade'" (Tieck 1797; Motley 1840).[31]

Blue Beard, or Female Curiosity! (1798)

Perhaps as significant as Samber's translation of the story into English, the Colman and Kelly production alters the English course of the story, far beyond the stage.[32] Further, the rich cast of secondary characters enabled the story to be transplanted and to evolve upon the stage. It was eminently adaptable for melodramatic, burlesque, and pantomimic renditions, on the public or the private stage, as will be seen.

George Colman the Younger's play *Blue Beard, or Female Curiosity!: A Dramatic Romance* opened at the Theatre Royal, Drury Lane, on January 16, 1798. A performer's copy of this play alludes to the 1791 harlequinade: "[Bluebeard] had frowned ferociously in a pantomime at Covent Garden, in 1791" (D. G. "Remarks"). The same author went on to note that the present production derived more from "a French piece, the *Barbe-Bleu*, played at Paris in 1746."[33] While such a play is referred to by Georges Doutrepont, and it is possible that a French piece could have played on a French stage in any given year following Perrault's publication of the *Contes*,[34] the play has long since dropped from popular or even critical consciousness. In his *Reminiscences* Kelly cited only Grétry's opera of 1789, and Colman himself stated in a preface (fourth edition) that "it would be as ungrateful, as impudent, to deny that I took the outline of my Store from the works of the celebrated Mrs. Goose," to whom he goes on to inscribe the Romance.[35] He further distinguishes his drama from any French precursor, with this claim to originality: "The following Trifle is not a Traslation [*sic*] from the French, nor any other Language:—I have an exclusive right to all it's [*sic*] imperfections."

The libretto is significant, because it introduces a range of new characters who will become enduring staples in the English dramatic and chapbook traditions of this story. The two-act drama opens with Fatima attempting to elope with Selim by escaping down the rope ladder at her window to his accompaniment of the song "Pit-a-pat." She is caught by her father Ibrahim: "Ah, traitress, have I caught you?" and sent indoors. Selim and Ibrahim argue, whereupon it becomes clear that Ibrahim has sold Fatima to the higher bidder: "He's richer. You have your merits, but he's a Bashaw—with three tails!" Selim vows revenge on his rival Abomelique and alludes more than once to his practice of "spells and magic" (perhaps alluding to Gilles de Rais). Irene, Fatima's sister, expresses her doubts about how suitable the match is and calls attention to the fact that Abomelique's serial monogamy is contrary to allowed practice in the Koran:

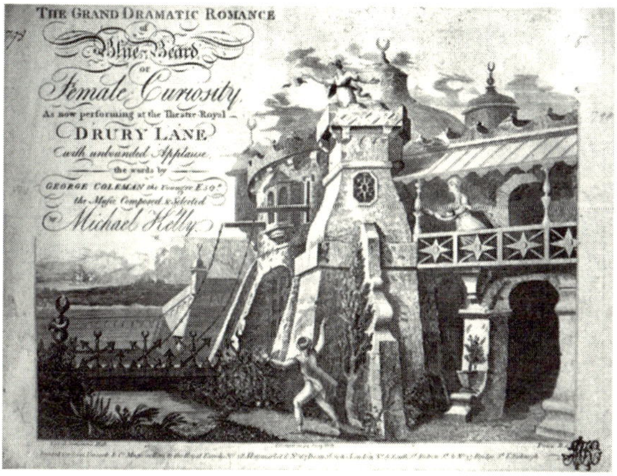

Bluebeard, or Female Curiosity! Colman and Kelly (1798), first page of piano vocal score, illustrated from the theater by R. Cruikshank. Reproduced by permission of the Royal College of Music.

IBRAHIM: I do think that a man's wives are punishment enough in themselves. Praised be the wholesome law of Mahomet that stinted a Turk to only four at a time!

IRENE: The Bashaw had never more than one at a time, and 'tis whispered that he beheaded the poor souls one after another, for, in spite of his power, there's no preventing talking (Colman 1798, 1983, 1.1).[36]

Abomelique arrives in a grand procession to the music of Kelly's famous "Grand March" and there are several conflicts. In the process, Abomelique "draws his saber" and the libretto indicates that it is Fatima in danger here: "Sabres are gleaming round the throat / Of beauty disobeying." It is revealed that Abomelique himself is haunted with a prediction: "that it is [his] fate to marry, and [his] life will be endangered by the curiosity of the woman whom you espouse."

Scene 2 shifts to Abomelique's castle, and the two courting servants Beda and Shacabac. Beda tries to draw Shacabac into discussion about the secrets he has been entrusted with; the audience finds out that Shacabac feels "tormented" when he goes into the Blue Chamber. But it also foreshadows the theme of female curiosity, as Beda is clearly curious and trying to find out just what secrets Shacabac and his master are keeping from her. They sing their duet to Beda's guitar: "Tink, tinka-tinka, tink." Abomelique returns and tells Shacabac they have employment in the Blue Chamber, and Shacabac reluctantly follows him.

Scene 3 opens on "a blue apartment. A winding staircase on one side. A large door in the middle of the flat. Over the door, a picture of Abomelique kneeling in amorous supplication to a beautiful woman. Other pictures and devices on the subject of love decorate the apartment." Dialogue here reveals both that the Blue Chamber is inhabited with "a few flying phantoms, sheeted spectres, skipping skeletons and grinning ghosts at their gambols!" and that these are Abomelique's former wives. Shacabac is to go in and place a talisman (a dagger) at the foot of a skeleton inside the chamber, which will keep Abomelique safe.

The audience's first view of the open chamber is spectacular: "The door instantly sinks, with a tremendous crash, and the Blue Chamber appears, streaked with vivid streams of blood. The figures in the picture of the door change their position, and Abomelique is represented in the action of beheading the beauty he was before supplicating. The pictures and devices of love change to subjects of horror and death. The interior apartment—which the sinking door discovers—exhibits various tombs in a sepulchral building, in the midst of which ghastly and supernatural forms are seen, some in motion, some fixed. In the centre is a large skeleton, seated on a tomb, with a dart in his hand, smiling, and, over his head, in characters of blood, is written: 'The Punishment of Curiosity'" (1.4).[37] As Shacabac lays the talisman in its place, the inscription changes to read: "This Sepulchre Shall Inclose Her Who May Endanger the Life of Abomelique." The Skeleton's dart is raised and lowered. Abomelique reads this as a "prosperous" omen for him and wishes: "May Fatima be prudent and avoid [rashness]."

Scene 4 reveals Fatima pining for Selim, singing "When pensive, I thought on my love," and then conversing with Irene, whose objections are assuaged by Abomelique's wealth. Fatima gives her a brief lesson on the moral use of money, a preview of how nineteenth-century wives in the fairy story will use their inherited wealth for public good works. Shacabac calls the women to the illuminated garden and stays to sing a commentary on Abomelique's practices: "A fond husband will, after a conjugal strife, / Kiss, forgive, weep, and fall on the neck of his wife. / But Abomelique's wife other conduct may dread: / When he falls on her neck, 'tis to cut off her head!"

In Scene 5, another subplot develops: the lecherous Ibrahim tries to seduce Beda, comically exaggerating the power of his position as major domo. The parallels with Abomelique's misuse of power are obvious: "Cheer up, little one, I rule the roost here; it shan't go worse with you that I have power and you have charms."

Act II begins with Selim's revenge in motion: the Spahis are gathered in the woods and prepare to launch their attack on the castle. In Scene 2, Abomelique tells Fatima he is to go away, gives her the keys (to Shacabac's dismayed interruption: "What, *all* the keys?"), and cautions her not to enter the Blue Chamber: "That door, and that alone, is sacred. Dare to open it, and the most dreadful punishment that tongue can utter will await you! It is the sole restraint I ever shall impose. In all else you have ample scope. Merit my indulgence and tremble to abuse it!" Fatima tries, unsuccessfully, to return this key to him, and Shacabac leaves with Abomelique, terrified that Fatima will pry into the forbidden chamber before he can even get back from opening the gate for his master. Irene, being told of the keys and the chamber, immediately wants to enter it: "Dear, now, I had rather see that room than any other in the Castle!" Irene mentions in an aside that she will try to persuade Fatima into it. Irene sings a song invoking Cupid, echoing the fate of Sister Anne (dowered and married off by Perrault) and perhaps foreshadowing the future Irenes (Annes) who will in Victorian dramas try to usurp her sister's place or get herself a husband by any means.

In the following scene, Ibrahim, now made "major domo" over all the household slaves, continues to pursue Beda and sings a song in praise of his own greatness: "'Tis a very fine thing to be father-in-law / To a very magnificent three-tailed Bashaw!"

In Scene 4, Irene has succeeded in bringing Fatima to the door of the Blue Chamber and coaxes her into disobedience. On two occasions, ghastly sounds are heard from within the chamber: an echo of the word "Death," just spoken by Irene, and a "deep groan." Finally, Irene succeeds because she convinces charitably minded Fatima that it would be inhumane not to help the soul who made the noise. The chamber is revealed to the audience for the second time, just as at first. Shacabac returns from opening the gate and discovers that the key has broken. Abomelique is heard returning "full six hours before his time," and Fatima implores Shacabac to save them.

In Scene 5, he has hidden the women out of the way and delays Hassan, a black eunuch, seeking Fatima for Abomelique. In Scene 6, Abomelique discovers the broken key and swears death to Fatima; she is granted some time to prepare herself, and Irene and Shacabac promise whatever assistance they can while Abomelique calls up from below. The quartetto here echoes that in the first scene: here it is Fatima, Irene, and Shacabac calling and answering whether anyone can be seen coming, and Abomelique calls insistently for Fatima. Abomelique snatches Fatima; the soldiers rush the gate as Shacabac directs them. In brief Scene 7, Ibrahim submits to his cowardice and comically flees the arrival of the soldiers. In the eighth and final scene, Abomelique (now with scimitar, instead of sabre) drags Fatima within the sepulchre, Selim fights him, and Fatima manages to take the talisman from the foot of the skeleton, prompting it to raise its dart. After a skirmish with Selim, and with a troop of horse visible behind the broken wall of the sepulchre, the skeleton stabs

Abomelique and drags him below stage: "A volume of flame arises and the earth closes." The final chorus celebrates the death of Abomelique: "to your gloomy caves descending, / His career of murder ending" and the forthcoming marriage of Fatima and Selim: "Hymen comes, with pleasure crowning / Happy love!"

In his *Reminiscences*, Kelly reflected on the first performance (in which he played Selim) and on the play's popularity with enthusiasm. This passage is worth quoting at its original length, as it captures the phenomenon (and comical glitches) from someone intimately connected with it:[38]

> The drama was immediately accepted at Drury Lane; orders were issued to the machinists, painters, and decorators, to bring it forward with the greatest possible splendour and magnificence; and it must be admitted, that nothing could exceed its brilliancy; the music, which fortunately became extremely popular, I composed, with the exception of two selected pieces, and the success of the whole was beyond expectation and precedent. It may be worth noticing, that the Blue Beard, who rode the elephant in perspective over the mountains, was little Edmund Kean, who, at the time, little thought he should become a first class actor.
>
> The 16th January, 1798, was the first night of its production. From the bungling of the carpenters, and the machinery going all wrong, at one time, as it grew near the conclusion, I gave it up as lost: but never shall I forget the relief I experienced when Miss Decamp sang, 'I see them galloping! I see them galloping!' She gave it with such irresistible force of expression, as to call from the audience loud and continued shouts of applause.
>
> At the end of the piece, when Blue Beard is slain by Selim, a most ludicrous scene took place. Where Blue Beard sinks under the stage, a skeleton rises, which, when seen by the audience, was to sink down again; but not one inch would the said skeleton move. I, who had just been killing Blue Beard, totally forgetting where I was, ran up with my drawn saber, and pummelled the poor skeleton's head with all my might, vociferating, until he disappeared, loud enough to be heard by the whole house, 'D—n you! d—n you! why don't you go down?' The audience were in roars of laughter at this ridiculous scene, but good-naturedly appeared to enter into the feelings of an infuriated composer.
>
> The next day, the piece was much curtailed; the scenery and machinery were quite perfect; and, on its next representation, it was received with the most unqualified approbation, by overflowing houses, and has kept its standing for six-and-twenty years. The music had an unparalleled sale,

> but I could not escape the shafts of envy and malice. The professional, would-be theatrical composers, the music-sellers and their friends, gave out that the music was not mine, and that I had stolen it from other composers. But I laughed them to scorn; conscious that I never even selected a piece from any composer to which, when I printed it, I did not affix his name; . . .
>
> The second act of Blue Beard opened with a view of the Spahis' horses, at a distance; these horses were admirably made of pasteboard, and answered every purpose for which they were wanted. One morning, Mr. Sheridan, John Kemble, and myself, went to the property room of Drury Lane Theatre, and there found Johnston, the able and ingenious machinist, at work upon the horses, and on the point of beginning the elephant, which was to carry Blue Beard. Mr. Sheridan said to Johnston, —'Don't you think, Johnston, you had better go to Pidcock's, at Exeter 'Change, and hire an elephant for a number of nights?' – 'Not I, Sir,' replied the enthusiastic machinist; 'if I cannot make a better elephant than that at Exeter 'Change, I deserve to be hanged.'
>
> In the grand march, where Blue Beard comes over the mountain, there was to be a military band. I was not sufficiently conversant with wind instruments, and therefore I went to Mr. Eley, a German, and Master of the band of the guards. I took my melody to him, and he put the parts to it most delightfully (Kelly 1826, 131–34).

The play was intended, by his own description, to make Kelly's name in England as a composer.[39] In his *Reminiscences*, he talked often of writing music, passing over his actual performances as a sought-after tenor almost as footnotes in his seemingly constant touring with the singer Mrs. Crouch.

Despite the play's popularity, Colman's "Preface" (1798c) included an *apologia* for his use of "Romance, and Legends" (an interesting comment on the status of fairy tales at the time), and on his use of magic: "I feel nothing upon my conscience in having substituted a Blue Beard for a Black Face. —I have not attempted to make Magick usurp that space of the Evening's Entertainment much better occupied by Dramas of Instruction, and probability. I have kept my Enchantment within the limits where rational minds, without pedantry, have not only long tolerated it, but have found pleasure in unbending with it, after they have been more solidly engaged. In short, my Syllabub does not make its appearance until after the substantial part of the repast is over."

That the play *was* immediately and hugely successful can be evinced in several ways, more objective than Kelly's boast in his memoirs that all the world had seen the play by 1824,[40] through its performance history, reprintings,[41] sales of music,[42] and the immediate incorporation of imagery from the play in chapbooks of the period. In 1804 Benjamin Tabart "advertised *Cinderella, Blue Beard and Valentine* and *Orson* 'each with coloured representations of the scenes contained in the last spectacle at Drury Lane'" (Darton 1932, 207). Later editions of Colman's play included, for instance, "a fine engraving From a Drawing taken in the Theatre by Mr. R. Cruikshank." Its American success was perhaps even greater.[43] The 1811 transatlantic revival was another stage phenomenon, this time using live horses from Astley's who made their debut on the stage of Covent Garden on 18 February 1811[44] in the adaptation. In its first forty-one nights it brought receipts of more than £21,000 (one-quarter of the contemporary annual average).[45]

The impact of George Colman and Michael Kelly's collaboration turning Bluebeard definitively into the stereotype of an oriental stage tyrant permanently introduced a powerful "new" Bluebeard into the burgeoning pantheon. This figure is the most enduringly popular English Bluebeard, perfectly poised as he was to become the blundering buffoon (Pantaloon) of nineteenth-century harlequinade and pantomime, the endearing butt of the lovers' joke.

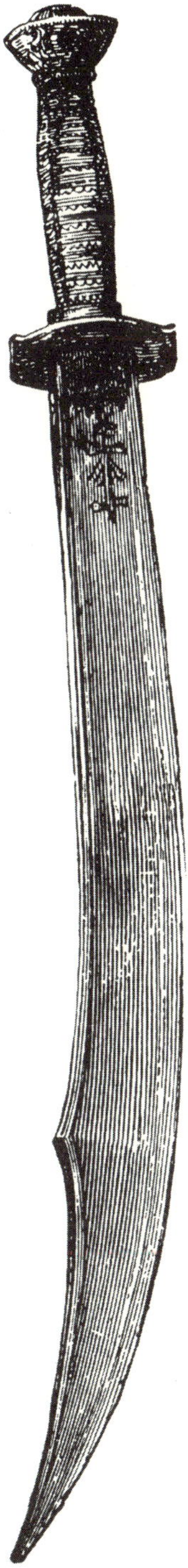

Part 3

Bluebeard in the English Nineteenth Century

Chapter 5

Cheap Thrills

Bluebeard in Chapbooks and Juveniles

Bluebeard came to prominence through the eighteenth century initially in the form of reprints and pirated knockoffs of *Mother Goose* tales, quickly breaking out into chapbook form. The term *chapbook* refers to small, cheaply printed books, crudely illustrated, and even more crudely sewn, which were in circulation throughout the British Isles by the hundreds of thousands in their heyday (1750 to 1850). These books were distributed to every rural area of Britain on foot by chapmen (also known more prosaically as traveling-, running-, or flying-stationers; peddlers, packmen, or hawkers). By the late eighteenth century, "Bluebeard" was headlining many of these same chapbooks alone or with one or two other tales, divested of the rest of the *Mother Goose* set (which of course continued to be reprinted, as they have been to the present day). It was through these cheap, ephemeral chapbooks, rather than the more expensive and elaborate printings of *Mother Goose*, that the majority of households of the period across all classes came to know Bluebeard.[1]

A common feature of chapbooks, which will have relevance to the study of extant Bluebeard chapbooks and the difficulty of distinguishing them, is that they were commonly pirated. Rival printers freely and routinely stole each others' texts, and copyright was largely ignored (Darton 1932, 70).[2] The chapbook phenomenon in England and Scotland in particular (little is known about Welsh and Irish production of chapbooks) is contemporary with that in other European countries. Chapbooks were printed and distributed in France from the time the printing press was invented and were known there as *livres de colportage*, referring to the neck (*col*) bag that was used to carry (*porter*) the books; or the *bibliothèque bleue* in reference to the books' cheap blue paper covers. While America imported these books by the tens of thousands for sale in peddlers' packs, Harry Weiss in his several studies of American chapbooks commented that there was never the same type of explosion of chapbooks in

America as in Europe (1942, 124). Nonetheless, they were imported in huge numbers.[3] The phenomenon peaked early in the nineteenth century, and chapbooks all but expired in the second half of that century. As early as 1882 in his major work on chapbooks, *Chap-Books of the Eighteenth Century: With Facsimiles, Notes, and Introduction*, John Ashton called them relics, in need of a rescue "from the limbo into which they were fast descending" (xii). As Ashton's work demonstrated, while they were dying out of popular culture, chapbooks were becoming a subject for scholarly collection and study for the first time. In the past, they may have been collected for their sentimental value, as they were notably by James Boswell, who returned to a bookseller to purchase and bind together a sample of the reading materials of his youth[4]; they were also collected from boyhood by Sir Walter Scott, who said he had them "from the baskets of the travelling pedlars" (Corson 1962, 203). But the first scholarly commentary on chapbooks both owes its derivation to the increasing scarcity of the now-prized "waifs of past popular literature" (Bergengren 1904),[5] and perhaps to the study of and credibility given to popular culture akin to the rise of folklore studies (by which means *Bluebeard* chapbooks could be interesting twice over).

In addition to being the means by which Britain came to know Bluebeard with great familiarity, these slight chapbooks are credited with preserving fairy tales altogether.[6] Fairy tales had a solid niche in the chapbook market, but the concept of a book market for children was comparatively new. John Newbery is credited with realizing the market potential in England for children's literature, beginning as late as the mid-1740s.[7] In her study of *Mother Goose*, Ségolène Le Men pointed to the shift in audience from adults to children, positing that this shift actually occurred in England (1992, 35).

Bluebeard Chapbooks

In chapbook form, it is fascinating to see what permutations the tale takes from the original and even from the first two major English translations (by Robert Samber and G. M.). Once firmly and thrillingly installed in the chapbook tradition and freed from the context of *Mother Goose* collections that more or less consistently followed the translations of either Samber or G. M., "Bluebeard" of course changed. The strain of orientalism, by which the nineteenth-century audience came to know Bluebeard as a Turk, his wife as Fatima, and which on the stage both comic and serious created a host of named "extras," took permanent root in the chapbook tradition. Given that it was in chapbooks that

Chapbook illustration, "Fatima in the Blue Chamber." Printed for N. Hailes, Juvenile Library. 1817. *Blue Beard: Adorned with Cuts.* Courtesy of The Lilly Library, Indiana University, Bloomington.

Bluebeard reached his widest audience, it is interesting to see just what story they were telling.

Charles Perrault claimed the tales from the oral tradition for children and rewrote them for an adult salon readership. In chapbooks, though, they were primarily returned to children, for whom these chapbooks were bought and by whom they were read and exchanged. Compellingly, the very first example of what an actual reader of chapbooks remembers reading in his childhood in the early 1800s, quoted in a book-length study of the chapbook phenomenon in England, is: *Bluebeard.*[8] The penchant for multiple illustrations in the chapbooks no doubt helped to ensure a broad audience.

Blue Beard (Dean & Son 1854–1856)

A representative chapbook is one published by Dean & Son,[9] who had several versions of the Blue Beard story in chapbook form throughout this century: *Blue Beard, or, Female Curiosity*. The chapbook is 12 pages and illustrated. It is already distinguishable from the lower end of rough-and-ready chapbooks by the fact that the illustrations are, for the most part, both pertinent to the story they are illustrating *and* consistent with one another. The cover is illustrated with a woman seated with a child, reading, on her lap. The back cover lists "13 sorts" in this series of "Children's Popular Tales," all at "1d. each, Plain, or

Chapbook illustration. From Dean & Son. 1854–1856. *Blue Beard, or, Female Curiosity*. Courtesy of The Lilly Library, Indiana University, Bloomington.

2d. Coloured," as follows: *Ali Baba and the Forty Thieves; Whittington and His Cat; Blue Beard, or Female Curiosity!; Butterfly's Ball and Grasshopper's Feast; Jack, the Giant Killer; Cat's Castle Besieged by the Rats; Little Red Riding Hood; Cinderella and Her Little Glass Slipper; Children in the Wood; Death and Burial of Poor Cock Robin; Jack and the Bean Stalk; Old Mother Hubbard and her Dog; Valentine and Orson*. More than half of these titles are familiar staples among chapbooks. In the center of the Bodleian copy's cover is the title: *Blue Beard, or Female Curiosity*. At the bottom is the name and address of the publisher, and the price: "Dean & Son, Threadneedle St, One Penny."

Directly on opening the chapbook, the interrelationship between illustrations and text is strikingly apparent. The verso of the title page has the title: BLUE BEARD above two half-page illustrations, while its facing recto page has yet another illustration above the text. Visually, nearly three-quarters of the two pages are illustrations of the story, and all precede the text. Somewhat unusually, restraint has been shown in not yet illustrating any of the three most iconic moments of the tale: the chamber discovery, the near-execution, or the simultaneous signaling and arrival of the rescuing brothers, which, if not already on the cover page, frequently serve as introduction to the tale. This Dean & Son version does make up for the lack by having *two* renditions of the near-execution depicted within the text: one before the wife has been granted her time to pray, and the other in its usual spot, after this time has elapsed. But at the beginning, this Dean & Son chapbook shows first, a woman sitting on a balcony, Bluebeard standing to her left, scimitar hanging below his waist, his left arm behind his back, his right arm over her shoulder. His cloak is trimmed with ermine. Below, in the bottom half of the page, Bluebeard is in the right foreground, unsheathing his scimitar, and there is a ship in the background taking up the left half of the picture. This picture, scimitar aside, is the only one not entirely consonant with the rest of the illustrations, which all depict Bluebeard dressed alike; in this one, he is in trousers instead of kaftan. In the third picture, the couple is walking by an elaborate fountain. Bluebeard is steering the woman with his left arm; with his right he is gesturing to the fountain. The images symbolize, in turn: courtship, power, and wealth. The overall effect in these first three illustrations, seen almost simultaneously, is the overwhelming presence of Bluebeard. In general, this version is representative of other chapbook versions in its economy of style. The key elements are here as they are in Perrault. When fitting the story into a fixed number of pages, as chapbooks must usually do, for any elaboration something must be lost. So, the main deviation in the ending of this version, which accounts for the final three paragraphs, is bought at the expense of other standard hallmarks, such as the delay in seeing the brothers arrive:

> Poor Fatimer [*sic*] had fainted, and was some days before she recovered; when [*new page*] finding herself so unexpectedly rich, she intreated [*sic*] her sister and two brothers never to leave her; and she also sent for her dear mother to live with her, and to share her fortune.
>
> Under their advice, she had the bodies of the unfortunate ladies buried with the greatest solemnity.
>
> And then, on condition that they paid just and liberal wages to their labourers, she very greatly reduced the rents of Blue Beard's tenantry. She built and gave pretty cottages, each with large gardens, without rents, to all the industrious working families on her large estates; and in performing such acts of goodness and mercy, she passed a long life, beloved and respected by all who knew her (Dean & Son 1854–1856).

The illustrations are a feature and an attraction to buyers of chapbooks, frequently advertised by the publisher, so it is not unusual to see that the text also gives ground to such a large number of engravings. As has been said, the pictures tell the story in counterpoint to the text rendition of it. The economy of style keeps the chapbook versions like this one in close contact with the fairy tale and oral traditions: cause and effect are boldly juxtaposed, without embellishments. The wife cannot clean the key; the husband returns; he asks for the keys the next day. In versions that do embellish, as the one quoted below demonstrates, these moments become heightened. The wife attempts to clean the keys with all manner of things (a catalogue that includes at various times sand, brick dust, and emery, and often includes naming soaps by brand). The midcentury comic version by F. W. N. Bayley elaborated: "With soap, lime, and ashes / She works and she washes, / In puddle and pail, / But it will not avail: / In meal and in malt, / In brandy and salt!" She finishes by roasting and boiling the key, which "Defies all the forces of fire and water" (Wm. S. Orr & Co. [ca. 1842], 27). In some of these chapbook variations, Bluebeard does not return before night, allowing the wife and her sister Anne a longer frightful period of waiting. They may then spend all night trying to clean the key before giving it up as a lost cause, as in the following example: "They spent a great part of the night in trying to clean off the blood from the key, which was the only evidence of Fatima's imprudence; but it was without effect. . . . Fatigued with their exertions they at last retired to bed: but the wretched Fatima, who could not sleep, lay ruminating on the awful scene she had gone through, and devising means for escaping the vengeance of her cruel husband Blue Beard" (Glasgow: For the Booksellers 1852, 10).[10] Occasionally, escape is fatally delayed: "she therefore resolved to escape from this dreadful mansion as soon as the entertainment which was appointed for the next day should have taken place" (Printed for N. Hailes 1817, 62). In one version, the cat and mouse game of asking for the keys is itself protracted; Blue Beard may ask for them on the pretext of needing to dress (W. Walker & Sons [185–], 5).

The orientalism of the Dean & Son version is minimal; it exists in name alone (Fatimer/Fatima) and to some extent in the nature of the illustrations, which while showing a coach instead of an elephant and livery instead of black slaves, as is often the case, and calling Bluebeard's blade a sword instead of a "scymitar," still depict oriental balconies and a beturbaned Bluebeard. It is less usual for Bluebeard to involve others in his activities, as when he calls out to his slaves to bring him his sword, but their role is fleshed out in much greater detail in the stage versions, as the secondary cast of characters. The chapbook *History of the Cruel Monster Blue-beard* (J. Bailey [1812–1813]) uses this cast and the plot outline from the Colman and Kelly 1798 play, likely due to its popular 1811 revival. Bluebeard is "Abomelique," the "barbarous Blue Bearded bashaw" with a servant named Shacabac who is included in his secrets and given a charmed talisman to place in the chamber; Fatima is sold to this husband by her corrupt father Ibrahim, as her lover Selim is not rich. When Bluebeard (Abomelique) is wounded by Selim, he is reclaimed by demons: "when a violent noise arose, and three or four infernal spirits were seen, who advanced to Abomelique, exclaiming his time was come; and the wound given by the youth had broken his charm which had hitherto preserved him from punishment, with these words they cast him into the furnace, which, with the infernal spirits and Blue Beard, sunk with a thundering sound, and vanished entirely from view" (J. Bailey [1812–1813], 17). This storyline is responsible for the chapbook illustrations, which show demons or lively skeletons and puffs of smoke pouring out of the chamber, as on the cover of S. Marks & Sons *Blue Beard* ([1876]).[11]

In orientalized chapbook versions it is not uncommon to begin by locating Bluebeard in Turkey: "In Turkey dwelt a wealthy man, / Whom maid and matron fear'd; / For frightful was his countenance,— / He wore a large blue beard!" (Samuel & John Keys [between 1873 and 1894]).[12] Some even comment on the difference in marriage laws, as the [1812–1813] chapbook also does: "Though Turkish laws allow every man the liberty to have as many wives and concubines as he can support, yet Abomelique, so far from availing himself of that privilege, never had more than one wife at a time; and it was not a little remarkable, that out of 12 young and beautiful damsels, to whom he had been married, no one lived more than a few months and for the major part were reported to be dead in only a few weeks after their marriage; and their funeral conducted in so private a manner, that none of their relatives had any opportunity of examining their bodies, to discover whether their death was occasioned by ill usage" (J. Bailey [1812–1813], 4).

The daughter's "vanity" is an issue in the Dean & Son example: "Among the guests, there were two sisters, daughters of a respectable widow, to whom Blue Beard paid particular attention; and this raised the vanity of the youngest so much, that she thought she should not object to become his wife" (1854–1856).[13] This vanity, instead of the mere greed implied by Perrault, is a feature sometimes editorialized upon in the chapbooks. Whereas Perrault's version leaves implicit that the courting is accomplished less by Bluebeard himself than by the show of his wealth and entertainments, the chapbooks focus instead on the younger daughter's vanity: "Personal attentions, even although paid us by an ugly creature, seldom fail to make a favourable impression, and therefore it was no wonder that Fatima, the youngest of the two sisters, began to think Blue Beard a very polite, pleasant and civil gentleman, and that the beard, which she and her sister had been so much afraid of, was not so very blue" (G. Caldwell 1828).[14] In some chapbooks, the mother also chastises her daughters for their prejudice against Bluebeard. An elaborate version of this vanity and prejudice is given in the N. Hailes miniature book, *Blue Beard* (1817), so that it seems curiosity is not to be the least of the wife's failings:

Such however is the thought-less emulation of young ladies, that scarcely any thing pleases them so well as an opportunity of surpassing each other in the vain trapping of finery. . . .

There is no strength of understanding, or variety of knowledge, or goodness of heart in making a shew of these childish embellishments; but a fondness for them certainly proves that the person who is so much attached to them, has very little else to be proud of. Indeed, so far from being a recommendation to a person; this foolish propensity for gaudy attire makes the nearest approaches to manners and dispositions of the most ignorant of mankind.

In all the places where savages are found, there is the strongest partialities for useless finery. In the islands of the Pacific Ocean, and in other parts of the world where knowledge has not yet enlightened the inhabitants, the uncivilized people decorate themselves with bits of glass, feathers, pearls, and shining stones. But they may be forgiven for this weakness; their minds have not been improved by instruction, and they have not art or science, or rational amusement to engage their attention.

But what can be thought of persons, who, surrounded by every allurement to useful and interesting employments, devote their minds to the decorations of dress: and who would foolishly think, that their glittering and fantastical ornaments give them superiority over the worthy and the wise? It would be advantageous to young folks to recollect, that so much attention to outward appearance betrays extreme vanity; and that vanity is the most degrading quality of the human heart, and the certain source of general contempt (Printed for N. Hailes 1817, 12–16).[15]

Whether the irony is intentional or not (and presumably it is not), lavish descriptions of the sumptuous castle and its trappings immediately follow this lesson. The same strain is visible even late in the nineteenth century, in the McLoughlin Bros. pantomime toy book *Blue Beard* [189–]: "Poor, foolish Fatima, you see, flattered herself that whatever might have been the trouble with his former wives, she would know how to manage him, and by means of his seemingly great affection for herself, would be able to retain her power over him forever. We shall see in the end, how miserably she was deceived in these notions, and the heavy price she was obliged to pay for her vanity and love of display" ([189–]).[16]

Instead of blaming the wife's curiosity outright, the Dean & Son chapbook gives the wife some nearly reasonable motivation: she "thought it strange" that she should not be allowed to go into this closet, and this is the cause of her final

Chapbook illustration. From W. Davison. 1808–1858. *History of Blue Beard.* Alnwick. Courtesy of The Lilly Library, Indiana University, Bloomington.

temptation. The suspenseful pause on the threshold is another of the heightened moments that prove irresistible to many chapbook publishers and later embellishers of the Bluebeard story. In some chapbooks, Anne tries to dissuade her sister at the door (one illustration shows Anne trying to pull her sister's arm away from the keyhole), to no avail.[17] As discussed in the next chapter, Anne's role here takes a significant shift, as she becomes the pantomime "villain" and betrays her sister.

Other wives are indignant that they should not be able to go into the chamber. In one late verse edition, Fatima and Anne both convince each other, after a week of obedience, to transgress: "They looked, and they longed, and they fidgeted round, / And whispered, 'We're not to obedience bound; / If a husband has secrets, it can't be a sin / For a good wife to know them'—and then they went in" (McLoughlin Bros. [189–]). Often, it is in the form of the following assumption: "Thinking as Blue Beard was so very fond of her that he would easily forgive her for disobeying him, she, with a trembling hand, applied the key to the lock, and opened the door" (G. Caldwell 1828, 12).

Another moment often embellished is the time given to the wife. Perrault's "half a quarter of an hour" has given all English translators some trouble: in Dean & Munday's *Blue Beard* (1821), it was given as "the eighth part of an hour," while in Thomas Nelson's *The Story of Blue Beard* (1900) it was: "seven and a half minutes exactly, and not a moment longer!"[18] The chapbooks reflect the difficulty of translating the time and range most commonly between five, ten, or fifteen minutes. But to heighten the dramatic moment, a countdown emerges in some chapbooks, so that the wife is given first a quarter of an hour. When that expires, she asks for five minutes more, then two, then one . . .; as each limit expires, the threat of death is again raised. Bluebeard is even complacent. She is completely in his power, so what is five more minutes?[19]

Another "untranslatable" expression that results in chapbook variations refers to the military ranks of the brothers. Perrault's "dragoon" and "musqueteer" do not translate well, so in English chapbooks they are officers "dressed in regimentals." Instead of purchased captains' commissions, as in Perrault, they are in one American version of 1797 awarded "colonel's commissions" (John M'Culloch 1797).[20]

While the variations in time are understandable, given the difficulty of translating the idiom, it is not in translation that the chamber becomes the "Blue Chamber" or the "Blue Closet" in many chapbooks, but in Colman and Kelly's melodrama (complete with blue fire).[21] The Colman and Kelly drama definitely referred to the Blue Chamber and underscored the point with liberal use of blue smoke during and at the end of the production. As early as Tabart's fifth edition there are illustrations in chapbooks captioned: "The Blue Chamber" (Tabart & Co. [1804 or 1805]).

Given that the readership of these chapbooks was children, a fact reflected in titles such as: *The History of Blue Beard: An Entertaining Story for Children*, and in use of nursery book or "Good Child" or "Juvenile Library" series titles, or "A Keepsake for Children" (London: Printed for the Booksellers [18–]), it is perhaps surprising to what extent the gore of the chamber is detailed, as it almost always is. In Samber's translation of Perrault's tale (1729), the description is given as follows: "But she could see nothing distinctly, because the windows were shut; after some moments she began to observe that the floor was all covered over with clotted blood, on which lay the bodies of several dead women ranged against the walls. (These were the wives that the Blue Beard had married and murder'd one after another.)" In chapbooks, the opportunity for embellishment is irresistible: "She found herself amidst the severed limbs and mutilated bodies of her husband's former wives! The scene was frightful! Her own future condition, she immediately thought, might add to these dreadful objects! Her blood chilled! Her very hair rose upon her head! Nor was her terror diminished, when she saw upon the wall these awful words: '*The fate of broken promises and disobedient curiosity*.'" (Printed for N. Hailes 1817, 57–58)[22] Perhaps it is as a result of captioned illustrations, as much as by the Colman and Kelly 1798 drama that used this device,[23] that the contents of the chamber are rendered literally legible. The wife's realization ("Her own future condition, she immediately thought, might add to these dreadful objects!") is spelled out: "she saw upon the walls these words: *The Reward of Disobedience and Imprudent Curiosity*" (Peter G. Thomson [n.d]). In one case, the heads themselves are each labeled: "An inquisitive wife" (Printed for J. Harris 1808).

In some chapbooks, there is an attempt to render a story of origins, the answer to the question: What did the first wife see when she looked inside? The originary story that circulates through chapbooks is surprisingly consistent: "Blue Beard's first wife was a bold-spirited woman, with whom he quarreled soon after marriage; and having in the heat of his anger murdered her, he concealed her body in this blue closet. The rest of his wives, who, like Fatima, could not refrain from indulging their curiosity, he had killed for acting contrary to his express commands; and the key had always betrayed their disobedience" (W. Walker & Sons [185–])[24] The tradition of originary myths for Bluebeard's chamber is now long and rich, but it is interesting to note that at its heart is always an unruly woman. Like Lilith, Eve's precursor in Eden, Bluebeard's first wife's transgression was to be "bold-spirited."

The last paragraphs of the Dean & Son version tell of perhaps one of the most interesting changes made in the nineteenth century to the Perrault version. In Perrault, the wife inherits Bluebeard's fortune and dispenses it to advance the situation of her siblings and herself: the brothers are bought captains' commissions, she and her sister Anne are dowered and marry. The monetary nature of the end of Perrault's story has been attributed to his lawyerly mindset. But it is still in starkly rapid contrast to the attentive descriptions of Bluebeard's lavish wealth and what it has bought him. In many Victorian versions, however, the details of how his wife proceeds once Bluebeard is dead, and how she then spends her fortune, are carefully rendered. But in contrast to the descriptions of lavishness (the "pomp and ceremony" of the wedding alone is sometimes given a page or two), the wife's disbursement of funds is much more charitably directed. Frequently, as in the Dean & Son version provided above, the house is opened to public view, and thereby a sort of exorcism is performed. In some cases, it is described in very practical terms: "The fatal closet underwent a complete repair, which removed every trace of his barbarity" (J. Innes [1830?]). The laws, rights and protections of community are restored through public rites, exorcising Bluebeard's anti-social secrets.[25] In these versions, there is often no mention of remarriage, but rather she becomes a "respectable widow," like her mother, with whom she may now live. Her family still benefits from Bluebeard's death, but does so by living together and behaving as good landlords to the tenantry. A long variation on this theme is given in the chapbook *History of Blue Beard*:

All those horrid murders which had been committed by Blue Beard, were unknown to his domestics, on whose credulity he imposed by falsehoods, which they had no means of detecting: Fatima and her brothers thought the most prudent way to act was to assemble them together, and then disclose the wickedness of their late master.

It was now that each of the domestics could recall to their memory the bitter sigh and heavy groan that had struck upon their ears, shortly before the wives of Blue Beard disappeared; yet the artful, and seemingly meek behaviour of their master, contrived to lull all suspicion of the atrocious fiend. It was with some difficulty that they made themselves believe that they had been serving this demon in human form.

By the directions of Fatima, her two brothers conducted all the servants to the dreadful scene of her husband's cruelties; and then showing them his dead body, related the whole occurrences which had taken place. They all said that his punishment was not adequate to what he deserved, and begged that they might be continued in the service of their mistress. As Blue Beard had no relations, Fatima was sole heir to the whole of his immense property; and mistress of the castle; in the possession of which she was confirmed by the laws of the country.

Immediately after the interment [*sic*] of the dead bodies, the company retired to Blue Beard's private chamber, and on examining his papers discovered a sealed packet, which, on being opened, contained a sheet of parchment, on which was written the names of his murdered wives, with the addresses of their nearest relatives, and at Fatima's request, her brothers, with as much delicacy and feeling as the distressing and mournful tidings would call forth, wrote to them a full explanation of Blue Beard's conduct, and a detailed account of the circumstances which led to the tragic termination of this infamous character.

Soon after this, Fatima gave a magnificent entertainment to all her friends, where happiness was seen in every face; and on this occasion the poor, who were assembled for many miles round, partook most liberally of her bounty. Though possessed of riches almost inexhaustible, Fatima disposed of them with so much discretion, that she gained the esteem of all who knew her. She bestowed handsome fortunes on her two brothers, who were the means of saving her life; and to her sister who was married about twelve months after, she gave a very large dowry.

The beauty, riches, and amiable conduct of Fatima, attracted a number of admirers; and among others, a young nobleman of very high rank, who to a handsome person, added every quality calculated to make a good husband; and after a reasonable time spent in courtship, their marriage was celebrated with great rejoicings (Glasgow: For the Booksellers 1852, 14–15).

If it is perhaps unseemly for Bluebeard's wife to profit so directly from his death, it certainly seems to be the case that she cannot be seen to profit so personally from her disobedience. One verse moral (directed to "Young Ladies") stated: "'Inquisitive tempers / To mischief may lead; / But placid Obedience / Will always succeed'" (Printed for J. Harris 1808).[26] Frequently it is moralized that the happy ending came at great cost: "But though his kind treatment soon made her forget Blue Beard's cruelty, she never forgot, that to her own indiscreet and foolish curiosity, she owed the terrible trial through which she had passed" (Pott & Amery [n.d.]); "Although the kindness of her second husband was equal to Blue Beard's cruelty, she never forgot that her own foolish prying was the cause of the terrible danger she had so narrowly escaped" (Thomas Nelson 1900, 119). The connection with her inheritance (rather than the kind treatment of a later husband) is most clearly made in the following formula: "Fatima used with discretion and liberality the wealth of which she had become possessed: but she never forgot that she should 'keep her promise; obey those who were entitled to her submission; and restrain her curiosity within moderate bounds'" (Printed for N. Hailes 1817).

Bluebeard does not entirely escape the moralizing trend either. The Miss Merryheart series of Dean & Son (printed by McLoughlin in America) all note that Bluebeard's conscience is awakened as he is killed: "Sudden as the attack of these brave men was, it was not quicker than the awakened conscience of this cruel man. All his deeds of blood instantly presented themselves to his mind. The image of every unhappy being whom he had destroyed, appeared to his imagination, and embittered the misery he now endured. After a few convulsive struggles, he fell back and expired" (Dean & Son [ca. 1860]).[27]

This moment is heightened in Hailes' 1817 miniature book version, whose castigation of the youngest daughter's vanity has already been quoted above, and is a lengthy dying speech from Bluebeard worthy of the stage. Still, in doing so, he nonetheless manages to heap further blame on his would-be victim:

The monster had yet sufficient life to speak: he raised himself on one arm; and looking on them all, thus spoke: "I am at last justly punished. By the splendour of my riches, I have induced many a beautiful woman to become my wife; but as soon as I discovered any deviation from truth, or disobedience to my will, she suffered death. I put Fatima's veracity to the test by obtaining her promise that she would not open the door of the blue closet; and by leaving the key with her, she broke her word; and the key, which has the property of preserving the stains of blood until it be rubbed with a peculiar oil, afforded the evidence of her guilt. By the same means I knew that she had disobeyed my desire. These two faults incurred my revenge. She has had but a narrow escape: yet I hope she will in future never break a promise; disobey those to whom she had promised submission; nor give way to the impulse of curiosity."

He grew faint, and having uttered a few prayers for forgiveness, he fell back and expired (Printed for N. Hailes 1817, 85–87).

In an example from the late eighteenth century, quoted above as giving "colonel's commissions" to the brothers, the title "with morals" entirely understates the case. Perrault's morals are given, which is not often the case in chapbooks, but in addition, an extra moral is provided at the end of the tale itself: "The curiosity of Blue Beard's wife had well nigh cost her her head; and this disposition will bring all of all sexes, who indulge it beyond the bound of prudence, into difficulties they can hardly escape from. Yet the reader is desired to take notice that there are two species of this turn of mind: the one *commendable*, when it leads to knowledge; the other *blameable*, when it only serves to gratify an idle inquisitiveness" (John M'Culloch 1797, original italics). It is unusual both in that the additional moral includes both sexes in its caution and in distinguishing between good and bad uses of curiosity, rather than castigating curiosity altogether.

A "Third" English Translation

Although it was common for chapbooks to be pirated and copied wholesale, a surprising discovery emerges from a survey of so many variations on the Bluebeard theme: a consistent "alternative" translation from Perrault to the dominant two by Robert Samber and by G. M. It has some of the characteristics of the Samber translation, using the term "collations," for example, and also several of the hallmarks of G. M.'s translation ("half a quarter of an hour"; "bawled"; "scimitar") blended together. But in addition, there is a series of hallmarks of this alternative version that are not present in either Samber's or G. M.'s translation and that are nevertheless astonishingly consistent. In these, Bluebeard entreats his wife to invite her friends "and to treat them with all sorts of delicacies"; he warns she must not enter the chamber, "nor even put the key

Chapbook illustration, the chamber. From E. Billing. 1839–1849. *History of Blue Beard*. London. Courtesy of The Lilly Library, Indiana University, Bloomington.

into the lock, for all the world"; he departs only "after tenderly embracing her"; and when she transgresses "she determined to venture in spite of everything." When she tries to recover from her shock at seeing the chamber's contents, she goes to her room "that she might have a little time to get into humour for amusing her visitors"; she tries to pretend she is "transported with joy" at her husband's unexpected return, and when he asks for the keys he tells her to bring them "by-and-bye." When he sees the key is bloody, he concludes that she must enter the chamber by saying "Vastly well, madam"; and the two officers who enter are "dressed in their regimentals" (Cunningham 1889).[28]

"Adorned with Beautiful Cuts": The Illustrations

The woodcuts and engravings that adorned chapbooks were often rough and recycled, but whatever the quality they seem to be a necessary component of the chapbook. The number and type of illustrations formed a major advertising point in the competitive publishers' lists. As Harry Weiss wrote: "Regardless of the crudeness of chapbook illustrations, they have a certain charm and quaintness and seem to be an integral part of the chapbook itself" (1942, 5).[29] They were integral, in other words, even when the illustrations were barely connected thematically to the text. As has been said, the illustrations were often a form of "filler" only tenuously linked to the subject at hand. This can lead to amusing results in Bluebeard's case. In some instances, such as J. Swindells [1830?], a couple of the illustrations depict a man with no beard. In the case of J. Pitts [1810?], Bluebeard is depicted properly bearded, except that in this case the *text*

Chapbook illustration. From J. March. [1864–1875]. *Blue-Beard.* Courtesy of The Lilly Library, Indiana University, Bloomington.

has described him as "clean-shaven," perhaps to accompany an earlier illustration.

It also seems that the illustrations, particularly the frequently repeated one of the near-execution, were an integral part of their first production, in Charles Perrault's manuscript edition of *Contes* (1695). Ségolène Le Men neatly situated the headpieces and composition of that first illustration of "La Barbe Bleue" and the resulting print edition (1697) within the emblematic tradition, which again argues how integral the illustrations are to the tale: "The organization of the illustrated page shared by [Perrault's] manuscript and the [1697] edition may suggest the reason why Perrault's tales were illustrated in the first place. Tales belong to an emblematic tradition, as do fables. . . . Emblems are a mixed medium rooted in the interplay between the concrete and the abstract, involving both text and image" (1992, 21).[30] Le Men also indicated that as "Each period added new pictures to the original group of single illustrations" (37), so the text was ultimately "evicted." In many chapbooks, this "eviction of the text" has already begun, in fact, as the illustrations grow in size and number to displace the text. The publishing restrictions (for cost and distribution) on chapbook size and page numbers dictate that the one must give way as the other usurps the limited space. More than merely decorative and perhaps, as Le Men argued, reminiscent of "pictorial pedagogy" (22), the chapbook illustrations of *Bluebeard* come to be repetitions of the same scenes from the text, to the point where they come to be the requisite iconography of the story.[31]

The Bluebeard chapbook illustrations are a series of "set pieces"; certain iconic postures repeated over and over again. The very first illustration, in Perrault's manuscript version of 1695, is in two forms: frontispiece illustration and in-text illustration (headpiece).[32] As Le Men described, Bluebeard is first recalled in the frontispiece illustration that draws visual elements from all the stories in the *Contes* in order to function as a rhetorical memory device. Bluebeard is recalled in "The carefully closed door and its visible keyhole" of the room in which "Mother Goose" is telling stories (the very door on which the sign "*Contes de mamere loye*" [*sic*] is nailed). The headpiece illustration derives directly from the story: "In Bluebeard, the picture is evenly split into two parts in order to show two settings and actions simultaneously: Bluebeard and his wife vis-à-vis the galloping horsemen; the inside vis-à-vis the outside of the castle" (1992, 32). Even the depiction of the near-execution is due to formal requirements: "the imminent danger and not the crime itself [is] pictured, as baroque pictorial conventions would dictate" (32).[33]

In keeping with this first illustrated headpiece, the illustration that most often represents the Bluebeard tale on chapbook covers and frontispieces is this moment of near-execution, except that it is now featured alone, while the imminent rescue is its own set piece.[34] Baroque pictorial conventions may have dictated this moment to some extent, but, in addition to being suspenseful and dramatic, it also depicts *erotic* violence. In the chapbook illustrations focusing on the wife's near-execution, Bluebeard stands over her, scimitar drawn. His wife is helpless and imploring, her head at or below his waist, pulling herself away as Bluebeard grabs and pulls her hair. It's not just Bluebeard's power, cruelty, and secrets being depicted, but sadistic, erotic violence. Even in comic versions such as F. W. N. Bayley's, the overtones are made clear: "Oh! hadn't a fair lady better be dead / Than be dragged down stairs by the hair of her head?" (Wm. S. Orr & Co. [ca. 1842], 41).[35] This, rather than the moment of women discovered in the chamber, is what is on the covers of Bluebeard chapbooks, and it is obviously connected to the corpses in the chamber.

The requisite illustrations grow through chapbook repetition to include standard "set pieces" for: the courtship (and/or the wedding procession), the giving of the key, the chamber, the call for rescue, the near execution, the killing of Bluebeard. The illustrations are sometimes captioned, and these captions and the order of illustrations (the first illustration going to the near-execution) tell the story a second time. The illustrations in *The History of Blue Beard* (W. S. Johnson 1850) are, with a couple of omissions, exactly the same illustrations as those in J. Innes [1830?] but with the addition of another on the first page: the near execution, as Bluebeard holds her by the hair and the brothers rush to the rescue. The others are captioned as follows: "Ann waving her Handkerchief to her Brothers at the time Blue Beard was going to murder Fatima"; "The First

Chapbook illustration. From W. Davison. 1808–1858. *History of Blue Beard.* Courtesy of The Lilly Library, Indiana University, Bloomington.

Visit of Ann and Fatima to the Castle"; "The Procession of Blue Beard after his Marriage"; "Blue Beard intrusting [*sic*] Fatima with his Gold and Jewels"; "Imprudent Curiosity of Fatima to see the Blue Chamber"; "Blue Beard asking how the Blood came on the Key"; "The Brothers Killing Blue Beard, to save their Sister."

The Chamber

The "beautiful cuts" of the chapbooks are gleefully rendered in the vision of the chamber, which has its own standard illustrations, but nevertheless also a surprising range of diverse elements. Despite an established readership of children, the contents of the chamber are usually rendered in all their gory detail (often colored by child laborers) liberally colored in swathes of red. The standard arrangement is: the wife reacting to the sight in horror, throwing her hands up and shielding her eyes; the key dropping to the floor in midfall; the bodies of several women lying or hanging or both, with and without their heads. *Blue Beard* [1861] shows an engraving depicting five headless corpses, eerily standing up, and six female heads on the floor, with blood. The description here is given with gusto: "She stood in the midst of blood, the heads, bodies, and mangled limbs of the murdered ladies strewed over the floor" (J. Bysh [1861], 4).

The key is usually oversized throughout these illustrations, and in the illustrations of the bloody chamber it is an integral and necessary element. In many cases, the key is visible in midfall; the illustration captures the moment of looking (discovery), and simultaneously the act of dropping the key that will result in the *other* discovery. In some chapbooks the key is depicted as

The Death of Bluebeard visually mirrors the chamber in its depiction of a corpse, balancing and redeeming the tale's violence with Bluebeard's own murder. Printed for J. Harris, successor to E. Newbery. 1808. *Blue Beard, or, The Fatal Effects of Curiosity and Disobedience, Illustrated with Elegant and Appropriate Engravings.* Courtesy of The Lilly Library, Indiana University, Bloomington.

broken on the floor; this was a prop resulting from stage adaptation, where a spot on a key would not be readily visible to the audience, but also helpful to the gradual bowdlerizing of the chamber in which there is first no blood, and finally no bodies. Instead, in response to the Colman and Kelly play, itself a gothic product, the contents of the chamber in illustrations become more lively and "supernatural"; skeletons appear alive, puffs of smoke issue from the room, and even demons fly about.

There are, of course, a few examples of editions with no bodies in the chamber at all. A late version, *Blue Beard and Puss in Boots* acknowledges that the child reader may have some qualms with the material in its dedication: "To Siegfried. / If the tale of Blue Beard / Should make you afeard, / As the time nears for bed! / "Puss in Boots" read instead!" (J. M. Dent & Co. 1895). By 1900, there is a giant key, dripping blood, pictured on a back cover of [*Ten*] *Favourite Stories for the Nursery, with Numerous Illustrations* (Thomas Nelson 1900), and not only are the chamber contents not depicted (the wife is shown from behind, as she looks in), but also the death of Bluebeard occurs "offstage";

the picture shows the brothers leaving him for dead, one stepping away from the body, the other already as far away as the doorstep.[36] The violence, like the chapbook phenomenon, has passed.

The chapbooks, "orphaned" and "rude" as they may have been, were the vehicle by which Bluebeard traveled across the British Isles and America, just as his counterpart was traveling across Europe. These chapbooks provide vivid evidence that while tastes in children's reading may not have changed, the publications marketed for children certainly have. The fairy tale thrived in this blunt format, and the illustrations were integral to its continued popularity. By sheer repetition, the orientalism introduced by the 1798 melodrama also took permanent hold, and it was a Turkish Bluebeard and a wife named Fatima who were most often projected to the reader of these chapbooks. The chapbooks also, importantly, blurred the distinctions between readerships; fairy tales were on a path to becoming children's fare, but chapbooks were widely read and not only by children. Furthermore, the memorable influence of childhood reading on future adult authors and artists, like Charles Dickens, also contributed to Bluebeard's hold on the English imagination.

Chapter 6

"You Outrageous Man!"

Bluebeard on the Comic Stage

In the dramas of the early decades of the nineteenth century, Bluebeard took his cue from the Colman and Kelly production, infusing contemporary chapbooks with imagery and characterization from this popular stage production (1798) and its popular revivals.[1] The stream of chapbooks that had taken their direction from Perrault translations was decidedly diverted. Here, Bluebeard is an oriental grotesque; his wife is named Fatima; she is sold by her mercenary father Ibrahim to the "three tailed Bashaw"[2] and rescued by her true love, Selim, along with her brothers and her sister Anne. Such was the story set by Colman and Kelly, illustrated from the theatre by R. Cruikshank, and thriving in the popular ephemeral chapbooks. Not surprisingly, therefore, this was the story told repeatedly from the stage, and in the first half of the nineteenth century in particular, the Colman and Kelly production was the persistent intertext with which these other works were in dialogue.[3] But after 1866, a rival "masterwork" entered the arena in *Blue Beard Re-Paired; a Worn-Out Subject Done Up Anew*, adapted by Henry Bellingham from a French comic opera by two masters of the form, Henri Meilhac and Ludovic Halévy. The plot is vastly different from that of Colman and Kelly's melodrama, the oriental cast is nowhere to be seen, and by 1868 the work had premiered in America, where, as in London, it remained popular throughout the last decades of the century, thriving in a climate encouraging to operetta.

An allusion in all types of Bluebeard dramas is Shakespeare's *Othello*, also featuring a wife-killer, a man "turned Turk." Already echoed in Robert Samber's English translation of Charles Perrault's fairy tale, the dramatic intertext was much more thoroughly brought to bear in stage representations of the Bluebeard tale, newly set in Constantinople or Baghdad, throughout the nineteenth century, creating comic disjunction between the tragedy of Shakespeare's play and the burlesque use made of it.

In the early decades, in light of extant records, it seems that audiences on both sides of the Atlantic were very pleased to see Colman and Kelly's drama itself. But with such an influential and "complete" precursor in the melodrama, there was an irrepressible upsurge of burlesque that began with making fun of this major intertext, so that the comic form in one way or another dominated the nineteenth-century dramatic representations of Bluebeard, whether Turkish (as he most often was) or not. In direct contrast to the trend on the German stage,[4] serious stage renditions of the Bluebeard story in England and America were almost entirely absent, save for a few of the amateur or parlor entertainments that act out Perrault's tale with little or no attempt at comedy.

Never presented on the English stage, Ludwig Tieck's five-act gothic drama *Blue Beard* was translated into English by John Lothrop Motley and published in two issues of the *New World* (1840). Motley was a writer who had studied in Germany and had already published translations of German works (of Schiller and of Novalis), both in 1839 for the *New Yorker*, and had reviewed Goethe for the *New York Review* (1839). The advertisement above the translation described Tieck as "the most popular living author of Germany" whose lighter pieces were very well known; the translation was presented as a "specimen" and an "experiment" to see if it would amuse the American reading public. The subject was introduced as one of a "Fantasie" series: a dramatized nursery play, which was "chiefly entertaining as being the vehicle for the author's delicate humor, satire, and romance." Tieck's play also demonstrates the influence of Shakespeare, whom Tieck had translated into German, but reveals the German writer's poetics of "nonsense" through making foolishness, rationality, and the ability to orate actual topics for the play's banter, and by making the Fool (Claus) wiser than the fools who employ him. The central plot concerns Agnes von Friedheim who is married to Hugo von Wolfsbrun, also called Bluebeard, by her brothers who desire a wealthy match. When she takes up residence there, with the gothic crone Matilda and her sister Anne (herself pining for her love Reinhold), she enters the chamber. The play does not show the moment of discovery, but revels in the description days after the fact. Anne notices that Agnes is behaving oddly and compels her to tell the story. Hugo, returning early, unleashes invective against his wife as a daughter of Eve: "Accursed curiosity! . . . The sin of the first mother of the human race has poisoned all her worthless daughters." While Agnes begs for mercy, he is unflinching: "You abominate me now." She is rescued by her brothers Simon and Antony, thanks to the former's dream prophecy. Subplots, which are extensive, concern the third brother Leopold and his elopement with Bridget, the sister of Reinhold and daughter of Agnes' godfather Hans von Marloff. There is a bevy of comic servants to offset the gothic drama.

The other possible exception to comic dramas on the subject is *The Female Bluebeard, or, The Adventures of Polyphemus Amador de Croustillac* by Thomas Higgie (first produced with some modifications in 1847 as *The Devil's Mount, or, the Female Bluebeard*).[5] The play uses the Bluebeard story for the eponymous Female Bluebeard, reputed to be wealthy, to have been a widow three times already, and to have turned to piracy. The story is set in 1685 and is a pirate story using Caribbean settings and characters to develop a love story of historical political intrigue and the necessity of disguise. Despite the use of Bluebeard's name and its interest as an early example of the "lady Bluebeard" label, it is anomalous as a serious drama on this subject.

By contrast, comic renditions of "Bluebeard" are abundant and fall into three major subcategories: harlequinade and pantomime; extravaganza and burlesque (including *opera bouffe*); and amateur or parlor plays for home entertainment (frequently as "children's" theatre). Whether amateur or professional, burlesque remained the dominant tone until the major twentieth-century Bluebeard operas.

Heigho! Bluebeard Harlequinades and Pantomimes

According to R. J. Broadbent, the French play called *Barbe bleu* on which Grétry based his Parisian opera in 1789 (which, as has been discussed, inspired Colman and Kelly), was a harlequinade to begin with: "'Blue Beard' was first dramatised at Paris, in 1746, when '*Barbe bleu*' was thus announced: —*Pantomime— representée par la troupe des Comediens Pantomimes, Foir St. Laurent*. It was afterwards dramatised at the Early of Barrymore's Theatre, Wargrave, Berks., and in 1791. After that the subject was produced at Covent Garden Theatre as a Pantomime" (Broadbent 1901, 204).[6] By 1791, when *Bluebeard, or, the Flight of Harlequin* was staged at Covent Garden, the concept of a harlequinade was already very familiar to English audiences, who had enjoyed pantomimes and harlequinades for more than a century,[7] and the genre had already spawned acknowledged masters in John Rich (at Covent Garden) and his rival Garrick (at Drury Lane), as well as public battles between the theatres for pantomime's lucrative ticket sales.[8] The precedent for using "Bluebeard" as a harlequinade in England had thus been set, but after Colman and Kelly's *Blue Beard* (produced, as it says in the preface, "to supply the place of a Harlequinnade"), the traditional Christmas and Easter pantomime[9] and harlequinades take on the

This Penny Pantomime sheet from London (ca. 1870) shows all the character transformations and set pieces from pantomime into harlequinade. From *Penny Pantomime of Blue Beard.* [1870?]. Courtesy of Harvard Theatre Collection, Houghton Library.

eastern cast as well. In 1811, during the popular revival of the Colman and Kelly production, *Harlequin and Blue Beard* burlesqued it, turning each of Colman's characters into traditional harlequinade figures.[10]

The harlequinade in England, as elsewhere in Europe, initially took its form from the Italian *Commedia del'Arte,* which used a number of stock figures, masked, in a "dumb show," accompanied by music. The term *harlequinade* (at this period in England it described the major portion of a pantomime) draws upon the figures from the *Commedia,* which in England devolved into four key players: Harlequin, the hero, able to do tumbling and direct the stage spectacles to appear as if by magic; Columbine, his lovely partner or a maid;[11] Clown, the machinating and gleeful menace, derived from the Italian Scaramouche figure, or servant; and Pantaloon, who became on the English stage an old man, never able to catch the couple he pursues and who is often described as having an "ambling gait".

Initially, the harlequinade elements were interwoven throughout the classical subject, as a continuing love story between Harlequin and Columbine, interspersing the unrelated action of the main story. But during the eighteenth century, the English pantomime structure changed to become a brief opening (usually based on a classical subject, fairy tale, or other universally known story), followed by a transformation scene that then initiates the harlequinade proper, using the same characters in order to resolve conflicts begun between them in the opening.[12] The structure and relationship of the traditional double-plotted harlequinade/pantomimes of the early nineteenth century were helpfully described by J. R. Planché, himself a popular and prolific author of burlesque extravaganzas (including *Blue Beard*, 1839). It is interesting to note from his generic description how easily the Colman and Kelly dramatic structure (the old father, the poor rival suitor, and servants) befits the pantomime genre to which it so quickly adapted:

> A pretty story—a nursery tale—dramatically told, in which "the course of true love never did run smooth," formed the opening; the characters being a cross-grained old father, with a pretty daughter, who had two suitors—one a poor young fellow, whom she preferred, the other a wealthy fop, whose pretensions were, of course, favoured by the father. There was also a body servant of some sort in the old man's establishment. At the moment when the young lady was about to be forcibly married to the fop she despised, or, on the point of eloping with the youth of her choice, the good fairy made her appearance, and, changing the refractory pair into Harlequin and Columbine, the old curmudgeon into Pantaloon, and the body servant into Clown: the two latter in company with the rejected "lover," as he was called, commenced the pursuit of the happy pair, and the "comic business" consisted of a dozen or more cleverly constructed scenes, . . . Again at the critical moment the protecting fairy appeared, and, exacting the consent of the father to the marriage of the devoted couple, transported the whole party to what was really a grand last scene, which everybody did wait for (Planché cited in Broadbent 1901, 172–73).

It can be safely assumed that the *Blue Beard, or, The Flight of Harlequin* at Covent Garden in 1791 followed this form, as most likely did *Harlequin and Blue Beard* (1811). But the pantomime changed again, even before the general use of speaking parts, in the 1820s and 1830s. Writing "On Pantomime" in 1817, writer Leigh Hunt praised pantomime for being so "real" (84). Writing again in 1831, he lamented that pantomime had devolved into "gratuitous absurdity without object."[13] One of the major changes in the interim had been the "ballooning" of the brief opening into a play of equal length as the harlequinade and sometimes even longer.[14] Although acknowledged masters in each of these roles received high praise and pantomime was consistently bankable entertainment, it had its detractors. Pantomime was low brow, and its slapstick pandered to crowds. While it remained a mute performance (set to lively music) it retained some of the best qualities of good acting performances. It remained a dumb show to get around restrictions on the minor theatres imposed by the patent theatres, until the patents were repealed and restrictions lifted by the Theatre Act of 1843. In 1830, a "speaking prologue" had been introduced, but as R. J. Broadbent wrote in 1901, pantomime "pursued the even tenour of its way" (220) until the mid-nineteenth century.[15]

The shift from melodrama (represented by Colman and Kelly's production)[16] to pantomime as a means of representing this fairy tale is significant and no doubt has many causes beyond simply the desire to mock a dominant precursor. Both melodrama and pantomime (especially pantomime, which reliably includes the rough treatments of Clown and Pantaloon and even stage murders) are "psychologically escapist" as Michael Booth noted, but they are also fundamentally opposed:

> The governing spirits of the Regency harlequinade were misrule and anarchy: the freedom to commit amusing capital crimes and set law and authority at nought was bestowed abundantly upon Harlequin and Clown. Thus the harlequinade was, like melodrama, psychologically escapist, offering audiences a release for sadistic impulses toward cheating, tricking, larceny, cruelty, wanton destruction, violence, and rebellion. Melodrama, however, idealized morality, revered the aged parent, rewarded virtue and punished vice; pantomime satisfied different desires and did the exact opposite. The same audiences enjoyed both genres, and both found common ground in a general hostility toward constituted and inherited authority. In melodrama this was largely a matter of class conflict, but in pantomime the same hostility manifested itself in vicious treatment of an oppressive father-figure, Pantaloon, and in his watchman or policeman surrogate (1976, 5.5–6).

By 1901, Broadbent could call Bluebeard "another familiar Pantomime subject" (203). Certainly there are a number of extant plays that indicate that the familiarity was warranted. In addition to the two already referenced, a good number of pantomimes called *Blue Beard* survive.

John Morton's pantomime *Harlequin Blue Beard, the great bashaw, or The good fairy triumphant over the demon of discord! A Grand Comic Christmas Pantomime* (first performed in 1854) is a sound illustration of the genre and of another principle used in it: the cross-dressed casting of several major parts, usually Sister Anne and Selim (but sometimes extending to other characters, such as "Mustiphustima," the sisters' mother, and even Fatima herself). The program in the printed edition of Morton's play (The Acting Edition) included what was likely the playbill, giving an extensive description of the plot by scene. In Morton's version, Rustifusti, the Demon of Discord, begins by inviting witches to help him fight the fairy. One of the witches, with his magic wand, summons an omen from a cauldron, warning that Bluebeard's life is in danger from his new wife's curiosity (wife number 22). It is revealed that the witch is in fact the fairy herself, and the other witches are also in disguise; the fairies keep Rustifusti's wand. There is a comic scene in Bluebeard's kitchen, largely comprised of physical humor (using hot pokers, a familiar instrument in the harlequinade sequences) and inventions out of control, culminating in an explosion. After pantomiming several routines in which Selim gets the upper hand on Ibrahim, Selim courts Fatima, with Ibrahim again trying to intervene and coming off the worse for it. Bluebeard enters (to the music of the now-ubiquitous march procession from Colman and Kelly) comically unsteady in his sedan chair and preceded by an hyperbolic brass band. These scenes are almost entirely mimed as the stage directions indicate. Bluebeard's nursery is shown with twenty-one children saying good night to their new mother. At word that poachers are shooting Bluebeard's game, he gives over the keys and enjoins Fatima not to open the blue chamber door. She immediately does, and amidst a number of special stage effects, including blue fire, one of Bluebeard's deceased wives, her head under her arm, delivers the bad news. The key has turned blue, and Fatima begins miming her futile attempts to clean it; she is surprised by Bluebeard (who tiptoes up behind her), and they immediately enter into the threat-of-execution stage of the story. A large illuminated clock shows five minutes to twelve and forms part of the background to the scene of Sister Anne at the tower. There is the common to and fro between Anne and Fatima, with the equally common additional commentary usually found in this scene. In this version, Fatima chastises Anne for talking about the flock of sheep: "Anne, you're a fool / All that great cry about a little wool!" Immediately after Selim kills Bluebeard, Rustifusti appears, changing the balance of power, but the Good Fairy also reappears and as the scene changes to Fairy Land, Rustifusti admits defeat and "like all Bad Geniuses in Pantomime, [goes] below." The Good Fairy then effects the transformation of each character into their harlequinade counterparts.

Thus, we see a fairly representative use of the Bluebeard story in pantomime and harlequinade. The addition of supernatural characters to oversee the action and effect the transformation is typical. Here, it is Rustifusti versus the

Good Fairy; in another, Despotino and his sidekicks are thoroughly trounced by Freedom and Britannia (Bridgeman 1860); elsewhere, Titania and Oberon team up against Bluebeard (Millward 1869).

In Charles Millward's program, a new cast appears for the harlequinade, following the transformation. In most cases, however, the regular cast doubles up into the harlequinade characters and continues the comic business there. The comic violence done to Ibrahim continues throughout his role as Pantaloon; Abomelique becomes the Clown, to continue his attempts to thwart the "good" characters.

Cross-dressed casting, from which no doubt much physical humor derives, is endemic. In the example of Morton's pantomime, both Sister Anne and Fatima (and therefore, at least initially upon transformation, Harlequina and Columbine) are played by male actors. Commonly, Sister Anne is played by a man. The comedy of the cross-dressed casting is further developed in pantomimes that elaborate on Sister Anne's own frustrated wishes to marry, usually by trying to frustrate her sister's relationship with Selim, marriage to Bluebeard, or both. Charles Millward's pantomime (1869) is a good example of this humorous subplot: on overhearing Selim's serenade to Fatima (on a banjo), she screams (no doubt comically), and then speaks in an aside to the audience: "ANNE: She talks of *hiding* him, to bill and coo, / I'd like to have the *hiding* of the two / (*aside*) Be still, fond heart, I really thought that he, / Instead of loving her, was 'spoons' on me" (7–8). Anne then tries to get Bluebeard to marry *her* instead of her sister and is rebuffed, but she is later proposed to by Shacabac. In Morton's version, Anne is curious for her own sake, "because it's woman's mission to be *curious*" (1854, 14), while her sister is not at all inquisitive. However, often, it is Anne's plan to encourage her sister into disobedience as part of her mission to gain a husband for herself, whatever the cost. As Sister Anne becomes more of a melodramatic villain, even quoting Iago at times, her own desire to marry leads her to hate her sister. Selim, in this version, is played by a female actor, as becomes very common over the course of the century. The same trend of cross-dressed casting continues in the amateur and home entertainments, with much being made of Sister Anne's "maidenly coyness" for instance.

Finally, the use of pantomime as a vehicle for topical and social satire is ubiquitous. In addition to thematically related comments about Mormonism (Millward 1869),[17] divorce court, and marital inequities, these pantomimes range far from the immediate subject matter to cast their topical allusions. While the deeds of public figures of the time are a matter now for historical research, others are self explanatory: "OBERON (*aside*): Were I a peer, would

I, with offspring blest, / Make one child rich, and *pauperize the rest?* / Blest if I would—yet there *are* peers who do it" (Millward 1869, 18, original emphasis). Sometimes Sister Anne's lookout sequence is used for this, as she names all manner of things that she can see coming, but which turn out to be illusions.[18]

Extravaganza and Burlesque

In addition to the pantomime and harlequinade, nineteenth-century comic theatre sported many other forms, of which a dominant one was the burlesque. The forms were "overlapping" but all distinguished from the "legitimate" comedy which, until the Theatre Regulation Act of 1843 at least, was limited by law to the patent theatres. The minor theatres used music and song to evade the strictures of the Licensing Act, as seen with pantomime. Extravaganza always uses elements of burlesque. In the later decades of the century, burlesque and extravaganza became interchangeable to the theatre-going public due to the evolution of burlesque into a more heavy-handed form (as was decried in the state of pantomime). Burletta was another subgenre derived from an Italian comedic form, but whose definition in English was intentionally vague because of its use as a means of satisfying the Licensing Act.[19]

Because of their impact and influence on dramas that followed in their footsteps, as well as their iconic status in the genres they straddle, the two burlesques considered here in more detail are the fairy extravaganza by James Robinson Planché and Charles Dance: *Blue Beard: an Extravaganza* (1839), and the influential *opera bouffe* by Jacques Offenbach, music by J. H. Tully: *Blue Beard Re-Paired* (Bellingham 1866).

Planché: Blue Beard: An Extravaganza *(1839)*

The dramatic negotiations with the legacy of the Colman and Kelly production took fixed burlesque form in 1839, in *Blue Beard: an Extravaganza*, by James Robinson Planché (another translator of Bluebeard and prolific writer of extravaganzas) and Charles Dance.[20] In at least one edition it is subtitled: *Very Far from the Text of George Colman.*[21] The play is the second in a long series of "fairy extravaganzas" by Planché that essentially created a new genre, for which Planché supplied more than twenty *exempla*. Planché's extravaganzas forged a long and successful collaboration with Madame Vestris, the actress-manager of the Olympic theatre, who also acted the role of Fatima in the first production of *Blue Beard*, after the opening night was delayed for that purpose (Planché 1858, 237–38).

The extravaganza is an irreverent take on George Colman's libretto, as indicated by its full title as given in the 1864 Lacy's Acting Edition: *Blue Beard: A Grand Musical, Comi-Tragical, Melo-Dramatic, Burlesque Burletta, in One Act.*[22] The setting is restored to France, and the play cites the legend of Gilles de Rais (although getting the details wrong). Planché noted in his *Recollections*: "'Blue Beard' was a great success. No longer 'a very magnificent three-tailed Bashaw,' as in Colman's well-known and well-worn spectacle, he appeared with equal magnificence in the mediæval costume, the scene of the piece being laid, according to the original legend, in Brittany, during the fifteenth century, and was run through, not only 'his wedding clothes,' but the season" (1858, 237–38). The tyrant, while charged in the drama with being a necromancer like de Rais, is also named "Baron Abomelique," even while the authors comment directly on the inaccuracy of having Bluebeard be a Turk: "The Melo-Dramatists of the past Century, converted Blue Beard into an Eastern Story, but every child knows that the old nursery tale, by Mons. Charles Perrault, is nothing of the sort. At Nantes, in Brittany, is preserved among the records of the Duchy, the entire process of a nobleman (the original of the portrait of Blue Beard) who was tried and executed in that city, for the murder of several wives, A.D. 1440. In accordance, therefore, with the laudable spirit of critical enquiry and antiquarian research which distinguishes the present aera, the scene of the Drama has been restored to Brittany" (Planché 1848, n.p.). Interestingly, though, the English reference also persists, as Abomelique swears twice "by Old Harry."[23] The matter is addressed within the play by having French names for the characters, reverting to the mother (instead of Ibrahim the father), and using the legend of de Rais to provide Bluebeard with legitimate cause to be gone from his wife. At the end of the play, the characters note for the audience's benefit that the lack of Turkish influence was deliberate:

JOLI. But there's another charge that may be made
By those who have not well the matter weighed;
They'll say this can't be Blue Beard; ask us where [*sic*] his
Horses, elephants, and dromedaries,
Real or stuffed?
FLEUR. To that the answer plain
Is—"Sir, the beasts belonged to Drury Lane,
And were but lent to Blue Beard, when—sad work—
They made him fly his country, and turn Turk."

Our Blue Beard's not a great Bashaw of three tails,
But a French gentleman of one—the details
Dished up, *a l'Olympique*, by the same cooks
Who for so long have been in your good books (1839, 28).

Fatima is named Fleurette, the military brothers are named "*longue epee*" (long sword) and "*bras de fer*" (arm of iron), Sister Anne is of course present, as is the mother Dame Perroquet. Fleurette is in love with Joli Coeur, who is thrown into Abomelique's dungeon on her account. But once she realizes the degree of Abomelique's wealth in rent rolls and that she may make a promising second match if he predeceases her, she forgets all about Joli Coeur, and is admonished for it by Anne. Bluebeard has married nineteen wives already and is looking to even the score. But despite claims to return Bluebeard to Perrault, the legacy of Colman and Kelly is the dominant intertext for the burlesque. The musical borrowings are thorough: it begins with the song from *Blue Beard* ("Twilight Glimmers"), and is followed by the "Grand March from the original Melo-Dramatic Opera of 'Blue Beard' composed by Michael Kelly"; Margot tries to usurp the heroine's line "In pensive mood—" but is cut off by O'Shac O'Back, her Irish lover: "Don't talk of moods or tenses!" They then sing their traditional duet ("Tink a Tink") but all about his fondness for drinking and her disapproval ("I think, I think, I think that drinking is a sin!"). Fleurette finally sings "As Pensive I Thought," and there is a trio "I see them galloping," all taken directly from *Blue Beard* (1798). Abomelique has made "an ugly bargain, with a still more ugly sprite" (1839, 13). Fleurette's decision to open the chamber is pragmatic: "And wherefore not, I should like to know? / If I'm to be the dame of this chateau" (16), and her response to the nineteen good women all with their heads under their arms (singing "nid nid nodding"), is equally unflappable, as she slams the door and goes about her business.

Planché's play introduced the most extensive allusion to *Othello* to date and established the trend in Bluebeard dramas for the remainder of the century:

Abomelique. That key—
Fleurette. [aside] I feel I've not an hour to live!
Abomelique. Did an Egyptian to my Mother give.
She was a fairy.
Fleurette. La, sir, you don't mean it?
Then would to goodness I had never seen it!
Abomelique. Wherefore?
Fleurette. He's like the black man in the play.

Abomelique. Is't lost? is't gone? Speak! Is't out of the way?
Fleurette. It is not lost; but what an' if it were?
Abomelique. Ha! fetch it! Let me see it. If you dare!
Fleurette. Of course I dare sir; but I won't before
You promise me to spare poor Joli Coeur.
Abomelique. Fetch me that key, I say—my mind misgives.
Fleurette. There's not a better natured fellow lives—
Abomelique. The key!
Fleurette. or on the horn can better play!
Abomelique. The key!
Fleurette. In sooth you are to blame.
Abomelique. Away! (21–22)

The allusion draws out the connection between Othello and Abomelique as "other," with overtones of witchcraft. Othello successfully refutes the charge in Act I of *Othello* of having won Desdemona by enchantment, but when he tells Desdemona that his mother bequeathed him an enchanted handkerchief that would betray a spouse and cause a marriage to fail, he has by this point in the play begun to turn into the racist stereotype he was charged with. The "fairy" element of this fairy tale of *Bluebeard* has always been the enchanted key, and the English translation early introduced the notion that it was given to Bluebeard by "a fairy" (rather than the key being "*fée*," or enchanted). The introduction of a love interest for Bluebeard's wife makes the allusion to *Othello* tidy and ironic. Desdemona has lost the handkerchief through no fault of her own because it has been picked up and taken by Emilia, but while innocent she is forced to tell the lie that the handkerchief is not in fact lost; Fleurette has a key that has turned blue to betray her transgression, and she is deliberately withholding it, but here tells the truth: "It is not lost." Whereas Othello's fears that Desdemona is having an adulterous affair with Cassio are founded on nothing but the "trifles" that Iago turns into evidence against them, Fleurette (or Fatima) is actually in love with Joli Coeur (or Selim).

Planché's "extravaganza" (burlesque, burletta) set the mold for the *Blue Beard* burlesques that follow it, of which there were many, but his style was considered more subtle than the burlesques that followed. There are barely any puns, and the ones that are used are subtle. O'Shac O'Back has been in the chamber dusting the heads and the bodies, presumably in order that Fleurette can realize the full effect once she opens the door; Abomelique's countdown to Fleurette is deliberately exacting (five minutes, four, two and a half, two and a quarter . . .), and Anne (who has been looking with a telescope) berates her brothers for coming on horseback instead of "by the rail-road." That is the extent of the exaggerated comedy of Planché's style.

Opera Bouffe

For the English comic tradition, the production that decidedly broke the mold set by Colman and Kelly, being a new import from a French *opera bouffe,* was: *Bluebeard Re-Paired: A Worn-Out Subject Done-Up Anew. An Operatic Extravaganza in One Act,* music by Jacques Offenbach, arranged by J. H Tully, the libretto by Henry Bellingham, adapted from the French of Henri Meilhac and Ludovic Halévy.[24] It was first staged in England at the Royal Olympic Theatre, Saturday June 2, 1866.[25]

At the point of Bluebeard's entrance at the king's court, the band strikes up Kelly's March, but is stopped with these words from the king: "Hold! Michael Kelly must tonight the *bâton* yield, / for Offenbach to-night commands the field" (26). Fleurette in the French becomes Flora in the English, and Selim becomes "Saphir" in both French and English versions. In the comic opera, Bluebeard's story is a parallel plot, not the only plot, and the affair of the lovers takes up a much greater portion of the drama by giving Fleurette a royal identity that has been kept hidden. The American edition published by Oliver Ditson and Co. gives both the French and a fairly close English translation of the French, with the Music of the Principal Airs (by Offenbach). The "Argument" provided gives the plot, with the names used in the original French. Boulotte, a "rustic maiden," is chosen by lot to be the Rose Queen and Knight Bluebeard's sixth wife. Fleurette, in fact Princess Hermia, long-lost daughter of King Bobeche, is discovered living in the village and returns to court. Prince Saphir, disguised as a peasant, follows her there. Bluebeard brings Boulotte to court with comic results. Spying Hermia, he determines that Boulotte should be poisoned so he can marry Hermia instead. Hermia is betrothed to Saphir, who is revealed to be the prince who had been disguised as a peasant. The alchemist who is to poison Boulotte does not kill her; she is revived in the company of the other wives. The prime minister reveals that he has likewise rescued several courtiers who had been doomed by the king. Bluebeard is denounced at court. His punishment is to keep Boulotte as his wife, while the other wives marry courtiers. Such is the French original on which the English version is based.

The English of Bellingham's libretto (published in London by Lacy) has a few substantive changes to this French template: the king does not execute his courtiers out of jealousy that they are meeting the queen, but out of mere pettiness. In addition, French allusions such as the aspirations of the prime minister ("Shall I be a Richelieu? Shall I be an Oliver?") are of course changed in Bellingham's version. In fact, the prime minister is changed to a different agent of the king entirely: Robert, the English bobby (a common target in nineteenth-century comedies), the "hi of the law." Robert is proud of his own deductive reasoning and speaks with stereotypical pompousness: "Them are secrets of state, Popolani, which, not knowing, it are not for me to divulge" (1866, 9). The second English stereotype incorporated by Bellingham is that of Jeames [*sic*], a courtier of the king and stereotypical English butler, punctuating his speech with many a "Haw!" The French original contains an ironic reference to the Bluebeard story that Bellingham for some reason removed: when the prime minister Oscar is to reveal that he has not in fact executed the king's men as he was ordered to, he produces the key of their hiding place: the alchemist refers to the key of the Bluebeard story by asking if it is blood-stained (*tachée de sang*), and Oscar replies: "No, not that" (36). Given that the alchemist has purportedly been *poisoning* the wives, the blood-stained key of Perrault only makes its appearance through this allusion.

Bellingham's anglicized version acknowledges the break that has occurred with English tradition as represented by Colman and Kelly. The first scene of the *opera bouffe* is pastoral; Flora the milk maid (later revealed to be the missing Princess Periwink) flirts with Saphir, the shepherd who is in fact a prince in disguise. Comic relief is in the form of Mopsa, a plain maid, in love with Saphir (her line: "My heart is pit-a-patting" [7] is an obvious allusion to Colman and Kelly's duet between Selim and Fatima). Robert enters the village to search for the princess, sent down the river in a cradle as an infant, and now eighteen. Coincidentally at the same time, Popolani, an alchemist, enters on the opposite side of the stage, in order to obtain a Queen of the May for Bluebeard to marry as his sixth wife. Mopsa throws in her lot, and wins the lottery. The drawing takes place using a cradle, engraved with "E.R." on the side; seeing this, Robert pantomimes "extravagant joy." The E. R. stands for "Earlypurl Rex," and Flora admits she is the child who came from that cradle. Flora now pledges herself to her "shepherd," Saphir: "Now our hearts with joy replete / Both in unison shall beat." Bluebeard arrives after they have left the stage to find his Queen of the May, Mopsa.

The second scene takes place at court, with a brief satire on the ways of court: "Who is prudent and discreet, / Let him study bowing, scraping; / Who would ruin be escaping, / Let him thus make both ends meet" (20). The king is proven as bad a tyrant in his way as Bluebeard: the king orders one of the courtiers to die because his obeisance falls short; this is the fifth man to be so condemned. Robert announces that Saphir will come courting that afternoon for the princess' hand, and Lord Bluebeard will present his sixth wife immediately after. The king's marriage to Queen Greymare is demonstrated to be a difficult one; they detest one another. The princess is averse to being married off to a prince, as she is in love with her shepherd; Prince Saphir arrives, and she realizes her error. Bluebeard arrives with Mopsa, who again provides comic relief by being unaware of the ways of the court. Bluebeard plans to murder Mopsa before Periwink can marry Saphir, so that he may marry the princess instead.

Scene 3 takes place in the Alchemist's Chamber. Popolani has had a vision that Mopsa will be Bluebeard's proverbial "last straw." He is ordered by Bluebeard to poison her like the others. Bluebeard shows Mopsa the chamber and forces her to read the headstones of the five wives, reserving the last for her. Popolani does poison Mopsa, but revives her with electricity. In a grim twist, all the previous wives have also been so revived, but are now a form of harem for Popolani himself: "Now, what doth remain to me? / Why, only dear Popolani!" Mopsa rises to the occasion and rallies them with the hope of future husbands.

Scene 4 returns to Earlypurl's castle for the conclusion. The marriage procession of Saphir and Periwink is interrupted by Bluebeard. When he is refused he threatens rebellion: "I've brought a handful of my guards, sire, / Twice fifteen hundred cannoniers; / One word, and like a house of cards, sire, / Your palace falls about your ears" (42). Bluebeard appears to win this round; he runs Saphir through with a sword and leads Periwink off. It remains to Robert and Popolani to scheme the outcome. Popolani knows the six wives live; Robert knows that the five courtiers condemned to die by the king are also still alive; they plan to revive Saphir to make the number even and arrive at the castle with the twelve dressed as gypsies. Back at the court, the gypsies arrive, and Mopsa reads the king's palm, revealing that the queen will outlive him, and that he had condemned five men to death. Bluebeard's six wives all unmask, and Saphir and Periwink are also reunited (although she has already been married to Bluebeard). The solution is to marry the courtiers to the wives of Bluebeard; Saphir and Periwink are a couple, as are Bluebeard and Mopsa. In their plea to the audience for applause, Bluebeard makes a traditional observation that he might be better understood by the men in the audience: "With the men p'raps I may go down, / But ladies at such freaks will frown" (49).

After 1866, Offenbach's *opera bouffe* was popular on stages on both sides of the Atlantic.[26] The music was noted as independently available from book and music sellers. There was also a spinoff in the form of *Boulotte*, which seems to be a title only used in America at this time.[27]

Amateur and Parlor Plays for Home Performance

Bluebeard was frequently performed at home, by adults and children in one-act drawing room dramas and even in charades. Charlotte Cushman, later a renowned cross-dressed Romeo of the Victorian stage, reputedly played the role of Selim (which became a female role during this period) at home in her mother's attic as a child.[28] At the other end of the century, younger sister of the future American president Roosevelt, Corinne Roosevelt, played the part of Alphonso (one of the two sons of Lady Grasping) in a parlor play called *Blue Beard*. While she was prompted by a typed script,[29] the play was a published one: *Blue Beard* by Sarah Annie Frost. Frequently, such plays came with stage business helpfully added for the amateur and juvenile actors at home.

By 1841, as seen in Francis Gower, Earl of Ellesmere's *Bluebeard; or, Dangerous Curiosity and Justifiable Homicide*, Bluebeard has reverted to the popular "Pacha of three Tails." The cast of characters includes Fatima, Anne, Schacabac (now their father, who like Colman's character Ibrahim, rhymes "father-in-law" with "three tailed bashaw"),[30] and as in the 1839 burlesque of Planché and Dance, the tone is obviously comedic. "Miss Fatty" is told that the fault of all of the previous Mrs. Aboumeliques [*sic*] is that they were "too fond of hurlothrombo pudding." Immediately she wants to know: "How is it made? What does it look like?" (24). Again the play alludes to *Othello* through the implicit reference to Othello's mother on her deathbed: "*Bluebeard*: My mother was a witch, and on her death-bed told me truly, / That womankind are all alike, rebellious and unruly, / And can't be trusted any more, her own expression was it, / Than in an hen-roost can a fox, or a cat in a china closet" (27). In the same exchange, the pudding itself is said to be enchanted: "Know, abandoned woman, the hurlothrombo pudding was a fairy. Therefore, as a *non-sequitur*, down on your knees and prepare for death" (27). A mock preface, dated in the future French Republic of 1870, accords the play the status of a found document, ascribed to John Milton. Reading through the humorous barbs directed at Shakespeare and via the French at the English, it seems as if the author's family acted the play privately, for Christmas. Gower's comments here about Milton's female characters (and precursors for Bluebeard's wife) are interestingly allusive themselves: "Nothing can be more consistent with his known tenets than the character which he gives the female sex through the mouth of Bluebeard, as elicited by the reprehensible conduct of the heroine Fatima. . . . The whole passage is worthy of the man, who, rising above the prejudices of his age and country, turned his wife out of doors, and advocated the doctrine of unlimited divorce. Fatima differs, indeed, from the Lady in Comus; but she bears a close

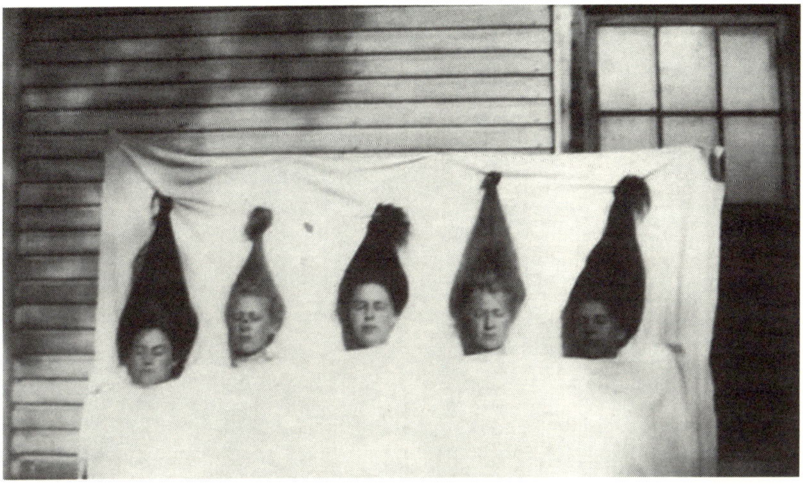

Parlor plays of the nineteenth and twentieth centuries gave information on how to make the "bloody chamber" scene. This photograph shows the results. Courtesy of Evan Finch.

resemblance, both in character and incident, to the Eve of his five-pound poem, and to Dalilah, the heroine of a piece which appears to have been written by Milton for one of the minor theatres of his day" (11). The epilogue, spoken in the persona of Captain Napier, counsels men to leave marrying at seven wives, rather than to add an eighth; women are to control their appetites, and by referencing the cover to the pudding makes an implicit connection between greed and sexual appetite: "And you, ye fair ones, who beheld with dread, / How nearly Fatima had lost her head, / Remembering that an appetite in you / At seven is vulgar, learn to lunch at two. / And dining with your husband or your lover, / Wait till he lifts, or bids you lift, the cover" (n.p.).

Much can be gleaned from this advice as to how these home productions were conducted. The play *Blue Beard, or Female Curiosity, A Sensation Drama in Two Acts and Two Scenes*, By an Experienced Amateur (Dean & Son 1871) is very short, and evidently aimed at young or very amateur performers in its easy, memorable rhyme ("It is no jest: look at those spots; / What say you to those crimson dots?" [7]) and easy actions ("FATIMA clasps her hands in an attitude of abject terror. BLUE BEARD folds his arms, and glares at her" [10–11]). The play text includes extensive information to assist with the production: a sample play-bill with the suggestion to print and circulate it, and costume ideas: Bluebeard's beard "can be made of blue fringes" (3). Selim can be "dressed either as a civilian, or as a common Turkish soldier" while the citizens can be dressed in "Every variety of Eastern costume that can be improvised" and their number can be reduced "if the effect is not so much the object as acting" (3). Finally, production advice includes the following: "A piece like BLUE BEARD can be made most effective by the expenditure at the fancy stationers' of a trifling sum in the purchase of gold-paper, gold-paper ornaments, tin-foil, and pasteboard" (3). Throughout, the script is interspersed with stage directions that often indicate what the action is supposed to mean: "She is supposed to impart the mystery of the Blue Room to SISTER ANNE, who seems petrified with horror and surprise, not unmingled with incredulity" (7). There is a reference to Anne Boleyn at the end of Act I, and to Mary, Queen of Scots, so that in the second instance Anne corrects Fatima: "Stop, dear, you make a trifling error; / Of course you're flurried in your terror. / A queen, and not a king, 'tis said, / Sent to the block poor Mary's head" (8). Act II begins with Kelly's "Blue Beard's March," "if it can be managed" (8). Sister Anne is able to do her lookout lines from a window, if there is one, changing the word "turret" to "window" to suit, or beside the stage, if not. There is helpful props advice given to accompany the final sword battle: "As they fight they should use the black iron swords sold at the toy shops, and, to make the combat effective, it would be well to practise so as to make the blades strike fire. This can be soon learnt" (13).

Finally, the script for a "Blue Beard" charade by Miss E. H. Keating in *Dramas for the Drawing Room; or Charades for Christmas* is similarly helpful in providing an insight into Bluebeard's use as parlor entertainments. Scenes are given for each syllable, and then for the whole word (blue beard). The scene for the first syllable (blue) is relatively lengthy, full of references to color (including two characters, Mr. Indigo and his wife Lady Violet), and many red herrings (volumes of references to current technologies and scientific lectures). But the clues are of course present: repeated references to "blue," lots of French expressions and discussion about the use of French in the house; the explosion in the kitchen of a device that perhaps recalls the pantomime scene where Bluebeard does the same; a reference to *Othello*, and Lady Violet having "no desire to become a domestic Desdemona" (9); a handkerchief (9); a reference to "tails from the Tartars" (10), and to human hair; and finally, where the syllable should be supplied at the end of the scene, the orchestral music "My Own Blue Bell" (12). The second scene is much less oblique; two men meet after they have both grown beards. They comment frequently on them. The final reference is "in case the Russians should invade old England, why we should be able to *beard them*" (17).

The final scene is longer, performed in "intensely Turkish [costumes] of the old school" (29), and contains a complete rendition of the Bluebeard story, using Colman and Kelly's template, without the Shacabac/Beda subplot (and keeping the name Irene for Fatima's sister), with Selim on a banjo, using music from the 1798 production in several instances. As seen in the same author's home play of the same tale, the ghost of one wife speaks to Fatima, warning her to escape, and the ghosts defer to one another trying to get back into order again. Also seen in Keating's play, the Bashaw has three pages, each holding up one of three tails; when the brothers kill him, they do so by severing these tails, at which point he lies down (and gets up again). There are topical references such as to a caricature (of historical novelist G. P. R. James) in *Punch* by Thackeray, "Barbazure." As had by then become a common motif, Abomolique [*sic*] plans to take a train and returns because he mistook it. In Scene 2, Irene coaxes Fatima to open the door "He meant you to go in, or else would he / Be such a goose as to give you the key?" (24). They send a page off for scouring drops to clean the key with, but Abomolique returns early, quoting Othello: "That key did an Egyptian with my mother barter / For two old hats, and Fox's Book of Martyrs" (26). He tells her to prepare herself "As tragic heroines do, by letting down your hair" (27) and gives her time to get some bill and wage-paying done. Not that it would be possible for an audience still to be in the dark this point, Selim mentions "he . . . in nursery story" (29) and finally states that Abomolique has gone "Down where the *Blue Beards* go" (29).

The popularity of "Bluebeard" as stage entertainment is not very surprising, given its inherently dramatic nature. It success in comic form is perhaps more surprising, but once the melodramatic mold of Colman and Kelly's production had been burlesqued, both in pantomime and extravaganza, it developed rapidly and inventively, until finally even the repetitions of comic motifs became clichéd. The persistent models for the fairy tale were those of Perrault, as adapted by Colman and Kelly and as burlesqued in a variety of comic forms. Despite the arrival of the Grimm's variants of this fairy tale in English in the midnineteenth century, the impact of these later arrivals was not registered in dramatic form. Through this popular currency Bluebeard assuredly would have been recognizable in nineteenth-century arts and letters drawing on the story to however wide an audience they aimed to reach.

Chapter 7

Bluebeard in Victorian Arts and Letters

Interestingly, Bluebeard's nineteenth-century popularity in chapbooks and drama was occurring at a time when the status of folk and fairy tales was in question in England, and this period was critical for their adoption by the middle-class readership. The widespread presence of the *Mother Goose* tales attests to their popularity, but not to their respectability. Jack Zipes noted that the Puritan suppression of morally dubious entertainment had far-reaching effects, and that the "'civilized' appropriation" of such tales by Perrault and other salon writers did not happen in England (1987a, xiv). The following suggestion by Maria Edgworth (1798) for how to bowdlerize "Bluebeard" is a case in point: "Just at the critical moment, when the fatal key drops from the trembling hands of the imprudent wife, the gentleman interrupted the awful pause of silence that ensued and requested permission to relate the remainder of the story." Such relation turns the wife into "a curious, tattling, timid, ridiculous woman" so that "The terrors of Blue-beard himself subsided when he was properly introduced to the company."[1] The religious and pedagogical value of the Bluebeard fairy tale was debated at some length in *Bitter-Sweet*, a monograph-length poem by Josiah Gilbert Holland (1858) set on Thanksgiving Eve in a Puritan household in New England. The dramatic verse story of Bluebeard told by one of the boys ends with four stanzas describing Bluebeard's remorse, the private funeral for Bluebeard and internment of his wives, and Fatima's good works (similar to the contemporary chapbook versions). The children who hear the story then comment, alternately wishing to have been one of the avenging brothers, marveling at the inheritance, and wondering whether Bluebeard drank. At this point, the adults in the poem debate the merits of "these bloody old romances" (1858, 156). Ruth argues "Story and comment alike are bad" (156), while her brother-in-law David argues instead that the negative example is useful: "So this ensanguined tale shall move / Aright each little dreamer, / And Bluebeard teach them how to love / The sweet Fatima" (159).

Following the massive multivolume English translations of the *Arabian Nights' Entertainments* and Grimms' *Die Kinder- und Hausmärchen*, and the antiquarian research into English folklore that ensued, "Bluebeard" became visible in the prose writings of several major Victorian writers' works. Among these are Charlotte Brontë's "Bluebeard novel" *Jane Eyre* and multiple works of both mid-Victorian writers Charles Dickens and William Makepeace Thackeray. In addition, the popular art of Alfred Henry Forrester, Thackeray (inspired by George Cruikshank), and Walter Crane contributed a store of nineteenth-century images of Bluebeard to rank alongside those by contemporary French artists Gustave Doré and "Cham" (Amédée de Noé).

Tales in Translation

The Arabian Nights' Entertainments

The Bluebeard tale had already been orientalized in the Colman-Kelly production of 1798 and consequently throughout the chapbooks and popular theater. In 1811, the same year as the hit revival of the Colman-Kelly play on both sides of the Atlantic, Jonathan Scott issued the first literary English translation of the *Arabian Nights' Entertainments* from Galland's French translation.[2] After Henry Torrens also began another translation from Arabic (1838), Edward Lane's multivolume translation appeared monthly between 1838 and 1841 and was then published in three volumes, with anthropological footnotes later published separately. Some forty years later, when John Payne issued his nine volumes of translation (1882–1884), followed by those of Sir Richard Burton (ten volumes, 1885), the print media debated the relative merits of the Lane translation over those of Payne and Burton, and such notables as Leigh Hunt and Andrew Lang weighed in. *The Arabian Nights* thus developed a scholarly context that included rival source manuscripts, controversies over apocrypha and "orphan" tales (those with no known manuscript source), the necessity of reading several languages, and development of English translation tools for Arabic.

The Grimm Tales

The nineteenth century also saw the English translation of *Die Kinder- und Hausmärchen* (*Children's and Household Tales*), which ensured the survival, popularity, and legitimacy of fairy tales in England. As noted in chapter 1, the story "Blaubart" was included in the first German edition published by the Grimms (1812 1:62), but was omitted from subsequent editions because it was thought to be Perrault's own tale. Moreover, and despite the inclusion of "Bluebeard" in the German tales published in 1845 by Ludwig Bechstein (the first English edition, *The Old Story Teller: Popular German Tales*, was published 1854 in London), this subordination of German variants of Bluebeard to French appears to have occurred even within the German tradition itself.[3] The Grimms' "Blaubart" was not published in English translation until Jack Zipes did so in 1987 with his translation of the omitted tales in *The Complete Fairy Tales of the Brothers Grimm*.

Aside from "Blaubart," the principal Bluebeard variants from the Grimm collections "Fitcher's Bird" (tale 46) and "The Robber Bridegroom" (tale 40) were also first published in 1812, substantially revised for the 1819 edition, and reappeared in the final (seventh) 1857 edition.[4] Other related Grimms' tales included in the 1812 edition were "Mary's Child" (tale 3: "Marienkind"), and "The Castle of Murder" (tale 73: "Das Mordschloss") which was omitted after the first edition[5], and in 1819 "Faithful John" (tale 6: "Der treue Johannes") and "The Hare's Bride" (tale 66: "Häsichenbraut"). These were available for Edgar Taylor to select for his English translation, which he derived from the 1819 German edition. However, of other "Bluebeard" variants in Grimm, "The House in the Forest" ("Das Waldhaus") did not appear in a Grimm edition until 1840, and "Old Rinkrank" ("Oll Rinkrank") was not published until 1850.

Taylor's (anonymous) translation of the Grimms appeared in two volumes (1823, 1826). They were illustrated by George Cruikshank, the popular English artist in his prime, and this was the first edition of Grimms in any country to be fully illustrated (Darton 1932, 216). Cruikshank made twelve etchings for the first edition and ten more for the second (Blamires 2006, 170); there is no illustration for "The Robber Bridegroom," however. Taylor's translations were popular and reprinted before being circulated in a one-volume form.[6] "The Robber Bridegroom" was translated for the second volume, that of 1826, after the popularity of the first volume encouraged Taylor in his efforts. He noted of the second selection that the tales "have more of the general character of fairy tales, and less of German peculiarity, than those of the first volume, in preparing which, the whole of MM. Grimm's collection was open for the choice of examples of all classes" (Taylor 1823–1826).

Taylor did not select "Fitcher's Bird" for translation in either volume, and thus it was not translated into English until 1853 in the two-volume *Household Stories* (Addey & Co).[7] But the first edition of *German Popular Stories* includes "The Robber Bridegroom." The tale provides an interesting case study for

Walter Crane, "The Robber Bridegroom." From Grimm, Household Stories (1866).

Taylor's translation principals overall. In his preface he noted that the translators have omitted select tales "which the scrupulous fastidiousness of modern taste, especially in works likely to attract the attention of youth, warned them to pass by" (1823–1826, 1:xi), and they were sometimes "compelled" to make alterations in tales, making notes to reflect such changes, but that "in most cases the alteration consists merely in the curtailment of adventures or circumstances not affecting the main plot of the story" (1:xi). The note provided for "The Robber Bridegroom" reflects that, although in Taylor's translation the ring alone flew into the maiden's lap, in the original it was the entire finger. Additionally, the note signals the tale's "general affinity" to "Bluebeard." However, the other significant changes Taylor silently made from the Grimm version similarly curb the brutality of the cannibal robbers. Instead of killing the woman by making her heart burst, she "fainted and fell down dead." The episode of ripping off her clothes, dismembering her, and salting the body to eat is omitted altogether.[8]

Perrault's "Bluebeard"

A new translation of Perrault's tales was undertaken by the scholar James Robinson Planché (author of the 1839 Colman-Kelly burlesque) for *Four and*

Twenty Tales (1858), including several fairy tales by other authors. His approach was scholarly, and he toured France in search of a first edition of Perrault's *Histoires* (Planché 1872, 356–60). His translation included footnotes (two for "Bluebeard") and appendices. His discussion of "Bluebeard" includes the disputed origin in Gilles de Rais, the translation of the "*fée*" key, and the difficulty of translating Sister Anne's speech from the turret: "unless we could say in English 'the sun that *dusts* and the grass that *greens*,' we cannot approach the terse and graphic description of dear Sister Anne" (517, original emphasis). His translation is clearly distinct from those of Samber and G. M. (see chapter 4), despite several phrases that directly repeat them, such as: "The poor wife was almost as dead as her husband, and had not strength to rise and embrace her brothers" (Planché 1858, 7).[9] Overall, he blends Samber's diction ("collation," "cutlass") with G. M.'s ("twice or thrice," "half a quarter of an hour"), and corrects both on the matter of the women "reflected" in the blood on the floor. The morals are translated in verse, but the translation is unique. A striking contribution is a direct address to the reader: "Behold them immediately running through all the rooms" (4).

Jack Zipes retranslated Planché's translation of "Bluebeard" for *Beauties, Beasts and Enchantment: Classic French Fairy Tales* (1989), noting that "to [Planché's] credit, his renditions contained a certain style and idiomatic characteristics that I felt helped recapture the highly mannered style of the French authors" (13). However, Zipes returned to the "quarter of an hour" translated by Samber, as opposed to the "half a quarter of an hour" of both G. M. and Planché (and Perrault). Elsewhere, modernized idiom in Zipes' translation loses some of the flavor of earlier translations (not to mention the *Othello* allusion). Bluebeard orders the key from his wife in Samber: "Do not fail . . . of giving it to me presently"; in G. M.: "Fail not . . . to bring it me presently"; and in Planché: "Fail not . . . to give it me presently." But in Zipes, Bluebeard says simply: "Bring it to me right now."

Andrew Lang championed Perrault in *Perrault's Popular Tales* (1888), reprinting them in French from early editions and including a scholarly introduction and headnote information on each tale. For "Bluebeard" he argued its archetypal nature, transcending the French national specifics of Perrault, but he argued at length how he "admirably handled" his materials (lx): "in point of art, Perrault's tale has a great advantage over its popular rivals. It is at once more sober and more terrible, and . . . possesses an epical unity of idea and action" (lxiv). Lang listed a range of international examples, including the English "Mr. Fox," in support of his argument. He also selected "Bluebeard" for inclusion in the first of his fairy tale series, *The Blue Fairy Book* (1889), using G. M.'s

English translation, but (significantly) altered "scymitar" to "sword." The alteration was in keeping with Lang's argument that Bluebeard was not a Turk, made in the edition's "Introduction." The story's two pen-and-ink illustrations by G. P. Jacomb Hood depict the chamber discovery (the wife viewed from within the chamber) and the near execution and rescue of the wife, but does so in orientalized dress for all characters. Bluebeard is dark skinned, with thick beard and mustache, and wields a short, curved scimitar over his head (in traditional contrast to the straight blades of the arriving brothers). In disagreement with his illustrator, Lang wrote: "[t]hey were all French folk and Christians; had he been a Turk, Blue Beard need not have been wedded to but one wife at a time" (358). There again he argues for its archetypal nature: "Punishment of disobedient curiosity is the motive of 'Blue Beard,' and of all the stories about forbidden doors, wells, trees, fruits, and so forth, which, among many races, are interwoven with the myth of 'The Origin of Death'" (354).

The English Tale "Mr. Fox"

In the preface to the 1826 translation *German Popular Stories*, Edgar Taylor noted that "The popular tales of England have been too much neglected" (iv), and his subject was one "little noticed" (xii). As late as 1888 in the introduction to his collection of Perrault's stories, Andrew Lang noted his opinion that English fairy tales were insubstantial: "No nation owes [Perrault] so much as we of England, who, south of the Scottish, and east of the Welsh marches [*sic*], have scarce any popular tales of our own save Jack the Giant Killer, and who have given the full fairy citizenship to Perrault's *Petit Poucet* and *La Barbe Bleue*" (xvi). Only two tales in Lang's *Blue Fairy Book* were English (Burne 1986, 143). After many decades of Grimm volumes, translations of *The Arabian Nights' Entertainments*, English translations of Hans Christian Andersen (appearing in 1846 by Mary Howitt[10]), and the now-canonical *Mother Goose Tales*, the time was ripe for editions of English stories.

In 1849, James Orchard Halliwell-Phillipps published *Popular Rhymes and Nursery Tales: A Sequel to the Nursery Rhymes of England*. He included both "The Story of Mr. Fox" and a related variant, "The Oxford Student," in full under the heading "Fireside Stories." In addition, he provided notes, stating of "Mr. Fox": "A simple, but very curious tale, of considerable antiquity. It is alluded to by Shakespeare, and was contributed to the varorium edition by Blakeway. Part of this story will recall to the reader's memory the enchanted chamber of Britomart" (47). In "The Oxford Student" he provided the rhyme that refers to the murderer as a "fox": "One moonshiny night, as I sat high, / Waiting for one to come by, / The boughs did bend; my heart did ache / To see what hole the fox did make." He contextualized the material as English antiquities in danger of disappearing and neglected by "antiquaries of the old school [who] considered such matters beneath their notice": "It may be that little of this now remains in England, but the minutest indications should be carefully chronicled ere they disappear" (275).

In 1878 the Folk-Lore Society was established in England. With a now legitimate subject matter and a primed readership, and in spite of Lang's claims for the inadequacy of English folklore, two other members of the Folk-Lore Society published English collections, in which "Mr. Fox" was again represented. Joseph Jacobs published the tale in *English Fairy Tales* in 1890,[11] and Edwin Sidney Hartland collected it in *English Fairy and Other Folk Tales* at the same time (ca. 1890), taking the tale from Malone's Shakespeare *Varorium* (1821, vol. 7).

Thackeray

The novelist William Makepeace Thackeray worked with the "Bluebeard" fairy tale repeatedly, and his use of the tale marks a radically new opening up of the intertext. Allusions to the fairy tale are scattered throughout his works,[12] but in novels like *The Memoirs of Barry Lyndon* (1844) and the unfinished play "[Bluebeard at Breakfast]" the allusion is direct and sustained. Thackeray also retold the tale parodically in pictorial format in *The Awful History of Blue Beard* (1833) and in short story format in both "Bluebeard's Ghost" (1843) and "Barbazure" (1847), which he also illustrated.[13] Despite the caricatures, his use of Bluebeard manifests a "sneaking sympathy" for him.[14] This can be seen in taking the first-person voice of Bluebeard for Barry Lyndon, "The Irish Bluebeard" (1844, 276), whose memoirs are reminiscent of Moll Flanders'. Lyndon writes frankly of his imprisonment and surveillance of his wife, his drunken beatings of her, and his periodic removal of her child in the spirit of self-justification. At one point he comments: "if I can prevent one of you from marrying, the Memoirs of Barry Lyndon, Esq., will not be written in vain" (255). The moral context is provided (and at the same time parodied) in the form of the memoir's "editor," Fitz-Boodle, whose notes in fact tend to sympathize rather than chastise: "From these curious confessions, it would appear that Mr. Lyndon maltreated his lady in every possible way; that he denied her society, bullied her into signing away her property, spent it in gambling and taverns, was openly unfaithful to her; and, when she complained, threatened to remove her children from her.

William Makepeace Thackeray's own illustration to his story "Barbazure" (1877).

Nor, indeed, is he the only husband who has done the like, and has passed for 'nobody's enemy but his own'; a jovial, good-natured fellow. The world contains scores of such amiable people; and, indeed, it is because justice has not been done them that we have edited this autobiography" (245 n.). As Lyndon ends in poverty, dying in prison of delirium tremens, the statement that "justice has not been done them" clearly situates Fitz-Boodle on Lyndon's side.

The play fragment sees Bluebeard discussing matrimonial woes over breakfast with boyhood friend Jack Butts, and Thackeray's sympathy is again clear. Butts points out that Lady Bluebeard spends many evenings with Captain Jones and is newly accustomed to the moneyed life, but Bluebeard is unwilling to understand him on the first point and defends his wife on the second. In the process, Butts reveals that he is "dev'lish tired of Mrs. Butts" (223), confirming Bluebeard's grim point that all marriages are alike: "There is cold mutton, Butts, in every house" (226).

The later of the two short pieces, "Barbazure," is a parody of George Payne Rainsford James, the popular historical novelist, published in *Punch's Prize Novelists*. It retells the traditional tale in florid prose, saturated with sensibility. Fatima's jilted lover Romané de Clos-Vougeot arrives from the Crusades to discover her marriage to Bluebeard. As the jilted knight, he challenges the Baron Raoul to a joust with untipped lances, which results in Fatima's imprisonment. The narrator then abbreviates: "(As it is impossible to give the whole of this remarkable novel, let it suffice to say briefly here, that in about a volume and a half, in which the descriptions of scenery, the account of the agonies of the baroness, kept on bread and water in her dungeon, and the general tone of morality, are all excellently worked out, the Baron de Barbazure resolves upon putting his wife to death by the hands of the public executioner)" (Thackeray 1847, 59). The executioner, revealed at the moment when he decapitates the Baron instead, turns out to be Clos-Vougeot himself. In "Barbazure," the secondary target of the satire is women, within the story and without. As Fatima goes unprotesting to the execution block, the narrator comments: "How few are the wives, in our day, who show such angelic meekness!" (60), while she is attended by a cousin who has already promised to marry Bluebeard next. This satire on women is extended in "Bluebeard's Ghost," which depicts Mrs. Bluebeard after Bluebeard's death being "haunted" by the ghost of her dead husband (in actuality, a disguised suitor). As in Perrault, female greed is a feature of the story, from the style of her mourning: "There was not a widow in all the country who went to such an expense for black bombazeen" (Thackeray 1843, 337), to her dispute with the Bluebeards over her inheritance: "'Your argument may be a very good one, but I will, if you please, keep the money'" (340). Throughout the story she refers to her deceased husband as a blessed saint, but the narrator gives her loyalty a different hue: "If anyone would but leave me a fortune, what a funeral and what a character I would give him!" (340).

The major contribution of Thackeray's comic and cartoon use of Bluebeard may be in opening the intertext to rewriting. Although the comic stage fleshed out the tale, adding the popular secondary cast, variations had kept the traditional character of Bluebeard even as it rendered him a dramatic ogre or a pantomime buffoon. Even as Thackeray's use of the names Fatima and, more particularly, Shacabac, demonstrate his awareness of the Colman-Kelly legacy[15] and signal his comedic treatment of his subject, "Bluebeard's Ghost" extends the confines of the original tale for perhaps the first time, while playing knowing intertextual games with the reader.[16] Beginning his story where "Bluebeard" traditionally ends, *after* the death of Bluebeard, the reader is immediately cast into new territory. At the same time, the fairy tale is both presupposed and called into question. Bluebeard's track record of wives and his diary of their deaths is offered to the reader as evidence that Bluebeard remains a serial wife murderer, at the same time as Mrs. Bluebeard argues against such calumny. The issue is left formally unresolved: "Whether it is that all wives adore husbands when the latter are no more, or whether it is that Fatima's version of the story is really the correct one, and that the common impression against Bluebeard is an odious prejudice, and that he no more murdered his wives than you and I have, remains yet to be proved, and, indeed, does not much matter for the understanding of the rest of Mrs. B.'s adventures" (339–40). Although there are hints that Widow Bluebeard had more to be afraid of than she allows ("Fatima once more had occasion to repent her fatal curiosity" [355]), it is certainly true that Thackeray's story is concerned with after, not before. His story traces the competition between rival suitors for Fatima's hand and fortune, and the chicanery they rely on to win her over. The ghost of Bluebeard presides over the story, but he is an imposter. In *Barry Lyndon*, presenting Bluebeard's first-person memoirs, Thackeray predated the defense written by Anatole France in "The Seven Wives of Bluebeard" (1909). Thackeray's treatment of the tale signals a much broader use of the tale's intertextual possibilities and with them the games narrators can play with their readers.

Dickens

Charles Dickens' essay "Frauds on the Fairies," published in *Household Words* (1853), argued for allowing fairy tales to thrive unmolested: "In an utilitarian age, of all other times, it is a matter of grave importance that Fairy tales should be respected" (57). He argued against his friend George Cruikshank who had altered the fairy tale "Hop o' My Thumb" to reflect "Total Abstinence, Prohibition of the Sale of spiritous liquors, Free Trade, and Popular Education." Whatever the agenda, Dickens argued that no one has a right to lay a hand on them, and he used Bluebeard as a primary example: "With seven Blue Beards in the field, each coming at a gallop from his own platform mounted on a foaming hobby, a generation or two hence would not know which was which, and the great original Blue Beard would be confounded with the counterfeits" (58).[17]

In his own writing Dickens did not censor the fairy tales so much as glory in their macabre humor and grotesquerie. The "Bluebeard" fairy tale is one of his favorites. He makes comic references to it in *The Pickwick Papers* (1837), *Barnaby Rudge* (1841), *Bleak House* (1853), *Hard Times* (1854), *Our Mutual Friend* (1865), *The Mystery of Edwin Drood* (1869–1870), and in his journalism.[18] But Dickens stamped Bluebeard in a full-blown "counterfeit" of his own, Captain Murderer, a "wretch" who "must have been an offshoot of the Blue Beard family" (1860, 150). But while Thackeray's Bluebeard in "[Bluebeard at Breakfast]" made "culinary metaphors" of women, Dickens' Captain Murderer actually eats them.

While "Captain Murderer" has become known as a literary fairy tale, it was in fact published as one story of the horrors of his nurse, a "female bard" who subjected the boy before the age of six to frightful stories. The tale is set within the "Nurse's Stories" essay of *The Uncommercial Traveller* (1860).

Captain Murderer is a cannibal ogre whose "mission was matrimony, and the gratification of a cannibal's appetite with tender brides" (150). In his courtship he always asked whether the woman could bake pie-crust, "and if she couldn't by nature or education, she was taught" (151). When he then produced a golden rolling pin and silver pie board a month after the wedding, she rolled her sleeves up to bake pie: "The Captain brought out flour and butter and eggs and all things needful, except the inside of the pie; of materials for the staple of the pie itself, the Captain brought out none" (151), prompting his wife to inquire what kind of pie it is to be: "Then said the lovely bride, 'Dear Captain Murderer, I see no meat.'" To this he would "humorously retor[t], 'Look in the glass.'" The joke is borne out at the point where the crust is completed and the bride looks up just in time to see her head cut off. The Captain courted twin sisters and married the fair one who loved him. The dark twin is suspicious of him, and notes the joke about house lamb, having peeped in the shutter and seen him file his teeth sharp. After her sister dies, she determines to be revenged, but does so through taking a strong poison before she is killed. Her posthumous revenge involves the Captain swelling, turning blue and spotty, and then exploding. The incident ends with a paragraph omitted when "Captain Murderer" is retold,[19] regarding his nurse's storytelling abilities:

> Hundreds of times did I hear this legend of Captain Murderer, in my early youth, and added hundreds of times was there a mental compulsion upon me in bed, to peep in at his window as the dark twin peeped, and to revisit his horrible house, and look at him in his blue and spotty and screaming stage, as he reached from floor to ceiling and from wall to wall. The young woman who brought me acquainted with Captain Murderer had a fiendish enjoyment of my terrors, and used to begin, I remember—as a sort of introductory overture— by clawing the air with both hands, and uttering a long low hollow groan. So acutely did I suffer from this ceremony in combination with this infernal Captain that I sometimes used to plead I thought I was hardly strong enough and old enough to hear the story again just yet. But, she never spared me one word of it.... Her name was Mercy, though she had none on me (153).

Victorian Women Writing "Bluebeard"

Unlike the heroine in Captain Murderer, who must kill herself to kill the ogre, the heroine of the literary fairy tale "The Ogre Courting" (1871, 1987) by Juliana

Horatia Ewing outsmarts the cannibal ogre on his own terms. It is said that "The Ogre only cared for two things in a woman—he liked her to be little, and a good housewife" (129). As he has eaten twenty-four women already, Managing Molly is aware that she is to be next and so plans ahead. She demonstrates such a degree of thriftiness that the ogre finally cannot bear the idea of marrying her, even as she has been the financial beneficiary of her efforts and is now well-dowered. In the Victorian fictions by women writers there emerges a dialogue, like this one between "Captain Murderer" and "The Ogre Courting," in which the traditional terms of the tale are deliberately renegotiated. Earlier in the century, this is begun in the novel *Jane Eyre*.

Charlotte Brontë's novel *Jane Eyre* (1847) has been called "the first adult, non-burlesque treatment of the Bluebeard theme in English literature" (Sutherland 1997, 68), although the dramatic Colman and Kelly production of 1798 is not a burlesque treatment, and the tale in chapbooks was arguably not produced for children.[20] The plot twist of the novel is that Jane discovers at the altar of her marriage to Edward Rochester that he has a living wife. Furthermore, this wife has been housed all along in the locked upper rooms of Thornfield Hall, in which Jane herself has been living as a governess. The novel describes the upper floor of the Hall as "looking, with its two rows of small black doors all shut, like a corridor in some Bluebeard's castle" (122), and at this very moment Jane hears Bertha Mason's "preternatural" laugh for the first time. Later, she describes Rochester as a "three-tailed bashaw" (302) while negotiating terms for her marriage to him.[21] The "madwoman in the attic" Bertha Mason was married for financial reasons under family pressure; her genetic predisposition to insanity was a secret her family kept from Rochester. Displaced from the West Indies to England, Bertha becomes increasingly unstable and is finally incarcerated, with a female "jailor," Grace Poole. Jane runs from Thornfield and is taken up on the point of starvation by the devout Rivers family. After a period in which she earns employment as a teacher, refuses a loveless proposal by St. John Rivers, and discovers that she is financially independent, she returns to find Thornfield Hall a burned ruin, and Rochester both blind and disabled by the events of the fire. Bertha's death in the fire she laid allows the couple to marry, and the novel concludes at the birth of the couple's first child. The novel was published pseudonymously, occasioning a public furor to discover the identity (sex) of the author. Critics commented that if the author was female, she was "unsexed" (Monsarrat 1980, 254); she had "forfeited the society of her own sex" (Rigby 1848).

Some three decades later in February and June 1871,[22] Anne Thackeray Ritchie published "Bluebeard's Keys" in her father's conservative *Cornhill*

Magazine aimed at "pleasant and instructed gentlemen and ladies" (Thackeray 1859).[23] Although the publication context should have dictated conservative treatment of the Bluebeard story, Ritchie managed to make claims for women's rights that escaped such censorious criticism.[24]

The gothic-flavored story is set in Rome: Ottavio Barbi has seduced "silly" Fanny de Travers with wealth and power, but she is not in love and is even frightened of him. Her sister Anne tries to save her before the marriage. The story opens with a verse argument telling the traditional version of "Bluebeard," and despite the wife being named "Barbara," the verse is otherwise orientalized (her brothers are named Osman and Alee). Part I contains Ritchie's version of the story, young Fanny de Travers' engagement to Enrico Ottavio Barbi. Ritchie made clear the connection between male power and violence, and "commerce": "Did Fanny expect to do as she liked when she married Barbi? Jealous, narrow, exclusive—a violent man, accustomed to rule and to dominate over all those who came in contact with him. There is nothing more curious than the dominion some persons now and then establish over others perhaps a hundred times cleverer, warmer-hearted, more tractable, wiser than themselves. A sheer strength of will seems to count for more in the commerce of life than all the grace, and accomplishment, and study, and good intention in the world" (Ritchie 1875, 24). The sisters are impoverished thanks to the vagaries of male relatives, whose wills they are written out of and back into at their benefactor's caprice. While Mrs. de Travers is castigated throughout the story, her need to sell her daughters for a good price is ascribed to the patriarchal economy, rather than personal vanity. Notably, Fanny becomes disenchanted with the engagement even before she discovers Barbi's sordid past (Rochester-like, he had courted one woman while a wife pined away): "Fanny's eyes wandered sadly round the room. Here her future life was to be spent, she thought to herself. There Barbi would sit" (28). It is less her husband she is afraid of than herself: "Fanny had begun to be afraid of herself" (27); "Fanny did not dare own it to herself, she had scarcely realized it hitherto, but a bitter disappointment was hers" (27). Barbi's injunction when it comes is traditional: "My present from this date belongs to you. Do not seek to know what is past" (26). He forbids Fanny access to a trunk in which she discovers first a mirror in the lid (the moment of reflection on the threshold is thus preserved), then clothes and letters revealing Barbi's past, and an ambiguous emblem: a "sort of whip or discipline, of long iron chain, rusted in places and fastened to a handle" (28). Unlike the traditional wives, "Fanny did not lose her presence of mind" (29) upon Barbi's return, but attempts to break off the engagement. Part I ends with Barbi insisting that she cannot break off the engagement, and the sisters shutting themselves away from his anger. The rescue of the two "brothers" (monks) comes in the nick of time, and Barbi is lead away to join them. The story is completed, but Part II exists to drive the point home.

In an Ozark version of "Mr. Fox," collected in the twentieth century, the decision to remain single is ascribed to trauma, after the young woman has seen Mr. Fox and two accomplices dig her own grave and plan to rob her. The story's last comment refuses to endorse her choice: "After that poor Elsie wouldn't go with nobody, because she figured men was all son-of-a-bitches. And so she never did get married at all, but just stayed around with the kinfolks. They was glad to have her, of course. But it is kind of sad to see a pretty girl bound and determined to be an old maid like that" ("Mister Fox" 1955, 97).

Because Fanny, merely eighteen, is likewise unmarried at the end of Ritchie's story, her "critic" wants to know how it ends: "what happened afterward" (Ritchie 1875, 30). The narrator comments that "the point of my story was, that they did *not* marry" (30). The rightness of this decision is emphasized throughout Part II. Fanny had been threatened with "a slow extinction of life" (30) in marriage to Barbi. Instead, as the story continues, Fanny embraces her narrow escape: "'Free!' she said to herself, drawing a long breath. She had not known until now how she had dreaded the thought of a life spent with that man" (31). Instead, alone, "she might be miserable, she might be lonely some day, but she was free" (31). Rather than returning to her old life reconciled to her lot, however, her epiphany has been life altering: "She herself was different, and she had found out that to every human being is granted a certain will and liberty of action and feeling which should be as much part of life as faith or affection itself" (33). The narrator also endorses this realization: "Happy those who find this out in time, and who have the courage and constancy to keep to the clue" (33). After tying up loose ends with Barbi and being gifted her financial independence, the narrator comments of Fanny: "She has never married. She is not one of the very happiest women of my acquaintance, but she is one of the most contented; her life is happier than the average, and bright and melancholy too" (41).

In 1875, Sabilla Novello published *The History of Bluebeard's Six Wives*, a quarto volume of some fifty pages telling the story of each of Bluebeard's wives in detail, and illustrated with color illustrations by George Cruikshank Jr.[25] The press notices being favorable enough, she followed this with *Bluebeard's Widow and Her Sister Anne: Their History Evolved from Mendacious Chronicles* (1876), illustrated by herself with pen-and-ink drawings. It is interesting for taking up the story after Bluebeard's death, as Thackeray did in "Bluebeard's Ghost," and concerning the next courting of Fatima (by the malapropistic Prince Adelbren). It depicts Fatima satirically as a greedy and vain woman, and Sister Anne is the genteel heroine of the work who is properly rewarded by fairyland characters for her good nature. A third volume, the story of Anne's children (named by their grandfather's first words upon seeing each): *HoHo and HaHa: Adventures Narrated and Illustrated* (by the author) followed in 1877. In a review of the reissue of *The History of Bluebeard's Six Wives* (1878), the *Dublin University Magazine* commended it as a "passable story" in a "decidedly clever and spirited style," but lamented the "vulgar" nature of the fairy tale itself: "To whisper, even under our breath, that the time-honoured legend of Bluebeard is just a little bit vulgar, would bring down upon us the wrath of the entire juvenile population, past, present, and to come. But though we have decided not to commit ourselves to so monstrous a libel, we yet are obliged to confess that the modern introduction to it is not so refined, either in thought or in tone, as nineteenth century taste would prefer." Ironically, while fairy tales had gained general respectability, Bluebeard was fast losing his.

It is in this context that Louisa May Alcott drew on the Bluebeard story as a coded commentary on the Victorian oppression of women's freedoms, intellectual ambitions, and sexuality. Rebellious from an early age and later an activist for woman's suffrage, Alcott gained public success and financial security from writing juvenile literature whose "moral pap for the young" (Alcott 1877b) she privately disdained. Her anonymous and pseudonymous writings (as A. M. Barnard) masked an alternative Alcott who revels in sensation fiction with "lurid" subjects, and the Bluebeard story is an apt vehicle both for her treatments of marriage ("the tragedy of modern married life" [Alcott 1868]), curiosity, and knowledge, as well as for her criticism of the gendered power dynamics of her times.[26]

In Alcott's juvenile novel *Under the Lilacs*, little Betty is told "to choose whichever one she liked best out of the pile of Walter Crane's toy books lying in bewildering colors before her": "'This one; Bab always wanted to see the dreadful cupboard, and there's a picture of it here,' answered Betty, clasping a gorgeous copy of Bluebeard to the little bosom, which still heaved with the rapture of looking at that delicious mixture of lovely Fatimas in pale azure gowns, pink Sister Annes on the turret top, crimson tyrants, and yellow brothers with forests of plumage blowing wildly from their mushroom-shaped caps" (1878, 162). Both Betty and Bab have a prurient interest in the contents of "the dreadful cupboard" (contents by now fast disappearing from juvenile illustrations). Betty herself is then compared to Bluebeard's wife: "Curious as Fatima, Betty went to look" (163). Even within Alcott's sanctioned writing for children, then, "Bluebeard" can appear as complex code: for female eroticism, books as the means to reveal censored mysteries, and the traditional depiction of gendered power dynamics, reiterated when the children put on their own parlor play in which Bab and Betty play Fatima and Sister Anne, respectively: "after a terrific struggle, the tyrant fell, and with convulsive twitchings of the scarlet legs, slowly expired, while the ladies sociably fainted in each other's arms, and the brothers waved their swords, and shook hands over the corpse of their enemy" (207).

It is no coincidence then that Alcott treated Bluebeard story more fully in the gothic novel *A Modern Mephistopheles* (1877a), published anonymously in the No Name series. (So different was the style from that of *Little Women*, the reading public were unable to guess the true author until it was made known a decade after.) An earlier version depicting a female Faust was rejected by the publisher.[27] In the novel Jasper Helwyze aims to corrupt Gladys Canaris by exposing her to erotic reading material and hashish. He is able to do this because of a pact he has made with Glady's husband, Felix, the Faustian figure, in which Felix gains literary success by allowing Helwyze to be his author. Helwyze also uses Olivia to distract Felix from his "work" with Gladys. The "one forbidden, yet most fascinating spot in all the house" (98) is the study in which the secret of authorship is hidden:

> Full of some pleasurable excitement, Canaris lead his wife across the room, threw open a door, and bade her look in. Like a curious child, she peeped, but saw only a small, bare *cabinet de travail*.
>
> "No room, you see, even for a little thing like you. None dare enter here without my keeper's leave. Remember that, else you may fare like Bluebeard's Fatima" (75–76).

Clearly, Victorian women artists were not burlesquing the story. Against the prevailing comic mode, these works borrow the marital dynamic of the Bluebeard story to engage with the role and rights of women within marriage. For women writers, the forbidden chamber is explored as a previously forbidden place of writing.

Bluebeard in Victorian Art

Although George Cruikshank did not illustrate "The Robber Bridegroom" when he illustrated *German Popular Stories*, and while they are not caricatures such as those on which his earlier career had depended, the style of the acclaimed illustrations he did create for the two volumes captures the comic element of the stories (Patten 1988, 26).[28] Thackeray's own illustrations of

Bluebeard are in the caricature vein, suitable for a student of Cruikshank's. The comic verse version by F. W. N. Bayley circulated with cartoon illustrations by Alfred Henry Forrester, depicting grotesquely exaggerated figures. Later in the century, however, the illustrations of Walter Crane reclaim the adult drama in poignant terms, better fitting the "heavy tragedy" Crane saw in the story.

Around 1875, Routledge published "Bluebeard" in the Walter Crane's Toybooks shilling series, whose cover illustrates emblems and pages from a number of recognizable fairy tales (ca. 1877, Opie: 013:101). The pictures take up most of the page, leaving space for small scrolled text boxes in a corner of each page. Crane's Bluebeard is courtly, and not orientalized; the French origins of the story are echoed in his motto "*Gardez le clef*" (keep the key/look after the key) both on his crest and carved in his furniture, and the word "*Barb*[*e*]" visible on the pennant fluttering from a spire. The scenes are all interior, with the exception of Anne at the turret, but in almost every illustration there is a secondary focus on something happening outside. In the first picture of Bluebeard handing the keys to his wife and enumerating them, a groom waits outside with Bluebeard's horse, anticipating his departure. The text stops at Bluebeard's marriage to a wife. In the second image, the wife hurries downstairs while over her shoulder and through the open doorway are seen the women admiring her goods. The text here explains their presence with Bluebeard's departing instructions to his wife, but he has not left yet; the text lags behind the image. In the third picture, his wife is opening the door and peering inside; behind her, the staircase she has descended beckons, but clearly she has descended into an underworld of experience and she cannot return to innocence, a reading supported by Crane's prominent use of Edenic imagery in several of the pictures. Both of his crests feature a horned head above them, cleft hooves, and in one a pointed tail; the demonic connection is clear even before the final picture depicting Bluebeard's face transformed into a devil. In the next, Bluebeard is angrily pointing at the keys, as his wife kneels imploring before him, her hair now unpinned and flowing loose. Anne walks past the open doorway in the background. In two panels of text, one on either side of the two-page illustration, the poetry has almost caught up with the image depicted. The next image shows Sister Anne gazing from the tower over a flat and extensive landscape. The text contrasts her languorous pose with the urgency of direct speech: Bluebeard threatens "You have been in the closet once, and you shall go again!" as the wife pleads for time, is granted it, and begs her sister to watch for their brothers. The penultimate image is particularly arresting; while the wife is central, reclining up the stairs through the center of the picture, Bluebeard is coming up (visible from his torso up and wielding a sword) and seems to have one hand on the hem of her dress. At the top of the staircase, in the top left of the frame, Sister Anne is bending over and waving. Above Bluebeard's head out of a casement window can be seen the two arriving brothers, still on horseback, their swords raised like his. In the final image, the two brothers take up most of the frame, while Bluebeard is on his knees struggling in the lower left quadrant. A brother has each of his hands pinned, his sword lies on the ground in the corner of the frame. In the extreme right edge behind the edge of a curtain can just be seen the two women, Bluebeard's wife on the floor.

Crane's illustrations take top billing, as seen in the marketing of *The Bluebeard Picture Book* (London: Routledge, after 1876). The cover states: "32 Pages of Design" and "By Walter Crane." The edition contains "Blue Beard," "Little Red Riding Hood," "Jack and the Bean-Stalk," and "Baby's Own A B C." It was printed in colors by Edmund Evans, as noted on the title page. A John Lane reissue of *Bluebeard's Picture Book* (Walter Crane Picture Books, large series, 1899) offers a different selection: "Bluebeard," "The Sleeping Beauty," and "Baby's Own Alphabet" with "the original coloured designs" as engraved by Evans. The cover offers images of all three personages: Bluebeard snarls as he points to the table of contents; he seems to inspire awe in the child representing "Baby," in his alphabet smock. The internal cover illustration by Crane shows Bluebeard riding on a horse, another of him leaving as his young wife (very different in appearance from the pre-Raphaelite woman in the original series) stands with keys in hand and Bluebeard waves farewell, and another shows a different turret scene with the brothers riding in on the same height as the tower itself. The preface to this reissue, also dated 1899, refers to the grouping of "Bluebeard" with "Sleeping Beauty" and the "Baby's Own Alphabet," and was thus written for the occasion, and signed with Crane's insignia. But it is also self-referential, depicting Bluebeard reading his own book: "Bluebeard's key, no doubt, unlocked many mysteries, and he may have had among his treasures a picture-book, if only to amuse his wives with, or to divert their attention from his own dark designs: but it must not be supposed that Bluebeard—although he is not free from the suspicion of having put several beauties to sleep—in presenting himself again with The Sleeping Beauty is at all responsible for her enchanted slumber, or that either Bluebeard or the Sleeping Beauty are concerned with Baby's Own Alphabet—except for the spelling of their own names." The preface also notes that Bluebeard is a "heavy tragedy" and this is perhaps the most striking contrast to the contemporary caricatures of Bluebeard. There is no comic element to the verse (which is unusual in verse versions of "Bluebeard") or in the illustrations. Instead, if Bluebeard's wife is shown submitting to the same temptation as Eve, she is nevertheless outmatched by the devilry of the

Bluebeard she has married, and the poignancy of her danger and the justice of her rescuing brothers are given full play in Crane's illustrations.[29]

Through the work of Victorian literary and visual artists, the Bluebeard tale once again became less of a laughing matter. Its innate doubling and doubleness was foregrounded through using it in a doubled way, retelling the story in a genre other than fairy tale and highlighting the tale's ability to address the themes of violence and gender inequality in a serious manner, no matter which stance on the theme the artist adopted.

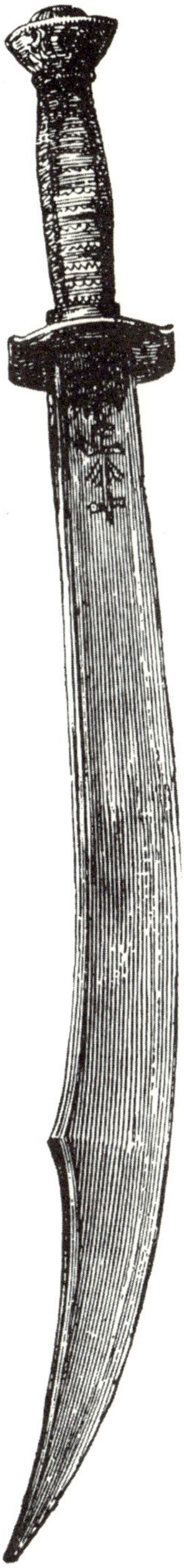

Part 4

Bluebeard in the English Twentieth Century

Chapter 8

Bluebeard in Crisis

At the advent of the twentieth century, the Bluebeard pantomime as Christmas fare had become thoroughly traditional. The 1901–1902 Drury Lane Christmas season pantomime *Bluebeard* (J. Hickory Wood and Arthur Collins) is exemplary: Mustapha has two daughters, Fatima, and Anne, the latter played to cross-dressed comic effect by the famed actor Dan Leno: "Seize me! Seize me! Why doesn't someone seize me?" (20). Fatima is in love with Selim, but is literally sold at the Slave Market to Bluebeard, "the millionaire collector" (17). Anne is part of the lot, slipped in by her father, but she believes herself to be the best wife for Bluebeard, lectures him on how to enter respectable society, and schemes to get Fatima to escape with Selim. But like pantomimes much older than this one, the play features a benevolent spirit, The Good Fairy, who watches over Selim and Fatima and gives Selim the means to summon aid (a magic bugle). At the same time, it is the Fairy legions who decide that Fatima should be taught a lesson, in order to cure her of her one fault, curiosity (exacerbated by the Spirit of the Fan, whose breeze fans her curiosity to a burning passion), and thus render her a perfect wife. The play includes a two-man elephant and concludes with a harlequinade sporting a Clown, Pantaloon, and a policeman. There is also comic business with Bluebeard's six old wives, all played by men, who later disappear into the Blue Chamber as talking heads on plates, and a botched play-within-a-play meant to awaken Bluebeard's conscience.

Similarly, in the Klaw and Erlanger burlesque *Mr. Bluebeard* (Solomon [ca. 1903])[1] an unambiguously villainous Bluebeard sings: "I love in gore my hands to steep, / I revel in villainy dire and deep; / As a fiend incarnate I'll admit / That I'm emphatically it" (13–14). Fatima sings of her virtue: "For I am not only as good as I am, But as good as I ought to be" (19), adding, however, that she is also a "somewhat shrewd girl" (18) and does not require a husband to pay her bills (17). The rescuing Selim's song features broad-stroke heroism: "'None but the brave deserve the fair,' / That shall my motto be, / And e'er the dawn

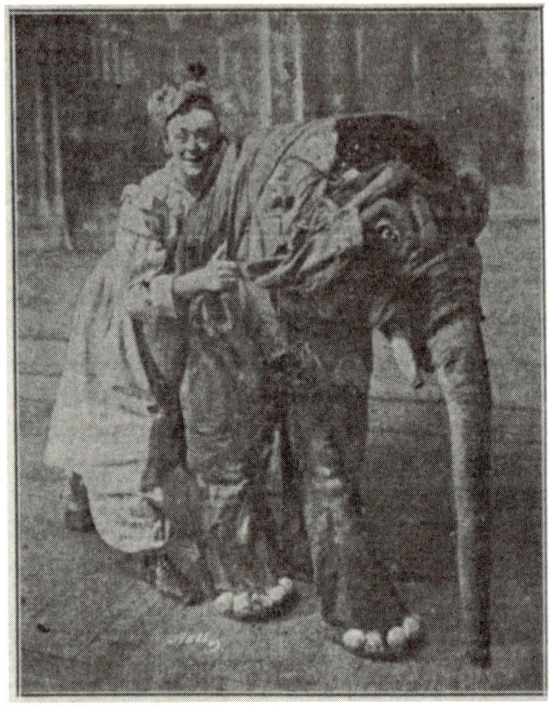

Eddie Foy as Sister Anne, with the Pet Elephant. This historical photograph shows a famous comedian (Eddie Foy) cross-dressed as Sister Anne, a staple of Bluebeard comedies. Foy was half-dressed in costume when he appeared on stage to calm the audience as the tragic fire that destroyed Chicago's Iroquois Theatre broke out. Billy Rose Theatre Division, The New York Public Library for the Performing Arts, Astor, Lenox and Tilden Foundations.

of another day / I'll set my true love free" (22). In its gleeful lack of ambiguity, its cross-dressed cast, Fairy interventions, National Tableaux, and Grand Transformation Scene, *Mr. Bluebeard* was also at the start of the twentieth century essentially a Victorian production in the prevailing mode: slapstick musical comedy. But with this very production the "Bluebeard" comedies lost some of their innocence in a horrific Chicago theater fire. The Iroquois Theatre fire of Christmas 1903 killed 602 people, mostly women and children, during a holiday matinee performance of *Mr. Bluebeard* at the new (and unfinished) Chicago playhouse. While the inadequacies of the theatre design and construction were in large part responsible for the inferno, the nature of the *Mr. Bluebeard* production itself contributed. The sets were deliberately extravagant: 280 drops were suspended from the flies, made of gauzy, sheer materials. Further, the equipment used to suspend an aerialiste so that she could fly out and scatter flowers over the audience, blocked the descent of the asbestos curtain.[2]

In the early years of the century, however, minor pantomimes, nursery and parlor plays, and juvenile renditions in the Victorian tradition nonetheless continued to be published and produced. Jenkins (1902) is typical in its burlesque

Chapbook illustration: typically the key is oversized, as here. Bluebeard is often dressed as a Turk, following the English orientalized version of him presented in the 1798 melodrama by George Colman and Michael Kelly. Surprisingly, his wife Fatima here is not orientalized. From Dean & Munday. 1821. Miss Horwood. *Blue Beard, or, the Effects of Female Curiosity in Easy Verse*. Courtesy of The Lilly Library, Indiana University, Bloomington.

In the iconography of the "bloody chamber" illustrations, the wife Fatima reacts physically to the sight. This illustration is essential to the chapbooks until around the turn of the twentieth century, when the women's bodies are no longer shown. From Dean & Munday. 1821. Miss Horwood. *Blue Beard, or, the Effects of Female Curiosity in Easy Verse*. Courtesy of The Lilly Library, Indiana University, Bloomington.

Walter Crane's illustration cleverly shows multiple sites of action: the wife refusing to come down, Bluebeard threatening to come up after her, and sister Anne in the turret waving on the brothers, who are visible arriving out of the castle window. From Walter Crane. 1899. *Bluebeard's Picture Book*. London: John Lane.

Arthur Rackham, "May Colven and the Parrot." A talking bird that can warn the trespassing woman can also betray her presence. Courtesy of the Bridgeman Art Library.

Bluebeard (as pirate) was a popular pier entertainment in the late Victorian period and early twentieth century; patrons enter and exit through Bluebeard's mouth. Courtesy of Harold Hartmann, curator of the Savin Rock Museum and Learning Center, http://savinrockmuseum.com.

Margaret Atwood, "Death as a Bride" (watercolor). Atwood has used the "Bluebeard" story repeatedly in her work. Atwood Papers, 1970. Courtesy of Margaret Atwood and the Thomas Fisher Rare Book Library, University of Toronto.

Cindy Sherman, Untitled, 1992, color photograph, 26 ½ x 40 inches. Courtesy of the artist and Metro Pictures.

treatment, but the play contributes the specific oddity that it is intended for a cast in black face, with all characters using "negro dialect." The Widow Kadiger speculates "we 'Merican moders don't care nuffin for rep'tations if our darters can marry wid de nobility" (4); Bluebeard sings of his own fame and of his plan for his wives: "She'll be the last, if she behabes, / But den I knows she won't" (6); Fatima calls: "Sister Ann, Sister Ann, does yer see nuffin?" and at the end Bluebeard returns from his apparent death scene and offers to "sign de pledge" (14).[3]

Women's suffrage is commented on directly in one *Bluebeard* children's play (Cummins 1922). Bluebeard refuses to give up his key at all, and so Fatma [*sic*] and her sister steal it while he is sleeping. Upon being fatally stabbed by his brothers in law, he denounces their folly in killing the man fighting their own battle, and murdering the masculine by the hand of the male:

In destroying poor Bluebeard you drive the last nail
In the coffin of "Power in the hands of the male";
You ensure that your sex shall be dashed from its heights
By a horde of wild women intent on their Rights!
Ah! I know all their mad aspirations by rote.
If you give them the keys they will ask for the Vote.
If you give them the Vote, they will capture the State,
And you'll mourn in their close silken fetters too late! (38)[4]

Bluebeard did not immediately disappear from juvenile literature, where he is later "most conspicuous by his absence" (Davies 2001, 58). Sir Arthur Quiller-Couch's collection of fairy tale retellings (1910), sumptuously illustrated by Edmund Dulac's watercolors, is among the more lavish Edwardian productions. Just as Perrault's version Christianized the pagan tale (instead of taking time to dress in wedding attire, he has Bluebeard's wife ask for time to pray), Quiller-Couch's tale is moralistic: "Scripture says we may not serve two masters, / And little keys have opened large disasters" (6–7 of 7). The contemporary illustrations of Dulac and Harry Clarke are svelte and gorgeous, but bloodless, and therefore far from the crude butchery so popular in old chapbooks.

Chapbooks, though rarer, also continued to circulate in the twentieth century. Wish Wynne's "Bluebeard" (published by Reynolds 1933) is a good example and captures an exaggerated return to the working class origins of the chapbook. The chapbook contains "Jack and the Beanstalk" (by permission of *The Radio Times*), "Bluebeard" and "Cinders." In a twentieth-century update of Perrault's "Mother Goose" frontispiece, with the female storyteller at the fireside surrounded by youthful listeners, the cover depicts a photograph with a woman seated in a doorway, mouth open as if midstory, holding an infant and surrounded by five children. All are fully dressed for daytime (this is not an image of bedtime comfort), and only one is seated; the others look as if they cannot pause for very long. The oldest is holding a broom. In the four-page story, Annie is sent to live with "Fatma" and Bluebeard ("old Blueface") out at their large eight-room house by Shepherd's Bush, outside London. They speculate as to whether he keeps his "booze" in his secret room, and the first thing they do after he leaves for London is to have a drink. (Similarly, in Ring Lardner's story "Bluebeard" [1925] the wife and all guests assume that the room contains his "hootch": "his Scotch and corkscrew." In keeping with the joke, the skeletons are described as "vintage.") The dialect and grammar of the female narrator (Wish Wynne) is working class: "They was all done in, hanging on 'ooks with their 'eads cut off. Looked just like Slater's the butcher's-shop at Christmas time, —only there wasn't no price on them" (1933, 11). A chapbook-like juvenile is the gruesome fairy play (Richards 1916) written for children in easy rhymes and set to popular tunes (Fatima pleads for her life to the tune of "Yankee Doodle Dandy"), which is illustrated on the penultimate page with the youthful brothers holding Bluebeard's dripping head and a sword also dripping gore (56). To the gleeful words: "Remove his ugly head!" Bluebeard is decapitated postmortem. Other juvenile examples, such as a juvenile version from A. L. Burt (1905), also defy the new trend and continue the chapbook focus on gore: "Their heads were severed from their bodies, and hung in a row upon the wall!!" (4).

An early example of the sanitizing that the Bluebeard story began to undergo can be found in *Blue Beard, or Tommy in Fairyland* (Thomas Nelson [1908]), which features a child telling an adult of his visits to Fairyland. Bluebeard is nothing like the Henry the Eighth he was expecting, but "more like our vicar than anybody I know" (24). He runs an orphanage, is kind to everyone, and only plays the part of Bluebeard because nobody else would, and without his sacrifice the tale would have disappeared from nursery books altogether. The forbidden chamber is described as a waxworks similar to Madame Tussaud's. Another example states its intentions outright in an introductory note: "As here told, they are free from the savagery, distressing details, and excessive pathos which mar many of the tales in the form that they have come down to us from a barbaric past" (Johnson 1920). The Victorian chapbook trend of the extended and very moral happy ending is also evident in this strain of sanitized juvenile literature. In "Bluebeard" by Louey Chisholm (1922), the last sentence is symptomatic: "And Fatima lived a long, happy, and *useful* life, beloved by all who knew her" (12, emphasis added).

But in addition to these essential Victorian forms, a new development emerges: a clutch of notable Bluebeard works that all problematize and challenge the traditional expressions of the Bluebeard story: Georges Méliès' film *Barbe-bleue* (1901); Maurice Maeterlinck's play *Ariadne et Barbe-bleue* (*Ariadne and Bluebeard* 1901, opera composed by Paul Dukas 1907); Béla Balázs' psychological drama *A kékszakállú herceg vára* (*Duke Bluebeard's Castle* 1907, opera by Béla Bartók 1912); and Anatole France's story "Les Sept Femmes de la Barbe Bleue" ("The Seven Wives of Bluebeard," 1909). While these artists are all European rather than English,[5] the influence of these writers' works on the English modernist expression of the Bluebeard tale is critical. What we see in all these versions is a darker vision of Bluebeard. These are explorations of gender relationships to fit the Freudian and Nietzschian generations; they question the mechanics of representation in addition to the story being retold, and they go beyond the marital focus to explore the human condition. The Bluebeard tale, more than ever before, turned *inward* in a way only glimpsed previously, through the gothic. Bluebeard's Castle, and its forbidden room, is no longer merely a prohibition and test, but a representation of his mind, his soul, his secret self. But as Bluebeard is humanized, becoming in a sense "Everyman," his wife runs the concomitant danger of becoming monstrous in comparison.[6] The modern man is *forced* to retreat from and preserve himself against not simply a curious and prying woman, but one who wants to claim his past and love everything about him, leaving nothing sacred. And if he lacks the cruelty to kill his wives, then he is cruelly outnumbered when the repressed wives return.

One significant source of this change of direction is the revival of interest in Gilles de Rais in the late nineteenth century, beginning with a number of important biographies.[7] One of the earliest, by Eugene Bossard (1885) published documents of his trial in 1440. Several other biographies and stage productions quickly followed; and Joris Karl Huysman's fiction *Là-Bas* (*Down There*, 1891) began the trend of rehabilitating the figure through portraying him as a suffering and spiritual individual in a full-length novel. With the Dreyfus Affair in France turning into a controversial debate over flaws in the justice system, it was a matter of French judicial history and public debate to revisit the Gilles de Rais trial and speculate as to whether it had been "rigged" by the influential Duke of Brittany in an effort to rob Gilles de Rais of his vast estates. Simultaneously, and lending additional force to the efforts to rehabilitate Gilles de Rais, his companion in arms, Joan of Arc, was the subject of a campaign for sainthood; she was beatified in 1908. Anatole France published a two-volume biography of Joan in the same year. As Gilles de Rais became humanized, so therefore did Bluebeard. These multifarious contemporary influences informed the French symbolists, from whom Maeterlinck and Balázs drew inspiration for their own librettos.

This chapter examines the impact of these important critical works, and then looks at how the English and American modernists and Hollywood films responded to them. Writers Sylvia Townsend Warner and Eudora Welty both reinterpreted the Bluebeard tale (in *Cat's Cradle*: "Bluebeard's Daughter" [1940], and *The Robber Bridegroom* [1942], respectively) in the light of modernist realignments of gender relations and narrative forms. At the same time, after the burlesque comedies of manners of the 1920s and 1930s, both on stage and then in film, the 1940s instead produced a clutch of American "Bluebeard" films (most of them literary adaptations) remarkable for their darker view of human nature.

BLUEBEARD IN EARLY FILM: SEEING DOUBLE

Although the Bluebeard figure in French cinematographer Georges Méliès' film *Barbe-bleue* (1901) is a familiar nineteenth-century caricature, the film represents perhaps the first modern European gesture for the Bluebeard story by virtue of putting it on film.[8] Méliès was one of the earliest creators of the fiction film: a narrative story in several scenes. In this ten-minute silent film, Bluebeard uses a display of his gold and jewels to obtain the hand of his eighth wife, much against her wishes. The first scene back at his castle is set in the kitchen (a staple set in Victorian burlesques) where, alongside the usual pratfalls (a cook falls into a cauldron and is cooked), is a parade of wedding food, including a giant bottle of Mercier champagne. After the wedding feast, Bluebeard comes upon his bride reading in a castle chamber, and explains he must leave, forbidding her to open a conspicuous door within the scene. He has no sooner left the scene followed by his customary train of servants before the wife has approached the door. She is then visited by a devil (played by Méliès) who overcomes her with curiosity, and she opens the door. The scene shifts to the interior of the forbidden chamber, where seven women are hanging in a row behind her.[9] The key grows to an enormous size, and the wife is chided by her fairy godmother for disobeying Bluebeard. In the next scene, the wife is tossing on her bed, haunted by a vision first of the women in the chamber, then Bluebeard himself, and finally a set of large, bouncing keys. Bluebeard returns while his wife is attempting to clean the key, and after granting her time to pray he paces about before following her out of the frame. On the two-level turrets, the wife implores Sister Anne to look out, before Bluebeard storms in and violently drags her off

From Georges Méliès, *Barbe-bleu* (1901). Although the iconography of the discovery in the chamber was familiar, the sight of hanging women in this early film would have been very shocking to the cinema audience.

down the staircase by her hair. In the exterior scene in which the wife had been cleaning the key, she is imploring now on her knees while the brothers can be seen hacking their way into the set and ultimately stabbing Bluebeard. He is pinned to a gatepost by the sword in his chest and flails continually throughout the remainder of the scene, in which the murdered wives appear as ghostly apparitions, revive, and are paired off with courtiers. Bluebeard only dies once they have left the frame, and the last scene is a grand *tableau* depicting that all has ended well.

It seems that Méliès was choosing a traditional route with his "Bluebeard," fitting it to a new medium rather than challenging or deconstructing the story. On closer inspection, though, the subtexts of gender relations are a timely commentary on the status of French feminism (and the need to be rid of legalized spousal murder). Further, the devil's power over the wife frees her from at least some of the culpability for her curiosity, usually heavy in French versions.[10] But the film is not simply filmed theater. Despite the highly stagey and spectacular nature of his *mise en scène*, the special effects implemented by Méliès in this film, as in others of his, are cinematic and create a radical new way to view spectacle.[11] The use of stop-motion cinematography often used by Méliès to substitute one object or person for another, or in the case of the keys to make them appear to grow, and to overlap dissolves where the new image appears superimposed over the previous image, which eventually then fades out, manipulate how the viewer sees things and, in the sense of medium as well as subject, thereby performs a deconstruction at the same time as a magic trick.

The film's inherent double vision is perfectly modern, encapsulating as it does the issue of representation, the notion of doubleness and the uncanny, and the Freudian and gothic return of the repressed. The revival of the murdered wives uses cinematic devices to perform the uncanny and is an example to add to those cited by one critic, who linked the new technologies of photography and film to the turn-of-the-century phenomenon of spirit photography.[12] The dissolve creates an overlay of images, which shows the act of retelling a known story in a new way and foreshadows the postmodern film treatments of the later twentieth century. Technological and narrative factors again converge as they did with the invention of blue fire used on stage in the Coleman and Kelly production of 1798, or when the mechanics of printing and distributing chapbooks occasioned an explosion of the "Bluebeard" juveniles. Méliès offered the reappearance of the repressed/dead using film's ability to revive them from still photograph to moving image. The film also creates uncanny doubling of images: Bluebeard's wives are uncanny in their multiplicity, but they have already been shown in the film first hanging in the chamber, then moving but also "hanging in the air" in the last wife's dream, and finally they fully revive at the end of the film. In its deployment of irony, Méliès used another form of double vision to deconstruct the story being told, one that links him with Anatole France's short story version several years later.[13]

REHABILITATING BLUEBEARD

Although separated by the first decade of the century (and by the two opera librettos), Méliès' film and France's story "Les Sept femmes de la barbe bleue" ("The Seven Wives of Bluebeard" in a collection of the same name, 1909) share the overt use of irony in representing the traditional story of Perrault. France's story provides a defense of Bluebeard, but the excuses given are largely the same as those perfected on the Victorian stage. What is different about France's version of Bluebeard's story is that it subverts the traditional genre separation of history and fiction, thereby undermining the idea of an objective reality and the possibility of recording it.[14] In "The Seven Wives of Bluebeard," Anatole France interwove the "authorized" story told by the "biographer" Charles Perrault with the "true story," arguing that Bluebeard has been slandered by those who survived him and who made him their victim just as Macbeth "whom legend and Shakespeare accuse of crimes, was in reality a just and wise king" (France 1909, 567). In France's fictional corrective, Bernard de Montragoux (Bluebeard) had in his castle Guillettes a room nicknamed the Cabinet of the Unfortunate Princesses, owing to its decorations: tragic Greek heroines were portrayed on the walls and the floors tiled in porphyry. In all his matrimonial dealings, de Montragoux is described not only as gallant, but as devoted to his wives and rather unmanned around them. He is uncertain in his dealings with women.

The women he marries are depicted not as aberrant specimens of womanhood, but as a misogynist's statistical sampling. The first wife left him, weary of being kept in one place by marriage. The second drank to excess and drowned in hysterics. The third was so preoccupied with ambition and social climbing that she finally pined away and died of jaundice. The fourth cuckolded him with so many men she was killed in the cabinet by one lover when surprised there with another. The fifth (prescribed by physicians to help de Montragoux combat his depressive grief) was foolish rather than cunning, but was abducted by a "mendicant monk" and most likely eaten by wolves. The sixth refused to consummate the marriage, and as de Montragoux would not force her, the union was annulled by Rome. Finally, Jeanne, younger sister of Anne and daughter of the scheming and penniless widow Dame Sidonie de Lespoisse, is privy to the plot to overthrow de Montragoux with her whole family and her lover the Chevalier de la Merlus with whom she frequently had trysts in the Cabinet. Her cruel sister Anne, while chaste, is the "soul of the conspiracy" (579).

France's plot itself is amusingly revisionist (although the misogyny is traditional), but the story's modernist contribution is asserted in the frame narrative of the historian/biographer who aims to correct the record on Bluebeard/de Montragoux. In this frame there is discussion of who writes history (the "unspeakable scoundrels" who perpetrated the crime), and of the need to correct omissions and biases in the telling. The business about the fairy key poses more of a problem for the historian-narrator: "a question which cannot be solved without leaving the limited domain of history to enter the indeterminate regions of philosophy" (580). Without "proof to the contrary," the philosopher allows the enchanted key to stand without correction, citing other sources for the likelihood of the supernatural. Yet because of the exaggerated care to which he sets about his task, this reader cannot take the narrator seriously. He is guilty of the very things he is criticizing other historians for having done: bias, omission, faulty logic, and requiring a deluge of supporting details to make his case.

The parody is not of the Bluebeard story so much as it is of "the impossibility of establishing objective truth" and the historical methodology that conveniently ignores such an impossibility. At the same time, the faultlessly inscribed revision of "Bluebeard" is now "a murdered myth" (Madeleva 1927, 10).[15]

"NEW WOMAN": THE TWO OPERAS

Adopting Bluebeard's voice for a sonnet (1917), Edna St. Vincent Millay wrote of this forbidden room: "An empty room, cobwebbed and comfortless. / Yet this alone out of my life I kept / Unto myself, lest any know me quite; / And you did so profane me when you crept / Unto the threshold of this room tonight / That I must never more behold your face. / This now is yours. I seek another place."[16] The speaker is a "postoperatic" Bluebeard; as in the short story by Anatole France, in both the opera by Nobel prize winner Maurice Maeterlinck and Paul Dukas, and that by Béla Balázs and Béla Bartók, Bluebeard is ennobled by suffering and his modern wives do "profane" him by their intrusions into his soul.

Ariadne and Bluebeard (1901, 1907)

Maurice Maeterlinck's symbolist libretto of *Ariadne et Barbe-bleue* (1901)[17] depicts Ariadne as the strong heroine who goes into Bluebeard's castle determined to discover the fates of his five missing wives, twice rescues Bluebeard himself, frees his previous wives from a dungeon and then, when they are incapable of finalizing their escape, she leaves the castle, the wives, and Bluebeard, too. The plot demonstrates the feminist force of the symbolist play, and its argument is that imprisonment in Bluebeard's castle is a state of mind, one that requires complicity. The use of the mythic name Ariadne recalls the heroine of the Cretan labyrinth, where Ariadne rescued Theseus from the Minotaur, only later to be abandoned by Theseus on a rock in the sea. Ariadne is known in myth then as a navigator of labyrinths, a rescuer of men, and subsequently (or perhaps consequently) as a betrayed and thwarted woman.

Maeterlinck's three-act libretto opens with the sounds of the milling crowd, unhappy that Ariadne is the next victim of Bluebeard who is already thought to have murdered five wives.[18] The nurse accompanying Ariadne is frightened, while Ariadne herself is confident that Bluebeard loves her and that it is her "duty" to discover his secret: "He loves me, I am beautiful and I will have his secret" (Maeterlinck 1901, 8, my translation). Given six keys of silver and one of gold, Ariadne literally throws down the silver keys, having no need of the jewels they release. Instead, the gold—the forbidden key—is the only one she requires. The nurse opens all the other doors in turn and various jewels cascade from the rooms.[19] Even Ariadne is swayed by the diamonds that pour from the sixth door, for their symbolic manifestation of the light that is her dominant theme. When she discovers the seventh door she opens it, but as she is about to go in, Bluebeard enters; yet despite his reproaches she insists on knowing his secret. He holds her arm and she cries out; at that moment a stone is thrown through the windows, and the crowd breaks through the doors the nurse has reopened. Ariadne faces down the crowd, reassuring them that she is unharmed, and firmly sees them out.

In Act II, Ariadne discovers the previous five women in a dungeon underground. She ultimately breaks a window to let the blinding light of the world outside break in (the literal light mirroring the diamonds of the earlier jewel scene),[20] and the act ends triumphantly as she leads them to freedom. In the third and final act, however, the women who have been magically prevented from leaving the castle adorn themselves with the jewels from the other rooms, encouraged by Ariadne, in order to release and see their own beauty. Bluebeard, who had left the castle, returns and is again attacked by the crowd. He is offered, wounded and bound, to the wives who are expected to kill him in revenge. Again, Ariadne dismisses the crowd then unties Bluebeard. The five wives, on their knees (recalling perhaps the execution stance usually assumed by Bluebeard's wives), refuse to leave him, and so she leaves them there together.

While the action of the libretto can perhaps easily be read today within a feminist matrix, comments by Maeterlinck and the treatment by Paul Dukas for his symphonic score belie a complex iteration of early-twentieth-century gender relations. Maeterlinck (later) disavowed any "moral or philosophical designs" to the piece, calling it a small "*opéra comique*" (1:22–23),[21] and indeed some of the first critics did laugh in print, but they did so in overt hostility to the feminism that many of them saw there.[22] Tellingly, Dukas did not agree with the author's reading of the play and reinterpreted it for the scoring. Dukas' orchestration sheds any *opéra comique* overtones, and he argued that Ariadne rescues Bluebeard.

Maeterlinck's subtitle, "*la délivrance inutile*" (the useless rescue), is omitted from Dukas' opera. The subtitle has frequently caused the opera to be read as a "failed" rescue. Ariadne does not succeed in rescuing Bluebeard's wives, her "sisters," which was her avowed mission. Whether the opera is read as "feminist" or not seems to turn on whether one believes Ariadne succeeded or failed.[23] It seems that a contemporary audience understood the libretto and the opera both to have feminist expression, but that the same contemporary audience, author and composer included, were uncomfortable defining it as such. In 1910, Dukas wrote an essay about this opera in which he rejected the idea of feminist motivations for Ariadne, but in doing so equated "feminist" with "man-hating": "But it is not by virtue of feminist convictions that she acts, but through the expansiveness of a superior nature, supernaturally good and active.... She does not hate Bluebeard at all."

The libretto remains ambivalent. On the one hand, Ariadne's rescue is successful. Ariadne releases light in all its many forms throughout the opera. The language is always of emancipation of light: "Behold the key unlocking your dawn!"[24] She succeeds in "rescuing" light, bringing the women into the light, and bringing the light out of the women: she releases their hair, arms, and shoulders, in every case stating that she is helping their light to shine. That it is a "useless" rescue is not Ariadne's tragedy; she leaves as determinedly as she arrived. Bluebeard's first five wives may choose to cleave to their enfeebled roles, but Ariadne serves as the herald of another type of woman. On the other hand, whether she "hates" him or not, Ariadne also seems to be the instigator of the figurative castration of Bluebeard. After Ariadne's first "rescue" of Bluebeard at the end of Act I, he is "disappeared" from the castle and from the libretto both. His last action in Act I is to look, eyes cast down, at the point of his sword (14). Ariadne then tells the nurse that he is defeated, but does not yet know it (16). When the women emerge from the dungeon they do not know where he has gone (Ariadne speculates), but when he reappears he is bound, choking, and remains silent for the remainder of the opera. His last gesture is "*inutile*" (useless): he makes a sign to restrain her as she leaves (34).[25] When the peasants give up the bound Bluebeard to her, Ariadne's reassuring phrases are condescending if not sarcastic: "You are heroes; you are our saviors. Leave us a while" (32). But even before Ariadne's arrival, Bluebeard collects and keeps women but does not kill them. Arguably, he does not have a secret worth hiding (his wives are alive and still love him), and he is incapable of keeping it or them from Ariadne in any case. At the same time, it is one of the first examples in the twentieth century of the act of collecting and keeping women as a symbolic equivalent to killing them (and, as Ariadne says, they are "dead" to the world because they are unable to free themselves [16]).[26] While in juvenile literature of the early twentieth century this bloodless type of Bluebeard made for milder nursery fare,[27] the opera expresses the crisis of impotence occasioned by the arrival of the "new woman."

Duke Bluebeard's Castle (1907, 1912)

Unlike the Maeterlinck production, best known for its symbolist libretto, the now-famous[28] twentieth-century Hungarian opera *A kékszakállú herceg vára* (*Duke Bluebeard's Castle*) is better known for Béla Bartók's music (1912) than for Béla Balázs' libretto (1907), which had already had some outings as a spoken play for some years prior (Banks 1991, 12). Balázs stated: "Bluebeard's castle is not a realistic stone castle. The castle is his soul. It is lonely, dark, and secretive: the castle of locked doors . . . Into this castle, into his own soul, Bluebeard admits his beloved. And the castle (the stage) shudders, sighs, and bleeds. When the woman walks into it, she walks into a living being" [ca. 1915]. The castle dominates the opera (it was listed as a *dramatis persona* by Balázs); the importance of the castle is also seen in the massive sets for various productions of this opera. Sometimes gothic, sometimes abstract, the characters are always dwarfed within it. The dominance of the castle emphasizes its modern symbolic function.

It represents a modernist bridge by uniting the old and new not simply through the libretto but simultaneously through musical expression. Balázs used Perrault's European fairy tale, but also a Hungarian variant in the Bluebeard-like *Ballad of Anna Molnár*.[29] Similarly combining old with new, Béla Bartók had been honing a personal musical style crafted from ancient Hungarian folk music, which he personally collected, and blended with contemporary influences.[30]

In *Duke Bluebeard's Castle*, there is very little direct action; instead the castle is the setting for an epic struggle within the self, played out as one between husband and wife. The symbolic use of the name Judith for Bluebeard's wife summons the biblical Judith, slayer of Holofernes.[31] At the outset, then, with the couple named Judith (beheader of men) and Bluebeard (beheader of women), the marital stakes of their conflict are fatally high. The set contains seven doors. Judith, Bluebeard's new wife, enters with him, and both remain on stage until Judith steps through the seventh and final door at the end, initiating the set's plunge into total darkness. She repeats that she loves him and that all doors must be opened so that (like Ariadne) she can let in the light and air. He cautions her repeatedly ("for us both be careful, Judith"), but after she has opened the first two doors (the torture chamber, the armory) she seems to be through his defenses and he welcomes her opening the progressively more "scenic" doors (treasure chamber, secret garden, all the lands of his dominion) even though they too are tainted with blood (represented in the opera by Judith's exclamations, lighting, and the musical "blood motif"). The fifth door represents a climactic turning point.[32] The light has returned (albeit with bloody shadows), Bluebeard exalts Judith and considers her work finished: "You deliver me from darkness. / Your fair hand has done this, Judith. / Come now, come now, let me hold you" (55). Judith repeatedly insists on opening the two remaining doors: "I won't have a single door here / Shut against me. If you love me" (56). Against his cries "leave it alone!" she opens the sixth door, to the lake of tears, and the hall immediately darkens. Judith realizes his former wives are alive and behind the remaining door: she insists on knowing of Bluebeard "Tell me of the way you loved them, / Fairer than me? Dearer than me?" (57). As she opens the seventh door, the sixth and fifth close; the end is now inevitable. As the three former wives emerge, symbolizing dawn, day, and evening, Bluebeard dresses Judith as his wife of night. Only now does Judith plead: "No more, no more! I am still here!"; "My beloved, spare me, spare me!" (59), but once she has submitted, the stage becomes utterly dark.

Whatever the subtleties of the equation (Judith has been criticized for her hen-pecking), it is clear that for Balázs and Bartók the opera represented a tragedy for both characters and for relationships between men and women in general. The opera is generally considered a bleak if compelling image of human loneliness and suffering;[33] the inability of lovers to commune with one another even in their most intimate relationships. However, the use of the name Judith and its allusive relationship with contemporary works that encoded *fin-de-siècle* anti-feminism seems to make the most powerful statement about early-twentieth-century sexual politics. In Hebbel's *Judith* (1841), which enjoyed a revival in the early twentieth century, Judith both attempted to seduce Holofernes and then decapitated him in revenge for her rape. With reference specifically to this play, Freud theorized his argument that decapitation is symbolic castration. And *fin-de-siècle* Judith was also confused with Salomé, another biblical woman responsible for a decapitation. In Wilde's play, she demands the head of John the Baptist out of revenge for having been spurned by him. In the confusion between the two,[34] Judith's murder of Holofernes becomes a further sexualized act of betrayal. By choosing this unusual name for Bluebeard's wife, Balázs offered a putative conflict whose resolution is actually a foregone conclusion. The outcome is inevitable; she betrays (and, arguably, even destroys) Bluebeard because that is her role, and he betrays and destroys her, because that is his. At the end of the opera, both are left in the darkness. Alternatively, she is Bluebeard's perfect match. She is given metonymic power to equal Bluebeard's. Therefore, the failure of their marriage underscores the universal impossibility of all unions; the balance must and will tip. His desire to remain closed, and her desire to open, are fundamentally opposed and cannot remain (at the fifth door) in even precarious stasis. One must destroy the other. Furthermore, Bluebeard adopts the stereotypically female traits: passive, silent, an onlooker in the drama, a keeper of secret interiors. Judith, by contrast, adopts traditionally male traits: she has the majority of lines, enacts the only actions of the drama (opening doors), and her entire motivation is to penetrate his interior spaces. Judith, the new woman, is both desirable and fatal to her male counterpart.

Extending the use of topical allusion in nineteenth-century comic versions of the Bluebeard tale, its value as a vehicle for social commentary became increasingly exploited in the early twentieth century with its renegotiations of gender politics. As Bluebeard became a sympathetic "everyman," Bluebeard's wife embodied both a powerful new woman and an anti-feminist backlash against her. The two operas of the period served as a powerful corrective to the prevailing comic mode, returning Bluebeard to the tragic. The doubleness inherent in the Bluebeard tale that was foregrounded by Victorian artists remained apt. The tale's self-referential possibilities were further explored both in using new technology in film and in the ironic mode that became a dominant trend in handling the complexities of the tale.

Chapter 9

Modernist Bluebeard

Modern treatment of the Bluebeard story is indelibly influenced by the two operas, that by Maeterlinck and Dukas and that by Balázs and Bartók, which themselves drew upon a wide range of European modernist ideas. Influences for the operas included the Dreyfus Affair and the Catholic Church's reexamination of the crimes of Gilles de Rais, as well as a desire to musically distinguish French and Hungarian music from German and French influences. Post–World War I, post-Freud, and post-Nietzsche, the Bluebeard story in the English tradition frequently reflected the modern dilemma. But as "Bluebeard" has always been used as a gendered commentary reflecting the state of the times, so the English modernists used the story to comment on the modern male dilemma: feminism. Bluebeard's wife has always been transgressive, and in many cases has insisted on her right to have no door barred against her; what is new is that she is increasingly cast, for better or worse, in the role of a feminist. Kate Wiggin's mock commentary on a fictional "Bluebeard" opera by Wagner was wittily accomplished. But it is framed as a lecture recital aimed at women wanting educated partners with them at opera recitals (Wiggin 1914, vii) and claims that the opera has an antifeminist aria occasioning the boycott of the opera: "It is these inexcusable lines which have caused the Feminist party to boycott (and perhaps rightly) any opera-house in which this drama is given, urging that they contain an insult which can be wiped out only with blood or ballots" (49).

In a twist on the "sad Bluebeard syndrome" cemented by the Balázs-Bartók opera, one gentleman tells a Lady in Blue in *The Inn of Disenchantment* that all men are Bluebeards and by way of proof provides the "true story of Bluebeard" in which his wife works to help her husband overcome what she believes to be secret sorrows. When he finally loves her with all of his heart, she is disappointed, and now curious to see what her love has "overcome": the chamber is empty, and she never forgives her husband for having nothing to forgive. In that way, summarized the gentleman, the true mystery is "the boring emptiness of absolute mediocrity," and all men are thus "poor pretenders" like Bluebeard (Ysaye 1917, 21).

There is no doubt about the antifeminist focus for the backlash in the modernist period. In the comedy of (female) manners *Blue Beard*, a fully realized fairy tale play (Merington 1916), Fatima is called an "emancipated specimen." She marries Bluebeard in order to get an inheritance (and won't forsake his money even after she has seen inside the chamber). One of her female neighbors recounts a bizarre dream "one in which women were equal with men, in the eyes of the law!" (188), and she repeats that "it was only a dream" (227; echoing the structure of "Mr. Fox"). She thus both performs an alarming story, reassures the male audience, and yet promises that the story will come true, all in one allusion to the tale: "it was only a dream." In an unsubtle later story Fatma [*sic*], the "Bluebeard's Daughter" of the story's title, has collected her husbands but not killed them, but is summarily killed on the floor of justice for being a "bad woman." Her crime is to confess: "I preferred to lock [my husbands] up, to civilize them, and have power over them. . . . I am also very much of a feminist" (Couperus 1947, 474).

The years of World War I and influenza pandemic of 1918 provided distractions enabling people to marry and murder multiple times before finally being detected. The tracking and capture of these contemporary criminals were highly publicized feats. However, the detective genre treatment of the Bluebeard tale remains traditional. The focus in these crime stories is not how to change the Bluebeard tale to best express the times, but rather how the story comes ready-fitted for the genre, whether the genre is true-crime serial "marriage for murder and money" or fictionalized hard-boiled detectives on the trail of same. Indeed, the strain of misogyny evident in these detective fictions (the dame may need rescuing, but the detective often feels more sympathetic to Bluebeard) indicates an unwillingness to tinker with the Bluebeard plot much if at all. (Instead, it was in the *noir* films of the first half of the century that the "crime novel" impulse was coupled with a modernist reassessment of gender roles.) In hard-boiled style, Ring Lardner in "Bluebeard" called the wife a "gal" and stated baldly the monetary reason for the marriage alluded to in Perrault: "they was a gal married a rich man named Bluebeard on acct. of he being rich. That was why she married him" (1925, 70).[1]

WOMEN WRITING MODERNIST FABLES

It was in this context of masculinist statements that revise but largely restate the gender issues at the heart of the Bluebeard fairy tale that three women writers interjected their replies. Beatrix Potter's novella *Sister Anne* (1932), Sylvia Townsend Warner's short story "Bluebeard's Daughter" in *The Cat's Cradle-Book* (1940), and Eudora Welty's novella *The Robber Bridegroom* (1942) explicitly addressed the Bluebeard story as a vehicle for commenting on gender relations of the early years of World War II in England and America. At the same time, each used the story as a vehicle for a modernist challenge to the traditional narrative.

Beatrix Potter's gothic horror story emerges from an unlikely frame: two mice beg a story from a third, to feature cats and a cupboard. The result is *Sister Anne*, a fully developed atmospheric novella set in a detailed feudal era, centuries past. Sister Anne is the rescuing heroine; Fatima sends a bird to call her sister, but that is her single act of self preservation. The novella's title is apt, as the focus throughout is on Anne's point of view and on the daily dangers the women face even before Baron Bluebeard gives over his keys to his eighth wife. Even before opening the forbidden chamber, Fatima has succumbed to the grim siege-state of life alone in a crumbling and fetid seaside castle, with no women and no male protectors and obsessively worries that "there are too many windows." In Bluebeard's daily absence, ransacking the region for exorbitant rents and courting his next wife, it is not safe for the women to descend within the castle. The porter-jailer Wolfram sings snatches of a ballad version of "The Twa Sisters," which tells a story of sisterly murder. While the litany of dismemberment reflects the fate Fatima faces, the story is contrasted by Sister Anne's rescue of her sister. Anne takes Bluebeard's keys and refuses to use them, until Bluebeard slips them directly into Fatima's purse. When Fatima opens the cupboard, she faints and does not recover her senses for the remainder of the story. It is through Sister Anne's courage and presence of mind throughout that the sisters survive to escape—and only after a prolonged siege in the upper quarters of the castle. To get her sister to climb up to the turret, Anne has to threaten her with pricks from a knife. As befits a tale told by mice, the sisters' actual rescue hinges not on the beacon Sister Anne has lit, but the third messenger pigeon first surviving the many castle cats and then getting past the falcons who ate the preceding two.

Sylvia Townsend Warner's frame story for "Bluebeard's Daughter," *The Cat's Cradle-Book*, has been used in recent years as an example of gendered modernist fiction and narrative criticism, and in terms of its use of "Bluebeard" is set in direct contrast to the precursor *Duke Bluebeard's Castle*.[2] The lengthy fictional introduction to the collection introduces an unnamed female narrator who understands the language of cats, and overhears one nursing feline mother beginning a story to her kitten reminiscent of one of Aesop's fables. William Farthing, the young man who keeps the cats and has become obsessed with recording their stories, cataloguing variants, and seeking ur-texts, is gently mocked by the female narrator for his approach to the cats as objects of his study: "With the collaboration of your cats? Or are they raw material rather than collaborators?" (1940, 21). His approach and the female narrator's descriptions are insistently masculinist. He does everything "intently" or "intensely." The narrator deliberately behaves "obediently" and draws attention to the constructedness of her response: "I said (hoping that my acceptance might sound sufficiently docile, sufficiently unobtrusive) that I would like to very much" (18). He tried to own and control the cat who was his first love, the Siamese cat Haru (the source for "Bluebeard's Daughter"). Shortly after, the cats all die of a disease, thought to be introduced by Farthing himself; as with Haru, the cats have first been objectified and then accidentally destroyed by the collector. While Farthing's methods are criticized, his discoveries are not: cats rather than humans are the original storytellers (the stories we tell are the stories cats have always told) and stories flow with the mother's milk. They are not, like other high modernist works, "merely works of art" but "nursery tales and education," examples of "the social function of literature" (22).[3] This, then, is the radical freight of the frame story for "Bluebeard's Daughter."

In Haru's short story, Djamileh is the eponymous daughter, a scholar, her mouth utterly blue, and Bluebeard had been a good father to her.[4] After Bluebeard's death, she is taken away by the avaricious Fatima, Ann, and "Uncle" Selim, before being returned to her inheritance by Bluebeard's will and his solicitor. She attempts to study but is not able to attend school, and her success therefore is mixed. When Djamileh marries her husband, Kayel, they explore the castle together (Kayel's delight in its riches echo that of Bluebeard's wives) before discovering a locked door on a hidden hallway with a scroll marked: "Curiosity killed the cat." Djamileh hides the key from Kayel, but both become competitive about which of them will open the door first. Finally, in Djamileh's absence, Kayel breaks open the door. The room was empty, but he fractured his collar bone in the process. Ultimately the couple decides to channel their natural curiosity into useful scientific pursuits: astronomy, to be precise.

The title and treatment of the story both lend themselves to symbolic reading: women are Bluebeard's daughters, marked by their heritage, but they are able to use it productively. The final paragraph of the story notes that

"Bluebeard's daughter is forgotten." Her identity has been subsumed by marriage into "the wife of Kayel the astronomer," whose "sympathetic collaboration" enabled her husband's scholarship. By naming the story after her, Haru (and the female narrator-editor) is unearthing Djamileh's story, yet the burial of the female voice repeats in the frame narrative as the female narrator is unnamed, while William Farthing is memorialized. The frame narrative also serves symbolically: as the stories of women (nursing cats) have been appropriated and told by men (Aesop, Homer, Perrault) they nevertheless thrive and can be recuperated by women (the unnamed female narrator, who becomes the editor), even if it is too late for them to reclaim their subject positions. Recalling that Haru was William Farthing's first and most passionate cat love, the story can be seen to encode a warning from Haru to her male collector of cat stories: in the process of pushing into the rooms of story, he may hurt himself. Better that he channel his interests elsewhere. But from the frame story we have also found that he unwittingly killed his Scheherezade, and later, by virtue perhaps of having collected too many cats, they are subject to the "murrain" or pestilence that kills almost all of the cat colony. In other words, William Farthing's curiosity killed his cats. Yet, Farthing also stated that this story is "the only one transcribed from memory and therefore not authentic" (30).

Like Warner's experimental story collection and its implicit challenge to traditional narrative expectations, Eudora Welty's *The Robber Bridegroom* (1942) performs a generic challenge to fictional and historical realism in its use of the fairy tale for fabulist elements. But unlike Anatole France's ironic undermining of the historian's enterprise in "The Seven Wives of Bluebeard," Welty's makes history and fairy tale into, as she said, "working equivalents," to "bind them together," and make them "interplay" (1975, 13, 18).[5]

In the novella, Rosamond, daughter of the planter Clement Musgrove, is sent out into the dangerous woods by her stepmother Salome, who was hoping to be rid of her. There, Rosamond meets the bandit Jamie Lockhart, his face stained with berry juice to disguise himself.[6] On the first encounter he robs her of her clothing, and when she sets out hoping for a second encounter he kidnaps her and "robbed her of that which he had left her the day before" (Welty 1942, 65). Rosamond sets out to discover his home in the woods and finds it a seat of bandits, warned off by a raven who says: "Turn back, my bonny, / Turn away home" (78); she lives there as the bride of the chief bandit. In the mistaken-identity double plot, after having sex with Rosamond, Jamie (without his berry juice disguise) is invited by Clement Musgrove to dinner. Rosamond does not recognize Jamie without his disguise, and Jamie never recognizes

Rosamond in her Cinderella state. After Rosamond's later abduction, Clement turns to Jamie for help finding his daughter, promising her hand in marriage as reward. Jamie promises reluctantly to help, not realizing that the daughter is in fact his common-law bride in the woods. Jamie's own darker double is Little Harp, one of the historical bandit brothers, who has the talking head of Big Harp locked in a trunk. It is Little Harp who, mistaking an Indian girl for her double Rosamond, enacts the closest parallels with the story of the novel's title: he drugs her, cuts off her finger (which bounces into Rosamond's lap), and rapes and kills her. The absence of any ring on her "wedding finger," the usual motivation for cutting it off in the story, points to the stark cruelty of the act.

The reception of the work was and is still deeply divided, reflecting the hybridity of the work itself.[7] Welty's agent Diarmuid Russell indicated that the publishing climate was inhospitable to "anything that seems out of the way," "everything that does not seem too familiar," "the original" (Marrs 2002, 48). John Peale Bishop, among the first reviewers in 1942, stated "what her tale adds up to, I cannot be sure," and Lionel Trilling in the same year criticized the work for being too self-consciously playful and linked it with similar works by "two other gifted women of our time," implying a gender connection in their "inevitably coy mystification."

In her article, Marilyn Arnold defended the same stylized simplicity criticized by Trilling by arguing a unification of the hybrid elements through parody: "Welty pretends to follow the fairy tale pattern by adopting a simple manner" (1989, 34). The novella "creates standard expectations in the reader; but she does not fulfill them" (33), thereby pointing out how the fairy tale falls short as a vehicle for expressing the complexities of life, or even of great fiction: "Delightful as fairy tales are, they are not great fiction; they are not the stuff life is made of" (33). While the analysis is a tidy one and provided with the caveat that "it is probably the warmest and most loving parody ever written" (37), the reading tries to reconcile the fairy tale elements with those of fictional realism by reading the story as a deliberately "failed" fairy tale, rather than as a modernist hybrid fiction incorporating elements of "fabulous realism," just as Sylvia Townsend Warner had done with her storytelling cats.[8]

Instead, *The Robber Bridegroom* points to the grisly Grimm canon, where robbers in the forest abduct, drug, maim, and kill women. In a darker twist, Rosamond is far from an innocent would-be victim of her robber bridegroom. Although she is hidden when the rape and murder of the Natchez Indian woman by Little Harp occurs, she is willingly living with Jamie in the forest, having sought him out and acquiesced in her own rape/seduction (the two pages preceding the loss of her virginity [65] are a catalog of stereotypical seduction tropes). Rejecting the full implications of the fairy tale elements involves having to deny and misread a good portion of the story.

Nevertheless, at certain moments the narrative tone is ironically distanced from the fairy tale characters' perceptions, as when Rosamond lives with Jamie but continues to be a "raped bride." The novel states: "But when she tried to lead him to his bed with a candle, he would knock her down and out of her senses, and drag her there. However, if Jamie was a thief after Rosamond's love, she was his first assistant in the deed, and rejoiced equally in his good success" (84). The musical stage adaptation by Alfred Uhry (1976) seems to exacerbate these problems. For instance, when Rosamund [*sic*] is robbed of her clothes: "Was you born of a woman? For the sake of your pore mother leave me my drawers. Imagine if somebody'd cum and done this to her." Jamie replies: "She'da loved it. Now gimme them thangs" (32). A major critic wrote in the *New Yorker* in 1976: "if the silent message of 'The Robber Bridegroom' is that women are inferior beings, who require rough handling both mentally and physically in order to become acceptable members of society and who, furthermore, *enjoy* being roughly handled, then I feel obliged to report that this is a very strange message indeed to be hearing in 1976" (Gill 1976, 61).[9]

The novel clearly expresses its generic hybridity, with fairy tale and fantasy on the one hand and historical fact and fictional realism on the other: "it was my firm intention to bind them together" (Welty 1975: 13). This hybridity proved confusing even to Welty's contemporaries familiar with modernist experimentalism. In her address to the Mississippi Historical Society some thirty years later, Welty repeatedly argued that her use of fantasy was necessary to get at the narrative truth of the matter. But the presence of the fairy tale genre serves not simply to provide a meditation on "human motivations" (21) but demonstrates a fruitful integration of "opposites" or doubles, just as the novel also thematizes.[10] The novel's use of the Grimms' fairy tale seems to be to recuperate fairy tale and fantasy as an archetypal narrative form for telling a historical story, as well as for the fairy tale acknowledgment of the dark doubles to life: murder, rape, dismemberment, even genocide. The narrative comment on the moment of taboo and trespass, the Psyche incident in the story, is revealing: "The only thing that could possibly keep her from being totally happy was that she had never seen her lover's face. But then the heart cannot live without something to sorrow and be curious over" (88). The novella's own employment and integration of doubles in the form of narrative genres becomes a demonstration of the heroic: "with the power to look both ways and to see a thing from all sides" (185).

Modern Film

The nature of modern film renditions of "Bluebeard" shifted from light-hearted comedies of the 1920s through a more intricate negotiation in the 1930s to an explosion of dark and complex psychodramas of the 1940s. The "Bluebeard" comedies of the 1920s were light-hearted adaptations usually from stage plays, such as *Bluebeard Jr.* (1922), *Bluebeard's Eighth Wife* (play 1923, film 1938), *Miss Bluebeard* (1925), and *Bluebeard's Seven Wives* (1926). In the play and silent film *Miss Bluebeard*, Bob Talmadge shows up at Larry Charter's apartment with a problem: he has "married" Colette but because he is married already and it was a misunderstanding, he has done so in Larry's name. Colette appears to be at a disadvantage, until it is finally revealed that in fact she had fallen in love with Larry when she nursed him during the war. She met his friends and made a bet (for charity) that he could be prompted to propose to her, which by now he has done. The play's dialogue is witty banter as the proposal shows: "Oh, my dear, marry me. It's the least that a wife can do for her husband" (Hopwood 1923, 68).

In contrast, the comedies of the 1930s depicted a much darker female trickery and were the inheritors of the earlier models by Maeterlinck and Dukas and Balázs and Bartók. In *Love from a Stranger* (1937), based on an Agatha Christie short story, Carol Howard (Ann Harding) marries Gerald Lovell (Basil Rathbone), becoming his eighth wife, after she has won a fortune in the lottery. When her fiancé, Ronnie, returns from the war he is disappointed that she is independently wealthy and doesn't need him. The Lovells buy a country place with Carol's money, but Gerald suffers from headaches and attacks, which appear to derive from shell shock in the Sudan war. The doctor who finally attends to Gerald and diagnoses a myocardial condition notes their shared interest in books of unsolved crimes, and they discuss the case of Fletcher, who has murdered three women. The doctor notes that his edition contains a picture of Fletcher. After Carol has seen the picture and thus realizes that Gerald is in fact Fletcher, the couple share a forced meal, a grim parody of married domesticity. Carol tries to convince Gerald that she is in fact a murderess herself, plying him with brandy and telling him she has poisoned his coffee. Although Ronnie and her former roommate, Kate, break in to rescue her, she has in fact incapacitated Gerald already. When the film was remade in 1947 with Sylvia Sidney and John Hodiak in the lead roles, Carol (now Cecily) is less able to rescue herself, requiring the physical assistance of her jilted fiancé, Nigel, and the Scotland Yard policeman he has enlisted. Her serial wife-murdering husband, Manuel Cortez, almost immediately realizes that she has not drugged his coffee.

Bluebeard's Eighth Wife *(1938)*

The film *Bluebeard's Eighth Wife* (1938), directed by Ernst Lubitsch and starring Claudette Colbert as Nicole and Gary Cooper as Mr. Brandon, is a case in point. The original theatrical trailer revels in the promise of misogyny; the "Method" that is described shows Gary Cooper striding toward the boudoir of Colbert, smashing a vase as he goes, marching in (all accompanied by military music) and, without a word, striking her across the face (the cheek that is slapped faces the camera). In case we missed it, the same is shown a second time, only this time Colbert's reaction (she slaps him back, across his face) is also included.

This moment is representative of the film as a whole. Mr. Brandon has had seven previous wives, has tired of each of them in turn (although one died, "of natural causes"), and has endowed each of them with a handsome pension of $50,000 a year for life. Nicole has fallen for him and is two weeks from the altar before she discovers this background (her future groom's bank account details were much more carefully discovered, by Nicole's father, an impoverished aristocrat), and she decides to beat him at his own game. She plays the game by his rules, but with twists of her own. In the end, Mr. Brandon admits "You win" and agrees to divorce; this has been Nicole's plan all along. Toward the end of the film, Brandon is in a sanatorium for a nervous breakdown and very unhappy (single for the first six-month period in his adult life, we are to understand). Nicole is able to effectively propose to him, no longer a dependent being auctioned off by her father, but "on equal terms" with the groom and having taught him a lesson. She calls this his first real marriage. We are led to understand that Nicole has had this plan in mind ever since she first learned of his previous wives and asks for double the annuity in her prenuptial contract should they ever divorce, and that she married him the first time with the intention to force him to divorce and thereby get his money.

At their first engagement, she turns the table on her mercenary father and she sells herself at auction ("my price goes up every minute"). The marriage march plays twice in the film, first at the wedding photo, the occasion of initial discovery of the problem, and again shortly after Nicole "sells herself" to Brandon. Immediately after the first wedding, however, the march becomes played as an ironic counterpart to the honeymoon woes; it plays as a drunken, wind-instrument underscore to the unhappiness Brandon is suffering at Nicole's neglect. It is implied that she is withholding intimacy; the second ironic echo of the wedding march accompanies the couple passing in *separate* Venetian gondolas. Brandon is buying books to "quieten his nerves," lamenting twice that he wouldn't need to if she would only "be a little nicer" to him. Her superiority at this point in the game, and its mercantile basis, is made clear: she threatens he will have a library of books before long, and says to the bookstore clerk: "charge them to me." That Nicole is having a much better time of it is also made clear at this point. She has made over her boudoir, is "never home before three in the morning," and declares it is wonderful not to be under "parental control" any more. She seems genuinely to be enjoying "stepping out."

But in the process, and despite coming out "on top," Nicole is subjected to several misogynistic impulses. On more than one occasion, Brandon comes close to strangling her. His aim to apply the lessons of *The Taming of the Shrew* (one of the books intended to "quiet his nerves") is ultimately disastrous, but nonetheless shows a certain glee in the attempt. After she has returned his slap across the face, he retires (to subdued martial music) but only to read more of the play, as if he had failed initially to read beyond the salient slap. He returns promptly, to martial music that has a renewed vigor to it, gets into position, and spanks Nicole repeatedly over his knee, announcing "Shakespeare" as he begins. It is not the last time in the film that Nicole's shrieks ("No, Michael, stop! Please!") are ignored and even used to heighten the comedy of the scene. The overt transaction between the father and Michael that has been grounded in financial terms now has other overtones; "out from paternal control" means that Nicole is delivered to the hands of her husband, who can put her over his knee like a child and spank her, to teach her a lesson. Again, however, Brandon's attempts are shown to be disastrous; we see him, disheveled, burning the Shakespeare book, and having iodine applied to his knee (reversing the parental overtones) as Nicole cheerfully admits she is happy to do this whenever she has bitten somebody.

Despite having come to an agreement ("no lovemaking, no quarrels"), the pair find themselves in the very next scene on the way to a repetition of this dynamic, which is the basic pattern of the film. He assaults (this time with alcohol, and his seduction is obvious even to Nicole, yet she is tricked into drinking more than she thinks she ought to); she is initially at a disadvantage and repeatedly tells him "No"; she comes to an advantage (she eats onions, to foil his planned kiss); he retaliates (calling her an animal, and puts his hands around her throat, asking "Why don't I?"); she seems to have triumphed, laughing at him ("I'm your worst investment . . . It's a holdup"); he counters ("My fundamental characteristic is tenacity") and threatens bodily violence again (I could "crush you like a matchbox . . . These walls are pretty thick"), and she ultimately wins.

In every scene, it is Nicole's cunning that is foregrounded, even as she is shown having to fight dirty to teach her husband to respect her as an opponent.

She outsmarts Brandon's hired detective, following him as he followed her, and threatening him with information that would have him at the mercy of his own shrew of a wife (she has a "vile temper"). This final episode of the besieged marriage plays out to the point where Brandon threatens "I'll kill you" but then quickly capitulates, "You win." It seems that if Bluebeard is not prepared to murder, then he will lose.

The film's conclusion, where Nicole proposes to Brandon, her ex-husband, contains the essential motifs. She is again traveling with her father, underscoring the father-husband-father transactions that have occurred. Nicole is unable to talk her way into the sanatorium and is repelled at the door by a nurse. The father uses cunning to get what he wants and then money (he buys the sanatorium so that she may enter it). That the money comes from the Brandon settlement is not merely ironic, but necessary to Nicole's plan that she be Brandon's equal before their marriage can really work. The father's comic interruptions assist in undermining the romanticism that the film has consistently resisted, but that has become a more pressing demand here at the film's romantic conclusion. Brandon is reduced to a straitjacket, protecting Nicole from him, but also putting him in her power, as she acknowledges. Three times in this section the father puts his head through the door, looks in the room, and says "Nothing" before leaving. The *King Lear* reference is not, as we have seen, the only Shakespeare quoted or ironically misquoted in this film. But Cordelia's famous refusal to quantify her love for her father, refusing outright the financial terms, "no-thing," on which the negotiations between the daughters and their father the king are turning, is here reversed. Nicole's father happily "sold" her to Brandon, and his primary motives seem to have been financial all along. When Nicole initially stalled on her marriage, there is a scream offstage, and mention of a "fainting spell"; amusingly, it is then the father who is carried in in a dead faint, not Nicole. Brandon is taught a lesson, but Nicole's father is relegated to the shadow of paternity. The last time he peers in the door he seems to be checking in to make sure his daughter is not being hurt by Brandon and finds them in something of an embrace (at which point he says "Nothing" and again retires). But since Brandon has struggled out of his straightjacket and his arms are in fact around Nicole's neck, the "embrace" could have been misinterpreted by a more fastidious father.

Bluebeard Psychodramas: Films of the 1940s

The 1940s saw a remarkable number of films participating in intertextual dialogue with the Bluebeard story. Yet with the exception of a strained Buster

Keaton comedy *Boom in the Moon* (a Spanish-language film in which he is mistaken for a Señor Bluebeard, and whose estranged wife shows up in the end to harangue him straight into prison), they overwhelmingly favor the psychological and cinematic devices of a subclass of women's film: the paranoid gothic. The term "women's film" groups a subset of films linked in their tendency to feature a woman as the main character and make some attempt to represent her point of view; they presuppose a female audience. The genres of film that offer examples of women's film include horror, *noir*, family melodrama, and feminist drama.[11] Mary Ann Doane, who dedicated a chapter to the "paranoid gothic" subclass of the women's film in the 1940s that coincides entirely with the list here, did not use the "Bluebeard" model for discussing the fact that the secret usually kept is one of wife murder, the "existence of a room to which the woman is barred access" (1987, 134), and the debated field being one of vision: "A crucial premise of the films is thus aligned with the very signifying material of the cinema and manifests itself as a crisis of vision in relation to sexuality: Is the husband really what he appears to be?" (124).[12] The woman's point of view is selectively limited, thus keeping the audience in the paranoid state with her as she attempts to discover the truth about the man she is with. At the same time, her own sanity or reasoning is frequently suspect: madness and neuroses are endemic to the subgenre.[13]

The persistence of the story in this medium in the 1940s was dubbed "the Bluebeard cycle" of films by Maria Tatar, who wrote that they seem to be as much in dialogue with each other as with the fairy tale, and that they are in direct opposition to the alternative prevailing fairy tale Hollywood models of "Cinderella" and "Beauty and the Beast," which played out in the 1930s comedies of remarriage.[14] At the same time in the 1940s context, it is important to note that these women's films play against the dominant *film noir* depiction of women as killers themselves: the "*femme fatale*" or "super-bitch killer beauties" (Frigon 2006, 17).

The films in the cycle include *Rebecca* (1940); *Suspicion* (1941); *Shadow of a Doubt* (1943); *Dark Waters* (1944); *Experiment Perilous* (1944); *Gaslight* (1944); *Jane Eyre* (1944); *Phantom of the Plains* (1945); *Spellbound* (1945); *Dragonwyck* (1946); *Hiss and Yell* (1946); *The Madonna's Secret* (1946), a remake of Ulmer's *Bluebeard* (1944) in which Bluebeard is *not* guilty; *Notorious* (1946); *Undercurrent* (1946); the remake of *Love from a Stranger* (1947); *Monsieur Verdoux* (1947); *The Two Mrs. Carrolls* (1947); *Secret Beyond the Door* (1948); and *Caught* (1949). In addition to the many Academy Award wins and nominations signified by this list and the draw of Alfred Hitchcock as a director of several of them,[15] the actors in this nexus of films represent the stars of the decade, many in repeating performances. The preponderance of successful leading men illustrates that these Bluebeards are of the operatic ilk, dignified and brooding, post–Balázs and Bartók. John Carradine, for instance, was cast in the role when Ulmer filmed *Bluebeard* in 1944 for PRC, a poverty-row studio infamous for churning out a massive number of films a year and where Ulmer himself was famous for his six-day shoots.[16] Carradine had a bizarre reputation, but he was fresh from a very successful performance in *Hamlet*. In *Bluebeard* he is dignified, brooding, artistic, and sexually betrayed. His first love, Jeanette, his painterly inspiration, cheated on him; he is compelled to kill women once he has painted them in spite of himself, in a futile effort to kill Jeanette symbolically. The film's approach made manifest what is latent in other films of the 1940s: that the killer (or suspected killer) is depicted with some compassion and by a well-known star. In the case of Cary Grant as Johnnie in *Suspicion*, the change in the ending from novel to the film was made in accordance with Grant's contract, to preserve the actor's reputation. In Frances Iles' novel *Before the Fact*, on which the film was based, wealthy wife Lina accedes to her own murder out of guilt for emasculating her gambling husband, Johnnie, and does so when she becomes pregnant, refusing to allow a monstrous duplication. While the novel firmly held Lina's point of view, the film ending has Johnnie explain himself and Lina does not die. However, when the car turns around, signifying a return to their marital home, the ending is torturous enough: Lina is going home with someone who still *may* be a murderer (Lina never drank the glass of milk she supposed to have been poisoned, and the death of Johnnie's friend remains suspicious), but who is *definitely* an abusive, lying, and callous husband.[17]

The Bluebeards themselves thus belie external demarcation as a murderer. They are stars, debonair and well-groomed charmers. The police ask in Ulmer's *Bluebeard* whether anyone in the crowd looks "unusual"; instead, the killer is hiding in plain sight as the puppeteer who has drawn the crowd in the first place. Charlie Chaplin transformed himself from the "baggy, comic character" into the extremely dapper serial wife killer Henri Verdoux for his black comedy *Monsieur Verdoux*.

As external objective sources of information prove untrustworthy, the other source of evidence foregrounded in these films is psychology, a popular theme in the 1940s Hollywood films in general. Further, the gothic genre on which these films draw uses madness as an endemic theme. In many cases Bluebeard is mad, and the investigative heroine must rescue herself with recourse to psychological investigations. *Spellbound* is set in an asylum, and Constance must "open the doors" in the mind of the amnesiac Anthony Edwardes/John Ballantyne to discover what horror he is hiding from himself. In *Experiment Perilous* the rescuer is a psychologist, and Nick Bedereaux tries to convince him that his wife Allida requires observation for the protection of their son, while in fact it is Nick himself, as the psychologist states: "You're mad, Nick. Completely mad." The insanity of Mr. Carroll in *The Two Mrs. Carrolls* is masked from his wife for most of the film by the expected quirks of an artistic genius, but the viewer sees him put hand to head repeatedly throughout the film. Finally his second wife must confront his condition and tells him: "You're sick!" Fritz Lang's *Secret Beyond the Door* is another quintessential expression of the "mad Bluebeard." The novel used for the adaptation, *Museum Piece No. 13* by Rufus King, makes the psychological investigation apparent: "I must cure him, Lily thought. I must help him all I can" (1946, 64). To do so, she is in frequent telephone contact with a psychiatrist. The novel makes overdetermined reference to the Bluebeard story to "diagnose" the situation as well. Lily goes to the library and finds that her husband has "gone in for the fable rather extensively" (182). Reading the tale, she makes the connections with her own situation.

Alternatively, in the course of being manipulated through fear, it is the paranoid heroine's sanity at issue. *Gaslight* foregrounds this as the Bluebeard figure (Gregory Anton) spends much of the film attempting to make his wife Paula believe she is insane, but other films in the cycle also question the heroine's sanity albeit, as in *Experiment Perilous*, as a red herring. In *Dark Waters* Leslie already suffers from a nervous condition after having survived a shipwreck and a lifeboat trauma that killed her parents. At the crucial point in the film, Dr. Grover pretends not to believe her, writing her a prescription and telling her to get some sleep (the "prescription," however, contains a note from him). In *Caught*, Leonora is prevented from sleeping while she is pregnant, and she is found in a nearly catatonic state and miscarries.

The films illustrate suspense: "suspicion," "doubt," and "undercurrent." Without depiction of a woman's corpse, the emphasis must remain on the female investigator who has no certain proof of a Bluebeard and therefore must look for evidence from other sources. The external, official, "verifiable" sources of information: newspaper, radio, poster, police, inevitably fail, as in the gothic. Bluebeard's wives do enjoy investigative pleasures, and they do rescue themselves, but not until after it has been demonstrated that no other form of rescue will be forthcoming. Police in Ulmer's *Bluebeard* set up a sting but are then unable to prevent their decoy from being killed, along with the man sent to protect her and tip off the police. In *Shadow of a Doubt*, Uncle Charlie is forced to elaborate lengths to take the section of family newspaper that would betray him, yet the police prematurely close the case by believing the real murderer has already been caught "out east." In spite of being courted and escorted by a detective on the case, his niece Charlie is personally endangered by what she knows.

As we have seen with Georges Méliès' film (*Barbe-bleue* 1901), it was immediately apparent that the Bluebeard story was particularly apt for film adaptation, and that a certain degree of spectator self-reflexivity is guaranteed by it. The film's audience is looking at the consequences of looking; the image of the hanged women would have been almost as shocking to the "defamiliarized" audience as it was to Bluebeard's wife. From early film examples, then, the Bluebeard story expresses not just audience anxieties about marriage, self-perpetuating secrets, prying wives, and murdering husbands, but also of depiction of the female body (alive and singular, dead and multiple) and issues of spectatorship, subjectivity, and the gaze. Bluebeard cinema is metacinema by definition. But in the Méliès adaptation, as in Perrault's fairy tale, the "Bluebeard" fairy tale illustrates *horror*. While suspense is present for the viewers who have expectations about what they will see when the wife opens the bloody chamber, the wife herself does not. Instead, she is rather suddenly horrified by the gruesome spectacle, and suspense (of her husband's return) is very brief as he arrives home that very evening, "unexpectedly." By striking contrast, the "Bluebeard" films of the 1940s *lack* the bloody chamber. The dead female body is absent, and although she haunts the film the possibility persists that she does not exist at all. While the bodies and wounds reappear with deliberate excess in the later twentieth-century "Bluebeard" films participating in the serial-killer genre, the 1940s paranoid gothic women's films are psychodramas first and foremost because the bodies are hidden.[18]

The modern woman posed an even greater threat to Bluebeard's authority and his patriarchal chambers, and the response of modern Bluebeards was correspondingly severe. Bluebeard's wife insists on her rights of access to patriarchal institutions, now to include her husband's own mind. Alongside depictions of the wife as a forthright new feminist, then, is a gallery of dangerously damaged men, with implications of a causal connection. The crisis of Bluebeard is rendered as a crisis of masculinity, the latest and most vehemently defended preserve.

Chapter 10

Contemporary Bluebeard

Bluebeard proliferated throughout the latter half of the twentieth century. As the protagonist of Loren Keller's novel *Four and Twenty Bluebeards* writes, "there was plenty of room in the 'postmodern' world, or any other, for my twenty-four versions" (1999, 257). In the contemporary landscape, these versions are simultaneous with one another. Charles Ludlam's avant-garde play *Bluebeard* (1987) features a Bluebeard who is part mad-scientist, part "Turk" (2.9), and it is set in part to Béla Bartók's music from the opera *Duke Bluebeard's Castle*. As Charles Dickens predicted, the "counterfeits" have taken the field.

"Bluebeard" works in the latter half of the twentieth century make full use of the tale's self-reflexivity, enhancing it through postmodern techniques.[1] As in the case of Keller's protagonist, who spends a "Bluebeard summer" acting the role of Bluebeard in George Bernard Shaw's play *St. Joan* and whose personal life becomes embroiled by living with a dyed beard for the duration of the run, the tale's characters become self-aware. The earlier one-act comedy *Bluebeard Had a Wife* (1957) resembles every other Victorian amateur production in every way, including slapstick (with a dead fish). However, in addition to a forbidden "cabinet," the tyrant Bluebeard also keeps a forbidden book, his memoirs: "BLUEBEARD (smiles contentedly as he reads aloud): 'There was a man who had fine houses, both in town and country, a deal of silver and gold plate, embroidered furniture, and coaches gilded all over. This man was so unusual as to have a blue beard—(He strokes his beard admiringly.)—which made all the townsfolk run away from him.' (He chuckles at the thought)" (Kelly 1957, 11).[2] The climactic revelation is in fact accomplished first with Anne suspensefully reading aloud from the book: The wife recognizes that "those are the very words he spoke to me" (18). When Anne reads aloud the discovery of the bloody chamber, the cook faints. Even in juvenile literature, postmodern self-reflexivity is the norm. In the illustrated children's book *The Three Naughty Sisters Meet Bluebeard* (Capdevila 1986), the sisters are sent back into story land by the Witch, help the wife open the forbidden door (discovering Bluebeard behind it), decide to trick Bluebeard, and save his wife. Under threat of crocodiles, they realize they can alter the story they are in and take an eraser to the crocodiles, thus defeating both Bluebeard and the Witch.

In addition to making the story the subject, these referential texts play cat-and-mouse games with the reader, foregrounding the reader's own complicity and processes in reading intertextually. The story is not only *about* Bluebeard; the story *is* Bluebeard. The text is Bluebeard's castle, while the act of reading is thereby allied with the wife's simultaneous acts of investigating and transgressing. Such is the case, for instance, with Donald Barthelme's story "Bluebeard" (1987), which continually thwarts the reader's intertextual presuppositions, and with Max Frisch's novel *Bluebeard: A Tale* (1982).[3] The pattern is characterized in "Bluebeard's Second Wife" by Susan Fromberg Schaeffer, in which the reader is first reassured: "you know all about the castle" (1988, 571) and then told there is a secret chamber nonetheless: "Of course, you think you know what happened next" (573). Méira Cook's story "Instructions for Navigating the Labyrinth" (1993) also sustains the conceit: it is fragmented and combines different genres within the story: riddles, direct address to the reader, and a Bluebeard story, all of which are interconnected through the reader. The story here is malevolent: a labyrinth that is impossible to escape: "How do you enter the labyrinth? / Reader, turn left turn left turn left" (107). Again, as in "Bluebeard's Second Wife," it encourages the reader to make equations with the Bluebeard story specifically in order to thwart them: "You know the rest" (108). At the same time, the text is informing the reader throughout that it is doing so: "This is the story of a red-herring so that you will recognize one the next time it swims past" (111).

This chapter charts the contemporary forms "Bluebeard" has adopted in the (now much broader) Anglophone tradition. As has been seen, self-reflexivity often takes the form of Bluebeard as an artist, writer, photographer, or art collector. By actualizing these self-reflexive gestures, postmodern texts explore various crises of artistic representation, most often around the display of murdered female bodies and the act of looking, as seen in Kurt Vonnegut's novel *Bluebeard* (1987). The contemporary tendency to self-reflexivity has been put to extremely productive use in feminist works using the Bluebeard story to challenge cultural assumptions about gender, violence, and artistic representation. The tradition of self-reflexivity inherent in depicting Bluebeard on film is also used to challenge traditional genre representations and constructions of the gaze, as seen in *The Silence of the Lambs* (1991) and *The Piano* (1993) to be discussed at greater length. Finally, the contemporary women writers Margaret Atwood and Angela Carter both return repeatedly to the Bluebeard story in their various works, as did Thackeray and Dickens in the nineteenth century. They also rewrite the tale, reflecting a feminist focus. Underscoring this, there has been a notable shift in the direction of Grimm variants and "Mr. Fox" with their tropes of dismemberment and cannibalism, but also female trickery and self- and "sister"-rescue.[4]

Self-Reflexive Artistry

Of course, more than simply a collector of women, Bluebeard has always been an "artist." While his grand house features gilded mirrors rather than paintings, foreshadowing the nature of his artistry, Charles Perrault's Bluebeard crafted the tableau of dead wives in the "forbidden" chamber presupposing a specific spectator: his transgressing wife.[5] He has deliberately crafted a *tableau mort* to reflect the living wife who will soon become part of the image she has seen, claimed by this uncanny mirror. He tells the wife: "as you have seen, so shall you be," transforming female spectator into "spectacle." The tale is thus predisposed to self-reflexivity and the use of mirrors and doubling, as well as the double and self-contradicting *moralités*, indicate that Perrault himself actualized this metadiscursive potential. Considering murder as death artistry is a common metaphor. Contemporary depictions of serial killers as death artists[6] owe a debt to writers such as Thomas de Quincey's "On Murder as Fine Art" and to the Marquis de Sade (whose novel *Justine* [1778] alludes to Bluebeard by name), as much as to the procedural relationship whereby the killer shapes the corpse tableau for the detective to analyze.

It is a short step from there to make Bluebeard an actual artist of some kind in addition to his tableau creation, further enhancing the tale's self-reflexive possibilities. The Victorians were familiar with referring to Bluebeard as a collector. As the song "Oh! Mr. Bluebeard" put it: "Now some collectors hunt for gems, / Others for guns and knives, / Pictures or lamps or slippers or stamps, / But he collected wives" (Chapin [1910], n.p.). In the English variant "Bloudie Jacke" (1842), recorded by the Victorians, the Shropshire Bluebeard is a cultured figure whose ladyfingers figure among Rembrandts and other rare pieces of art. The woman's intrusion seems uncultured:

She roams o'er your Tower by herself;
She runs through, very soon,
Each boudoir and saloon,
And examines each closet and shelf, Your pelf,

All your plate, and your china—and delf.
She looks at your Arras so fine, Bloudie Jacke!
So rich, all description it mocks;
And she now and then pauses
To gaze at the vases,
Your pictures, and or-molu clocks;
Every box,
Every cupboard, and drawer she unlocks (203).

In the twentieth century in particular, Bluebeard emerges not just as an art collector but as an artist in his own right. The 1949 Avon cover of Ward Greene's novel *Lives and Loves of a Modern Mister Bluebeard* (1930) depicts an artist drawing a woman who is naked from the waist up, herself tied to an easel, mirroring a scene in the novel in which the model finally faints, unnoticed by the artist. In the 1947 film *The Two Mrs. Carrolls,* one of the 1940s "Bluebeard cycle" of films,[7] Humphrey Bogart plays an insane Bluebeard figure who paints his best work when he has decided to kill the woman who is its muse. The painting "The Angel of Death" representing his first wife hangs ominously over the mantle in the home he shares with his second wife. He tells the second Mrs. Carroll, once he has completed his skeletal painting of her and has resolved to kill her in favor of another: "You made my work live again. Now there's nothing more from *you*. So I must find someone new." In Edgar Ulmer's film *Bluebeard* (1944), Bluebeard is a painter and puppet maker, and one of his paintings is taken into court to be analyzed: to discover its artist is to discover the murderer.

Three later twentieth-century works in particular demonstrate the critical exploration of representational practices at work when Bluebeard is a visual artist. Edward Dmytryk's film *Bluebeard* (1972) thematizes photography and plays cinematically with the viewing audience. Kurt Vonnegut's novel *Bluebeard* (1987) deconstructs both realism and abstract expressionism, attempting to arrive at a postmodern theory of art that can express humanism. Cindy Sherman's photographs in *Fitcher's Bird* (1992) invite spectators to be self aware in their role in relation to the photography that is viewed.

Dmytryk: Bluebeard *(1972)*

Edward Dmytryk's film *Bluebeard* depicts Baron Kurt von Sepper (Richard Burton) as an artist whose images derive from photography. He photographs women's faces when they are dead and traces them into unrecognizable intri-

Avon cover (1949) for Ward Greene's *Life and Loves of a Modern Mister Bluebeard* (1930). Bluebeard has often been identified with an artist, creating a tableau of women for other women to see. Copyright © 1930 by Ward Greene. Avon reprint edition copyright © 1948 by Avon Publishing Co., Inc. Reprinted by permission of HarperCollins Publishers.

cate line drawings. The face is so embedded that the image is on public display in his mansion. The serial murder of his wives is represented in the film by increasing the number of pictures on the wall in a series of brief, juxtaposed shots. The women incorporated in them are not shown until much later in the film, as flashbacks. In some scenes the baron or his housekeeper is able to watch the new wife looking quizzically at the image: a face looks at a face through a face; the last wife Anne comes face to face with her likeness even before she opens the forbidden chamber.

Through the perspective of the last wife Anne, the secret chamber is finally depicted. The entrance is through a life-sized hunting portrait of the baron and this reveals a room that is a freezer. The baron's wives are literally frozen within this room. The act of opening the door triggers a hidden camera to photograph the evidence of transgression; first the frozen image is formed, then the women are frozen into these images. The baron takes Anne into the darkroom to show her the photograph of herself that he has developed, inviting her to see herself as he sees her. Again the film's representation of this image is redoubled, by virtue of Anne's previous discovery of a room filled with headless dressmaker's mannequins from whom these frozen women are at first indistinguishable.

The film is self-aware and even parodic to an extent. The casting and frequent nudity of the international female stars was contrived to fulfill foreign distribution requirements. The murder of the first wife for her incessant singing ("How else could I shut her up?") is followed by other overdetermined motivations. Raquel Welch plays a chaste nun who, once she has agreed to marry the Baron von Sepper, disburdens herself of an endless confession of male lovers accompanied by an increasing state of lurid undress, driving von Sepper to shut *her* up in a coffin. Yet the brash Anne, played by Joey Heatherton, who attends his funeral with the gold key prominently around her neck, is unable to rescue herself (she requires help) despite buying time for rescue by trying to get her husband to talk himself into a cure. In a psychoanalytic echo of Scheherezade's role, she will be killed at dawn but she prompts him to heal himself by telling her everything in flashback of his previous wives. By analyzing his pattern, she diagnoses him contemptuously. He is unaware of his own impotence and the fact that he kills his wives at the point when they demand a sexual relationship.

The choice of photographer-artist for von Sepper is interesting given his choice of forbidden chamber, which is the freezer. The frozen image is represented multiple times in the film. These are the forms of the baron's death artistry, effectively set in contrast with the moving image that is embedding all these representations. The film outlives the baron; just as Anne was shown from behind, photographed in the moment of transgressing, she is again shown from behind as she walks away from the baron lying dead (and posed) at his funeral.

Yet for all its domestic focus, the film attempts to depict a broader ramification of von Sepper's cruelty and impotence. It is implied that his impotence derives from his wartime experience. He is depicted as a returning war hero at the outset of the film and his blue beard is the result of being shot down and burned. Called to one of his honeymoon beds, he faints and is put to bed by the doctor instead, who insists on the rest that all war heroes deserve. His impotence and its wartime cause are inextricable. Further, the way he speaks about women as monsters who "only began to look human when they were dead" objectifies them in ways linked with his anti-Semitic politics. Thus, although he is incapable of seeing the connection, von Sepper's Nazism and his order to raze a Jewish quarter sow the seeds of his downfall by the hand of a man whose parents were killed. The depiction of the holocaust does more than extend von Sepper's characterization. True to the trope, the last wife survives Bluebeard's attempts to freeze her in (his) frame; by spilling out from the embedded flashbacks into the present, in which the baron is killed and Anne is saved, the film both depicts images of holocaust and yet does not contain them. The survivors (Anne and the unnamed Jewish man) are allied with the moving image itself.

Vonnegut: Bluebeard *(1987)*

Depicting Bluebeard as a photographer in a film gives rise to self-reflexive commentary on the art of representation. Using an abstract expressionist painter, Rabo Karabekian, as the main character for his novel *Bluebeard* (1987), Kurt Vonnegut provided a metaphor for his own artistic engagement. Karabekian's house guest, Circe Berman, tells him his art is solipsistic: "What's the point of being alive . . . if you're not going to *communicate?*" (35, original emphasis). This criticism prompts Karabekian to open up his secret museum in the potato barn. Here, he has locked away a large painting depicting the "unutterable" sight as he saw it on D-Day, May 8, 1945. The painting is called "Renaissance" and it unites representational realism with his previous abstract expressionist works.

The novel comprises a debate between the ancients and the moderns as well, in the form of mimetic realism on the one hand and abstract expressionism (and modern art in general) on the other. Karabekian, a child of Armenian refugees, a seventy-one-year-old painter and art collector, began his artistic career apprenticed to a fascist "Bluebeard," Dan Gregory. Gregory's thinly disguised fascist sympathies are made analogous to his photorealistic art. Gregory's art uses realism as a weapon and repels the spectator. He is an admirer and advocate of Mussolini who would, he says, "burn down the Museum of Modern Art and outlaw the word *democracy*" (132). Rabo Karabekian's father says of a camera: "all it caught was dead skin and toenails and hair which people long gone had left behind" (76). By making his art camera-like, Gregory is likewise a brilliant "taxidermist" (82). He is further linked with Bluebeard in that his house has a Gorgon-head knocker on the front door and eight human skulls on one of the mantles. The photographs of his wife, Marilee, in which she is posed and costumed in different ways renders her unrecognizable to Karabekian, who sees her in Gregory's paintings as "nine different women" (77).

If Dan Gregory is Bluebeard, Karabekian is his apt apprentice. He tells his house guest Circe Berman: "'I am Bluebeard, and my studio is my *forbidden chamber,* as far as *you're* concerned'" (46, original emphasis). Now writing his autobiography in his Long Island gallery/mansion, under Berman's tutelage, he is undergoing his second resurrection. Karabekian's description of his career illustrates a layered process through at least three discernible and distinct phases, each expressed by an artistic work on the exact same canvas at three different times. After mimetic realism, the second represents abstract expressionism. The third, entitled "Renaissance," is a new communicative act for Karabekian, despite its being locked in the potato barn that Circe is forbidden to enter.

Karabekian's own talent as a "camera" (44) who can "capture the likeness of anything [he could] see" (43, 236) remains his hidden "reserve" when he turns to the new school of abstract expressionism, which prevents these works from being the form of expression he is hoping for. In the orange field titled "Hungarian Rhapsody," Karabekian first sketches a caricature of his friend intended to display his talents, but this face remains and reemerges after the demise of the painting, when the paint flakes off the canvas. In attempting to escape history by painting over it, he has only achieved a camouflage. Even the seven strips of tape on this orange canvas are not the "pure abstraction" (256) that they masquerade as. To Karabekian they "secretly" represent six deer in a glade and the lone hunter who has them in his sights (256). Like Gregory's art, which is antagonistic to the viewer because of the absoluteness of the mimetic vision, these abstract expressionist works are "*meant* to be uncommunicative" (35, original emphasis). The works produce responses like the following, from Karabekian's cook: "They just don't *mean* anything to me . . . I'm sure that's because I'm uneducated. Maybe if I went to college, I would finally realize how wonderful they are" (127).

The third painting is a "Renaissance" (265) in that it involves a turning away from the self-sufficient forms of either photographic realism or abstract expressionism and is instead an attempt to communicate. It depicts representative humanity in 5219 figures in a D-Day vision of survivorhood. David Rampton contrasted this with Bluebeard's art in his comments on Vonnegut's novel: "In Bluebeard's secret chamber is death; in Rabo's, a painting that depicts life and death, the survivors of a six-year nightmare of bloodletting caused by people who make Bluebeard look like Mr. Rogers" (1993, 22). There is a story for every figure, but after the barn is opened to the public, as the painting already in a sense has been, the painting becomes "activated." This signals Karabekian's return to a world of community and communication after his seclusion. The painting's name also signals return: "Now It's the Women's Turn." Lawrence Broer interpreted this in the context of the Bluebeard story: "By contrast to the obscenely destructive male of the seventeenth-century tale by Charles Perrault, Rabo notes that it is the female of the species who plants the seeds of something beautiful and edible" (1989, 168). Like Karabekian, Broer was quoting Marilee's comparison of men planting mines and women planting seed. Earlier, Gregory's wife Marilee summed up abstract expressionism as a male artistry about "The End." In turning back from the end, this work is a turning back on the threshold of Bluebeard's chamber. Karabekian's "forgiveness" is opening his work to the viewer: "'Make up your own stories as you look at the watchamacallit'" (270).

Sherman: Fitcher's Bird *(1992)*

The book of Cindy Sherman photographs *Fitcher's Bird* is self-reflexive, like all of her photography, in which she tends to serve as both photographer and subject. But like the fictive painter Karabekian, she actively separates her pieces from overdetermination by the artist in order to open them up to reader's narrative engagement with them.[8] She does not title the majority of her photographs; even one of the History Portraits depicting her posing as Judith of Holofernes is untitled (#228). Sherman's gestures are highly postmodern: rejection of genre stratifications, use of borrowing and pastiche, and use of photographic medium to create nonphotographic art (confounding "high" art culture of painting with traditionally "low" genre photography). At the same time, what Sherman represents throughout her work is the female body. Sherman's artistry enlists the viewer to acknowledge objectification of the image by oscillating back and forth over the surface/depth schism.[9] Sherman's photographs are not static but filmic and narrative. She repeatedly stresses the narrative engagement the photographs encourage of the spectators. The role of the camera (and thus the location and directing of the spectator's gaze) in her work is immediately self-reflexive in a way that a novelistic description of a painting is not and works to deconstruct the camera's construction of gaze. Her work then functions less as model of static visual art than as a useful feminist deconstruction of what is at work in mainstream filmic representations of women's bodies.

Fitcher's Bird is representative of her work on the female body in that it uses dolls, masks, and medical prosthetics, Sherman's favorite props when she is not herself deliberately masquerading as the model. The photographs of the *Fitcher's Bird* series feature high-key lighting and vivid color saturation. The grotesque is juxtaposed throughout with the pathetic, whether it is in the form of the grubby fingers and dirty feet next to pristine hands and shiny eggs, or the contrast between viewing Fitcher seen from an extremely low angle as a predator or the second time from above, reflecting the power shift as he struggles to carry the basket hiding one of the sisters inside back to their parents' house. In all cases the frame is filled with close-ups and extreme close-ups: there is no comfortable distance from which to assume the role of a passive spectator. The artistically decorated skull with jewels is suspiciously clean and fresh looking next to the dirty, hairy, and sweaty figures who are "alive"; the irony is that Sherman's pristine "art" is prepared to get dirty. The choice of "Fitcher's Bird" also highlights a shift in focus to female artistry and its role as a strategy for self-rescue, and both the feathered bird and the decorated skull are appropriately two of Sherman's set pieces.

Feminist Revisionism

In 1961, Sara Henderson Hay's poem "Syndicated Column" targeted traditional gender platitudes through ironic use of a traditional genre and using an even more traditional poetic form, the sonnet:

Dear Worried: Your husband's actions aren't unique,
His jealousy's a typical defence.
He feels inadequate; in consequence,
He broods. (My column, by the way, last week
Covered the subject fully.) I suggest
You reassure him; work a little harder
To build his ego, stimulate his ardor.
Lose a few pounds, and try to look your best.

As for his growing a beard, and dyeing it blue,
Merely a bid for attention; nothing wrong with him.
Stop pestering him about that closet, too.
If he wants to keep it locked, why, go along with him.
Just be the girl he married; don't nag, don't pout.
Cheer up. And let me know how things work out.

While feminist treatment of the Bluebeard tale is arguably embedded within the variants themselves, with "trickster" women figures like Scheherezade and all the women who rescue themselves through wit, courage, and trickery, it was an increasingly insistent phenomenon through the course of the twentieth century to take the fairy tale and retell it, further privileging the woman's own agency and empowering her within a format that has, like Hay's "Syndicated Column" writer, enculturated girls into subservience, silence, and passivity. Traditional and misogynist forms do persist. Alongside Bluebeards for mature readers in the three-part *Bluebeard* comic series by James Robinson (1993) and illustrated by Phil Elliott[10] is the Mills and Boon/Harlequin romance version of the tale: *Bluebeard's Bride* (Holland 1985).[11] These are the two sides of the same cultural coin, as Fay Weldon wittily indicated: "The transformation from ugly duckling to swan fills the prepubertal child with unreasonable hope. After the wintry ice of rejection, the warmth of sun and acceptance will surely come. Well, perhaps, and hi there, Mr. Fox" (1998, 330).

Like Hays' poem, in the short stories by Shirley Jackson, "The Honeymoon of Mrs. Smith" (in two versions) thought to have been written in the 1960s, the reader is invited through tragic irony to share the intertextual secret. The two stories are most interesting for being two complete versions of the story by the same author, neither of which was previously published. In each, Mrs. Smith has married a man, strongly suspected of drowning six previous wives in the bathtub and burying them in the cellar, on very little acquaintance. All the townsfolk are aware of her precarious position. In each version, however, the treatment is radically different. In "Version I" the townsfolk gossip about her but seem paralyzed and unable to talk to her about their suspicions, except for her downstairs neighbour whose concerns the wife dismisses as macabre fancy. The reader becomes aware of the wife's predicament, but—as is the case with tragic irony—she never does. In "Version II: The Mystery of the Murdered Bride," however, the townsfolk are unable to warn the wife of her predicament because she is perfectly well aware of it, having recognized the man from the moment he sat down beside her. But in this case, the irony is that foreknowledge has contributed nothing. She is fatalistic, complicit, seeing her election as inevitable destiny. Despite "seeing then the repeated design which made the complete pattern" this wife maintains "tactful respect for her husband's methods" (83) and awareness of the role she is expected to play in the tragedy: "Everyone is waiting; it will spoil everything if it is not soon" (87). At the end of the story it is Helen prompting her nearly reluctant husband: "'Well?' 'I suppose so,' Mr. Smith said, and got up wearily from the couch" (88).

With metafictional techniques, the reader is invited more directly into the intertextual situation. In "Bluebeard's Second Wife," the reader is told: "Reader, if you find that castle, if you hear the voice of many women laughing, do not go in" (Schaeffer 1988, 578). In A. S. Byatt's "The "Story of the Eldest Princess," the narrator states just as baldly: "Keep away from the Woodcutter, if you value your life" (1992, 22). But the advice to avoid Bluebeards is ignored by the protagonists who are, like Mrs. Smith, increasingly self-aware but also empowered to alter the pattern instead of submitting to it. As in Byatt's story, the postmodern self-awareness of Bluebeard's survivors extends to awareness of the story they are in. Just as the princess says, "I am in a pattern I know" (16), the Bluebeard women know the pattern they are "caught" in. In Dora Knez's *Five Forbidden Things* (2000) another "Bluebeard's wife" states: "Well, she thought, there is always one thing forbidden to women" (26). In Annie Proulx's short fiction "55 Miles to the Gas Pump" (1999), Mrs. Croom climbs to the roof to saw a hole in the attic to find what she knew to be there: "just as she thought:

the corpses of Mr. Croom's paramours" (491). The wife in Joyce Carol Oates' "Blue-bearded Lover" only asks why she cannot go in to the chamber because she knows this to be her role in the drama: "for I saw that he expected it of me" (1988, 183).

Most tellingly, women are themselves dangerous in their cunning. In "The Wife Killer," Lydia Millet wrote: "In the postmodern world Mrs. Blue Beard doesn't take the bait" (1998, 230). This strategy is not always successful, as shown in another story where the heroine refrains from taking the bait to no avail. She tells her husband: "'I think you're entitled to a room of your own.'" However, her refusal to play the role still results in her death: "This so incensed him that he killed her on the spot" (Namjoshi 1981, 64). More often, though, being aware of the story and its assigned roles enables women to be tricksters themselves. In the poem "Visiting," Jay Macpherson wrote: "Takes one to know one: he / Never fooled me" (1981, 92). This stance is reminiscent of all the "youngest sisters," who always know how to deal with a murderer. These women have the knowledge of Bluebeard already, and by having "forbidden knowledge" these women are themselves dangerous. Sylvia Plath's untitled poem from her juvenilia declares: "I am sending back the key / that let me into bluebeard's study" (pre-1956, 305). The speaker has already been into Bluebeard's study, after all, and so has knowledge of it. By referring to the forbidden space as a study, knowledge becomes at once literary and thus metafictive. In this context, "sending back the key" suggests the act of writing, and the act of writing about Bluebeard becomes the very means of outwitting his plot. As another narrator writes: "I will rewrite the story of Bluebeard. The girl's brothers don't come to save her on horses, baring swords, full of power at exactly the right moment. There are no brothers. There is no sister to call out a warning. There is only a slightly feral one-hundred pound girl with choppy black hair, kohl-smeared eyes, torn jeans, and a pair of boots with steel toes. This girl has a little knife to slash with, a little pocket knife, and she can run" (Block 2000, 165).

In some cases, "it takes one to know one" becomes more literal, as women are depicted as "Bluebeard in drag"[12] themselves, with their own murderous secrets. In Celia Fremlin's story "Bluebeard's Key" (1985), the wife has a secret of a domestic murder she keeps from her husband, burying the evidence, a door key, in their back yard. In Neil Gaiman's story "The White Road" (1996), while "Mr. Fox" is being beaten to death at the end of the story he sees the woman who has told the story that has caused his downfall, and she has a brush tail between her legs.

As this last reference illustrates, it is notable if not surprising that references to "Mr. Fox" become more prevalent in feminist revisions, as well as the use of the Grimm variants "The Robber Bridegroom" and "Fitcher's Bird." As has been seen, Cindy Sherman also uses the "Fitcher's Bird" variant from Grimm rather than Perrault's version. The 2003 collection *The Poets Grimm* reprinted both Allen Tate's and Margaret Atwood's poems entitled "The Robber Bridegroom," and in both cases the severed finger is essential: "He will cut off your finger / And the blood will linger" (Tate 2003, 52); "He would like to kill them gently, / finger by finger and with great tenderness" (Atwood 1984b, 304). These variants are both more gruesome in their images of dismemberment and cannibalism, but also feature a heroine who rescues her murdered sisters and who is not herself rescued by outside agency but by her own wits. Usually, her escape relies on trickery and forms of storytelling, and even by using Bluebeard's own artistry against him. Fitcher's "bird" disguises herself; many of these heroines make effigies of themselves to trick Bluebeard into believing she is still there (unable to distinguish between a live wife and a dead one). In most, she tells the story disguised as a story to enact justice, an elaborate and gleeful feature that prolongs the revenge Bluebeard must suffer. The numerous feminist revisions of the Bluebeard tale all make thorough use of the tale's inherent self-reflexive qualities and of postmodern techniques to enhance them.

As seen from the early cinematic representation of "Bluebeard" by Georges Méliès in 1901, film's ability to engage the spectator becomes particularly metacinematic when the Bluebeard story is in play. In feminist terms, this inherent potential becomes the means of commenting on construction and ownership of the cinematic gaze, as we see with two contemporary "Bluebeard" films, *The Silence of the Lambs* (1991) and *The Piano* (1993).

Demme: The Silence of the Lambs *(1991)*

The Bluebeard story has obvious thematic connections with standard tropes of horror, thriller, and serial-killer film.[13] Marina Warner said, "The Bluebeard story can be seen as one of the slasher film's progenitors" (1994, 270). Although the Bluebeard cycle of films has had no exact equivalent since the 1940s, the contemporary popularity and controversies of the serial-killer genre draw on the Bluebeard model explicitly. Jonathan Demme's film adaptation both represents the broad transformation of the "Bluebeard" film into contemporary serial-killer films: seriality is central; women are collected and killed. Although the film's relationship to several traditional genres is at issue, the arguments revolve around gaze, the spectacle of the woman who looks and is traditionally punished for it: "One thinks of the many instances in films where the woman, having heard a noise, looks down in the basement, or 'behind that door', and is promptly murdered, seemingly for daring to do so" (Dubois 2001, 300). At the same time, Demme's film is controversial in its self-reflexive challenge to

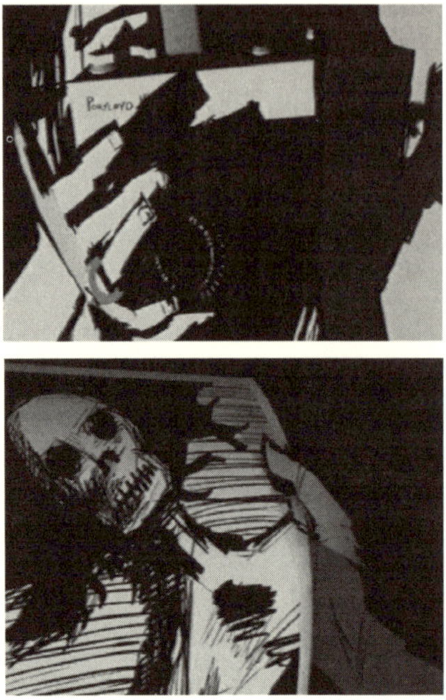

As stills from this film show, the camera is used to effect, but now by Bluebeard's wife. The film plays in postmodern ways with adaptation issues, using cut paper figures digitally created and employed in a three-dimensional environment. Courtesy of James Merry.

the genre through the reappropriation of gaze by Clarice Starling, played by Jodie Foster.

In Thomas Harris' novel *The Silence of the Lambs*[14] the serial murderer Jame [*sic*] Gumb has inherited a house with a basement "maze" (1988, 137, 203) in which he rears exotic butterflies, has chambers of tableaux made of corpses, and keeps the women he kidnaps in order to "harvest" their hides for his own metamorphosis. He is making "a girl suit out of real girls" (163, 320).[15] Clarice Starling, a neophyte FBI agent working with her mentor Jack Crawford, is tracing Gumb by means of another serial murderer in captivity: the psychiatrist Dr. Hannibal Lecter. Lecter draws Clarice's attention to the "first principles" in Gumb's motivation: he covets; you covet what you see. His basement already contains a number of rooms containing series of "tableaux" (354, 360) he has made with corpses. Gumb clearly sees himself as an artist. Although Gumb is the motivation for Starling's investigation, the film is centrally concerned with the relationship between Starling and Lecter.

The film is particularly interesting for the controversies between critics who seized upon the character of Clarice Starling and the casting of Jodie Foster in the role as a feminist appropriation of the male detective role and those who see the film as simply a variation on the inherently misogynistic serial-killer genre.[16] Starling's point of view is privileged throughout the film, and she is not punished for looking. At the point where the audience is invited to adopt the traditionally privileged gaze of the killer stalking the female detective in the dark with night vision goggles on, the audience is "punished" for doing so: Starling shoots directly at the camera.[17]

Campion: The Piano *(1993)*

Jane Campion's period film *The Piano* is overtly concerned with deconstructing the mechanics of representation and through it challenging the traditional cinematic gaze. The film contains an embedded "Bluebeard," represented as the amateur Christmas pantomime produced on a community stage in the New Zealand bush. The wives' "decapitated" heads poke through a curtain.[18] Bluebeard wields his axe in shadow play. The representation is already ironically quoted out of context: the setting is uncanny to the transplanted English; the play and its mechanics of representation are uncanny to the indigenous Maori in the audience, who disrupt the performance to "save" the threatened women. At the same time, the frame story of Ada, her husband Stewart, and her lover Barnes is also a Bluebeard story. As in the fairy tale, there is an indelibly stained "key," which in this case is the proof of Ada's infidelity with Barnes: she burns a message into a piano key for Barnes, who cannot read, but the message is delivered to her husband Stewart instead. The key is then replaced with Ada's own finger. A shift has occurred between Perrault's "Bluebeard," deconstructed and now "harmless," and Grimms' "The Robber Bridegroom," the "real" story and not harmless. The shadow play of pantomime is revisited in the brutal dismemberment of Ada by her husband, cutting off her finger with his axe. Again, the film thematizes the cinematic gaze. Barnes lies under the piano to gaze at Ada; what begins as exploitative is then transformed into complicity as Ada becomes dependent on Barnes' gaze to play. Stewart is also shown peeping through a crack in the wall and then another in the floor, watching his wife's infidelity with Barnes. As Sue Gillett summarized: "It is able to offer female spectators a kind of sympathetic engagement with and confirmation of their subjectivities along with an escape from the usual sorts of containment they receive in patriarchal cinema" (1995, 287).

Angela Carter and Margaret Atwood

The feminist and revisionist use of the Bluebeard tale is typified through the contemporary work of both Angela Carter and Margaret Atwood, who both have made repeated use of the tale in various ways and across a range of genres.

Angela Carter's revisionist use of the Bluebeard story in "The Bloody Chamber" (1979), titling that collection, can be set in the context of her translations of Perrault's "Blue Beard" and editing of Virago collections to include "Mr. Fox" and "Old Foster," as well as allusions within other of her fictional works.[19] The most obvious revision of Perrault's story in "The Bloody Chamber" is the very point on which Margaret Atwood objects to the French version of this tale: the rescue of the heroine. In Perrault, the wife's soldier brothers ride in to kill Bluebeard in the nick of time. In Carter's story, it is the heroine's own mother who rides up over the causeway and shoots Bluebeard between the eyes, thereby rescuing her daughter. It is a decisive comment on the original, and one that revises not only Perrault's story, but the rules of the fairy tale genre, which dictate that mothers abandon their daughters either actively or by default when they die or are "disappeared" from the tale. It is this moment celebrated in the woodcut by Corinna Sargood, a frequent illustrator of Carter's works, in which the avenging mother is in the foreground, depicted in the act of shooting Bluebeard.[20] The antiquated style of the woodcut itself echoes nineteenth-century fairy tale illustration, reflecting the collection's strategy of revision to a traditional model.[21]

But while the punchline is most obviously revised, the story also offers another defamiliarizing viewpoint: female complicity in masochistic relationships through first person confessional narrative. The story is set in the early twentieth century (and is saturated with the aesthetics of *fin-de-siècle* decadence).[22]

Atwood has often stated in interviews that she read the unexpurgated Grimms at the influential young age of six and that she "loved it." She focused her comments on the heroine's capacity for self-rescue in these stories, explicitly comparing them to the French versions: "The unexpurgated Grimm's Fairy Tales contain a number of fairy tales in which women are not only the central characters but win by using their own intelligence. Some people feel fairy tales are bad for women. This is true if the only ones they're referring to are those tarted-up French versions of 'Cinderella' and 'Bluebeard,' in which the female protagonist gets rescued by her brothers. But in many of them, women rather than men have the magic powers" (1978a, 115). She stated elsewhere that "Fitcher's Bird" is her second favorite tale (1978b, 70–71), and that "Nobody raps *her* knuckles for being curious" (1998, 34). She went on in this essay to analyze the heroine's symbolic bird transformation, shedding her bodily form and adopting the guise of her soul-form, summarizing: "In fact, she accomplishes her own resurrection. It's a powerful feat, and if this is how it's done, we should all start collecting honey and featherbeds immediately" (36).

Atwood's poems "Hesitations Outside the Door" (1971) and "The Robber Bridegroom" (1984b), the short story "Bluebeard's Egg" (1983a) that titles the collection, and the novel *The Robber Bride* (1993b) as well as allusions within other of her works and several watercolors all testify to an enduring interest in the Grimm version of the tale.[23] The early novel *Lady Oracle* (1976) features an overtly gothic subplot drawing on the Bluebeard tale; her novel *Bodily Harm* (1981) had a working title of *The Robber Bridegroom*; and a section of the short fiction "Alien Territory" (1992) is a retelling of the story, beginning "Bluebeard ran off with the third sister, intelligent though beautiful, and shut her up in his palace" (82). Throughout these works, Atwood was preoccupied with "Bluebeardian sexual politics,"[24] female transformations, and escape strategies and consistently worked metafictively. In Atwood's terms, engaging with the story is always a dangerous business, but as Sally, the protagonist of "Bluebeard's Egg" discovers, ignorance is much more dangerous.

"Bluebeard's Egg" uses a very obvious technique for metafiction by having Sally enrolled in a creative writing course, "Forms of Narrative Fiction." When they get to the folklore section, the teacher reads "Fitcher's Bird" to the class, and the students are asked to rewrite that story from a different point of view. Sally focuses on the egg. In the frame story, she thinks of her husband as this egg: "blank and pristine and lovely. Stupid too. Boiled, probably" (159). But Sally is forced to confront her preconceptions when she discovers that Ed is a man with secrets.

This story is a useful emblem for the revisionist strategy women writers often use: rewriting a known story from an unfamiliar point of view, defamiliarizing the intertext and opening it up to new readings.[25] At the same time, this strategy often allows a previously silenced character a voice of their own. Individual fairy tales have all been explored this way, but each revision of a traditional fairy tale simultaneously comments on the entire corpus and the constructions of the genre itself. The cautionary note in Atwood's story is when Sally misreads her own marriage in the light of an apparently demystified Bluebeard story. Taking her cue from Jane Austen's *Northanger Abbey* in this and other of her fictions, Atwood suggests that domesticity is the territory of contemporary gothic, rather than the sign of its absence.

In the poem "Hesitations," Atwood's metafiction is signaled by the unreliable speaker and by the ability to propose an "Alternative version." The poem posits the "house" of the Bluebeard paradigm as a third party, but one beyond

Bluebeard's control. Bluebeard's own story is not expressed architecturally so much as determined by it (reminiscent of the felicitous rooms of *Museum Piece No. 13* [King 1945], which determine what happens in them). The house seems to dictate the terms of the relationship that takes place inside: "Whose house is this / we both live in / but neither of us owns" (1971, 135). Another familiar Atwoodian gesture reflected here is to depict the Bluebeard as the oppressor, and then deflate that depiction, demonstrating instead a conspiracy between both speaker and so-called Bluebeard to play these roles of victim and oppressor together. The Bluebeard figure is gothicized, then romanticized, but then the apparently passive speaker tells Bluebeard to get out while he can, demonstrating that the roles are trapping them in their respective behaviors. Here, the speaker realizes that the house is purely symbolic: "This is not a house, there are no doors" (137). Finally, in the last two numbered sections of this multi-stanza poem of many rooms, the story in the closed room is knowledge of the other (as it has always been in the Bluebeard story). Both speakers tell lies to the other: they tell stories about what is in the room, each knowing the other lies. The poem, despite its apparent finality, "In the room we will find nothing / In the room we will find each other" (138), remains unresolved. The door is not opened; the binary is a paradox, itself an example of Bluebeardian politics, the dictum of "either /or." Where the Bluebeard story is fixated on teleology, the closed ending, Atwood's storytellers are always more interested in the creative possibilities of escape artistry: transformation and self-resurrection.

The many contemporary Bluebeards in English—the pirates and Turks, the lilies and dog breeds—masked somewhat the ever-present wife murderer of fairy tale origin who retreated from early childhood reading and Christmas pantomimes but who persisted in adult art forms. The archetypal shape-shifter, Bluebeard is the aristocrat, the gentle husband, the animal groom, the male psyche, the creative impulse, Death as a groom. The fairy tale invites a postmodern deconstruction, turning the story inside out and making it over again. However, the persistence of reworkings of the tale by artists of both sexes and in different art forms points to its inexhaustibility. The tale cannot be emptied or neutralized by its many postmodern deconstructions. Instead, its enduring themes have been recast to reflect changing preoccupations and forms of expression, and the Bluebeard tale has earned its permanent place in the English artistic landscape.

Epilogue

Bluebeard Today

In the postmodern present, all Bluebeards are simultaneously possible. In the pantomime *Bluebeard* (2003) by Paul Reakes, the treatment of "Bluebeard" is entirely traditional.[1] Contemporary references to *Buffy the Vampire Slayer* and *Wallace and Gromit* are the only clues that the pantomime is less than a hundred and fifty years old, and the pantomime delights in the traditional comic business, the kitchen scene, *ad lib* interaction with the audience, and the pantomime dame as Sister Anne (Ruby, played *en travesti* by a male actor), whom no one wishes to marry.[2] Symbolically present in this traditional pantomime are the dozens of traditional Bluebeard pantomimes and harlequinades that precede it on the British stage, as well as more recent postmodern exploitations of the form and postcolonial dialogues with it (such as the Jamaican Bluebeard pantomime, *Busha Bluebeard*).[3] In the same year, S. P. Somtow's extravagant novel *Bluebeard's Castle* (2003), a compulsively allusive, postmodern sprawling pop-culture, gothic fantasy set in Bangkok, attempts to include within it many Bluebeards both real and counterfeit.

Two of the most recent "Bluebeard" works are a collection of poetry and a collection of short stories, both of which use the allusion to the fairy tale in their titles. The new poetry collection *Bluebeard's Wives* (edited by Boden and Brigley 2007) again embraces the creative possibilities of reimagining the Bluebeard story and telling it from multiple points of view (the wives', Bluebeard's, even his sword). At the same time, the prior intertext is not simply the Bluebeard tale ("Mr. Fox," in one poem and "The Robber Bridegroom" in another), but the influential Balázs and Bartók precursor opera, *Duke Bluebeard's Castle* (1912). An English National Opera production at Birmingham Symphony Hall was the direct inspiration for a women's poetry project; many of the poems published in *Bluebeard's Wives* derive from it. Some voices contradict the terms of the opera, while others pay homage. The collection is prefaced by the sonnet of Edna St. Vincent Millay,[4] claiming another important precursor text, specifically a poem by a progressive feminist. Sophie Hannah's reading of the sonnet in the preface to *Bluebeard's Wives* is of a female speaker claiming preserved space, a right traditionally accorded to Bluebeard alone, for herself. Even as the poems create other secret spaces, as a group they refuse the status of sacred space for the Bluebeard intertext itself; they dare to "profane" by using it freely. Interestingly, the poets refer to themselves as Bluebeard's Wives and as a harem, but beyond this notion of a collective the twenty-four poets and their personae have little in common. As a result, though grounded in the particulars of the Bluebeard story and the iconography of the modernist opera, and intertextually aware of each other, the poems are universalized expressions: all women, all lovers, and all wives are envisioned.

Pierre Furlan's short story "Blue-beard's Work-shop" (2007), translated from the original "L'atelier de barbe-bleue" (2002) in a New Zealand collection of the same title, encapsulates both the lasting desire that we have for the Bluebeard story and the unexpected influence it has on the stories we tell about it. Like Margaret Atwood's "Bluebeard's Egg" (1983), the metafictive story is set in a writer's workshop, this time in a sultry Belgian summer, in a "fake" eighteenth-century castle. The postmodern knowledge of the workshop is offered as a writer's "key to success": rewrite a known story because, as the teacher of the workshop says, "People's subconscious hasn't changed over the last five centuries, really" (23). The male protagonist decides also to exploit this "tacky story" (27) in order to exploit the teacher's masochistic desire to be not Sister Anne, who knows the truth and sounds the alarm, but Bluebeard's wife. At the same time, the control he exercises over his own desire is quickly revealed to be an illusion: the companion to "hormone-fuelled desire" (24) is "insan[e] jealous[y]" (27). Once again, and just as it has done from the very beginning in Charles Perrault's version, in "Mr. Fox" and "The Robber Bridegroom," those stories about storytelling, and "Fitcher's Bird," the story about transforming the known story into a new disguise, the tale escapes the frames, spilling out of the embedded story into the Belgian summer and out into the remainder of the stories in *Blue-beard's Work-shop*. Although the themes are archetypally consistent, once again the story takes protagonist and reader alike to a place they did not expect.

It seems unlikely that Bluebeard will reenter English cultural parlance as a children's nursery story. The image of Bluebeard the "pirate" now firmly occupies the vacuum left when Bluebeard the serial wife killer was censored out of fairy tale collections for children. But as gender politics both endure and evolve, so will artistic engagement with the Bluebeard fairy tale.

Notes

Preface

1. In 1973, *Evening Standard* graphic strip writer Peter O'Donnell published a strip of Modesty Blaise over a year called "The Bluebeard Affair." When the strip was collected in 2006, he wrote in the preface: "The name still appears in modern dictionaries and was generally known in the early decades of the twentieth century, but then seems to have faded from the vocabulary. I've now asked a number of people about it but nobody under about seventy knew what it meant. That being so, it was pretty dumb of me to use it in the title, wasn't it?" (O'Donnell and Romero 2006). Kurt Vonnegut in *Bluebeard* has his main protagonist write: "I meant to mention Bluebeard in this book. I wanted to know if I had to explain, for the sake of young readers, who Bluebeard was. Nobody knew" (1987, 45).

2. Maggie Pearson and Gavin Rowe (2000). Alternatively, "Bluebeard" is listed as "antique" by Judy Mastranglo's *Antique Fairy Tales* (Perrault 1988).

3. T. Allston Brown (1903): "all the dresses which had been made for 'Bluebeard' were likewise consumed" along with the show animals (elephants, lions, bears, leopards).

4. See Balanchine's "Chronology" (Balanchine and Mason 1977, 738). This *Bluebeard* is based on the 1866 Offenbach operetta.

5. Darnton's example seems limited, however: "The English versions seem almost jolly in comparison. 'Peerifool' begins in Peter Rabbit fashion . . . and it ends with some good, clean giant killing (by boiling water)" (1984, 46).

6. Manfred Grätz (1988), quoted by Meredid Puw Davies (2001, 6–7): "Grätz goes on to show that it is more likely that the German *Märchen* were in fact modelled on the highly fashionable, seventeenth- and eighteenth-century French *contes de fées*, which were sophisticated literary products of a high salon culture, rather than unsullied transcriptions of peasant narrative, although their authors, as in the case of Perrault, did sometimes make such claims." Focusing on the tale and close variants, Josef Herzog in *Die Märchentypen des "Ritter Blaubart" und "Fitchervogel"* (1938) analyzed a large set of international variants (thirty-one, with multiple variations for each) by comparing their motivic content. However, his hopes for locating its source through ethnographic study did not yield a result.

7. Emil Heckmann (1930) quoted by Harriet Mowshowitz (1970, 16).

8. Meredid Puw Davies (2001) cited Bottigheimer (1987, 1993) on the Grimms and uses largely German scholars: Suhrbier (on how the German tradition blunts the tale's subversive elements), Gräz, Heckmann, and Saintyves. In a chapter surveying the scholarly tradition, largely German, she surveyed mythology, anthropology, social history, and folklore studies in turn. Mythology: Kretschmer (1901) and Heckmann (1930) and Gabory (1926); Astrology: Pancritius (1930); Social Practice: leprosy, beards and their significance, tarring and feathering, cannibalism, werewolfism, eliminating matrilineal inheritance; fear of death in childbirth, Perrault's proto-feminist comment on married women's lack of legal and property rights; Psychology: Jungian primarily (Mowshowitz, Suhrbier, Lüthi [via Jacoby], Hedwig von Beit, Verena Kast, Helmut Barz, Bettelheim, and Annemarie Dross). Notably, she did not include any more recent (non-Jungian) feminist studies.

9. Roger Schlobin was more specific: Bluebeard would fall under the "femivore" archetype, the "lovable bastard" that includes Don Juan, Romeo, lady killer, Casanova types, and others. Still, "the couplings of femivores and victims repeat archetypal patterns in which they both seek individually and mutually destructive power" (1989, 96).

10. For the sun theory applied to Bluebeard, Saintyves cited: H. Husson, *La Chaine Traditionnelle* (Paris: A. Franck, 1874, 34–41) and A. Lefèvre, *Les Contes de Perrault*, lxvi–lxix (Paris: C. Marpon & E. Flammarion, 1875). He noted that for F. Dillaye in *Contes de Perrault* (Paris: 1880, 218–19), the struggle of day and night explication is not essentially any different and depends on the same arguments as Husson (362 n.). At the same time, Saintyves links with this discredited theory that of Bluebeard as Kronos or Saturn, in a struggle to kill the new year (363–64).

11. Jean-Pierre Bayard (1955) similarly universalized the gender of the initiate, concluding that curiosity is a prevalent and eternal theme pertaining as often to men as to women. Derek Brewer also universalized the theme of escape from death: "We all have to open the door of the little room, where our predecessors have gone" (1980, 40).

12. See also Bayard (1955), Mowshowitz (1970), and Brewer (1980).

13. The first wife was killed for looking into a forbidden room; one hid the fact she was "bandy legged", and another that she was black. All other wives, from different nationalities, are unfaithful to Bluebeard.

14. See Shuli Barzilai (2009). She has applied Freudian and Lacanian approaches to the tale previously.

15. Essentially, Clarissa Pinkola Estés' (1992) reading was the same in *Women Who Run with the Wolves*. Bluebeard is a predator. Being curious is the "key" to psychic individuation. The bride learns to summon her animus (her two brothers) to overthrow the predator. Ann and Barry Ulanov also agreed that Bluebeard is representative of a "killer animus" who functions aggressively, the solution to which is to "transform it into something positive" (1994, 284). He is a contrasexual archetype; the Bluebeard negative animus complex in women would be an anima complex in men (284).

16. Both Mowshowitz (1979) and François Flahault (1979) offered similar readings. Jack Zipes (2006) cited his agreement with Philip Lewis' reading of the crisis of

phallotocracy. In publishing the secret to phallocratic power, Perrault revealed the unrevealable. Janel States argued in "Confronting the Forbidden" (1996) that Bluebeard is threatened by his wife's inability to reflect his gaze perfectly and thus in frustration destroys her; he wishes his wife to occupy an object rather than a subject position.

17. Studies such as that by Jennifer Welch looked at the use of the tale as a revisionist tactic: "When revisionists challenge the *Märchen* paradigm, they also implicitly comment on the method of storytelling. As with all works of art, form and content are inseparable" (1994, 12).

Chapter 1

1. See Davies *The Tale of Bluebeard in German Literature* (2001: 60–65) for her criteria for *Blaubartmärchen* and a brief discussion of the difficulties of classifying the tale, calling it "more elusive than some other tales" (61).

2. There are numerous variants within each nationality also. In their catalogue of French and francophone fairy tales and folklore, *Le conte populaire français* (1957), Paul Delarue and Marie-Louise Ténèze also added a subcategory: AT 312B, a Christianized version of AT 312, citing three of these and giving one in full: "*Le diable et les deux petites filles*." Other tales are often fruitfully compared with selections from these three AT categories, such as Grimm's "Castle of Death" or "The Murder Castle" ("Das Mordschloss"); "The Hut in the Forest" ("Das Waldhaus"); "Our Lady's Child" ("Marienkind"). "Faithful John" ("Der treue Johannes"), on the other hand, reverses the usually brutal consequences of transgression to bring its male protagonist great fortune. This example of apparent double standards running through many of the tales was analyzed by Maria Tatar in "Taming the Beast" (1987, 167). Tatar read this standard in, among others, the Russian folktale "Marya Morévna" in which Prince Ivan's violation of a prohibition happily brings him wealth and marriage. The AT system has been criticized for being Eurocentric. Nevertheless, European variants have most strongly marked the English tradition.

3. In variants, particularly French, the bride stalls by dressing elaborately in wedding clothes. In "The White Dove," for instance, she requires dress, veils, skirts, train, cap, etcetera. Harriet Mowshowitz conjectured that details of dressing would have offended Perrault's courtly audience (1970, 23).

4. In one French (Vendéen) variant of Bluebeard the dog is named Sarène, an evident cognate for sister Anne: *Soeur Anne* ("Barbe Bleue," variant in Bødker).

5. In *The Folktale*, Stith Thompson noted: "The tale in approximately this form (AT 311) is known over most of Europe from Germany eastward. Its area of greatest popularity is found in the Baltic states and in Norway. In the north, it seems to go no further east than the Urals, but it is found in Palestine and has several versions in India. It has also been carried to the Eskimos and to Puerto Rico. The story has never been thoroughly studied, but a cursory examination of the variants suggests Norway as at least an important center of dissemination of this tale, if not its original home" (1946, 36).

6. There are many translations of this enigmatic title. Most common are "Fitcher's (or Fetcher's) Fowl" and "Fitcher's Bird." The origin of the German title is unknown, but

it is presumed to be connected with the bird disguise the heroine adopts. The Grimms associated it with the Icelandic word *fitfugl*, a web-footed or water bird (Zipes 1987a, 730–31 n.). Elsewhere, "Fitcher" becomes "Fezzy the Fetcher" (of women).

7. In many variations, the punishment for seeing the forbidden is to be struck blind, as in "The Story of the Third Calendar" (*The Thousand and One Arabian Nights*), and "Mary's Child."

8. The latter, by Ludwig Bechstein (1845), is a hybrid of "Fitcher's Bird," because in addition to creating the effigy of a straw doll dressed in her clothes and cap, the "young bride" covers herself in honey and feathers to escape recognition. But she is escaping a robber's den, where she has been a captive for several years.

9. The 1823, 1826, and 1834 editions of *German Popular Stories* are identical in typesetting and pagination and contain the note to "The Robber Bridegroom": "in the original, the finger is chopped off, and is carried away by the bride, as well as the ring upon it" (201 n.).

10. The trail of blood is used in the English Squire King Caley variants "Cellar of Blood" and "Doctor Forster."

11. In the Afro-Caribbean tale "Jack and the Devil," they cook the ogre and eat him. In the Sicilian tale "The Story about OhMy" the test is whether the girl will eat a dead body part; the first two sisters throw it away, but it is called back by OhMy. The third is advised by the soul of her dead mother to burn it and grind the powder so that it cannot be called back to disprove that she ate it. This command to eat a body part is a consistent alternative to the prohibition.

12. As in "The Girl Who Got up a Tree," "Lass 'at Seed Her Awn Graave Dug," "Lonton Lass," (although she is spared by the premonition dream of a nearby farmer), "The Oxford Student," and "Riddle Me, Riddle Me Right."

13. The rhyme here is very close indeed to "The Girl Who Got up a Tree": "I'll rede you a riddle, I'll rede it you right, / Where was I last Saturday night? / The wind did blow, the leaves did shake, / When I saw the hole the fox did make" (1970).

14. Francis Child, creator of the Child Ballad classification, lists six variants for Child Ballad #4: "Lady Isabel and the Elf Knight."

15. A Caribbean variant on this is "Jack and Old Bluebeard," also a Jamaican pantomime (1960s). Another is the Greek tale "The Underworld Adventure."

16. Similar help is given by the third daughter in "The Widow and Her Daughters" and in "Peerifool."

17. Hürlimann also noted that the provenance of some stories leads back to Persia and India (1959, 1963, 26).

18. Translated by Richard Burton (who also had earlier translated *Arabian Nights* for the Victorians); Burton may even have modeled his translation of this episode on "Bluebeard."

19. Andrew Lang also quoted the French Romantic writer Charles Nodier (1780–1844): "Odysseus, Figaro, and Othello are not more certain to be immortal than Hop o' My Thumb, Puss in Boots, and Blue Beard, the heroes whom Charles Nodier so pleasantly called 'the Ulysses, the Figaro, and the Othello of children'" (1888, xxxv). Nodier

(through Lang) is also quoted in J. Saxon Childers' edition of Perrault's and (G. M.'s 1763] *Histories* (1925, 123–24).

20. The existence of frescoes at St. Nicholas de Bienzy and another nearby church dating from 1704 and discovered in 1850 demonstrate the cult of Triphine has been interwoven with the Bluebeard story in popular imagination. Renée Van Raamsdonk summarized the images in the frescoes: "first, the saint's marriage with a Breton lord; second, her receipt of several keys from her husband; third, her discovery of a room where seven female corpses hang from a wall; fourth, her husband's return, his anger, and her evident dejection; fifth, the saint at a window praying with a woman who is presumably her sister. In the sixth and last frescoe, the saint, Tropheme [Triphine], has been hanged, but St. Gildas resuscitates her, while her two brothers kill the murderous husband" (1976, 6–7; see also Flahault 1979). The 1912 modern gothic novel *Château Bluebeard*, by Mrs. Leeds, uses the legend for its setting and the lineage of the novel's villain, the Count de Kerouac.

21. As summarized by Brigitte Cazelles in "Arthur as Barbe-Bleue" (1999). Cazelles looked in detail at a nineteenth-century French play that turns King Arthur into the tyrannical husband of Triphene, manipulated by a false advisor into condemning her to death first for matricide, then for adultery: *Saint Tryphine et le roi Arthur. Mystère breton en deux journées et huit actes*, trans. F. M. Luzel, ed. M. l'abbé Henry (Quimperlé: Clairet, 1893). This variant does not appear to be widely known outside of Breton tradition.

22. The duke had written: "25 March, 1858 . . . Mr. Planché there reports with good reason that one of the supposed precursors for Blue Beard is the Maréchal de Rais who was burned in Nantes in 1440. It is the opinion the most widely given, [but] I doubt that it has any foundation. I have retrieved in my archives an old copy of the trial of the Maréchal, who was, I regret to say it, a very notable Lord and a very brave soldier. He was tried and condemned for a number of ghastly crimes, but entirely different from those of Blue Beard" (Planché 1872, 359–60, my translation).

23. Harriet Mowshowitz went to great lengths in her dissertation "Bluebeard and French Literature" (1970) and in her article "Gilles de Rais and the Bluebeard Legend in France" (1973) to untangle the historical figure Gilles (and his own legends) from the legend of Bluebeard. In her thesis, "Gilles de Rais in Life, Literature and Legend" (1986), Elena Baca Odio concludes that *both* Comôr and Rais were the joint precursors for the Bluebeard tale, reappearing in this form after centuries in which the historical tales had been circulated in an oral tradition.

24. Harold Dearden noted that before Rais was fourteen years old, two arranged marriages resulted in the death of the brides "almost immediately after the ceremony" (1937, 575), and elsewhere it is reported that two fiancées died before the wedding. Cazelles did mention one story about wives cited by Bossard, an early biographer of de Rais: "One evening, Gilles welcomes two travelers in his castle of Rais (between Elven and Questembert): the count Odon de Tréméac, lord of Kervent, and Blanche de l'Herminière, his betrothed. Gilles de Laval, whose beard is of a most beautiful red hue, has Odon thrown into a dungeon cell and tries to force Blanche to wed him. Upon a

promise that he will be hers 'body and soul,' Blanche finally accepts and soon reveals her true identity; she is the devil in flesh, who is come to notify Gilles de Laval that because of the crimes and misdeeds he has committed, henceforth he belongs to Hell. The devil makes a sign, and Gilles's beard changes from red to blue" (Bossard 1885; Cazelles 1999, 137). Clement Wood's bizarre fairy tale *Bluebeard and His Eight Wives* (1926) describes de Rais fulfilling a prophecy in wedding eight "women": Tiphaine and Beatrice, his wife Catherine, a household traitor Marie, Joan of Arc, a spirit Leopard Lady who fled into the forms of all the children he murdered, Gilla, and finally Morta: Death.

25. Subtitle of Rais' first major biography by the Abbé Eugène Bossard (1885).

26. Website of the Conseil Général de la Vendée: "Tiffauges: Château de Barbe-Bleue", http://www.chateau-barbe-bleue.com/pages/menprin.asp.

27. Leonard Wolf's scholarly biography *Bluebeard: The Life and Crimes of Gilles de Rais* drew together the scattered source materials in one place, and confirmed that Rais is not known to have had a blue beard (or, indeed, any beard at all), and that a black beard that shows blue is a plausible but fanciful notion (1980, 156–58). In the note to the appended story by Perrault, Wolf added: "What is curious and poignant and worth mulling over is that in the process by which Gilles's name and Blue-beard's have been confounded, the child murderer has been transformed and softened into a man who murders his wives" (218).

28. Wheeler also quoted Holinshead's reference to another "Bluebeard," in the reign of Henry VI, anno 1450 (1866). A similar suggestion was made by A. A. ([18]66): "Blue Beard in England": "In Caxton's *Polychronicon* (54, 6, *recto*, A.D. 1449) is the following passage: 'After relating the troubles in Flanders; the loss of the towns in France, Pont l'Arche and Rouen; the arrest and return of the unpopular Duke of Suffolk; the anger of the Commons for the deliverance of Anjou and Maine, the loss of Normandy, the author goes on to say,— 'And in especial for the death of the good duke of gloucester, in soo moche that in somme places men gadred togeders and made hem Captaynes as *blew berd* and other, which were resysted, and taken and had Justyce and deyd. And thenne the sayd parlement was adiourned to leycetre.' Can this 'blew berd' be the original of the truculent hero of the fairy story? Of course we often hear of Jacke Strawe, Hob Miller, and such names, but I do not recollect among any of the mob leaders a Blue Beard'" (original italics).

29. The association of Henry Tudor with Bluebeard was made by Jane Austen, according to her nephew's "Memoir," where she says of Henry VIII that he was "held to be an unmitigated tyrant, and an embodied Blue Beard" (Austen-Leigh 1869, 331). One verse chapbook frequently reprinted throughout the nineteenth century made the allusion: "he did *marry* / As many fair dames / As our eighth English Harry" (J. Harris 1808). In Anne Thackeray Ritchie's "Bluebeard's Keys" two men in the street comment on "Barbi's" chances of getting another wife in the following terms: "he will not find much difficulty. Remember Henry Tudor, and the Sultan in *Arabian Nights*" (1875, 28). In Broadbent's *History of Pantomime*, he began by stating that the pantomimes of Blue Beard are thought to be based on "a satire on our King Henry VIII," but went on to talk of it being in fact

Gilles de Rais (1901, 200). The novel by Emma Cave, *Bluebeard's Room* (1995), casts the persecution of fiancée Lucy as a vague extension of her ancestors' religious persecution by King Henry. Catherine Howard was called "the fifth wife of Bluebeard" in a book of that title by Olivia Leigh (1969).

30. "[W. C.] Taylor locates the tale as before the time of the Tudors since the text seems to indicate no surprise that a man would have the right to kill his wives" (Taylor 1848, 136).

31. "The dramatic Blue Beard is a bashaw with three tails, who has cut off the heads of his seven wives; consequently, our eighth Harry is a wife or two in arrear with the Turk."

Chapter 2

1. See Cordingly (1998, xii–xiii). The book is still widely listed under Defoe's name in bibliographies.

2. Named for the Belgian town of Ramillies and the British victory there in 1706. The wig is braided down the back and tied with ribbons.

3. Lee wrote, "There has not been found any authenticated record or any statement of the identity of the girl whom Blackbeard married. Tradition has it that the girl's name was Mary Ormond, and there exists a letter written by a relative of Mary Ormond so stating" (1974, 74 and note). The footnote dates the letter 1947, however, and the genealogy has not been proven. Lee's own research did not turn up any "legitimate" descendents of Blackbeard with his surname or any of the accepted variations upon it (198n29).

4. Lee noted "neither in Spotswood's letters nor elsewhere is there any evidence that Eden ever had improper dealings with Edward Teach" (1974, 141) and quoted Johnson's five-paragraph retraction. Lee quoted Johnson as his oldest source for Eden performing the ceremony: "Writers have seized upon this marriage performed by Governor Eden as sufficient proof that Blackbeard and the governor were bosom friends allied in the commission of piratical acts. Such a conclusion reveals ignorance both of the laws and of the conditions existing in North Carolina in 1718 with respect to marriages." Lee was a Professor of Law, who published on North Carolina law.

5. Even with such a history, Teach did not feature at all in the 1924 publication *Love Stories of Some Famous Pirates* by A. Hyatt Verrill.

6. Lee also cited: "It has been said that, prior to his formalized wedding of 1718 in North Carolina, he had been married on at least thirteen occasions and even had a wife living in London" (1974, 25). Lee's source for this information is more reputable: a letter from Governor Walter Hamilton to Council of Trade and Plantations, dated January 6, 1718, Cal State Papers, XXX (Aug. 1717–Dec. 1718), sec. 298. This letter predates Johnson's account, which also mentioned the same information and was cross-referenced by Lee along with a 1962 account (Michael Craton, *A History of the Bahamas*) that no doubt drew on the former.

7. The expanded fourth addition in 1726 and the expanded edition of 1734 increased the original number of pirates in the book.

8. Robert Lee argued that Blackbeard did not reap cash treasures but rather ships' stores, which he used or sold, and that he was a notorious spendthrift; thus, it was unlikely that he ever buried much, if any, treasure at all (1974, 171–72). That has, of course, not stopped people from searching for it and evidence of digging still occurs at all major Blackbeard/Teach sites, even those that have not been authenticated.

9. See also "Bluebeard's Castle," n.d.

10. Subtitle of Harold Schechter's book on Holmes. The term "multimurderer" was coined by a Chicago journalist (Schechter 1994, 258).

11. The confession is problematic; it is the fullest confession of his crimes, but he described killing several people who were not in fact dead and is suspected of killing many more than he confessed to. He provided rooms for tourists during the Chicago World Fair, and "as many as fifty tourists who took rooms at the Castle never returned home from their trip" (63). See Schechter (1994).

12. Newspapers took to calling him "the Modern Bluebeard" (Schechter 1994, 258).

13. Walz stated that the "ultimate proof of Landru's crimes was the simple assertion [by the press] that he was the 'Bluebeard of Gambais'" (2000, 100).

14. See Le Queux (1966).

15. The actual number is not known. In a 1926 account, "The Stockyards Bluebeard," Edward Smith wrote: "The total number of the man's wives has been placed as high as fifty, though I think thirty-five more like the correct number. Bluebeard had seven wives and has become a legend" (1926, 101).

16. See *Encyclopaedia of Murder* (Wilson and Pitman 1961, 283–84). This entry on Gufler used "Bluebeard" as an adjective, lowercase, and twice as a noun. The waltz of this name is used to effect in both the Claude Chabrol film (1963) when Landru waltzes with one of his victims to this music in his blue villa, and again in the Edward Dmytryk film (1972) as background to Richard Burton's activities. Further, it appears in the title of a pantomime listed by Georges Doutrepont (1926, 420): *Barbe-Bleue ou la Sorcière du Danube* (1830).

17. Harold Schechter's article "The Bloody Chamber" discussed the facts and the films in terms of the fairy tales "Bluebeard," "Fitcher's Bird," "The Robber Bridegroom," and the epigrammatic warning from "Mr. Fox" and drew on E. Sidney Hartland's 1885 essay on the forbidden chamber cycle.

18. In reference to South African Daisy de Melker, by her biographers (Bennett and Rousseau 1934).

19. Holbrook is also author of "Belle, the Female Bluebeard" *American Mercury* 53.212 (August 1941): 218–26. This title echoes the entry of a circa-1920 crime detective pamphlet (Crimes of Love and Passion no. 2): "Belle Gunness: 'The Female Bluebeard'" by Henry K. Vernon (cited in Langlois 1978, 159 n.).

20. Anderson picked up the "Lady Bluebeard" moniker presumably from the press of the period, as his book reproduced a *San Francisco Chronicle* headline describing her as "Mrs. Bluebeard."

Chapter 3

1. The first five stories of the eight that became *Contes de Ma Mère l'Oye* were present in this manuscript, discovered in Nice in 1953, now in the Pierpont Morgan Library, New York (see Perrault 1695). The debates over authenticating original authorship between the father and son derive from the name on the publishing license, which was that of the son. Percy Muir stated: "at the time of original publication, and throughout the lifetime of Perrault senior, the son's authorship was generally accepted" (1954, 49). The opposite opinion holds sway in most scholarship on the topic. Jacques Barchilon provided an even-handed survey in "The Authorship of the Tales," in the first chapter of the *Facsimile*, and for the first time also performed a handwriting analysis of the manuscript original, concluding: "the facts available are not absolutely conclusive. On the basis of different contemporary statements either the father or the son could be the author of the *Contes*. The manuscript does show apparent evidence of the father's work in the dedication inscription and in a few corrections, and the scribe who copied the tales also copied another manuscript for Perrault in the same year" (Barchilon 1956: 32, 35).

2. Barchilon noted in his "Foreword" to the Samber reprint (*Authentic Mother Goose*): "The text which he used for his translation was the French edition of 1721 or its reprint of 1729 published in Holland. In these, the sequence in the original Perrault edition of 1697 has been changed" (Barchilon and Pettit 1960, 47).

3. Muir ascribed the (mis)translation of this title to Samber: "Samber, the first translator, was responsible for the switch from *La Belle au Bois Dormant* to *The Sleeping Beauty in the Wood*, which is probably accountable to a faulty acquaintance with the French language" (1954, 49).

4. Claire-Lise Malarte-Feldman wrote: "This error in authorship is not unique to Samber. We know that from the beginning of the eighteenth century, cheap editions were sold all over France; these were the blue books of the *bibliothèque de Troyes*. It is not too farfetched to imagine that Samber may have seen some of those editions in which often Perrault was mistakenly presented as the author of Mlle L'Héritier's tale" (1999, 187). She also added in a footnote that Catherine Velay-Vallantin (1987, 145) noted that this novel was "erroneously attributed to Perrault as early as 1716" (Malarte-Feldman 1999, 196). Andrew Lang also footnoted an example of its inclusion from 1721 (1888, xxvi) and commented that it "holds its place even now"; Barchilon noted that these were the Dutch editions of 1721 and 1729 (Barchilon and Pettit 1960, 49). Interestingly, editions of the translator G. M. also include it. In his book on French chapbooks, Pierre Brochon also stated that the erroneous attribution derived from the French chapbook tradition (1954, 76).

5. See Percy Muir (1954, 50) for a description of the comparison between editions.

6. "The story of Blue Beard . . . Gent's translation from Perrault" (book no. 451). "The master cat; or, Puss in Boots, a tale. To which is added, An historical story of Blue Beard. . . . Both these are from Gent's English version of Perrault" (book no. 538). He went on in

the next paragraph with even greater sarcasm about their use of "Gent" as the surname: "This family was so numerous that almost every literary man of the sixteenth, seventeenth, and eighteenth century, who had no other title, was admitted to membership" (Saxon Childers 1925, 122–23).

7. In his Notes, he says "the designs for these wood cuts were borrowed from the 1687 edition of *Contes de ma Mère l'Oye*" (Saxon Childers 1925, 122). Ironically, this is a slip for "1697." As Percy Muir (1954, 50) noted, the earliest edition of any of the tales is several that appeared in the *Receuil* of Moetjens (the Hague), beginning in 1694.

8. Samber's edition clearly includes them, even in the title: *Histories ... with Morals*. Furthermore, his Dedication to the Countess of Granville emphasizes their importance, as Michael Patrick Hearn underscored in his preface to the Garland edition of Samber's 1729 text (Perrault 1729, xv). In addition to the passage Hearn quoted, Samber wrote in the Dedication that, like the instructive fables, the tale "carries notwithstanding in the Bottom, a most solid Sense, and wraps up and infolds the most material and important Truths" (Perrault 1729). Percy Muir, in his *English Children's Books 1600–1900*, summarized the history of the 1719/1799 misprint and its discovery, which is otherwise rarely discussed (1954, 49).

9. Percy Muir is the only author I have found to begin a list dividing "Samber" editions from "G. M." editions (1954, 51), but his list in either case is brief, only giving the editions that attribute a translator. It is not merely the eleventh edition of 17[99] that credits "G. M." with the "Englishing" of Perrault, and a list of prominent extant editions from the eighteenth century and after demonstrates the enduring intertwining of translations. Where square brackets are given around the translator the attribution is my own, made by comparing the text with known translations by both translators: 1729: R. S., Gent (London: Pote and Montagu, and 3rd corrected ed. London: Pote and Montagu, 1741); 1763 G. M., Gent (Salisbury: B. Collins, and London: W. Bristow, and 7th corrected edition, Salisbury: B. Collins; also sold in London: Carnan and Newbery, and London: S. Crowder, 1777; 8th corrected edition, Salisbury: B. Collins and London: S. Crowder, 1780; 11th edition, Salisbury: B. Collins, the misdated edition, 1799); 1764 R. S. (London: S. Van den Berg, bilingual edition; ascribed to Samber by Hearn in the prefatory material to his reproduction of the 1729 translation [xxiii], and by the British Library); 1785 [G. M.] (Brussels: B. Le Francq, bilingual edition); 1790 R. S. (Dublin: Richard Cross; predating this, a Dublin: Richard Cross edition of d'Aulnoy's *The history of the tales of the fairies* (1785) was the first to include "The Blue Beard," and similarly used Samber's translation of it); 1794 [G. M.] (1st American edition, Haverhill, MA: Edes; Malarte-Feldman is not correct when she ascribes this as a Samber reprint [1999, 185], as are Barchilon and Flinders [1981, 112]); 1796 [G. M.] (London: T. Boosey, bilingual edition); 1798 [G. M.] (New York: John Harrison; the copy filmed for readex was imperfect, but the first three pages of "Blue Beard" are included, and suffice to determine the translator); 1800 [G. M.] (Edinburgh, Morrow and Cowgate); 1803 G. M., Gent (London: J. Harris, successor to Newbury); 1817 [G. M.] (Glasgow: Lumsden); 1888 [G. M.] (Clarendon: Oxford University Press; Andrew Lang's *Blue Fairy Book*. Glenn Burne attributes it to Samber

incorrectly in his article "Andrew Lang's *The Blue Fairy Book: Changing the Course of History*" [1986, 142]); 1925 G. M. (London: Nonesuch Press, Ed. J. Saxon Childers); 1928 G. M. (London: Fortune Press).

10. In Lang's introduction to *The Blue Fairy Book* which also includes "Blue Beard," he stated: "I have given his tales of *Mother Goose* in the words of the oldest English translation I can procure. . . . Though published in 1697, Perrault's *Contes* . . . do not seem to have been Englished till 1729. A version is advertised in a newspaper of that year, but no copy exists in the British Museum. The text we print is from a very pretty little edition of 1763 which I purchased in Paris. The French and English face each other. . . . Clearly the English version was not made from Perrault's first edition, but followed a later and slightly altered text" (1889, 356). Claire-Lise Melarte-Feldman, in her brief study of the English and American translations from Perrault, "The Problems of Translating Perrault's *Contes* into English," used as two of her major twentieth-century editions Philip and Simborowski's *The Complete Fairy Tales of Charles Perrault* (1993) and Jack Zipes' *Beauties, Beasts, and Enchantment: Classic French Fairy Tales* (1989). Melarte-Feldman noted that Philip and Simborowski retranslated Lang's 1889 edition; thus, apparently unwittingly, G. M. (Philip noted in "Translating Perrault" that Lang used the 1697 text [1993, 129], but he omitted Lang's own reference to the source being an "old English version of the eighteenth century" in Lang's "Preface" of 1889.) Zipes instead retranslated James Planché, who seems to have followed Samber.

11. For the G. M. transcription I have used the Salisbury 1763 edition, attributed to him, from the Lilly Rare Book Library, Bloomington, Indiana. For the Samber text I have used the 1977 Garland reprint edition. A scanned facsimile of the 1729 edition is also available online as part of the Eighteenth-Century Texts online. It is also available (minus the morals) in Opie and Opie (1974, 137–41).

12. My colleague, Dr. Lyle Morgan III, generously leant a linguist's eye to the two versions. He concluded that the results were frustratingly indeterminate. Whoever G. M. was, he was generally contemporaneous with Samber, and the diction does not therefore help to date G. M.'s translation more closely. Morgan commented: "Grammatically, both translations are equally accurate with G. M.'s most often, but not always, demonstrating a patina that is stylistically more elegant and formal. Samber's translation often appears stylistically tighter; he most generally uses fewer words to express the same thought, and more often tends toward an idiomatic colloquial usage as you can see throughout the text. However, this apparent difference is somewhat schizophrenic. At times, Samber lapses into the more 'elegant' usage of the Elizabethan English of an earlier age such as is seen in the King James Version of the Bible of the early 17th century. 'I beg you' in G. M.'s translation is rendered as 'I desire thee' in Samber's, and so on. In these instances, Samber reverts to an older, more 'stylish' usage. However, this does not hold true throughout. What G. M. renders as 'I shall,' Samber renders by the more vernacular contraction 'I'll'" (personal communication, 26 January 2006). Similarly, Barchilon and Flinders noted the juxtaposition of styles in Samber's translation: "In 'Bluebeard' there is an oddly colloquial and modern question: 'How comes this blood upon the key?' In the same tale, we find it

quaint that the wife and her sister address each other with the archaic 'thee' and 'thou'" (1981, 112).

13. Malarte-Feldman commented: "Where the tales speak the universal and timeless language of the marvelous, their morals fix them in the time and space of the late 1600s, often providing Perrault with the opportunity to mock the miraculous content of his own narrative. Samber, Johnson, Zipes, and many others have attempted to produce a translation in verse whose tone might to some extent render the savor of Perrault's affected and *précieux* style" (1999, 191).

14. Barchilon, Flinders, and Foreman note in the *Concordance* that Perrault uses a vocabulary of 2676 words for the *Tales*, using a concordance prepared in 1968, while Corneille or Racine used printed vocabularies of 4088 and 5000 words, respectively (1977, viii).

15. This word is highlighted by Malarte-Feldman as posing a special difficulty for English translators: "In the lexicon of the *Contes*, there are two recurrent terms with meanings deeply rooted in the language of the late 1600s: '*honnête/honnêteté*' and their opposite '*malhonnête/malhonnêteté*.' The *Dictionnaire de l'Académie* (1694) proposes '*poli*' or '*courtois*' as the definition for '*honnête*,' which in English is quite adequately reflected in words such as 'polite,' 'kind,' 'civil,' or 'mannerly.' On the other hand, '*malhonnête*' (meaning, according to the same dictionary, '*qui ignore les règles de la politesse et de la bienséance*' [that which ignores the rules of politeness and *bienséance*] is most often erroneously translated into 'rude' or 'rudeness' ('*grossier*' or '*rustre*' in French). The word is especially problematic for translators because it alludes to a past way of life and a culture particular to a period when *les bonnes moeurs* and *la bienséance* constituted elements of a rigid social code which ruled over France's upper society and was reflected in the literary style" (1999, 190; italics for French are added). Meredid Puw Davies in *The Tale of Bluebeard in German Literature* (2001) made this issue central to her interpretation of Perrault's comments on civilization.

16. This is one example where there was a substantive revision made between the 1695 dedication manuscript and the publication of 1697. In the first instance, Bluebeard adds: "*et que ie vienne a le scauoir*" (and if I come to find out about it), which is later omitted. Perhaps more important is the change of verb from "fear" (*craindre*) to "expect" (*attendre*), leaving the punishment both clear and at the same time unspecified: "*Il n'y rien que vous ne deuiez craindre de ma colere*" (there is nothing that you may not *fear* from my anger).

17. I am indebted to my colleague in Modern Languages at Pittsburg State University, Dr. Myriam Krepps, for confirming this and my reading of Perrault's French.

18. This last sentence, spelling out the reality of the spectacle and thus the consequences of seeing it, was added after the 1695 dedication manuscript.

19. Interestingly, Malarte-Feldman used this last sentence as a representative example of the challenges of translating Perrault. She said: "Often we found out that American English enabled more modern and looser translations: for example, Blue Beard's wife, after having discovered the corpses of her husband's former wives hanging in the forbidden room, returned to her bedroom, but 'she could not relax because she was too upset' according to Zipes' translation (*Beauties* [1989] 32). In the Clarion edition, Neil

Philip ([1993], 38) translated the same passage as 'but she was so distressed that she fainted on the way,' which, besides being inaccurate, underlines the challenge translators were up against when they had to interpret Perrault's enigmatic formula '*mais elle n'en pouvait venir à bout, tant elle était émue*' [but she could not come to the end of it, so much was she emotional]" (1999, 187).

20. It is unlikely that Guy Miège would have mistranslated from Perrault's French; but whoever G. M. was, it appears that either Samber or G. M. grounded their translation primarily on the other English translation, rather than on Perrault. Barchilon and Flinders missed the G. M. connection altogether when they stated: "The bizarre translation quoted above was reproduced in the first American edition (1794) and thus proves that the American publisher simply reprinted Samber's translation" (1981, 112). In fact, the American edition (Edes) used G. M.'s version; see note 9 above.

21. Another (twentieth-century) example gives "One mere hour to live," in order to give the brothers time to arrive on "the swift Arab horses" (William Cowper [192–?, n.p.]).

22. Malarte-Feldman also commented on the possessive adjective used here. Perrault's wife uses "my" brothers, and Anne also responds, here come "my" brothers; neither woman uses the more expected "our" brothers. Malarte-Feldman said: "As a whole, English translations respect the incongruities in Perrault's text, particularly as concerns Perrault's sometimes surprising use of possessive adjectives. . . . One would more logically expect that the two sisters, sharing as they do the possession of the two brothers in question, would refer to them with the possessive adjective 'our' rather than 'my.' The Clarion edition took upon itself to rectify Perrault's puzzling grammar by using the plural 'our' (Philip [1993] 41)" (1999, 190).

23. Except that, as Planché commented in the Appendix following his translation, it is not possible to translate the "dust" and "green" as verbs, as in the original (*perdoyer, verdoyer*): "I wished to point out that unless we could say in English 'the sun that *dusts* and the grass that *greens*,' we cannot approach the terse and graphic description of dear Sister Anne" (Planché 1858, 517, original emphasis).

24. Hannon (2001) argued that the instrument is a reflection of his true class and cowardliness, in that the cutlass is the instrument of a mere executioner (*bourreau*), and Bluebeard is someone who does not know how to handle the more aristocratic "*épée*."

25. Barchilon and Flinders noted that Perrault was trained as a lawyer and the "legalistic precision" of his fairy tale endings (1981, 108).

26. See chapter 4 for description and analysis of the English orientalized version of "Bluebeard."

27. Samber and G. M. were the first to translate these morals aiming for the "spirit" rather than the literal letter. Theirs is as follows: "O Curiosity, thou mortal bane! / Spite of thy charms, thou causest often pain / And fore regret, of which we daily find / A thousand instances attend mankind: / For thou, O may it not displease the fair, / A flitting pleasure art, but lasting care; / And always costs, alas! too dear the prize, / Which, in the moment of possession, dies. / Another. / A Very little share of common sense / And knowledge of the world, will soon evince, / That this a story is of long time

past, / No husbands now such panick terrors cast; / Nor weakly, with a vain despotick hand, / Imperious, what's impossible, command: / And be they discontented, or the fire / Of wicked jealousy their hearts inspire, / They softly sing; and of whatever hue / Their beards may chance to be, or black, or blue, / Grizzled, or russet, it is hard to say / Which of the two, the man or wife, bears sway." Nonetheless, the translation is more literal than, for instance, the Philip and Simborowski translation, which went so far as "Once the wife's made up her mind, / The husband meekly trails behind" (1993, 44).

Chapter 4

1. The "three tails" refer to horses' tails worn in the shield as a mark of rank (Colman 1798, 1983: 184 n.).

2. As discussed in the previous chapter, the earliest G. M. attribution is 1763, although it is not a first edition.

3. See Kelly's *Reminiscences* (1826, 130–31).

4. In the introduction to the *Broadview Anthology of Romantic Drama*, containing a reprinting of Colman's 1798 libretto, the editors noted: "As popular dramatic pieces, *Blue-Beard, Timour the Tartar*, and *Harlequin and Humpo* do more than reveal popular styles and changes in theater technology and dramatic technique. Like many pieces of popular culture, they engage with the topical issues, anxieties, and fascinations that held the attention of their respective publics. Thus the plays' ritualistic treatment of gender—*Blue-Beard*'s tale of violent misogyny, . . . all echo with key concerns in the age of Wollstonecraft and the subsequent backlash against her and other women writers and intellectuals. Even more striking are the 'orientalist' motifs invoked in *Blue-Beard* and *Timour*, which show Colman, Lewis, and their wartime audiences constructing a collective fantasy of Asia. Both plays direct their viewers to consider the importance of the 'East' just as England comes to dominate India, as Napoleon moves into Egypt, and as diplomatic and military manoeuvring intensifies in the Balkans and around the Black Sea. It is no accident, then, that audiences of *Blue-Beard* drew parallels between Abomelique's minister Ibrahim and George III's prime minister William Pitt" (Cox and Gamer 2003, xxiv).

5. The tales themselves "so far as we know, found their way into ms in Arabia round about 1545. The provenance of some stories, however, leads back to Persia and even to India" (Hürlimann 1959, 26). Marshall's list of chapbooks in 1708 includes the title *Arabian Nights' Entertainments* (Muir 1954, 26 n.). Harvey Darton wrote in his study of children's literature: "The Eastern tales [*Arabian Nights*], already present in some sort in *Aesop*, and to a less extent in details of the *Romances* and *Gesta Romanorum* —even in Chaucer's Squire's Tale—spread over Western Europe in the eighteenth century like an epidemic. The first serious European translator of them was the French diplomat Antoine Galland, whose *Mille et une Nuits* appeared in twelve volumes between 1704 and 1717. . . . The *first* English translation, from such of Galland's edition as had appeared, came out between 1705–8; no perfect copy seems to be known" (Darton 1932, 91).

6. *Banbury Chap-books*, by Edwin Pearson, shows three woodcuts for Bluebeard; the orientalized one bears the note: "This woodcut did duty for 'Arabian Nights,' 'Bluebeard,'

etc; probably designed by Cruikshank, engraved by Branstone" (1890, 116). Ros Ballaster made a compelling case in her study of the oriental influences on eighteenth-century English literature that *Arabian Nights* established the Turkish spy as a male, despotic, scopic figure in contrast to the female, survivalist, vocal figure of Scheherezade. Of Scheherezade and Schahriar, Ballaster noted: "Her agency is that of the tongue and of time, his of the eye and of the masterful control of space" (2005, 78). The connection with the Turk as a scopic figure is interesting, given the idea that he controls the castle and his wife's gaze and that he knows of her transgression almost as quickly as it happens. The other major text in the English eighteenth century according to her study was *Letters Writ by a Turkish Spy*, which ran to 600 letters (dates) and occasioned a sequel by Defoe: *A Continuation of Letters Written by a Turkish Spy* (1718). This text perpetuated the same dichotomy, but cast a male spy who in turn must fear for his life (as Caleb, of *Caleb Williams*) from a Turkish despot.

7. See "Othello Turns Turk" by Daniel Vitkus for a precise examination of English Protestant fears of the Ottoman invasion expressed through *Othello*. Vitkus also noted that Othello, while not a Turk, easily slips into the "othered" position for English protestant audiences: "Othello, the noble Moor of Venice, is not, however, to be identified with a specific, historically accurate racial category; rather, he is a hybrid who might be associated, in the minds of Shakespeare's audience, with a whole set of related terms—'Moor,' 'Turk,' 'Ottomite,' 'Saracen,' 'Mahometan,' 'Egyptian,' 'Judean,' 'Indian'—all constructed and positioned in opposition to Christian faith and virtue. More than being identified with any specific ethnic label, Othello is a theatrical embodiment of the dark, threatening powers at the edge of Christendom. Othello's identity is derived from a complex and multilayered tradition of representation that includes the classical barbarian, the Saracen or 'paynem knight' of medieval romance, the 'blackamoor,' and (an early modern version of the medieval types of lust, cruelty and aggression) the Turk" (2003, 90). Vitkus later discussed that for contemporary audiences a black skin was conventionally associated with damnation, and damned souls on stage, from medieval miracle plays on, were represented in black paint or black costumes (102–03).

8. Adultery is central to the cultural fear: the threat is not simply to Christendom, but to sexual virtue. Vitkus wrote of Othello: "The transformation of Othello, the 'Moor of Venice,' from a virtuous lover and Christian soldier to an enraged murderer may be read in the context of early modern conversion, or 'turning,' with particular attention to the sense of conversion as a sensual, sexual transgression" (2003, 84). Later: "Iago brings on the 'conversion' of Othello, and that conversion is dramatized as a fall into a bestial, sex-obsessed condition" (87).

9. Ysaure is also the name of the heroine in Untermeyer's "Bluebeard," *Tales from the Ballet* (1968), but the hero is Arthur.

10. Of this story, Daniel Vitkus wrote: "This story was dramatized on the London stage in at least four different versions during the sixteenth and seventeenth centuries. It was printed in both prose and verse forms and was widely disseminated" (2003, 99). Vitkus deferred to Chew, and both list: George Peele's lost play *The Turkish Mahomet and Hyrin the Fair Greek*; Thomas Goffe's *The Couragious Turke, or Amurath the First*, "written

after, and influenced by, Shakespeare's *Othello*" (Vitkus 2003, 99) but dramatizing an already well-known story; Lodowick Carlell's *Osmond the Great Turk* (ca. 1637–1642); and Gilbert Swinhoes' *Unhappy Fair Irene* (ca. 1640).

11. After looking at earlier anecdotal examples, a fuller version from William Paynter was given by Chew in *The Crescent and the Rose* (1937): "Mahomet—'not the false prophet,' the narrator is careful to note, but the Conqueror of Constantinople—fell in love with a fair Greek named Hyrenee and became 'a prey to his darling,' neglecting the affairs of state so that the people murmured against him and sedition would have arisen but for dread of his cruel rigour. For a long while the 'bewitched' despot was 'overwhelmed in beastly pleasure.' Among the courtiers was a frank and courteous gentleman, one Mustapha, who had been since boyhood the Sultan's intimate friend. He ventured to remonstrate with him and in order to inspire emulation recited to him the heroic deeds of his ancestors. He warned Mahomet that the Pope was organizing against him a coalition of all Christendom; and if Europe joined with the power of the Persian Sophy the Ottoman Empire would be destroyed. Mustapha suggested that if the Sultan could not overcome his infatuation he could take the lady with him to the wars. Mahomet was at first angry with his friend but presently saw the justice of his remonstrances. For a day and a night he had his pleasure of the fair Greek; and then after a banquet he commanded her to appear, decked and adorned; and in the presence of the nobility he caught her by the hair and with his falchion struck off her head. 'Now,' he exclaimed, 'ye know whether your Emperor is able to represse and bridle his affections or not!'" (Paynter 1566 1.30).

12. Of the last Chew stated it "is too well-known . . . to require comment."

13. "Selim" appears to be a common name in Eastern-themed English dramas; in addition to *Barbarossa* and *Bluebeard*, there is also a Selim character in the contemporary *The Forty Thieves*. J. N. Ireland indicated that Sheridan sketched the outline, the dialogue was written by his brother-in-law Ward, the music composed by Kelly, and the drama revised by Colman (1968, 257). It first appeared on the New York stage in March 1808. Chew (1937) is a good source for these, including *Selim the Grim*.

14. Burke prosecuted Hastings' impeachment trials from 1788 to 1795.

15. The different versions were discussed and collated by William McBurney in his scholarly edition. Lillo's play was first briefly produced by Henry Fielding at the Little Theatre in the Haymarket. After a first run of seven nights during the spring of 1736, it was withdrawn, "refurbished" somewhat by Henry Fielding, and replayed for eleven nights in 1737. McBurney noted: "Lillo lost both champion and stage, and the tragedy was not presented again before his death in 1739" (1966, xi). It had "sporadic" revivals through the midcentury. "Between 1782 and 1784 two rival adaptations of the tragedy, by George Colman the elder and Henry Mackenzie, appeared on London stages and bookstalls. Eventually, the Colman text (1782) surpassed in popularity not only Mackenzie's version but also Lillo's original" (x). In addition to the versions listed by McBurney, including the "influential collection, *The British Theatre* (London, 1808)" by Elizabeth Inchbald, the version reprinted in *The Select London Stage* (1827) under Lillo's name is also Colman's version, unattributed, determined according to McBurney's collation. As McBurney commented, the most notable effects of Colman's alterations are to cut the play from an

already economical 1244 lines to 1050 lines (xvi n.). Interestingly, it was Lillo's play referred to in a chapter entitled "Woman's Curiosity" by T. Thiselton-Dyer, as late as 1906.

16. McBurney's Appendix, "The Source of *Fatal Curiosity*," cited a black-letter pamphlet of 1618: *Newes from Perin in Cornwall of a Most Bloody and un-exampled Murther very lately committed by a Father on his owne Sonne (who was lately returned from the Indyes) at the Instigation of a mercilesse Step-mother* (1966, 55). But the introduction also footnoted William E. A. Axon, "The Story of Lillo's 'Fatal Curiosity,'" from *Notes & Queries* 6th Series, V (1882): 21–23, which cited several international analogues to it (xii).

17. McBurney noted the convention of double titles: "The first title stated a norm or a problem, and the second implied or stated a complementary aspect of the problem. Thus, in *Guilt Its Own Punishment; or, Fatal Curiosity*, Lillo suggests that Old Wilmot and Agnes, who commit 'this horrible deed that punishes itself,' are complemented by their son, whose 'curiosity' brings disaster to himself and to his parents" (1966, xx). He footnoted that "the title was reduced to *Fatal Curiosity* after the first performance, perhaps in imitation of those plays such as *The Fatal Dowry* and *The Fatal Marriage*." Colman's edition was first published as: *Fatal Curiosity . . . With Alterations* (London: Printed for T. Cadell, 1783).

18. McBurney (1966, xiii) noted the Shakespearean allusions rife in Lillo's play, including *Othello*.

19. The libretto was published in Amsterdam in 1791 by G. Dufour.

20. Kelly's claim, repeated in volume 2 of his *Reminiscences*, at the point where he discusses the first productions of *Blue Beard*, that he used none of Grétry's music is not accurate. Critics are clear on the fact of his borrowing, but nevertheless praise his abilities in selecting and adapting music. See in particular Porter (1990, 63–66) and also Porter (1994, xii–xxiii).

21. The libretto consists of 20 handwritten leaves, without music.

22. Also interesting is the use of a key "form'd of gold" (*Blue Beard*, "Recitative"). Such a golden key crops up occasionally in chapbooks also. Another less obvious gothic effect made its first appearance in this play: immediately prior to the finale, during the quartetto in which Abomelique calls for Fatima while she, Irene, and Shacabac try to get assistance, trombones are played. In her edition of the play in *British Opera in America*, Susan Porter quoted Roger Fiske who said, "it is the first occurrence in trombones in eighteenth-century theater music, and is intended to produce a 'spine-chilling effect'" (Fiske 1973, 283).

23. This may in part be due to generic considerations. Philip Cox reminded us that "The relationship between a novel and its dramatic adaptation in the Romantic period would, of course, have had very different cultural resonances: the drama had an established literary genealogy which invested it with a potential cultural respectability whereas the novel was, historically, a relative newcomer which was often denied such respectability as a result of the very popularity which rendered it so culturally prominent" (2000, 5).

24. Initially the play was a "Spectacular failure" that was performed "only four times" until the more successful revised version was staged and "received sufficient acclaim to heal the author's wounded pride" (Colman 1798, 1983: 60). Damian Walford Davies noted

the play's success and legacy: "George Raymond remarked in 1844 that the play became 'a stock-piece in the acting drama' (*Memoirs of R. W. Elliston*, 2 vols., London, 1844–1845: 1:74) and Bagster-Collins notes that '*The Iron Chest*, stand[ing] somewhere between tragedy and melodrama' held the stage for 'longer than forty years' and that 'Most of the great tragedians of the nineteenth-century played it and scored personal triumphs. It [the 1815 production Hazlitt saw] was one of Edmund Kean's greatest performances' (Bagster-Collins, *George Colman*, 100–01 n.; Colman 1798,1983, 63). The last major staging of the play was Sir Henry Irving's at the Lyceaum in 1879; the *Times* described it as 'a curious fossil' and the *London Figaro* as being of 'purely antiquarian' attraction, but the *Daily Telegraph* recorded that it took 'a deep hold on the people'" (Davies 2002, 532).

25. See Philip Cox's chapter "*Caleb Williams* and *The Iron Chest*" (2000, 25–43). In "The Politics of Allusion: *Caleb Williams, The Iron Chest, Middlemarch* and the *Armoire de Fer*," Damian Walford Davies also suggested that in playing down the critical commentary posed by Godwin's highly political and "thoroughly allusive" novel, Colman made the subject palatable for the stage: "The stage has now no business with Politicks: and, should a Dramatick Author endeavour to dabble in them, it is the Lord Chamberlain's office to check his attempts, before they meet the eye of the Publick" (Colman 1796, xxi). In an interesting coda to this sort of remark, Colman himself was made Examiner of Plays in 1824, and is widely recorded to have been vicious in the prosecution of his duties. Robert Hume noted a practical reason for the rise of melodrama in the acoustics of ever-larger theatres: "The new Drury Lane of 1794 held more than 3,600 people—with disastrous effects on the audibility of the dialogue. Covent Garden was likewise inflated—from a capacity of some 1,400 in 1732 to about 3,000 in 1792. The Licensing Act prevented the erection of more theatres, and in consequence the patent houses bloated themselves on their monopoly. Given the difficulty of hearing dialogue clearly in such barns we cannot be surprised that ranting melodrama flourished while wit comedy languished" (1981, 7).

26. Another critic who argued that Godwin uses the locked trunk motif in a way that transcends the mere gothic use of it (per Colman) is W. M. Verhoeven: "while Colman mistakenly assumes that the meaning of the trunk *is* its contents—Godwin realized that the true significance of the locked trunk lies in the very act of opening it. While Colman's interest in the trunk is merely dramatic, therefore, Godwin is interested in the locked-trunk motif because it opens up possibilities for psychological and epistemological analysis and speculation" (1995, 212–13).

27. Davies does not cite the source, other than to call it "A widely circulated contemporary print."

28. Verhoeven wrote that "little use of [the *armoire*] was made at the king's trial, [but it] entered history surrounded by myth as the revelation that proved his treachery and sealed his fate" (1995, 527). He quoted Andrew Freeman (1989) in support.

29. "Both horrible and sensual (all those wives!), Bluebeard is perhaps a more comfortable figure when he is the Other, the Outsider, the Foreigner, and not one of us" (Windling 2002, 6).

30. Winfried Menninghaus analyzed in book length this example of a Romantic poetics of nonsense. She provided all quotations from the work in English. The tale is

also the subject of a German dissertation by Klaus Buschmann: "Everything Was Empty: Ludwig Tieck's Bluebeard Adaptations" (Universität Wien, 2006).

31. See chapter 7 for more on Tieck's play at the time of its English nineteenth-century translation.

32. The orientalization of Bluebeard has had a permanent impact. However, by the last decade of the nineteenth century, the London Stage calendar (Wearing 1976) did not list a single version of *Bluebeard*, English or French, drama, opera, Christmas pantomime or otherwise, and the only Colman piece to appear in London that decade was another comedy, *The Heir-at-Law*.

33. This information is repeated in library catalogues of Colman's drama, citing "Barker" as their source. In the section "Bluebeard in Theatre" in Harriet Mowshowitz's study (1970), she cited Doutrepont as the source for this date. Alone of the critics consulted, R. J. Broadbent in *The History of Pantomime* (1901) provided more information on this play, and he was possibly still quoting a source (the magazine *The Drama*, from the early 1800s, source not given): "'Blue Beard' was first dramatised at Paris, in 1746, when '*Barbe bleu*' was thus announced:—*Pantomime—representée par la troupe des Comediens Pantomimes, Foir St. Laurent*. It was afterwards dramatised at the Earl of Barrymore's Theatre, Wargrave, Berks., and in 1791. After that the subject was produced at Covent Garden Theatre as a Pantomime" (Broadbent 1901, 204).

34. As Harriet Mowshowitz noted, "the bearded wife-slayer was adapted wholeheartedly by the [French] theatre. . . . One finds him in all varieties of popular theatre: in pantomimes, in vaudeville, in operettas and in burlesques" (1970, 85).

35. In *Biographica Dramatica; or, a Companion to the Playhouse*, Stephen Jones also ascribed the orientalism to Colman: "Mr. Colman has made him [Bluebeard] a bashaw of three tails; presuming, we may suppose, that the murderer of seven wives must have been a very Turk indeed. The original Blue Beard, however, was none other than Gilles, Marquis de Laval" (1811, 2:62).

36. "And if ye fear that ye shall not act with equity towards orphans of the female sex, take in marriage of such other women as please you, two, or three, or four, and not more" (*The Koran*, chapter 4, Bath, 1795 [*sic*], 92; cited in Colman 1798, 1983).

37. Colman shifted this scene in later editions to keep the chamber mysterious.

38. Kelly had a share in management of Drury Lane Theater for many years. He was a first-hand witness to its destruction by fire, and it is possible that the originals of *Blue Beard* burned with the theater, as Kelly commented later in his *Reminiscences* (1826, 252–53).

39. Kelly similarly noted the practice of handing off work to Colman, his friend of decades, in his *Reminiscences* (1826, 2:204–05). For his part, Colman noted in his preface to *Blue Beard; or, Female Curiosity!* the largesse of allowing Kelly to make his reputation as composer with this piece: "I have given an opportunity to Mr. Kelly of fully establishing his reputation, as a Musical Composer, with a Publick, whose favour he has long, and deservedly experienced as a Singer. Crouded [*sic*] audiences have testified the most strong, and decided approbation of his original Musick, in *Blue-Beard*; and amply applauded his taste, and judgment, in Selection" (1798c).

40. Debate does not seem to be over whether the play was popular, but whether (as melodrama) it was "good." J. W. Lake noted representatively, in *The dramatic works of George Colman the Younger: with an original life of the author*: "If popularity is any indication of merit, the dramatic romance of *Blue-Beard, or Female Curiosity* is a *chef d'oeuvre* of its kind, and excited in an extraordinary manner the curiosity of the play-going public of both sexes. It was brought out at Covent Garden, with all the pomp and display of scenery and machinery, dresses and decorations for which that theatre is so justly celebrated in getting up such pieces.... The march over the mountains, when Abomelique comes in oriental magnificence to claim the fair, but unwilling, Fatima, as his bride, is one of the finest ever produced on the stage" (1823–1824). In the preface to the Oxberry edition of the play, the editor P. P. wrote: "The poetry, we admit, is not of a very high order; the puns are vile, the sentiments stale, and the language in general bombastic. Yet, the author, who had little in view beyond manufacturing a convenient vehicle for the display of gorgeous scenery and shewy [*sic*] processions, has effected his intention with a cleverness, which many who may think meanly of the performance, would find some difficulty in equaling; and, what probably was to him but the pastime of an evening, has on numerous succeeding evenings imparted gratification to thousands" (1823, iv).

41. Extant copies at the British Library alone show that the play was in its 7th reprinting by 1800. See Porter (1990, 1994) for other major editions. The play continued to be printed even much later in the century, as evidenced by a "one penny" edition of around 1854, which changed Beda to Gulnare but otherwise remained the same as Colman's libretto: *Blue Beard; or, Female Curiosity*, Boys of England Edition (London: Skelt). It is dated 1854? by the *National Union Catalogue Pre-1956 Imprints*: 61:686.

42. Apparently, "The March in Bluebeard," even accompanied sailors on a North Pole expedition in 1810 and was described as "one of the smash hits of the era" (Roberts n.d.). Susan Porter commented: "Of the more than two hundred separate issues of Kelly's works published in American cities during his lifetime, one of the most popular was the 'March' from *Blue Beard*" (1994, xxi). See Porter for more on music statistics (1990, 66–70).

43. Porter noted: "By 1810, it had been performed more than 120 times in theaters in New York, Philadelphia, Baltimore, Boston, and Charleston; it was one of the ten works most performed in America between 1790 and 1810" (1990, 61).

44. See Cox and Gamer. "P.P." wrote in the prefatory remarks to the 1823 Oxberry edition of the play that this was the first use of live horses on stage (see Colman 1823). Michael Kelly also wrote of the event in his memoir (1826, 263). Porter noted that live elephants had been used in a New York staging in 1806 (1990, 67).

45. Saxon (1968) wrote about the revival in *Enter Foot and Horse*: "At a time when the annual average receipts amounted to approximately 80,000 pounds, the season of 1810–1811 brought in 100,000 pounds, of which more than 21,000 pounds was produced by the first 41 nights of *Blue Beard* alone." The annual profits from the 1810–1811 season exceeded the contemporary average by that much or more (Frederick Reynolds 1826, 2:403–04). Saxon quoted the initial review in *The Examiner* at greater length, which gave details of the performance. Saxon also cited a lengthy excerpt from Kemble's biographer

James Boaden, who described the horses' choreography and well-acted death throes in particular (1825, 2:541–42). The spectacle was another smash hit to which Covent Garden had recourse whenever profits were slow (Alfred Bunn 1840, 2:216–17), and it launched a trend: *Timour the Tartar* joined *Blue Beard* as a new equestrian spectacle in April 1811. But critics were unhappy with the equestrian *Blue Beard*, as Saxon illustrated. The tenor of protest is at the mixing of genres. Covent Garden is a stage for legitimate theater, while Astley's horses allegedly belonged to another genre entirely. But as Saxon summarized: "Spectacle, not Shakespeare, was what audiences now paid their money to see" (1968, 93). The same year also saw the French play *Barbe-Bleue ou les Enchantements d'Alcine: Tableaux en Trois Actions* (Paris, 1811), which features a German Bluebeard: Rodolphe Barbe-Bleue (Prince Souverain d'Allemagne, "Sovereign Prince of Germany," my translation), recalling Tieck's *Ritter Blaubart*. But the additional cast of characters and storyline follows the template begun by Grétry and developed by Colman and Kelly: young, poor, and beautiful Aglaure, her sister Anne, Aglaure's true love Arthur (a rich young lord), and a secondary cast of servants. However, Aglaure's sister is still Anne, they have two brothers (Verther and Mederic), and their mother Mathilda. The French play does not adopt the Turkish scenario of the mercenary father.

Chapter 5

1. This grandiose claim for chapbooks is echoed throughout chapbook studies. John Ashton wrote in 1882 that they went "to every village, and to every home" (v). In 1904, Ralph Bergengren described the chapbook readership as "the entire rank and file of the British nation" (39). Harvey Darton noted: "They were the books of the people of England" (1932, 70). Victor Neuburg wrote in *The Penny Histories* that they "formed the most important and numerically the most considerable element in the printed popular literature of the eighteenth century" (1968, 3).

2. One comparison demonstrates how little deviation there could be: *The Popular Story of Blue Beard, or, the Effects of Female Curiosity* (G. Caldwell 1828) and *The Popular Story of Blue Beard, or, Female Curiosity* (J. Innes, [1830?]), whose illustrations reappear with different text entirely in *The History of Blue Beard* (W. S. Johnson 1850). The text and typesetting of the Caldwell and Innes versions are identical, but slight deviations show whichever text is the later (dating of Innes copy is uncertain) being somewhat devious about the wholesale borrowing.

3. There is no doubt that English chapbooks were imported and sold in America just as were other books. William Williams, a printer of Utica, New York, in the "Patriot and Patrol" of August 18, 1818, advertised for the wholesale and retail trade, "8,000 Chap Books, 60 kinds," and "27,000 toy books, 33 kinds," and previous to that date there are booksellers' advertisements relating to definite importations from abroad (Weiss 1938, 22). While it is not possible to know whether copies now in American libraries were imported then or since, the 1905 *Catalogue of the New York Public Library* lists several versions of Bluebeard chapbooks. A "home grown" version attests to the story's popularity in the early

1800s in the Northeast: *A New History of Blue Beard, written by Gaffer Blackbeard, for the Amusement of Little Lack Beard and his Pretty Sisters* survives in twenty or so editions from a handful of different publishers in the northeastern states; see note 11, below.

4. In a journal entry dated 10 July 1763, Boswell noted: "I must mention that some days ago I went to the old printing-office in Bow Church-yard kept by Dicey, . . . There are ushered into the world of literature JACK AND THE GIANTS, THE SEVEN WISE MEN OF GOTHAM, and other story-books which in my dawning years amused me as much as RASSELAS does now. I saw the whole scheme with a kind of romantic feeling to find myself really where all my old darlings were printed. I bought two dozen of the story-books and had them bound up with the title CURIOUS PRODUCTIONS" (Boswell 1763). Margaret Spufford commented on such evidence: "If Johnson and Boswell, Burke and Morris all read the chapbooks as schoolboys . . . the gap between the culture of the elite and popular culture was not complete" (1981, 75).

5. Their French equivalents are similarly described: "*Vagabonde, humble et méconnue*" (Brochon 1954, 92). In 1900 Charles Gerring, who otherwise copies wholesale from Percy Cropper, called them: "Uninviting, poor starved things, printed in the rudest manner on the roughest of paper, decorated with the most villainous of cuts" (1900, 100).

6. Harvey Darton wrote similarly that fairy tales were an endangered species: "It is easy to condemn that huckstering trade and its products. [But] . . . they also, *and they alone*, found a home in print, among all the treasure and the rubbish they preserved, for two higher, more immortal things, the Fairy-Tale and the Nursery Rhyme" (1932, 82, emphasis added); "The chapmen gave them their true juvenile vogue in print" (1932, 94). Interestingly, as part of the slow death of the chapbook, fairy tales may have enjoyed a longer shelf-life than other types in the catalogues. Victor Neuburg noted in *The Penny Histories* that when the main trend was over by the early decades of the nineteenth century, "It was no longer the most important element in popular literature; and it was now entirely intended for child readers" (1968, 65). He does not date the actual death of the chapbook (current revivals notwithstanding) until the 1880s, with the close of W. S. Fortey's business, as the last owner of the Catnach Press (a renowned chapbook publisher). The seventy intervening years, then, are left to these "child readers" and their favorite chapbooks, of which *Bluebeard* was undoubtedly one. Neuburg situated the chapbook as the only source of fairy tales during this period: "More important from the point of view of young readers was the fact that fairy tales were available to them only in chapbook form. The rich tradition of English fairy mythology survived in the eighteenth century almost entirely because of chapbooks. Like the medieval romances, fairy legends and tales had remained popular amongst educated people until about the middle of the seventeenth century, and they declined similarly about this time. Through chapbooks, children had immediate and ready access to a very considerable range of traditional literature that their more sophisticated elders had, for better or worse, outgrown" (1968, 15–16).

7. As in Gloria Delamar: "John Newbery was to gain recognition as the first publisher to devote a line to the publication of books expressly for children" (1987, 6).

8. The quote is given in chapter 3. W. J. Bowd states in "The Life of a Farm Worker" that his father James Bowd was "what we call Maneger [*sic*] over the haymakers" and, as the title and autobiographical content of the excerpt from Bowd's 1889 journal indicates, the man recalling the chapbooks of his childhood was a farm worker in later life, supporting the argument that chapbooks were not limited to the educated classes (1955, 293–94).

9. The years 1854–1856 were dated by the Lilly Library (IN). The identical Bodleian Library version (filmed for the Opie Collection) suggests the year 1860. The cover pages are different: the Bodleian Library chapbook cover is adorned with a repeating border of floral tiles, larger inset corner tiles, and borders around each section of text. The first section has the series title: "Children's Popular Tales." But text and images are the same, save that where the Bodleian version has the name as "Fatimer" in the text, the Lilly version has "Fatima."

10. The W. Walker & Sons *Blue Beard* [185–] and the Peter G. Thomson [n.d.], respectively, describe this sequence: "They spent a great part of the night in trying to clean off the blood from the key, but without effect" and "they passed a sleepless night in trying to clean off the blood from the key, but without effect."

11. The Colman-Kelly storyline and characters are also used by the American verse chapbook: *A New History of Blue Beard Written by Gaffer Blackbeard for the Amusement of Little Lack Beard and His Pretty Sisters*, that circulated in multiple editions from presses in the northeastern states from 1800 (John Babcock 1800) through around 1822 (Watson, David). Editions were printed in Philadelphia (John Adams); Montpelier, Vermont (Park's Press); Windsor, Vermont (Farnsworth, Josse Cochran); Albany, New York (Hosford); New Haven, Connecticut (Sidney's); and Stonington, Connecticut (Trumbull). The chapbook is unusual in praising Fatima for her learning: "She wrote immediately to Selim. Now only think what a fine thing it is to be a scholar, for if Fatima could not have wrote to her lover, nobody else would have done it for her, and what would have been the consequence you will find by and by; so above all things learn to read your book, that your daddy and mammy may learn you to write too" (Printed by John Adams 1804, 11–12).

12. In *History of Blue Beard* (J. L. Marks [1835–1857]) it goes as follows: "There lived a rich Turk in Con-stan-ti-no-ple, / Who had a blue beard—and whiskers as well."

13. The Dean & Munday version [not after 1847] repeats this theme, with more elaboration: "the younger of the two was thought to be unusually handsome, and was therefore noticed rather more than her sister. It often happens that beauty is a misfortune, because, if a young lady has not good sense as well as beauty, it will make her vain; and a vain girl often falls into misery or trouble." It is repeated in Dean & Son [not before 1882].

14. Also: J. Innes [1830?]; W. Walker & Sons [185–]; and Peter G. Thomson [n.d.]. Greed is directly addressed in the later comic version by Bayley, at Bluebeard's entertainment: "And *didn't* she gobble, and *didn't* she stuff? / And *wasn't she sorry when she'd had enough!!*" (Wm. S. Orr & Co. [ca. 1842], 10, original emphasis).

15. This version is used for "Blue Beard, or Female Curiosity" in Dean & Munday [not after 1847].

16. It is unclear how her "love of display" is relevant to the story as it is told in this version. It goes on further: "you would have thought she was a Queen at least, making a tour of her dominions. This was all very pleasant for the vain and giddy Fatima: so much so, indeed, that she was in no hurry to fix a date for the marriage."

17. See *Blue Beard* (Pott & Amery [n.d.]): "At this moment her sister, who wondered at her absence, and had gone in search of her, came up, and tried to keep her back; but all in vain, so her sister left her." In the illustration, Anne has both hands on her sister's arm, trying to prevent her from using the key. Similarly: "Her sister, who alone knew what she meant to do, followed and tried to bring her back; but all in vain, so her sister left her" (Thomas Nelson 1900, 115).

18. Same text as *Blue Beard* (Pott & Amery [n.d.]).

19. "He knew she was in his power, and that her escape was impracticable; her beauty had also some effect: he gave her five minutes more" (Printed for N. Hailes 1817); "I'll give you ten minutes / I'm not in a hurry" (McLoughlin Bros. [189–]).

20. In one example, they are "one a captain of foot, and the other of horse" (J. M. Dent & Co. 1895).

21. A French version printed in London also gives it as "*La Chambre bleue*" (Tabart et Co. 1804), but they also printed more than ten English editions of the same, and the French version has a list of "Idioms in the foregoing story, with their proper Interpretations," so it perhaps originated in English (Tabart et Co. 1804.)

22. In another example the word *gore* is itself used: "Fatima beheld the floor crimsoned with human gore! which had flowed from the bodies" (T. Richardson [not before 1838], 8).

23. The practice of labeling important places and people for audience edification was long established in dramatic terms through the pantomime, where it was often necessary.

24. The same is seen in 1828: "Bluebeard's wife was a bold-spirited woman, with whom he quarreled soon after marriage; and having in the heat of his anger murdered her, he concealed the body in the blue closet" (G. Caldwell 1828, 13; J. Innes [ca. 1830]).

25. One version even uses the word *lawful* to describe her inheritance, either out of anxiety over her riches, in contrast to Bluebeard's unlawful behavior, or both: "as Blue Beard had no heirs she found herself the lawful possessor of his great riches" (J. March [1864–1875], 8).

26. This moral is reprinted on the cover of J. Pitts [1810?].

27. Same as McLoughlin Bros. [ca. 1856–1870].

28. This "variant" version is quoted by Cunningham (1889).

29. See Harvey Darton (1932, 71).

30. Le Men went on to link the morals provided by Perrault to this tradition: "The image appeals to the sense and emphasizes the concreteness of the text, that is, the story. The rhymed epigram, or 'morality,' belongs to the emblem's abstract aspect, its moral lesson. The motto is used to link image and text, and it has a double meaning: the first is related to the picture preceding the tale; the second is discovered with the 'morality' at the

end, which becomes integrated only upon a second reading. This format is indicative of how involved illustrations are in the reading and rereading process" (1992, 21).

31. Whether by accident or design, all illustrations in one edition are out of order. If not accidental, it demonstrates the disregard for the order of events in the narrative: what matters is not the order, but the inclusion of the illustrations. They show, first, one brother killing Bluebeard; next, Ann waving from the turret; third, a woman looking at herself in a mirror, another woman behind her; Bluebeard giving the key, the near-execution, courtship or departure with Bluebeard bowing to a woman seated before the parted curtains of a tent (S. Marks & Sons [1876]). The cover of this chapbook shows the wife reacting to the contents of the chamber: billowing smoke and skeletons.

32. While Perrault did not make the illustrations himself, his dedication and presentation of the maquette to his niece is a form of approval of the manuscript: "No one knows who drew these illustrations, even though the frontispiece was signed by an engraver named Clouzier. He was probably someone close to Perrault, as was the scribe of the manuscript. And, presumably, Perrault himself approved the illustrator's interpretations since he gave the illuminated manuscript to 'Mademoiselle'" (Le Men 1992, 34).

33. Le Men also added here that "the violent scenes of Bluebeard . . . expressed with simple gestures, are close to the style of popular broadsheet imagery" (1992, 32). In *L'Histoire des Contes* (1992), Catherine Velay-Vallantin provided three Bluebeard illustrations, one from a chapbook, one from a broadsheet, and one from a juvenile collection. All three show the iconic near-execution: the wife is on her knees, held by the hair, Bluebeard has his cutlass raised. Taken representatively, the imagery is consonant with English chapbook illustrations. See also her *Les Usages de l'imprimé* (1987, 155–56) on the blue book iconography of the "interrupted execution."

34. This is evident even when more than one tale is shown on the cover, as in *Blue Beard: Pleasing Picture Book* ([G. Bishop & Co.] [185–]), where scenes from six tales are shown in medallions. Bluebeard is shown top right, and is the moment of near-execution: Blue Beard holds his wife's hair, she implores him on her knees, his sword is raised overhead, the curve of the scimitar matching that of the medallion.

35. Earliest extant is Hurst & Co. (1840).

36. The text is the same as that used in the Pott & Amery [n.d.] version. The Dulac illustration shows the wife frontally, but as she is looking out at the reader, the fourth wall is broken and if there are bodies, they are out here with us, the readers. Another version dated sometime in the twentieth century similarly does not show a chamber, but does depict an axe and chopping block (Printed in Bavaria 19–).

Chapter 6

1. The line "You outrageous man!" is from Sister Anne to Bluebeard, in *Droll Dramas for Christmas Comedians and Parlour Performers* (Evans 1846, 20).

2. See note 1, chapter 4.

3. David Mayer, in *Harlequin in His Element*, noted first that the gothic template (used to such effect in the Colman-Kelly melodrama) heavily influenced pantomime (1969, 90–91). He also noted that the fad for exoticism pervaded the pantomimes of the period: "The most pervasive foreign and exotic style was the potpourri of Indian and near-Eastern styles variously called Asiatic, Hindu, Eastern, or Persian. . . . In pantomime, however, the Eastern style was the apex of splendor and luxury and was well established as a fashionable decor by the 1790's" (156–57). He added: "innumerable pantomimes were enriched with Asiatic or Persian settings and costumes. Many pantomimes whose libretti give no indication that their milieu is Eastern appear, when reproduced in the juvenile drama, to have been costumed and decorated in some variant of that style" (160).

4. See Meredid Puw Davies, "Laughing Their Heads Off" (2002). Her thesis is that in contrast to the French and English comic tradition of Bluebeard on stage, the German tradition was a serious one, with several exceptions, which are the focus of her study in this article (using 12 works, dated 1797–1895).

5. The French source is Eugène Sue's *Le Morne au Diable* (1842), translated as the novel *The Female Bluebeard* (1844).

6. Possibly still quoting *The Drama* magazine from the early 1800s, source not given.

7. Broadbent wrote: "The year 1702 marks the appearance of the first Pantomime introduced to the English stage, written by John Weaver, a friend of Addison and Steele's, and entitled 'Tavern Bilkers.' It was produced at Drury Lane" (1901, 137). Cyril Beaumont refuted this specifically, and cited several instances of native harlequinades in England before then, including one by Aphra Behn (1926, 87).

8. Drury Lane began by mocking the popular trend, but quickly changed their stance when the lucrativeness of pantomime production became known. Leo Hughes described the eighteenth-century chronology in "Afterpieces: Or, That's Entertainment," noting that when Drury Lane burlesqued John Rich's Harlequin in 1723, the burlesque was hissed. Whereupon "Drury Lane shifted their strategy from ridicule to imitation" (1981, 62). All critics agree that the holiday pantomimes made the money on which the theatre depended for the rest of the year's offerings. One critic commented that Laura Keene's failing season (1857) was "redeemed by a Christmas Pantomime, *Harlequin and Bluebeard*" (Mowry 1993, 39).

9. Pantomimes were holiday fare, but not until much later in the century were they merely Christmas fare (opening on Boxing Day). Booth noted that they were staged in the major theatres at Easter and Christmas, and sometimes in November, while the minor theatres staged them at Easter and midsummer.

10. Booth, in *English Nineteenth Century Plays*, noted: "The rage for spectacular displays of horsemanship on stage was also parodied in Charles Dibdin's *Harlequin and Bluebeard* (1811), in which the Genius of Burlesque transforms the main characters of Colman's newly equestrianized spectacle-melodrama *Blue-Beard* into the harlequinade stereotypes" (1976, 5.30). David Mayer further noted that Grimaldi, England's most famous Clown, possibly played Sister Anne, and then was Clown in Dibdin's production: "When *Bluebeard* was produced as a melodrama at Covent Garden in February 1811,

Charles Dibdin, Jr., responded by offering *Harlequin and Bluebeard* with the summer's entertainment at Sadler's Wells. Of his parody, Dibdin observed: 'In the Town Scene, in which the Trio and Chorus "I see them galloping" is introduced (of which my Trio was a Parody), Grimaldi was very happy in his caricature of the action and manner of Miss Decamp (now Mrs. C. Kemble) the heroine of Bluebeard, who (as I was informed) witnessed the performance of our Pantomime, and joined heartily in the laughter and plaudits of the audience'" [Citing Charles Dibdin, Jr.]. Mayer added: "although no libretto of Dibdin's pantomime survives to reveal the extent of the parody, puffs for the pantomime in the daily newspapers revealed that the villainous Bluebeard transformed by the Genius of Burlesque became Pantaloon, Selim and Fatima were likewise transformed into Harlequin and Columbine, and Grimaldi was added as Clown. The horses were not neglected, for the piece concludes with 'a grand Gallimaufry Combat, Bipeds and Quadrupeds; the Quadrupediant department under the direction of Mr. Grimaldi'" (Mayer 1969, 78–79). A play called *Harlequin Bluebeard* also played at the Royal Pavilion Theatre, Whitechapel, in 1840 (noted in reference to the set design by William Beaumont, "People Play UK" website). A *Harlequin Bluebeard* was also recorded by John Kenrick (1996) as being played on Broadway, opening December 26, 1864 at the Hippotheatron (circus), and running for fifty-six performances. Similarly, a circus "Grand Pantomime of Blue Beard" is noted in the British Library, with an illustrated poster (Sanger's Hippodrome, Circus and Menagerie, Lambeth, Evanion Catalogue), dated circa 1881. It notes the use of "20 elephants, dromedaries &c."

11. Broadbent noted of Columbine's origins: "About 1695, Columbine appeared in a parti-coloured gown like a female Harlequin, and in the piece '*Le Retour de la foie de Besons*,' acted at the *Comedie Italiene*. As the innovation was much liked, the part of Columbine came to be dressed like the Harlequin. The Columbine dressed in short muslin skirts is a creation of modern times. In the French Comedies Columbine was often Harlequin's wife, but she never had the powers of a magical wand" (1901, 125).

12. Booth attributed the change to Sheridan's *Robinson Crusoe*: "This pattern had changed little from the years of John Rich's pantomimes at Covent Garden and Garrick's at Drury Lane, except that after Sheridan's *Robinson Crusoe* (1781) the harlequinade scenes constituted the second and greater part; instead of being interwoven with the serious and refined scenes. They were also directly related to what became known as the 'opening' (the first part) by the transformation of the principal characters in that opening . . . into the regular personages of the harlequinade. . . . At the same time the supernatural being effecting the transformation awarded Harlequin his wonder-working bat, which, slapped upon the scenery, floor, or object, gave the cue for the transformation whose purpose was to hinder pursuit or bewilder, frighten, and torment the pursuers; this ritual existed in England from the earliest days of eighteenth-century pantomime" (1976, 2–3).

13. Hunt, *The Examiner* (1817). For his writing in *The Tatler* (28 December 1831), I am indebted to the quotation provided in Booth (1976, 8–9).

14. Booth and Beaumont attributed this to the loss of Grimaldi, who as Clown was a main attraction. Presumably also the lapse of patent theatre restrictions led to the demise

of harlequinade, as it was no longer as necessary as a means for the minor theatre to stage dramatic spectacles that did not rival the patent theatre offerings.

15. Beaumont wrote: "During the eighteenth century there had been isolated speaking-pantomimes . . . Opening scenes were sung until 1830, when Mark Lemon wrote a burlesque to precede the harlequinade in *Harlequin Fat and Harlequin Bat, or, The Giant's Causeway*, produced at Covent Garden" (1926, 94). Planché discussed the restrictions imposed on the minor theatres critically: "no one had a legal right to open his mouth on stage unaccompanied by music; and the next step was to evade the law by the tinkling of a piano in the orchestra throughout the interdicted performances" (1872, 289).

16. Although Booth distinguished specifically between melodrama and "melodramatic spectacle," using this play as an example of the latter (1973a).

17. Bluebeard comments: "I'm par excellence, the mormon of the day," (6) and sings "I rather like polygamy," while Oberon comments: "How they would welcome him in Salt Lake city" (4). The practice of aiming salvos at public figures was lamented by Planché, who wrote in his autobiography that the emendations required by the Licenser of plays are all but ignored (1872, 315).

18. In another, elaborately extended pantomime version of this scene (Millward 1869), it is the source for protracted commentary on topical events and politics: "BLUE BEARD *Five minutes*, and no sharper blade is seen./ FATIMA What else see you, sister, now?/ ANNE Quite a miracle, I vow,/ *An election free from bribery and wrong!* / FATIMA: That's *too distant* to serve me,/ ANNE But the ballot too, I see!/ And a *Gladstone Bill* is with it as it now creeps along" (and so on; 19–20).

19. Booth wrote: "Because of the various licensing laws, governing the minor theatres in the 1830s, the early Olympic extravaganzas were called 'burlettas,' a word whose vagueness of meaning legally permitted the performance under that name of a wide variety of drama, except legitimate comedy and tragedy, outside the patent theatres" (1976, 10–11). David Mayer likewise noted that the nineteenth-century definition of *burletta* was intentionally ambiguous: "The burletta, loosely defined at best, was described by George Colman, the actor-manager and Examiner of Plays, as 'a drama in rhyme, which is entirely musical; a short comic piece consisting of recitative and singing, wholly accompanied, more or less, by the orchestra.' That Colman, charged with the duty to enforce the Licensing Act, could so ambiguously define its provisions is evidence of the latitude granted performances at burletta houses" (1969, 20, citing Watson Nicholson's quotation of Colman, *The Struggle for a Free Stage in London*, Boston, Archibald Constable, 1906, 282). (There is of course an additional irony in Colman being Examiner of Plays, and in Planché using the term *burletta* in order to burlesque Colman's own play *Blue Beard*.)

20. First performed at the Royal Olympic Theatre, January 2 (according to the 1848 edition) or January 1 (according to the 1864 edition), 1839. Planché's style of extravaganza was unique, as noted by Peter Thomson: "these are Planché's seminal contribution to comic drama. The theatrical trick was to present fairy tales in quirkily rhyming couplets that could accommodate puns and topical references and cheerfully descend to doggerel, in elegant settings and tasteful costumes and through actors who gave the appearance

of taking them seriously. Later writers of outrageously punning Victorian pantomimes owed much to him" (2006, 201). Thomson called these an "overlapping network of dramatic categories [so that] burlesque and travesty are not easily distinguishable from extravaganza, which shares a bed with pantomime" (201). Indeed, as Booth noted, in the specific context of Planché's fairy plays, "the fairy extravaganza is essentially a pantomime with the harlequinade removed and the comedy and magic tricks transferred to the opening" (1976, 19).

21. Play Submitted to the Lord Chamberlain, London (original copy in the British Library) MS 42950 (17), reproduced in microfiche Readex (New Canaan, CT), Nineteenth Century English drama series [198–].

22. *Lacy's Home Plays*, "An inexhaustible source of harmless amusement, occupation and interest, adapted for all stations and localities, to any age, to either sex" (Planché 1839, 19).

23. Elsewhere the same reference is made by Bluebeard, "a ferocious Turk": "I'm like King Harry, with his numerous wives; / He never scrupled to destroy their lives– / No more do I – 'Twas *only* six he had, / And history sets him down as monstrous bad" (*Blue Beard: a Christmas Masque* [1884?], 3).

24. In *Operetta: A Theatrical History*, Richard Traubner noted that Meilhac and Halévy along with W. S. Gilbert were "the undisputed masters, indeed, the creators" of operetta (1983, xiv–xv).

25. Under the theatre management of Horace Wigan. A footnote to the program of the Lacy edition noted: "Since this piece was written, the Irish nationality of its hero [Mr. W. M. Terrott, as Bluebeard] has been discovered. By the addition of 'Faix!' and 'Bedad!' to the dialogue at suitable intervals, the language of the modern-stage-Irishman will be faithfully represented."

26. It debuted in America at Niblo's theatre (1868) and demonstrated several things, according to Gerald Bordman in *American Musical Theatre*: "In this Gallic version Bluebeard is tamed by his sixth wife, the country wench Boulotte. M. Aujac and Mlle. Irma starred. [H. L.] Bateman's faith and determination [in forming an Opera Bouffe Company] were justified. The work was a resounding hit, running twelve weeks. *Barbe Bleue*'s popularity assured the reign of opera bouffe over the musical stage for several seasons. But its success did something else. The people flocking to Niblo's box office convinced many a manager that audiences would buy musical entertainments even during hot weather when they would not attend 'legitimate' attractions. Within a year, even Wallack's, the most august of the 'legitimate' houses, offered its summer-darkened auditorium to producers of lyric pieces. The notion of the frivolous, space-filling 'summer-musical' was born" (2001, 24). Bordman noted productions of *Barbe Bleue* in 1869 (Théâtre Française), 1871 (Lina Edwin's Theatre), and Farnie's extravaganza of 1884, an adaptation of Offenbach, a six-week run at the Bijou theatre with Jacques Kruger in the title role (2001, 75).

27. According to Bordman, in 1875 "The Henderson and Colville company opened the season on August 19 with a reworking of *Barbe Bleue* called *Boulotte*. The piece ran until

the beginning of September" (2001, 38). A fourteen-night run was noted at Wallack's, beginning August 19, 1875 (Kenrick 1996). As *Bluebeard Re-Paired* is the title frequently given for Offenbach's opera bouffe, *Boulotte* may well be yet another variation on this theme.

28. Stebbins quoted a reminiscence from "H. W." that she played Selim to her friend's Abomelique: "I may fittingly insert here portions of a letter I have received from a friend of her childhood, which refers to these days. She says:—'. . . She recalled with the greatest zest, and laughter long and loud, an earlier stage début than the world had seen, when, in our school-days, her mother, my eldest sister, and perhaps one or two of our neighbors, made up the audience to our first representation of the operetta of Bluebeard, in the large attic chamber of her mother's house. This was before the days of popular private theatricals, and marks the mind to dare and do at that early age. Fatima and Irene have gone to their graves before her. I was Abomelique. She, with her then good voice, which afterward became such a rich and wonderful contralto, was the lover, Selim. Even now I seem to hear the cheering song of the young soldier, in his white Turkish trousers, close jacket, red sash, wooden scimetar, and straight red feather, which, if not that of the Orient Turk, was of the Western Continentals, as, mounted on some vantage-ground, a chair, or wooden steps perhaps, he bravely sang out loud and clear,—'Fatima, Fatima, Selim's here!'" (1878, 17). Clara Erskine Clement similarly noted "During her school days she made her mark in theatricals in her mother's attic, and 'brought the house down' as Selim, the lover, in 'Blue Beard'" (1882, 2). That she "brought the house down" indicates a comic rendition.

29. The typescript has a manuscript notation at the top of the first page: "Corinne Robinson—Alphonso" and Alphonso's lines are underlined throughout in pencil. The typescript is not dated, but Corinne Roosevelt became Corinne Robinson by marriage to Douglas Robinson April 29, 1882. The print edition of the same play is also not dated, but estimated by the Houghton Library to be 1890–1899.

30. "Bluebeard's March" plays as Bluebeard arrives (Gower 1841, 20), so Kelly's well-known music is present as well.

Chapter 7

1. See also Sarah Kirby Trimmer's negative review of the Benjamin Tabart fairy tale collection (1803) containing "Bluebeard," for the influential *Guardian of Education*.

2. See Irwin, *The Arabian Nights: A Companion* (1994), whose information is summarized here.

3. Davies wrote: "First, while the *KHM* [*Kinder- und Hausmärchen*] has been central in the definition of what constitutes a Märchen, the first edition of 1812, the only one to contain the *Blaubartmärchen*, is hardly ever used as a basis for anthologies. This situation certainly explains the subordination of 'Blaubart' to 'Fitchers Vogel' in such works of reference as Bolte's and Polívka's. But although it is tempting to assume that this alone would account for the omission of 'Blaubart' from the contemporary German *Märchen*

canon, the issue is more complex, particularly since 'Fitchers Vogel' too is missing from the anthologies explored above. Moreover, Ludwig Bechstein's *Deutsches Märchenbuch* (1845), which did include 'Das Märchen vom Ritter Blaubart,' was better known and more popular than the Grimms' book in the nineteenth century, and a wealth of other nineteenth century 'Blaubart' texts exists too" (2001, 64).

4. For "Fitcher's Bird" the Grimms' sources were Friederike Mannel (1783–1833) and Henriette Dorothea (Dorchen) Wild (1795–1867). D. L. Ashliman translated the 1812 version, which is simpler but in essence the same as the revised version of 1819 and after. For "The Robber Bridegroom" the Grimms' source was Marie Hassenpflug (1788–1856) and other sources. Ashliman also translated the 1812 version of the latter tale to illustrate its greater differences from that of 1819 and after: the maiden is a princess instead of a miller's daughter, and the robber bridegroom is a prince; he ties ribbons on trees rather than leaving an ash trail; an old lady is killed instead of a young maid. Additionally, the bride does not wait until the wedding celebration to reveal her knowledge to the bridegroom, but he arrives the next day to ask why she missed her appointment with him.

5. Omitted "due to its Dutch origins and similarity to 'Bluebeard'" (Zipes 1987a, 739).

6. See Brian Alderson, who stated they were reprinted "at least twice before 1834." He also noted three rival English translations of the nineteenth century and weighed their comparative merits (1978, 69–71).

7. While there were some exclusions from the 1853 edition, "Fitcher's Vogel" is not among them. David Blamires noted the first complete translation of the *KHM* dates from 1884, by Margaret Hunt (2006, 173).

8. English translations by Zipes, Ashliman, and Tatar, all based on the 1857 version, are consistent. Blamires analyzed Taylor's selections, arguing that the resulting collection paints a "skewed . . . picture of the Grimms' collection" (2006, 166). Taylor "zealously avoided using any of the tales with a religious dimension" so that "Marienkind," another Bluebeard variant, is excluded. "Taylor tended also to avoid stories that contained too much of a frightening character," which may account for the exclusion of "Fitcher's Bird." Blamires noted "It is surprising that [Taylor] actually included 'The Robber Bridegroom'" (167), despite excising the cannibalism from this story and others.

9. Samber and G. M. both add "enough" after "strength."

10. *Wonderful Stories for Children* includes ten translated tales. Two additional volumes followed the same year.

11. Glenn Burne noted that Lang in fact meant specifically "English," as opposed to Scottish, fairy tales and had published several tales of his own before *The Blue Fairy Book* (1986, 144).

12. In her introduction to the play fragment "[Bluebeard at Breakfast]", Juliet McMaster noted Thackeray's references to Bluebeard both by name and indirect allusion in *Barry Lyndon, The Rose and the Ring, Pendennis, Philip,* and *The Newcomes* (Thackeray 1971, 206–07, 210). She also noted the reference in *Vanity Fair* (1848) to Michael Kelly's "March in Bluebeard" from the Colman-Kelly production of 1798. There are two further: to Sister Anne's lookout on the tower (Thackeray 1848, 68), and another focusing on

female materialism: "a title and a coach and four are toys more precious than happiness in Vanity Fair: and if Harry the Eighth or Bluebeard were alive now, and wanted a tenth wife, do you suppose he could not get the prettiest girl that shall be presented this season" (1848, 93).

13. McMaster reproduced Thackeray's illustrations (1971, 200–01) for the picture book from a copy at Princeton Library, Robert Taylor collection.

14. So labeled by Juliet McMaster (1976, 19), who posited that in depicting Bluebeard other than as a villain, "The work would run afoul of those of Thackeray's critics who objected to his comic handling of evil, and the consequent tendency of his works to confound good with evil" (1971, 214). The fact of Thackeray's own marital tragedy whereby his wife suffered from long-term depression, ultimately housed in confinement abroad, lends force to McMaster's discussion of his investment in the tale and his representation of Bluebeard as a beleagured "Everyman." McMaster speculated that the play remained unfinished "because the action [of wife murder] is not really compatible with the agent he has created to perform it" (Thackeray 1971, 215), in keeping with Thackeray's "notorious reluctance to plunge into action" (215).

15. Fatima's surname is Shacabac. Also, the theatre manager in the story lends a gong and blue fire, both of which were features of the 1798 spectacle.

16. See Hermansson (2001) for more on the use of intertextual presupposition in the story.

17. In a published reply, George Cruikshank (writing as "Hop o' My Thumb") defended his "editor" with examples of the horrific details in fairy tales and asking how they can be considered a "pretty example for children" (1854, 6).

18. Allusion is also made in *Old Curiosity Shop* (ch. 28); noted by McMaster (1976), who also cited Mr. Murdstone in *David Copperfield* (["Bluebeard"]). There is a reference to Dickens by name and to *Old Curiosity Shop* in Bayley's comic verse version of *Blue Beard* (the earliest extant edition of which is 1840 [New York], the same year as *Old Curiosity Shop* was serialized). (See Barzilai 2004.)

19. As in Briggs' *A Dictionary of British Folk-Tale in the English Language* A.1 (1970), where "Captain Murderer" is listed as a variant of AT 311.

20. However, Anne Brontë's *The Tenant of Wildfell Hall*, which could be read as a serious response to novels like Thackeray's *Barry Lyndon*, was published close afterward, in 1848. Jane Austen's earlier novel *Northanger Abbey* parodies Catherine Morland's gothic reading and her consequent conviction that General Tilney is a Bluebeard, but there is no explicit reference to Bluebeard in the novel (for *Northanger Abbey* as Bluebeard intertext, see Hermansson 2001).

21. Jane seems aware of the Bluebeard reference, and mockingly states her intention to enter into a harem to stir mutiny in the women: "I'll be preparing myself to go out as a missionary to preach liberty to them that are enslaved—your harem inmates amongst the rest. I'll get admitted there, and I'll stir up mutiny; and you, three-tailed bashaw as you are, sir, shall in a trice find yourself fettered amongst our hands: nor will I, for one, consent to cut your bonds till you have signed a charter, the most liberal that despot ever yet conferred" (Brontë 1847, 302).

22. It was also printed in *Littell's Living Age* CVIII (March 11, 1871) and CX (July 15, 1871) and reissued (with revisions) as *Bluebeard's Keys and Other Stories* in 1908 (Odio 1986, 116 n.).

23. Moore also pointed out that the *Cornhill* had published an essay about keys, to which conversation the story appears to address itself, assisted by the extended opening: a musing on keys. The essay "A Few Thoughts on Keys" (whose own epigraph refers to Bluebeard's key), published six years prior, was addressed to men, and "mocking the carelessness of their wives" (Moore 2002, 164). Moore discussed Ritchie's story at length, in the context of other writings in the *Cornhill* at the time, and Ritchie's other fairy tale rewritings, arguing that it offers subversive commentary on destructive mothers, dangerous marriages (domestic violence), and gender inequality. In 1861 Ritchie wrote "Toilers and Spinsters," in praise of single women (189).

24. Jack Zipes grouped the story by name into the bracket of authors using fairy tale rewritings to "reconcile themselves and their readers to the status quo of Victorian society," and as such are "exercises in complicity with the traditional opponents of fairy tales, for there is rarely a hint of social criticism and subversion in their works" (1987b, xxiii). However, the story does appear to offer several nontraditional comments on the subject; as Emily Moore summarized: "To study her is to marvel at her ability to rewrite fairy tales to advance a political position in a publication that avoids politics" (2002, 191).

25. The "Contemporary Literature" review section of *The British Quarterly* (1876) was unsympathetic: "The vermillion and ultramarine employed in the broad farcical illustrations of the story do not give us any very high idea of the taste or skill of Mr. George Cruikshank, jun. The drawing, colour, and posé of the figures are, it is true, in harmony with the rough and brutal hyperbole of the whole legend."

26. Among other motifs in Alcott's "alternative" writings, in "Behind a Mask" the actor Jean Muir assumes the role of Judith of Holofernes in a *tableau vivant* as a coded gesture (see chapter 9 for the role of Judith in the "Bluebeard" story). Elsewhere, in chapter 4 of *Work*, Alcott revised the plot of *Jane Eyre*, giving Christie work as a governess. While reading *Jane Eyre*, the protagonist tells her employer: "I like Jane, but never can forgive her for marrying that man." She goes on to say: "If he has wasted his life he must take the consequences, and be content with pity and indifference, instead of respect and love. Many good women do 'lend a hand,' as you say, and it is quite Christian and amiable, I've no doubt; but I cannot think it a fair bargain" (Showalter 1988, 293).

27. "A Modern Mephistopheles, or The Fatal Love Chase" (1867). Manuscript at Houghton Library, Harvard (Showalter 1988, xxii).

28. Patten also notes that in costuming his illustrations he "derived in part from English rather than German theatrical and pictorial precedents" (1988, 20), so the "Englishing" of the German tales is reflected in the illustration.

29. Another Bluebeard illustration by Crane is on the cover of O. B. Dussek's *Fairy Songs and Ballads for the Young* in which Fatima is opening the door and looking surprised; the key is falling, the wives are hanging (in shading) by their hair on either side of the door, forming a triptych for the viewer in which "Fatima" is in the center. The verse version refers to Bluebeard as "a Bashaw," his wife as Fatima, and his cutlass as a "scimitar."

Chapter 8

1. The play was a burlesque of *Bluebeard, Jr.*

2. The history of the tragedy was given in researched detail in Nat Brandt's *Chicago Death Trap* (2003). A spark emanating from an exploding light set one of the drops alight, sending a massive fireball through the auditorium. The tragedy made a permanent mark on laws governing safety of public theaters. One of the avowed heroes of the day was Eddie Foy, an already-famous comedian, who was performing the role of Sister Anne (with Pet Elephant, a two-man costume that burned in the fire). As the fire broke out Foy went on stage, looking incongruously comedic in his makeup and female dress, and urged the panicking crowd to stay calm. F. J. T. Stewart, superintendent of the Chicago Underwriters' Association, noted that the building's "unfinished condition . . . together with the highly combustible scenery of the 'Mr. Blue Beard' spectacle, combined a remarkable number of very unfortunate circumstances" (Brandt 2003, 125 citing the Superintendent of Inspections, Report of Fire, 2–4, Chicago Historical Society).

3. See Marion Adams (1904); Marguerite Merington (1916); Caroline Thomason (1921); Lyle Cummins (1922); Alice Monro Foster (1924); and T. E. Ellis (1930). While not comic, Edward Rush Duer's drama *Bluebeard in Bologna* (1929) is traditional in form. Bluebeard pantomimes also continued to be popular. The third annual Pantomime "Bluebeard" by the 28th Division, Macedonia, was shown on tour during World War I to more than thirty thousand military personnel in five months, December 1917–May 1918 (Horrocks and Jacques, preface by Lt. Col. R. Henvey, 1918, 13). The 1948 pantomime by K. O. Samuel uses the full Colman-Kelly (1798) cast: Abomelique, Shacabac, Fatima, Anne, their father Ibrahim, Fatima's lover Selim, and Beda (Bluebeard's French maid).

4. A similar reference was made in *Home Acting*: "She talked of her 'rights,' said 'her soul was her own,' / Addressed me in quite in impertinent tone, / I told her no souls our great prophet had given / to women" (Valentine [19–], 12).

5. Méliès, France, and Dukas were French, Maeterlinck a Belgian (francophone), and Balázs and Bartók Hungarians. Balázs, though, was German-Jewish, changed his name to a more Hungarian one, and was later exiled from Hungary for all but the last three years of his life. Dukas was also Jewish. In each case, the issue of nationalism in their art is highly complex. See Suschitzky (1997; on Dukas) and Leafsted (1995; on Balázs).

6. "Monstrous Wives" is the title of Maria Tatar's chapter in *Secrets Beyond the Door*, which includes discussion of the two operas discussed here. The desire to know the husband's secrets is itself monstrous: in the 1912 story "Solomon Bluebeard" by Charles Marriott, Lady Frances expresses "the woman's need for everything, the weakness as well as the strength—the kinks, the twists, the false starts; the man, the boy, the child" (655). In 1973 an avowed "Homage to Bartók" underscored that this is the ironic legacy of the opera: "'Alas, Judith, my Judith! It's not what I did to them. It's what I failed to do. And they're not locked in. I can't persuade them to leave.' / 'Ah, my poor Bluebeard, let me console you. You'll be safe with me. It will all be all right with your Judith. I love you.' / 'Yes, my Judith. That's what I'm afraid of'" (Brophy 1973, 50).

7. I am heavily indebted to Leafsted's section "The Emergence of a Sympathetic Bluebeard in Turn-of-the-Century Literature" (1999) for his detailed discussion of the Gilles de Rais rehabilitation through the biographies, the Dreyfus Affair, and the efforts to have Joan of Arc made a saint. In addition, he provided examples of works on both Bluebeard and de Rais between 1880 and 1920 (174–75).

8. According to Bernard Bastide in his analysis of Perrault in the earliest French films, "Bluebeard" was apparently the first to be adapted to film (2005, 25), and in fact the first film of Bluebeard predates that by Méliès: an anonymous *Barbe bleue* of 1897, shown in Lyon in 1898. The film *Bluebeard* by Étienne Arnaud (1907) dates two months after the opera of *Ariadne et Barbe-bleue*. In this latter, the wives are not murdered at all, but kept in a cupboard. It is notable for being one of the first French films largely filmed on location and outdoors. The 210 meters of film make 12 scenes of 9–10 minutes' length (*Essai de reconstitution du catalogue français de la Star-Film* 1981, 98). In calling the character in the film a "devil," I am following the terminology in the catalogue description of the film cited by Bretèque (2005, 63).

9. The sight of the hanging women is judged to have been very shocking to an audience in 1901, "*encore vierge de tout choc visuel de ce type*" (never having seen shocking visual scenes of this nature) (Bastide 2005, 26). It is thought that Méliès did not color the scene for that reason (31).

10. See Hiltbrunner (2005a). It is worth noting, further, that the "sale of the daughter to Bluebeard by the greedy father" motif to the Bluebeard story is not present in the original Perrault, although it has become a commonplace variation in the English tradition. It is unusual that a specifically French retelling of Perrault's tale would present this alternative, and thus more of a commentary is perhaps being made on the story than has been acknowledged.

11. It is common to refer to Méliès' cinema as "cinema of attractions," but usually to the detriment of his narrative development or as an example of "primitive" film. Instead, André Gaudreault argued that "cinematic spectacle is not synonymous with 'theatricality'" (1987, 112) and that Méliès' extensive editing of his films goes largely unacknowledged. Further to my present point, Gaudreault added that "his films by their very construction always already point to their illusionary and 'screen' existence. . . . many of the filmic elements in this system exist precisely in order to remind viewers that they are watching a film" (113).

12. Tom Gunning (1995) cited Méliès' use of the same theater (Théâtre Robert-Houdin) in which spiritualist shows with a magic cabinet had been performed, a lost Méliès film, *L'Armoire des Frères Davenport* (1902), "which may be based on the original Robert-Houdin version of the brothers' séance" (*158 Scénarios de Films Disparus de Georges Méliès* 1986, 46–47), and another called *The Spiritualist Photographer* (1903).

13. Méliès' use of irony was noted by Bretèque (2005, 66, my translation): "This ironic treatment of the 'marvellous' is a sort of cultural coding which functions as in the operettas of Offenbach and which is a wink at the cultivated public."

14. There were several English translations of France's story on both sides of the Atlantic in the 1920s. The notion of redeeming Bluebeard by telling the "True Story" was

picked up in an amateur operetta: *Bluebeard* (Foster 1924). The foreword stated: "This operetta has been written in the laudable endeavor to correct the misleading and unjust ideas of Blue Beard's character which so universally prevail." He has indeed murdered so many women he requires an alphabetical "matrimonial ledger" to keep track of them, but all was done under the enchantment of his beard, which he is tricked into losing before the play is done. Similarly, Arthur Quiller-Couch's story was largely a rendition of Perrault's, using Samber's translation as its base, but it offered two or three extended digressions that echo France's approach.

15. Harriet Mowshowitz said the same in her thesis "Bluebeard and French Literature": "taking murder out of the situation amounts to robbing Bluebeard of his stuffing" (1970, 90–91). While Bluebeard is ably rehabilitated as "a victim in the sex war," still "France's transformation of the legend does nothing to improve upon it" (108).

16. In "In Bluebeard's Closet: Women Who Write with the Wolves," Cheryl Walker noted of her Bluebeard sonnet that it is a "surprising" (1996, 16) adoption of the Bluebeard voice by a female writer. She used it to argue against the therapeutic line popularized by Clarissa Pinkola Estés, that women must confront the intruder, the shadow animus, and overcome it in order to function wholly. Instead, Walker argued that literature depicts aesthetically that "women who write with the wolves *are* Bluebeard as well as the wife" (17, original emphasis).

17. Carl Leafstedt suggested that this play in fact represents a significant change of stylistic direction: "Unlike the plays that brought Maeterlinck acclaim earlier in the 1890s, Ariadne features considerable dramatic interaction between the characters. It is also less overtly symbolic than previous plays, less mysterious, and less gloomy. Oblique allusions to life's eternal mysteries are correspondingly few" (1995, 132).

18. The angry mob demanding justice is a reminder of the class differences pronounced in Perrault's "Bluebeard" (1697). A parallel idea was raised in Walter de la Mare's version of Perrault's "Bluebeard" (*Tales Told Again*): "the country people hated Bluebeard, and refused even to sell him their butter and eggs and pigs and fowls" (1927, 155).

19. The symbolic use of stunning color in each of the successive cascades of jewelry (in detailed stage directions in the libretto) is rendered in Craig Russell's graphic novel adaptation (1989) of the opera in striking color sequences.

20. Interestingly, as Peter J. Somogyi noted, as a result of the glass breaking, the "castle" theme in the music "temporarily vanishes from the score. It only reappears towards the end of the third act as the wives begin to tend to the wounds that the Duke has acquired from the battle with the peasants" (1985, 79).

21. Austin B. Caswell argued that Maeterlinck was ambivalent about Georgette Leblanc both in his life and thus in his play and that this ambivalence plays out in numerous ways through the libretto and the author's ownership of Ariadne (1988, 203).

22. Caswell (1988, 210, 212) cited examples.

23. Caswell compromised by concluding that the opera is feminist "by accident" and that "Ariadne is a strong figure in spite of the conscious intentions of both of its authors" (1988, 220).

24. My translation. Ariadne says this as she takes the stone and prepares to smash the window with it. Anja Suschitzky argued a nationalist symbolism for the light in Dukas' opera: "Light is an image of freedom from Wagnerism, of true and essential Frenchness in music, a torch leading to the future" (1997, 148). Further, she argued that Maeterlinck's revisions to the song sung by the five wives of Bluebeard, "Les cinq filles d'Orlamonde," (with reference to a well as the source of the key, rather than a cave as in the original poem of 1893) point to the allegorical figure of Truth and its use in period cartoons with reference to the Dreyfus Affair: "The well brings a specific topical context, in the form of a famous brave woman—the allegorical figure of Truth—who, according to tradition, lives at the bottom of a well" (152).

25. "*Barbe-Bleue fait un mouvement instinctif pour la retenir. Elle se dégage doucement.*" Even this gesture is usually translated as "as though to" prevent her from leaving (Hermann Klein's translation). In fact, the French is clear: he makes the sign to prevent her from leaving; it fails.

26. In the French symbolist Bluebeard poem by Henri de Régnier [1892] the collection is represented by a collection of dresses, not women. It is represented early in a song dated [1910] by Anna Chapin, "Oh! Mr. Bluebeard": "Now some collectors hunt for gems, / Others for guns and knives, / Pictures or lamps, or slippers or stamps, But he collected wives." (In the humorous chorus, these women are prepared to "take a chance" despite the unluckiness of his wives: "Oh, Mister Bluebeard, I'm awfully stuck on you!"). In Merington's play *Blue Beard* (1916), Bluebeard had bequeathed his collection of wives to the Constantinople museum: "I will not deny that I have collected wives, as other men collect works of art, also that I have hung them in a gallery, like rare paintings, as indeed they were" (242).

27. Another example from later in the twentieth century is in fact reminiscent of Maeterlinck's libretto: the wife finds seven women in the chamber and tries to think of some way to help them escape. The gold key had, however, turned "as black as soot" after use (there is no blood in the chamber to mark the key). Finally, Bluebeard runs from his foes "but they soon caught him and tied him up and he was taken away" (Perrault [1961]).

28. An acknowledged masterpiece, the opera's early reception was mixed. The fist production was "rejected as unperformable" and delayed until 1918 (seven years after composition), whereupon the symbolist libretto was generally disliked and the performance was pulled after a mere eight performances. It was not performed in Hungary again until 1936. (See Banks 1991.) Balázs first offered it to Zoltán Kodály, who passed on it but he introduced Balázs to Bartók, who felt an affinity with it immediately, beginning work on it most likely in 1911. Balázs published the play in *Mysteries: Three One-Acters* in 1912 (see Leafstedt 1995).

29. The plot that follows is from one version collected by Zoltán Kodály, with whom Bartók collected folk songs (three variants of the ballad were included in published collections of folksongs by Bartók; Leafstedt 1999, 166). A translation by Peter Sherwood and Keith Bosley of a version sung by Samu Szabó in Transylvania (1872) is provided in *The Stage Works of Béla Bartók* (1991, 23). In the ballad, a young lady is persuaded to leave

her husband and young son and go with a mysterious suitor who promises her his seventh mansion. On the way, they lie down to rest under a tree, and he warns her not to peep up into the tree while he sleeps. She does, and sees six women hanging in it. Her tears drop on his face and wake him, so she tells him she was thinking of her own son left behind. He tells her to climb the tree, but she persuades him to go first, and once he turns his back she kills him, dresses in his clothes, and rides his horse home. Once there, she pretends to be a stranger until she is assured of her welcome and takes her place again. The ballad is in keeping with international folk variants of the Bluebeard tale, and is interesting in the echo of Cupid and Psyche (her tears fall on his face, waking him), and her quick-wittedness enabling her own escape. But the fact that she has a child already, leaves of her own free will, and must disguise herself and prove her worth before risking revealing herself to her husband are a unique combination. The ballads of Annie Miller, Lady Isabel and the Elfin Knight, and May Colven are variants of one another (Marina Warner grouped them; Arthur Rackham has also illustrated May Colven). (See chapter 1 for more on variants.)

30. Debussy formed an important influence after Bartók's exposure to his music in Paris. However, *Duke Bluebeard's Castle* is considered unusual for its time in the almost complete exclusion of motifs (the "blood" motif excepted). Simon Broughton quoted Bartók: "It seems . . . that, in our age, modern music has developed along similar lines in countries geographically far apart. It has become rejuvenated under the influence of a kind of peasant music that has remained untouched by the musical creations of the last centuries." Balázs similarly stated: "'We believed that the completely new could be transplanted only from the completely old'" (1991, 17; no source given). Other influences include Wagner's *Lohengrin*, which drew upon the Zeus and Semele myth, another Bluebeard story (discussed by Mike Ashman 1991, 37), although musically, like Dukas, Bartók is credited with bringing contemporary opera out from under Wagner's shadow (see Grant 1991, 25). Carl Leafstedt also discussed Herbert Eulenberg's play *Ritter Blaubart* (1905), the only other bluebeard story to use the name Judith for the wife and from which an opera was later based, and Alfred Döblin's story "Ritter Blaubart" (1911), which follows a similar story arc as the Balázs and Bartók opera (1999, 183).

31. See Leafsted's chapter "Judith: the Significance of a Name" (1999), and the book by Margarita Stocker *Judith: Sexual Warrior* (1998), which contains a chapter on *fin-de-siècle* allusions.

32. Carl Leafstedt (1995) argued compellingly that this is the point of no return, for Judith trespasses (with "tragic self-assertion") when she continues to the sixth and seventh doors. He posits that Balázs' doctoral study of Hebbel (1906–1908) influenced the German romantic style and specifically drew upon Hebbel's theory of "tragic guilt," which is why Judith steps more or less willingly into the seventh door and into perpetual night at the end of the opera. Further, Hebbel authored a drama entitled *Judith* (1841), another plausible influence for Balázs. Musically, the turning point is also represented: "the music pays lip service to this [story arch] in a tonal scheme, starting in F#, reaching C major in the centre and returning to F# at the close" (Grant 1991, 26). The arrival at C upon

opening the fifth door is frequently noted, however Paul Banks noted the foreshadowing of what is to come: "Here, at the opening of the fifth door, Bluebeard proudly reveals his lands to her accompanied by resounding triads for the full orchestra doubled by the organ. Judith acknowledges the vista, and in doing so uses an unadulterated pentatonic phrase. But Bartók suggests that she is disturbed and confused by this insight into Bluebeard's soul and that it distances her from him: instead of adopting the 'white notes' of the unequivocal C major of the orchestra's final chord, Judith sings to a tonally remote 'black-note' pentatonic scale. The irony of her response is perfectly captured" (1991, 10).

33. As George Steiner used the opera in his critical essay *In Bluebeard's Castle* (1971) as a metaphor for the human urge to open doors, and as (ungendered) social criticism, both the opera and Steiner's book were cited together by Jane Marcus as examples of "recuperations, misreadings and rehabilitations" (1992, 31). In "Sylvia," she argued further: "This appropriation of the oppressed victim as representation of man's plight . . . is one of the characteristics of the modernist rewriting of history" (1990, 536).

34. Nadine Sine, in "Cases of Mistaken Identity: Judith and Salomé at the Turn of the Century" (1988), argued that the many representations of both Judith and Salome around the turn of the twentieth century were backlashes against the various suffrage movements across Europe. The portraits of both women were skewed by their representation in influential plays by Hebbel (*Judith*, 1841) and Wilde (*Salomé*, 1891). Hebbel's play was widely performed in the wake of Wilde's, and Max Reinhardt's production of it in 1909 was critically successful. Sine noted: "Thus, between 1893 and 1911, images of Salome and Judith were much in evidence. According to these radically new interpretations of biblical stories, decapitation results from a sexually-related act of revenge by a woman: the virgin Salome seeks revenge for John [the Baptist]'s rejection of her advances [as in Wilde's play]; Judith avenges the assault on her virginity [as in Hebbel's play]" (14). Stocker's book title, *Judith: Sexual Warrior* (1998), emphasizes the standard reading of Judith.

Chapter 9

1. Other "hard-boiled" examples include the Sam Spade radio play *A Bluebeard Caper* in which Sylvia is "forcing" her Bluebeard to marry her, because he's "so courtly" (Hammett 1980). See also Bruce Sanders (1951) and Kerrigan (1945). A recent but typical example is that of Alistair Boyle's *Bluebeard's Last Stand* (1998) in which Gil Yates, P.I., quickly finds himself "feeling sorry for Bluebeard" (29).

2. Jane Marcus (1990, 536; 1992, 31) referenced the Balázs-Bartók opera and its rehabilitation of Bluebeard in contrast with Warner's stories and "Bluebeard's Daughter," in particular.

3. If Farthing realizes the social function of literature, presumably espoused by Warner as a member of the British Communist party, he nevertheless evinces the high modernist hierarchical approach to narrative, disparaging fairy tales: "I can't have it coming out like a story-book for children" (Warner 1940, 31; the narrator points out that these *are* in fact nursery stories). This ironic comment frames Warner's own publication here of a

collection of fables; she also published other elfin stories, and her "fantastic realism" is a hybrid precursor to "magic realism."

4. Jane Marcus commented: "I cannot help but read the mark of the patriarchy on Djamileh's mouth and tongue, as the ink of all the patriarchal texts on which women have been nurtured as their father's daughters" (1992, 30–31).

5. The novel was in the public view in other ways in 1975 also, with the opening of the musical adaptation of it by Uhry and Waldman. In its runs in 1975 (the Play Lab, the Saratoga Performing Arts Festival, where Kevin Kline was in the cast, and a first run in Los Angeles) it was nominated for two Tony awards. Reception was mixed, but it was picked up (and revised) for a New York run on Broadway in 1976 (with Barry Bostwick winning a Tony as best actor in 1977).

6. Welty herself acknowledged the use of the myth of Psyche and Cupid, and by using berry juice she "binds it" with historical reality (1975, 17).

7. See Barbara Carson (1988, 64) for a survey.

8. Ironically, in stating that the fairy tale world fails because it is either/or, black/white, right/wrong, Arnold rejected the novella's fairy tale properties (by arguing a successful if loving parody that undermines the genre) because of the same either/or mentality: "as a fairy tale, it cannot be significant fiction" (1989, 32). In "Fairy Tale of the Natchez Trace," Welty referred once to the "ironic modification" she effected from the fairy tale, specifically in reference to Rosamund's pragmatism. However, throughout that essay Welty wrote that the fairy tale and fantasy genres were the best incarnation for her material: "In my story, I transposed these horrors—along with the felicities that also prevailed—into the element I thought suited both just as well, or better—the fairy tale. The line between history and fairy tale is not always clear. . . . And it was not from the two elements alone but from their interplay that my story, as I hope, takes its own headlong life" (1975, 18). Later in the essay she wrote: "Fantasy is not good unless the seed it springs from is a truth, a truth about human beings. The validity of my novel has to lie in the human motivations apparent alike in the history of a time and in the timeless fairy tale" (21). Her writing does not support Arnold's thesis.

9. The novel is set just before 1798; however, Suzanne Marrs came closer to a unified reading by looking at the historical and fairy tale material as an aesthetic projection of wartime reality, drawing upon Welty's personal correspondence in support of her reading of the novella as the "aesthetic distance" needed "to confront issues relevant to the war-torn present" (2002, 53). With the rise of fascism, anti-Semitism, and German military aggression reported from the mid-1930s in Welty's two local papers, and ultimately her two brothers leaving in 1942 for their military training, Welty was highly aware of the implications of the war and recorded her revulsion for it. One expression of it is in the violence of the novella and the (future) genocide of the Natchez Indians haunting it. Kreyling stated: "the rape and murder of the Natchez girl operate symbolically as the genocide of her nation" (1999, 46) and that the guilt of genocide "hovers over the novella" (45). Welty later stated in the process of converting it to screenplay that the rape needed to be there, as a shadow deed to what happened to Rosamund but also as "a reality of the times" (Welty 1948; notably, Uhry's libretto removes the Indian subplots

altogether). Other critics note that the positive character Clement Musgrove, Rosamund's father, expresses the awareness that the Indians are enacting their "end time," and that the end of other nations will follow it. Another element is the "destructive nature of self-glorification" (56) that occasions such acts of violence, and third in Marrs' analysis is the nature of memory, which is not static and fixed in the novella but evolving. At the same time, a weakness of Marrs' reading is to elide the violence against women as "only a feminist statement" (58); the use made of the allusive material of *The Robber Bridegroom* is demonstrably a working out of both the global and personal concerns of the war, but it is also marked by gendered violence. The rape and murder of the Natchez girl is not *merely* symbolic. Marrs went on to state: "Violations of women are representative of violations more far reaching in nature" (58). The symbol itself, however, is not as transparent as Marrs suggested.

10. See Barbara Harrell Carson (1988) on the doubleness and the work of the novella focused on integration of the self by realizing the interdependence of contrasting states in the natural order. As well as doubleness of character, most of the plot incidents are also paralleled or inverted elsewhere in the novel.

11. Mary Ann Doane most fully defined the women's film in her book *The Desire to Desire: The Woman's Film of the 1940s*: "The films deal with a female protagonist and often appear to allow her significant access to point of view structures and the enunciative level of filmic discourse. They treat problems defined as 'female' . . . and, most crucially, are directed toward a female audience" (1987, 3). Doane argued for a subversiveness to these films: "there is a sense in which the woman's film attempts to constitute itself as the mirror image of this dominant cinema, obsessively centering and recentering a female protagonist, placing her in a position of agency" (129). Her study explores the full implications for construction of female spectatorship and female subjectivity in cinema. See also Laura Mulvey's controversial study, "Visual Pleasure and Narrative Cinema" (1975; and a counter to it in relation to Hitchcock's films by Keane 1986). For the "women's film" subset (they are not generally given genre or subgenre status due to the variance in film types they represent), see also Elsaesser (1987) and Haskell (1973).

12. For films that have a "secret room" she listed *Gaslight* (the attic), *Dragonwyck* (the tower room), *Jane Eyre* (the tower room), and *Secret Beyond the Door* (the locked room). Her chapter "Paranoia and the Specular," as well as another devoted to *Rebecca* and *Caught*, is thoroughly useful to the present study, although her list excludes the Bluebeard film titles. She argued further that these paranoid gothic films "in their articulation of the uncanniness of the domestic, and more especially in their sustained investigation of the woman's relation to the gaze, the gothic films not only reside within the 'genre' of the women's film, but offer a metacommentary on it as well" (Doane 1987, 125).

13. For instance, madness is explicit in the narratives of *Love, Rebecca, Experiment Perilous, Gaslight, Jane Eyre, Undercurrent, Secret Beyond the Door,* and *Caught*. It is implied in Ulmer's *Bluebeard* (he kills the women he has painted, in spite of himself) and *Spellbound* (in the amnesia that results in the suspected Bluebeard playing the main psychiatrist at a mental asylum). Interestingly, in Beatrix Potter's grisly *Sister Anne* (1932), Fatima is just such a "paranoid" heroine and the plot is similar to that of *Gaslight*.

14. Tatar in her chapter "Investigative Pleasures: Bluebeard's Wife in Hollywood" (2004) charted select films from *Gaslight* (1944) through several Hitchcock examples, Fritz Lang's *Secret Beyond the Door* (1948), to *Caught* (1949), discussing three in more detail (*Gaslight, Secret,* and *Notorious*). After briefly setting the context for these films around World War II, what she discovered is that the films offer a female investigator/would-be victim, powerfully motivated by terror and desire. As in traditional *noir* films, the investigator is also a passive observer. Her paranoid characterization frequently belies her very real imperiled state. Tatar argued that the women in the Bluebeard cycle must contribute to their own rescue but that overall the films contain women's investigative threats to the domestic arena and thus the happy endings are a "let down."

15. Hitchcock also edited *Witches' Brew,* which contains "The Gentle Miss Bluebeard" by Nedra Tyre (1959). With deft ironic humor, the story describes an elderly woman who realizes she has been in training for murder all her life: she was nicknamed Mary Ann Bluebeard in childhood. She sets about killing elderly and ill people within a five-block radius of her own apartment.

16. See Gregory Mank (1994). Initially, Boris Karloff was touted in the Carradine role but in 1934 Universal fired Ulmer, and it was not until 1944 that he would direct *Bluebeard* for PRC.

17. Mary Ann Doane (1987) pointed out that the verbal lacks weight to overturn the more powerful visual images to which the audience has been privy, many of them out of Lina's subjectivity and thus carrying the authority of third person omniscient, such as the glass of milk Johnnie carries up the stairs. Hitchcock placed a light within the milk so that it glows ominously. The poisoned milk device is echoed in *The Two Mrs. Carrolls* (1947), and scenes of Bogart carrying the glass of milk on a saucer to both his first wife and, later, his second, overtly recall the Hitchcock film.

18. As Mary Ann Doane wrote of this subgenre: "violence is precisely what is hidden from sight" (1987, 134).

Chapter 10

1. In a brief exploration, Cristina Bacchilega studied different postmodernisms manifest in different contemporary rewritings of fairy tales against models proposed by Jameson, Lyotard and Alice Jardine, as well as drawing on Linda Hutcheon's theorization. While types vary, all emphasize their self-reflexivity: "Postmodern fictions then hold mirrors to the magic mirror of the *Märchen* [tales] and play with the images it frames in a desire both to expose its artifice and to multiply its refractions" (1998a, 315).

2. The farce *Too Much Bluebeard* by Gertrude Jennings (1944) is similarly self-aware, but one of the characters having read the story of "Bluebeard' to her grandson then finds herself as Fatima in her dream. Only her knowledge of the story enables her to manipulate the desired ending.

3. Although translated into English from the German, the novel has not necessarily impacted the English tradition so much as reflected that postmodern European treatments are similar to it.

4. Mererid Davies cited Atwood and Carter when noting the utopian potential expressed by English women writers, contrasting that with the German tradition (2001, 70).

5. See Hermansson chapter 5: "Death Artistry" (2001). Maria Tatar (2004) also offered a chapter focusing on Bluebeard's artistry: "The Art of Murder: Bluebeard as Artist and Aesthete."

6. Simpson wrote of serial murder that it "substitutes repetition for creativity, pattern for design, and the spilled blood of corpses for paints" (2000, 18).

7. See chapter 9.

8. Sherman confirmed this idea in several interviews. In one she said: "I don't want to make art that looks self-referential. I'd rather make things that anybody could relate to without having to have a degree in art or art theory or art history or criticism" (Howell 1995, 5).

9. Laura Mulvey (1975, 1991) extensively theorized Sherman's challenge to the construction of femininity as "to-be-looked-at-ness," which is a term Mulvey also used.

10. The erotic *Bedtime Stories for Women* by Nancy Madore (2003) similarly features "Bluebeard," a sado-masochistic sexual fantasy that Madore alleged in her preface is what women want.

11. See also Resa Nelson, "The Key to Bluebeard's Heart" (1994).

12. Reference is from "Object Relations" by Australian poet Tracy Ryan (1996) and forms the title of her collection.

13. Bliss Lim noted of *The Stepford Wives*: "This ghastly tableau is what brings slasher and serial killer movies into the compass of the Bluebeard tale" (2005, 170).

14. There is a Finnish article that read *The Silence of the Lambs* in relation to Bluebeard: "*Fran Riddar Blaskagg till Hannibal*," *Finsk Tidskrift* (Finland) 232–232.3(1992): 110–23.

15. The detail links the film to *Psycho* and *The Texas Chainsaw Massacre*, both of which use the Ed Gein story. Among the horrors of his house were found "a skin-vest, complete with breasts" (see Schechter 1984, 75).

16. Diane Dubois (2001) included references to Taubin (1991) and Rich (1991), both of whom endorsed the film as feminist. Dubois focused her analysis on the use of the gaze, both on screen and off.

17. This scene is at the crux of arguments on both sides of the issue; Dubois' reading of it (2001, 301) is the one offered here. See also Linda Williams (1984) on the use of the gaze in horror films.

18. Exactly as illustrated in "The Way to Show the Heads" in Mrs. Valentine's *Home Acting for Amateurs* (n.d.), and the "Description of Bluebeard's Closet" for the 1921 juvenile play by Caroline Thomason.

19. As with Atwood, an interest in depicting "Bluebeardian sexual politics" broadens Carter's use of the tale to include most of her works, such as feathered woman Fevvers in *Nights at the Circus*, which suggests the bird-woman symbol of "Fitcher's Bird." For Carter's use of the "Bluebeard" tale, see in particular, Duncker (1984); Lokke (1988); Waite (1993); Walker (1996); Renfroe (1998); Benson (2000); Hermansson (2001, 186–94, 205–14); Moore (2002, 115–32); Tatar (2004, 114–19); Pyrhönen (2007).

20. The woodcut was intended as the frontispiece to *The Bloody Chamber*, but was not used. Instead it appears on the title page of *Angela Carter and the Fairy Tale*, ed. Danielle M. Roemer and Cristina Bacchilega (Detroit: Wayne State University Press, 2001). See also Sargood in Bacchilega (1998b).

21. The same was used by Maurice Sendak for "Fitcher's Feathered Bird" in *The Juniper Tree*. The cut deliberately evokes "a sense of an earlier age" (Bodmer 2003, 129–30).

22. Benson (2000, 245) dated it as "the latter half of the 1910s." He argued an "interrelation of contemporary and *fin-de-siècle* treatments of the [Bluebeard] tale" (246), using Carter's story and those of John Updike, "George and Vivian" and "Bluebeard in Ireland" (1994).

23. Throughout Atwood's works, such as *The Handmaid's Tale*, in which the protagonist Offred is a captive second "wife," couples negotiate the Bluebeard paradigm. The same is true of same-sex relationships, of which *The Robber Bride* is only the most obvious example. See in particular Sharon Wilson (1986, 1988, 1993), Kathleen Manley (1996), and Karen Stein (2003) for surveys of intertextual use of Bluebeard across Atwood's work. For select works in this context see: McMaster (1976); Grace (1984); Walker (1996); Hermansson (2001, 229–37, 240–44); Moore (2002, 132–49); Tatar (2004, 108–14); Barzilai (2005, 2006).

24. The phrase is Sharon Rose Wilson's.

25. Another example would be "Bluebeard's Children," by Meredith Steinbach (1987), in which two children of Bluebeard reveal the violent fragmenting of subjectivity that domestic violence has caused them.

Epilogue

1. So is that by Martin Ladbrook (2005), although focused for much of the play on secondary characters.

2. In Trudy West's 1952 pantomime, Sister Anne is referenced as "the typical dame of pantomime dressed in loud, exaggerated clothes" (3).

3. Bennett and Vaz (1949–1950). It was first presented at the West Indian Festival 1958. Jean Rhys' novel *Wide Sargasso Sea* (1966) is another postcolonial engagement with a "Bluebeard" master text, *Jane Eyre* (1847).

4. Quoted in chapter 9. Aline Kilmer's story "The Case of Bluebeard" (1923) is also prefaced by four lines from the sonnet, but rather than diverging from the traditional perspective it endorses the castigation of Fatima as someone who sinned and was not cleansed of her sin or even aware of the need for it: "Not since I reached the age of reason have I sympathised with Bluebeard's wife" (93).

Bibliographies

The following repositories are at these locations:
British Library, London
Harvard Theatre Collection, Pusey Library, Harvard University
Houghton Library, Harvard University
Lilly Library, Indiana University
Loeb Music Library, Harvard University
Opie Collection, (microfilm) Wells Library, Indiana University
Osborne Collection, Lillian H. Smith branch, Toronto Public Library
Thomas Fisher Rare Book Library, University of Toronto
Wells Library, Indiana University
Widener Library, Harvard University

Bluebeard Variants

Abbreviated titles in this list indicate full reference in Primary Sources or Secondary Sources.

"Barbe-Bleue." 1970. Mowshowitz, Harriet. Appendix I. "Bluebeard and French Literature." 223–24. Taken from Sebillot's *Littérature orale de la Haute Bretagne*, 41–43.

"Barbe Rouge." 1970. Mowshowitz, Harriet. Appendix III. "Bluebeard and French Literature." 225–26. Taken from *Mélusine* III, E. Rolland (1856–1887), 330–31.

"The Beggar with the Baskets." 1958. Marie Campbell. *Tales from the Cloudwalking Country*. Bloomington: Indiana Univ. Press. Reprint Westport, Conn.: Greenwood, 1976. 200.

"The Bloody House." 1955. Leonard W. Roberts. *South from Hel-fer-Sartin: Kentucky Mountain Folk Tales*. Lexington: Univ. of Kentucky Press. no. 7B.

"Bloudie Jacke of Shrewsberrie: The Shropshire Bluebeard." 1842. *The Ingoldsby Legends*. 2nd ser. Ed. Richard Harris Barnum. London: J. M. Dent, 1960. 201–11.

"Bluebeard." 1818. *Grimms' Other Tales: A New Selection by Wilhelm Hansen*. 1956. Ed. and trans. Ruth Michaelis-Jena and Arthur Ratcliff. Edinburgh: Canongate, 1984. 135–39.

"Bluebeard." 1977. Trans. Angela Carter. *The Fairy Tales of Charles Perrault*. London: Gollancz. 31–41.

"Blue Beard." 1982. Joanna Cole. *Best-Loved Folktales of the World*. Garden City, N.Y.: Anchor/Doubleday. no. 4.

"The Blue Beard." 1974. Opie. *Classic Fairy Tales*, 137.

"Blue-Beard." 1963. *European Folk Tales*. European Folklore Series, vol. 1. Ed. Laurits Bødker, Christina Hole, and G. D'Aronco. Copenhagen: Rosenkilde & Bagger. 158.

"Bluebeard: The Wife-Murderer." 1895. *The Hero of Esthonia and Other Studies in the Romantic Literature of that Country*. Compiled from Esthonian and German Sources by W. F. Kirby. 2 vols. London: John Nimmo. (Section III: Cosmopolitan Stories.) http://www.sacred-texts.com/neu/hoe/hoe2-03.htm.

"Bobby Rag." 1970. Briggs. *A Dictionary of British Folk-Tale in the English Language*. A, vol. 2. 375.

"The Brahman Girl That Married a Tiger." 1890. Ashliman. *Folklore and Mythology Electronic Texts*. Source: Mrs. Howard Kingscote and Pandit Natêsá Sástrî. *Tales of the Sun; or, Folklore of Southern India*. London: W. H. Allen & Co. no. 10.

"The Cannibal Innkeeper." 1915. Ashliman. *Folklore and Mythology Electronic Texts*. Source: Abstracted from M. Gaster. "Why Does the Duck Feed on Refuse? The Story of the Cannibal Innkeeper." *Rumanian Bird and Beast Stories*. London: Folklore Society. no. 85. 259–61.

"Captain Murderer." 1970. Briggs. *A Dictionary of British Folk-Tale in the English Language*. A, vol. 1. 175[–77].

"The Cellar of Blood." 1970. Briggs. *A Dictionary of British Folk-Tale in the English Language*. A, vol. 2. 390.

"Devil Gets Tricked." 1985. Elizabeth Mathias and Richard Raspa. *Italian Folktales in America*. Wayne State University Folklore Archive Study Series. Detroit: Wayne State Univ. Press. no. 4.

"Disobedience Punished." 1980. Arewa, Erastus Ojo. *A Classification of the Folktales of the Northern East African Cattle Area by Types*. New York: Arno. 200–02.

"Doctor Forster." 1970. Briggs. *A Dictionary of British Folk-Tale in the English Language*. A, vol. 1. 214[–16].

"Don Firriulieddu." 1885. Thomas Frederick Crane. *Italian Popular Tales*. Boston: Houghton-Mifflin. no. 76.

"The Enchanted Pig." 1890. *Red Fairy Book*. Ed. Brian Alderson. Harmondsworth, Middlesex: Kestrel, 1976. 84–98.

"The Fäderäwisch." 1966. *Folktales of Germany*. Ed. Kurt Ranke. Trans. Lotte Baumann. Folktales of the World. Chicago: Univ. of Chicago Press. no. 24.

"The Fair Young Bride." 1845. *Fairy Tales of Ludwig Bechstein*. 1967. Trans. Anthea Bell. London: Abelard-Schuman. 138–40.

"The Fellow That Married a Dozen Times." 1958. Marie Campbell. *Tales from the Cloudwalking Country*. Bloomington: Indiana Univ. Press. Reprint. Westport, Conn.: Greenwood, 1976. 246.

"Fitcher's Bird." 1819. Grimm. *Tales*, no. 46.

"The Giant, the Princesses, and Peerie-Fool." 1975. Ernest W. Marwick. *Folklore of Orkney and Shetland*. The Folklore of the British Isles. Totowa, N.J.: Rowman & Littlefield. 144.

"The Girl Who Got up a Tree." 1970. Briggs. *A Dictionary of British Folk-Tale in the English Language*. A, vol. 2. 405.

"The Girl Who Married a Ghost." 1982. Joanna Cole. *Best-Loved Folktales of the World*. Garden City, N.Y.: Anchor/Doubleday. no. 181.

"The Girl Who Married the Devil." 1966. *Folktales of Germany*. Ed. Kurt Ranke. Trans. Lotte Baumann. Folktales of the World. Chicago: Univ. of Chicago Press. no. 25.

"The Girls Who Married the Devil." [1924]. Martha Warren Beckwith. *Jamaica Anansi Stories*. New York: G. E. Stechert for The American Folk-Lore Society. http://www.sacred-texts.com/afr/jas/jas_00.htm.

"The Hare's Bride." 1819. Grimm. *Tales*, no. 66

"The Hen Is Tripping in the Mountain." 1964. *Folktales of Norway*. Ed. Reidar Christiansen. Trans. Pat Shaw Iversen. Folktales of the World. Chicago: Univ. of Chicago Press. 228.

"How the Devil Married Three Sisters." 1885. Thomas Frederick Crane. *Italian Popular Tales*. Boston: Houghton-Mifflin. no. 16. [78–81].

"How the Devil Married Three Sisters." 1974. *One Hundred Favorite Folktales*. Ed. Stith Thompson. Bloomington: Indiana Univ. Press. no. 8.

"How Toodie Fixed Old Grunt." 1955. Vance Randolph. *The Devil's Pretty Daughter and Other Ozark Folk Tales*. New York: Columbia Univ. Press. 63–65. Reprint *Stiff as a Poker and Other Ozark Fairy Tales*. New York: Barnes & Noble, 1993.

"Ímarasugssuaq, Who Ate His Wives." [1921]. *Eskimo Folk-Tales*. Collected by Knud Rasmussen. Ed. and trans. W. W. Worster. [London]. Html by Christopher M. Weimer, May 2003. http://www.sacred texts.com/nam/inu/eft/eft11.htm.

"Jack and His Master." 1955. Leonard W. Roberts. *South from Hel-fer-Sartin: Kentucky Mountain Folk Tales*. Lexington: Univ. of Kentucky Press. no. 34.

"Jack and Old Bluebeard." 1985. *Jack Tales: More than a Beanstalk*. Sound Recording. Coll. Richard Chase. Perf. Donald Davis. Weston, Conn.: Weston Woods.

"Jack and the Devil." [1924]. Martha Warren Beckwith. *Jamaica Anansi Stories*. New York: G. E. Stechert, for The American Folk-Lore Society. http://www.sacred-texts.com/afr/jas/jas115.htm.

"Jurma and the Sea God." 1984. *Scandinavian Folk and Fairy Tales: Tales from Norway, Sweden, Denmark, Finland, Iceland*. Ed. Claire Boos. New York: Avenel Books. 554.

"King Bluebeard." 1999. Trans. Ashliman. *Folklore and Mythology Electronic Texts*. no. 38. From Ernst Meier, *Deutsche Volksmärchen aus Schwaben*. Stuggart: C. P. Scheitlin's Verlagshandlung, 1852, 134–37.

"The Lass 'At Seed Her Awn Graave Dug." 1970. Briggs. *A Dictionary of British Folk-Tale in the English Language*. B, vol. 2. 87.

"The Leopard and the Girl." 1980. Erastus Ojo Arewa. *A Classification of the Folktales of the Northern East African Cattle Area by Types*. Folklore of the World. New York: Arno. 207.

"The Little Blue Ball." 1952. Vance Randolph. *Who Blowed Up the Church House? and Other Ozark Folk Tales*. New York: Columbia Univ. Press. 59(–59).

"The Little Blue Ball." 1955. Leonard W. Roberts. *South from Hel-fer-Sartin: Kentucky Mountain Folk Tales*. Lexington: Univ. of Kentucky Press. 27–28. no. 6A

"The Lonton Lass." 1970. Briggs. *A Dictionary of British Folk-Tale in the English Language*. B, vol. 2. 256.

"The Lord of the World Below." 1953. *Modern Greek Folktales*. Ed. and trans. R. M. Dawkins. Oxford: Clarendon. Reprint. Westport, Conn.: Greenwood, 1974. [89–95]. no. 17.

"Man-Snake as Bridegroom." [1924]. Martha Warren Beckwith. *Jamaica Anansi Stories*. New York: G. E. Stechert, for the American Folk-Lore Society. http://www.sacred-texts.com/afr/jas/jas085n.htm.

"The Marriage of a Queen and a Bandit." 1980. Italo Calvino. *Italian Folktales*. Trans. George Martin. New York: Pantheon Books. no. 169.

"Mary, the Maid of the Inn." 1970. Briggs. *A Dictionary of British Folk-Tale in the English Language*. B, vol. 2. 263.

"The Merchant and His Three Daughters." 1963. *European Folk Tales*. European Folklore Series, vol. 1. Ed. Laurits Bødker, Christina Hole, and G. D'Aronco. Copenhagen: Rosenkilde & Bagger. 173.

"Mister Fox." 1955. Vance Randolph. *The Devil's Pretty Daughter and Other Ozark Folk Tales*. New York: Columbia Univ. Press. 95. Reprint *Stiff as a Poker and Other Ozark Fairy Tales*. New York: Barnes & Noble, 1993. 95–97.

"Mister Fox." 1970. Briggs. *A Dictionary of British Folk-Tale in the English Language*. A, vol. 2. 446.; 1849. Halliwell-Phillips. *Popular Rhymes and Nursery Tales*. 47–48; Jacobs, Joseph. 1890. *English Fairy Tales*. London: David Nutt. 148.

"Mister Fox's Courtship." 1965. *Folktales of England, Folktales of the World*. Ed. Katherine M. Briggs and Ruth L. Tongue. Chicago: Univ. of Chicago Press. no. 43.

"Mister Fox's Courtship." 1970. Briggs. *A Dictionary of British Folk-Tale in the English Language*. A, vol. 2. 448.

"Mr. Bluebeard." 1904. *Jamaican Song and Story: Annancy Stories, Digging Sings, Ring Tunes, and Dancing Tunes*. Collected and edited by Walter Jekyll. New York: Dover, 1966. no. 10. 35–37.

"Mr. Fox." 1993. Jimmy Neil Smith. *Why the Possum's Tail Is Bare, and Other Classic Southern Stories*. New York: Avon. 95–101.

"The Ogre Courting." 1871. Juliana Horatia Ewing. *Victorian Fairy Tales*. Ed. Jack Zipes.

"Old Bluebeard." 1925. Amabel Williams-Ellis. *Fairy Tales from the British Isles*. New York: Frederick Warne, 1964. 209–15.

"Old Bluebeard." 1925. Collected by Isabel Gordon Carter from Jane Gentry of Hot Springs, North Carolina. *The Journal of American Folklore* 38.149 (July–September 1925). Jimmy Neil Smith. *Why the Possum's Tail Is Bare, and Other Classic Southern Stories*. New York: Avon, 1993. 47–51.

"The Old Dame and Her Hen." 1888. Peter Christen Asbjørnsen and Jørgen Moe. *Popular Tales from the Norse*, 3rd ed., Edinburgh: David Douglass. Reprint *East o' the Sun and West o' the Moon*. Trans. George Webbe Dasent. New York: Dover, 1970. 14.

"Old Foster." 1964. *Buying the Wind: Regional Folklore in the United States*. Ed. Richard M. Dorson. Chicago: Univ. of Chicago Press. 192.

"Old Rinkrank." 1819. Grimm. *Tales*, no. 196.

"The Oxford Student." 1970. Briggs. *A Dictionary of British Folk-Tale in the English Language*. B, vol. 2. 103; 1849. Halliwell-Phillips. *Popular Rhymes and Nursery Tales*. 49–50.

"Peerifool." 1970. Briggs. *A Dictionary of British Folk-Tale in the English Language*. A, vol. 1. 446.

"The Poor Woman and Her Three Daughters." 1890–1893. J. F. Campbell. *Popular Tales of the West Highlands: Orally Collected*, 4 vols. London: Alexander Gardner. Reprint Detroit: Singing Tree, 1969. vol. 2. 288.

"Pretty Polly." 2000. Collected by Emory L. Hamilton, Wise, Virginia. AppLit. http://www.ferrum.edu/applit/bibs/tales/PrettyPolly.htm.

"A Pueblo Bluebeard." 2003. *Pueblo Indian Folk-Stories*. Charles Lummis [1910]. no. 28. Sacred Texts.com, scanned by J. B. Hare (December 2003). http://www.sacred-texts.com/nam/sw/pifs/pifs00.htm.

"Riddle Me, Riddle Me Right." 1976. Edith Fowke, *Folklore of Canada*. Toronto: McClelland and Stewart. 141.

"The Robber Bridegroom." 1819. Grimm. *Tales*, no. 40.

"The Robber Bridegroom." 1826. Trans. Edgar Taylor. *German Popular Stories*, vol. 2.

"The Robber's Bride." 1854. Trans. Ashliman. *Folklore and Mythology Electronic Texts*. Source: Carl and Theodor Colshorn, "Die Räuberbraut," from an oral source. *Märchen und Sagen*. Hanover: Verlag von Carl Rümpler, no. 38. 125–28.

"The Secret Room." 1960. Amabel Williams-Ellis. *Fairy Tales from the British Isles*. New York: Frederick Warne, 1966. Reprinted from the *Journal of American Folk-lore*, "Folk-lore from Schoharie County, New York." Recorded by Miss E. M. E. Gardner.

"Seven Cauldrons Bubbling." 1986. *Arab Folktales*. Ed. and trans. Inea Bushnaq. New York: Pantheon Books. 315.

"Silver Nose." 1980. Italo Calvino. *Italian Folktales*. Trans. George Martin. New York: Pantheon Books. no. 9. [26–30].

"Sir Richard Baker." 1970. Briggs. *A Dictionary of British Folk-Tale in the English Language*. B, vol. 2. 353.

"The Story About OhMy." 2004. *Beautiful Angiola: The Great Treasury of Sicilian Folk and Fairy Tales Collected by Laura Gonzenbach*. Ed. and trans. Jack Zipes. New York: Routledge. 287–94.

"Story of the Third Calendar, Son of a King." 1898. *The Arabian Nights Entertainment*. Andrew Lang. New York: Dover, 1969. 102–21.

"The Three Cauliflowers." 1880. *Tuscan Fairy Tales*. London: W. Satchell. 63–74.

"The Three Chicory Gatherers." 1980. Italo Calvino. *Italian Folktales*. Trans. George Martin. New York: Pantheon Books. no. 142.

"The Three Sisters." 1984. *Gypsy Folk Tales*. Ed. John Sampson. Salem, N.H.: Salem House. 24.

"The White Dove." 1956. Paul Delarue. *The Borzoi Book of French Folk Tales*. Trans. Austen E. Fife. New York: Knopf. 36.

"The Widow and Her Daughters." 1890–1893., J. F. Campbell *Popular Tales of the West Highlands: Orally Collected*, vol. 2 of 4. London: Alexander Gardner. Reprint Detroit: Singing Tree, 1969. 279.

Bluebeard Chapbooks and Juveniles (by Publisher)

[A. Collins]. [1901]. Jay Hickory Wood. *Blue Beard, or, the Curse of Curiosity*. [London]. Toronto Public Library.

A. L. Burt. 1905. J. Watson Davis. *The Story of Bluebeard and Other Stories*. New York.

Addey & Co. 1853. *Household Stories, collected by the Brothers Grimm, with two hundred and twenty four illustrations by Edward H. Wehnert*. London. Osborne Collection.

Printed in Bavaria. 19–. *Bluebeard*. [England]. Opie Collection.

C. Jeffreys. [between 1869 and 1873]. *Blue Beard: the story versified by W. F. Vandervell, the Music Adapted and Arranged by Rose Jeffreys*. London. Score. Osborne Collection.

Cameron & Ferguson. [ca. 1850]. *The History of Blue Beard*. Glasgow. Osborne Collection.

Cassell & Co. Ltd. 1895. *Fairy Tales, far and near, re-told by Q.* [Sir Arthur Quiller-Couch]. *With illustrations by H. R. Millar*. London, Paris, Melbourne. Osborne Collection.

Chapman & Hall. 1855. Peter the Friar. *Blue Beard, or, Fatal curiosity: semi-burlesqued, for private theatricals*. London. Osborne Collection.

Chez Baumgaertner. 1847. *Histoire de Barbe Bleue qui egorgea ses femmes, ornee de 10 gravures coloriees*. Leipsic. Lilly Library.

Cory, Marshall & Hammond. [1830?]. *Bluebeard; or The fatal effects of curiosity and disobedience. Embellished with elegant copperplate engravings*. Providence. Filmed from the holdings of the Harris Collection, John Hay Library, Brown Univ., Providence, R.I.

D. Lothrop & Co. [1878]. Clara Doty Bates. "Blue Beard" in *More Classics of Babyland*. Boston. British Library.

Darton & Clark. [ca. 1851]. *Fairy tales, in verse*. London. Lilly Library.

Dean & Munday, Printed for the Booksellers. [1811–1847]. *History of Blue Beard*. London. Lilly Library.

———. 1821. Miss Horwood. *Blue Beard, or, the effects of female curiosity in easy verse, embellished with four colored [sic] plates*. London. Lilly Library.

———. [not after 1847]. "Blue Beard, or Female Curiosity" (39–72) in [Five] *Popular Tales of the Olden Time. Corrected, and adapted to Juvenile Readers of the Present Time. By A Lady*. [169 pp]. London. Opie Collection.

Dean & Son. [between 1847 and 1854]. *Blue Beard, or, Female curiosity*. [London]. Opie Collection.

———. 1854–1856. *Blue Beard, or, female curiosity*. London. Lilly Library.
———. 1856. *Blue Beard. The history of blue Beard*. [1856, Miss Merryheart Series]. London. Lilly Library.
———. [1856]. *Blue Beard. The history of Blue Beard*. London. Lilly Library.
———. [1859]. "Blue Beard." *Our Old Friends' Ball*. Mamma Lovechild's Series. London. Osborne Collection.
———. [ca. 1860]. *Blue Beard*. London. Opie Collection.
———. [not before 1873]. *Blue Beard*. Dean's Mammoth Series no. 3. London. Opie Collection.
———. [1880]. *Blue Beard*. London. British Library.
———. [1881]. *Blue Beard, arranged and drawn by the designer of Dean's Pantomime Toy books*. London. Osborne Collection.
———. [not before 1882]. *Blue Beard, Sleeping Beauty, Hop-o-My Thumb. Favourite Tales No. 2*. London. Opie Collection.
———. [188–]. *Blue Beard Dean & Son's Pantomime Toy Books with Five Set Scenes and Nine Trick Changes*. London. Houghton Library.
E. Billing. 1839–1849. *History of Blue Beard*. London. Lilly Library.
Edwin Pearson. [n.d.]. *Blue Beard* [wood cuts]. *Banbury Chap-books*. London, 1890. Reprint New York: B. Franklin. 1966.
Frederick Warne & Co. 1868. "Blue Beard." *The Book of Nursery Tales: Keepsake for the Young*. London. 235–43. Opie Collection.
———. [1881]. Edmund C. Nugent. "Blue Beard." *Charades for Acting: In Town or Country*. London. 87–101. Osborne Collection.
[G. Bishop & Co.]. [185–?]. *Blue Beard: Pleasing Picture Book*. London. Opie Collection.
G. Caldwell. 1828. *The popular Story of Blue Beard, or, the Effects of female curiosity*. Paisley. British Library.
Gall & Inglis. [1870]. Charles Perrault. *Blue Beard*. Edinburgh. Lilly Library.
George Routledge & Sons. [1875]. *Bluebeard*. Routledge's new sixpenny toy books, no. 113. Illus. Walter Crane. [London]. Houghton Library.
———. [after 1889]. "Blue Beard" in *Bright Fairy Tales, with Thirty Illustrations*. London. Opie Collection.
Glasgow: Printed for the Booksellers. [183–]. *The Story of Blue Beard, or, The effects of female curiosity: to which is added The murder hole: an ancient legend*. Opie Collection.
Glasgow: For the Booksellers. 1852. *History of Blue Beard*. Lilly Library.
Goode. [between 1859 and 1879]. *The Popular Story of Blue Beard*. London. Opie Collection.
Grant & Co. 1875. Sabilla Novello. *The History of Bluebeard's six wives: a veracious account of how each of these predecessor[s] to Fatima met her tragical end. Collected from the mendacious chronicles by Sabilla Novello, who affectionately dedicates it to her nieces Porzia and Valeria dei Conti Gigliucci in memory of byegone [sic] "Tell-us-a-story" days*. London. Osborne Collection.
Griffith, Farran, Okeden & Welsh. [1890]. *The Story of Bluebeard*. [catalogued as *Blue Beard*] Illus. A. Chasemore. Old Corner Series. London. British Library.

Hamilton, Adams. [n.d.]. *The Story of Blue Beard.* In *Amusing Prose chap-books, chiefly of last century.* 1889. Ed. Robert Hays Cunningham. London. 230–36.

Henry Altemus Co. 1905. *The Story of Bluebeard.* Banbury Cross Series. n.p.

Hodder & Stoughton. [1915]. Edmund Dulac. "Blue Beard." *Edmund Dulac's Picture Book for the French Red Cross.* London, New York, Toronto. Osborne Collection.

Hurst Co. 1840. F. W. N. Bayley. *Crowquill's Fairy Book.* New York.

J. & J. Colman. [189–?]. *Blue Beard.* London. Osborne Collection.

J. Bailey. [1812–1813]. *The History of the Cruel Monster Blue-beard. To which is added, the comical adventures of Jack Who by strategem killed many giants.* London. British Library.

J. Bysh. [1861]. *Blue Beard.* London. British Library.

J. Fairburn. [1820–1839]. *The Spoiled prince and little white rabbit.* London. Indiana University.

Printed for J. Harris, successor to E. Newbery. 1808. *Blue Beard, or, The fatal effects of curiosity and disobedience, illustrated with elegant and appropriate engravings.* London. Lilly Library.

J. Innes. [1830?]. *The Popular Story of Blue Beard or, Female Curiosity.* Embellished with superior colored engravings. London. British Library.

J. L. Marks. 1820s. *The Wonderful History of Bluebeard.* London. Buffalo and Erie County Public Library.

———. 1835–1857. *Blue Beard.* London. Lilly Library.

———. [1835–1857]. *History of Blue Beard.* [London]. Opie Collection.

J. Lumsden & Son. 1830–1850. *The Story of Blue Beard or, the Effects of Female Curiosity. Embellished with beautiful coloured plates.* Glasgow. Lilly Library.

———. [ca. 1835]. *The Story of Blue Beard; or, The effects of female curiosity, Embellished with Beautiful Coloured Plates.* Glasgow. Opie Collection.

J. M. Dent & Co. 1895. *Blue Beard and Puss in Boots.* Illus. R. Heighway. Banbury Cross Series, no. 6. London. Opie Collection; British Library.

J. MacKenzie. [ca. 1802]. *The Whitsuntide present, or, Fairy tales: containing, Blue Beard, The fairy, and Little Red Riding Hood.* London. (W. S. Betham, printer). Opie Collection.

J. March. [1864–1875]. *Blue-Beard.* London. Lilly Library.

J. Pitts. [1810?]. *The History of Blue Beard, or, the Fatal effects of curiosity and disobedience.* London. British Library.

J. Swindells. 1796–1853. *Blue Beard: or female curiosity: An entertaining Fairy Tale.* Manchester. Lilly Library.

———. [1830?]. *Blue Beard: or, Female Curiosity.* Manchester. British Library.

J. T. Wood. [n.d.]. *The Story of the Cruel Bluebeard and His Many Wives.* London. Elizabeth Nesbitt Chapbook Collection, Univ. of Pittsburgh.

J. Wrigley. [n.d.]. *Blue Beard.* New York. New York State Library.

James Burns. 1845. "The Story of Bluebeard." *The Book of nursery tales: a keepsake for the young.* 3rd series. London.

———. [1845]. "Blue Beard." *The Book of Nursery Tales: A Keepsake for the Young.* London. Osborne Collection.

James Robins & Co., Joseph Robins. 1827. *German Popular Stories.* Translated from the *Kinder und Haus Märchen,* collected by M. M. Grimm, from oral tradition. London & Dublin. Osborne Collection.

Printed by John Adams. 1804. Charles Perrault. *A New History of Bluebeard* (*Gaffer Black Beard*). Philadelphia. Indiana University.

John Babcock. 1800. *New History of Blue Beard, written by Gaffer Blackbeard, for the amusement of little Lack Beard and his pretty sisters.* Hartford. Indiana University.

John & Charles Mozley. [ca. 1845]. *Blue Beard, or, Fatal curiosity.* Derby & London. Osborne Collection.

John M'Culloch (No 1 North Third-Street). 1797. *Little Red Riding Hood, The fairy, and Blue Beard; with morals.* 24mo. Early American Imprints, first series, no. 48226. Philadelphia. Indiana University.

John Murray. [1846]. *The Fairy Ring. A New collection of Popular Tales, translated from the German of Jacob and Wilhelm Grimm, by John Edward Taylor, with Twelve Illustrations by Richard Doyle.* Jacob Grimm. London. Osborne Collection.

Jordison. [1889]. W. Morgan. *Blue Beard.* Howard & Wyndham's seventh Grand Pantomime. London. Toronto Public Library.

L. & F. Lockwood. 1818. Charles Perrault. *Blue Beard, and, Little Red Riding Hood: Tales for the Nursery with Three Copperplates. A New Edition.* New York. (Birch & Kelley). Early American Imprints. Wells Library.

London: Printed for the Booksellers. [18–]. *The History of Blue Beard: an entertaining story for children.* Opie Collection.

Marks & Spencer. [192–]. William Cowper. *The stories of John Gilpin and Blue Beard, Beautifully Illustrated.* Manchester. Opie Collection.

McLoughlin Bros. [1856–1870]. *Blue Beard. The History of Blue Beard.* Miss Merryheart's series. [New York]. Indiana University.

———. [189–]. *Blue Beard.* New York. Lilly Library.

Methuen and Co. [1895]. S[abine] Baring-Gould. "Blue-Beard." *A Book of Fairy Tales, retold by S. Baring Gould, with pictures by A. J. Gaskin.* 2nd ed. 160–68. Osborne Collection.

Printed for N. Hailes, Juvenile Library. 1817. *Blue Beard: Adorned with cuts.* London. Lilly Library

Oliver & Boyd. [ca. 1815]. *Mother Grim's* [sic] *fairy tales: containing the stories of Blue Beard, The little white mouse, the two serpents, and the Queen of Gor.* Edinburgh. Osborne Collection.

———. [ca. 1825]. *The popular story of Blue Beard; or, The effects of female curiosity. Embellished with neat wood cuts.* Edinburgh. Toronto Public Library.

———. [ca. 1828]. *The Popular Story of Blue Beard, or, The effects of female curiosity.* Edinburgh. Osborne Collection.

Orlando Hodgson. [between 1832 and 1835]. *Blue Beard, or, Female Curiosity; an Eastern Tale.* London. Osborne Collection.

———. [ca. 1835]. *Blue Beard; or, Female curiosity. An eastern tale. Embellished with eight coloured engravings.* London. Toronto Public Library.

Peter G. Thomson. [n.d.]. *Blue Beard.* Cincinnati. Donald Beaty Bloch Collection, Univ. of Colorado–Boulder.

Printed for Pinnock & Maunder. [between 1817 and 1820]. *Blue Beard, or, Female Curiosity: and Little Red Riding Hood.* London. Osborne Collection.

Pott & Amery. [n.d.]. *Blue Beard.* Pott & Amery's Nursery Toybooks (#13). Cooper Union, N.Y.. Donald Beaty Bloch Collection, Univ. of Colorado–Boulder.

Reynolds. 1933. Wish Wynne. "Bluebeard." *Wish Wynne's Bedtime Stories.* Book 2. London. 9–13.

Ryle & Co. [ca. 1845]. *The popular story of Blue Beard, or Female curiosity.* [London]. Osborne Collection.

———. [between 1846 and 1859]. *The popular Story of Blue Beard, or, Female Curiosity.* London. Osborne Collection.

S. Marks. 1858. *Blue Beard.* London. Lilly Library.

S. Marks & Sons. [1876]. *The History of Blue Beard.* London. British Library.

Samuel & John Keys. [between 1873 and 1894]. *The History of Blue Beard, or, Female curiosity.* Devonport. Opie Collection.

———. [ca. 1840?]. *The History of Blue Beard, or, Female Curiosity.* Devonport. Osborne Collection.

Sanderson & Co. 1817. *Fairy Tales. Containing Little Red Riding Hood, Blue Beard, Princess Fair-star and Prince Cherry, The Fairy, Ebouli Sina, and The Fairy Song.* Edinburgh. British Library.

T. & J. Allman. [1817–1825]. *Blue Beard.* [London]. Lilly Library.

T. Goode. [186–]. *The History of Blue Beard.* London. Osborne Collection.

T. Harvey. [1823]. *The History of Blue Beard, or, The Fatal Effects of Curiosity.* London. Osborne Collection.

T. Richardson. [not before 1838]. "Blue Beard; or, Fatal Curiosity." *Holiday gifts for good boys and girls: Containing the Surprising and Diverting Histories of Blue Beard, Jack and the Bean-stalk, and Tom Thumb; with a Coloured Engraving.* Derby. Opie Collection.

Tabart et Co. 1804. *Barbe Bleue, et le petit chaperon rouge: contes pour les enfants.* London. Lilly Library.

Printed for Tabart & Co. [1804 or 1805]. Charles Perrault. *Blue Beard, or, Female curiosity; And Little Red Riding-Hood: tales for the nursery/from the French of C. Perrault; with copperplates.* 5th ed. London. Lilly Library.

Tabart & Co. 1806. *Blue Beard; or, female curiosity: and Little Red Riding-Hood: tales for the nursery. From the French of C. Perrault.* 10th ed. London: [by W. Henby, Printer, 76 Fleet-Street]. Lilly Library.

B. Tabart & Co. 1809. *Blue Beard.* (June 1, 1809). London. Osborne Collection.

Thomas Nelson. 1900. "The Story of Blue Beard" in [Ten] *Favourite Stories for the Nursery, with Numerous Illustrations.* London, Edinburgh, and New York. Opie Collection.

———. [1908]. *Bluebeard, or Tommy in Fairyland.* London. British Library.

Thomas Richardson. [ca. 1830]. *The popular story of Blue Beard.* Derby. Osborne Collection.

———. [1840?]. *The History of Blue Beard.* Derby and London. Osborne Collection.

———. [1840?]. *The History of Blue Beard.* Derby and London. British Library.

Printed for the Travelling Stationers. [1820?]. *Blue Beard, or Female Curiosity: An Entertaining Story.* Warrington. British Library.

Valencia: n.p. 1830. *Barba Azul, ó la Clave encantada.* British Library.

W. & J. Deas. 1809. "Blue Beard." *The young lady's and gentleman's library: consisting of voyages, travels, tales and stories: carefully selected and abridged for their amusement and instruction.* Vol. 6 of 6. Edinburgh. Osborne Collection.

W. Davison. 1808–1858. *History of Blue Beard.* Alnwick. Lilly Library.

———. [1840?]. *History of Blue Beard.* Alnwick. British Library.

W. Fortey. [n.d.]. *History of Blue Beard.* [Title-page: *The Story of Blue Beard.*] Bloomsbury. Elizabeth Nesbitt Chapbook Collection, Univ. of Pittsburgh.

W. S. Fortey. [1860–1885]. *Popular Story of Blue Beard or, female curiosity.* London. Lilly Library.

W. S. Johnson. 1850. *The History of Blue Beard.* London. British Library.

Printed by W. Lewis, for J. Bysh, C. Penny, J. & C. Evans, W. Paley. 1820. *The history of Blue-Beard: a tale for the Nursery.* London. Osborne Collection.

Walker & Sons. [184–?]. *Blue Beard.* Otley. Osborne Collection.

W. Walker & Sons. [185–]. *Blue Beard.* Otley. Opie Collection.

———. [189–]. *Blue Beard.* London. Opie Collection.

Walter Scott Ltd. [1893]. *English Fairy and Folk Tales, Selected and edited, with Introduction by Edwin Sidney Hartland; thirteen illustrations by* G. [i.e., C.] *E. Brock.* Ed. Edwin Sidney Hartland. London. Osborne Collection.

Whittingham & Arliss, Juvenile Library. [1815–1817]. *Blue Beard Adorned with Cuts.* [London]. Houghton Library.

Wm. Charles. 1815. *Bluebeard, or, The fatal effects of curiosity and disobedience.* Early American Imprints, Second Series, no. 51526. Philadelphia. Indiana University.

Wm. S. Orr & Co. [ca. 1842]. Frederick William Naylor Bayley. *Blue Beard.* 2nd ed. London. Toronto Public Library.

———. 1844. F. W. N. Bayley. *Comic Nursery Tales with illustrations, humorous and numerous. Blue Beard. Beauty and the beast. Robinson Crusoe.* London. Toronto Public Library.

Primary Sources

Adams, Marion. 1904. *Bluebeard. A Nursery Tale Play for Boys and Girls.* Illus. Brinsley Le Fanu. Books for the Bairns. 105. Opie Collection.

The Airs, Glees, Choruses &c. in the New Pantomime of Blue Beard, or the Flight of Harlequin. As performed at the Theatre-royal, Covent Garden, London. 1791. *Songs Sung at Covent Garden 1784–1803.* London: T. Cadell. British Library.

Alcott, Louisa May. 1872. "Work: A Story of Experience." Reprint *Alternative Alcott.* Ed. Elaine Showalter. New Brunswick, N.J.: Rutgers Univ. Press, 1988. 239–349.

———. 1877a. *A Modern Mephistopheles.* Reprint New York: Bantam, 1995.

———. 1878. *Under the Lilacs*. Reprint New York: Gramercy, 1996.

Allingham, Margaret. 1962a. "Three Is a Lucky Number, or Bluebeard's Bathtub." *Classic Crime Short Stories*. CSA Word, 2005. Sound File. Audible.com.

———. 1962b. "Bluebeard's Bathtub." *This Week*. Reprinted as "Three is a Lucky Number." *The Allingham Case-Book*. New York: Morrow, 1969.

Ancliffe, C. 1924. *The Bluebeard Blues*. Vocal score. British Library.

Anderson, Brian. 1970. *Bluebeard: An Operetta in Two Acts Composed by Jacques Offenbach*. London: Chappell.

Anderson, William C. 1994. *Lady Bluebeard: The True Story of Love and Marriage, Death and Flypaper*. Boulder, CO: Pruett.

Angus, Keith. 1879. "Bluebeard." *Children's Theatricals: Being a Series of Popular Fairy Tales Adapted for Presentation in the Drawing Room*. London: Routledge. 68–100.

Arnold, Gertrude. 1919. *Sister Anne! Sister Anne!!* Toronto: McClelland and Stewart.

Ashliman, D. L., ed. and trans. "Bluebeard." Folktales of Aarne-Thompson types 312 and 312 A about women whose brothers rescue them from their ruthless husbands or abductors. http://www.pitt.edu/~dash/type0312.html. *Folklore and Mythology Electronic Texts*. Univ. of Pittsburgh.

———, trans. "Fitcher's Bird." Jacob and Wilhelm Grimm, "Fichters Vogel" [*sic*], *Kinder- und Hausmärchen* (Berlin, 1857), no. 46. http://www.pitt.edu/~dash/grimm046.html. *Folklore and Mythology Electronic Texts*. Univ. of Pittsburgh.

———, ed. and trans. "How the Devil Married Three Sisters and Other Folktales of Type 311." http://www.pitt.edu/~dash/type0311.html. *Folklore and Mythology Electronic Texts*. Univ. of Pittsburgh.

———, ed. and trans. "The Robber Bridegroom and Other Folktales of Aarne-Thompson type 955." http://www.pitt.edu/~dash/type0955.html. *Folklore and Mythology Electronic Texts*. Univ. of Pittsburgh.

Atwood, Margaret. 1971. "Hesitations Outside the Door." Reprint *Power Politics: Selected Poems 1966–1984*. Toronto: Oxford Univ. Press, 1990. 135–38.

———. 1976. *Lady Oracle*. Reprint London: Virago, 1987.

———. 1981. *Bodily Harm*. Toronto: McClelland and Stuart.

———. 1983a. "Bluebeard's Egg." *Bluebeard's Egg*. Toronto: McClelland. 133–66.

———. 1983b. "Murder in the Dark." Reprint *Murder in the Dark: Short Fictions and Prose Poems*. London: Jonathan Cape, 1984. 29–30.

———. 1983c. "The Page." Reprint *Murder in the Dark: Short Fictions and Prose Poems*. London: Jonathan Cape, 1984. 44–45.

———. 1984a. "Doorway." Reprint *Interlunar: Selected Poems 1966–1984*. Toronto: Oxford Univ. Press, 1990. 290.

———. 1984b. "The Robber Bridegroom." Reprint *Interlunar: Selected Poems 1966–1984*. Toronto: Oxford Univ. Press, 1990. 304.

———. 1985. *The Handmaid's Tale*. Reprint London: Virago, 1986.

———. 1990. *Selected Poems 1966–1984*. Toronto: Oxford Univ. Press.

———. 1992. "Alien Territory." *Good Bones*. Toronto: Coach House. 75–88.

———. 1993a. "Grimms' Remembered." *The Reception of Grimms' Fairy Tales: Responses, Reactions, Revisions.* Ed. Donald Haase. Detroit: Wayne State Univ. Press. 290–92.

———. 1993b. *The Robber Bride.* Toronto: McClelland.

———. 2003. "The Robber Bridegroom." *The Poets' Grimm: 20th Century Poems from Grimm Fairy Tales.* Ed. Jeanne Marie Beaumont and Claudia Carlson. Ashland, OR: Story Line. 132.

Austen, Jane. 1818. *Northanger Abbey.* Reprint *Northanger Abbey, Lady Susan, The Watsons, and Sanditon.* New York: Oxford Univ. Press, 1991.

Balanchine, George, and Francis Mason. 1977. *Balanchine's Complete Stories of the Great Ballets.* Garden City, N.Y.: Doubleday.

Balázs, Béla. 1907. *Duke Bluebeard's Castle.* Reprint Trans. John Lloyd Davies. *The Stage Works of Béla Bartók.* London: John Calder, 1991. 45–60.

Barchilon, Jacques. 1956. *Perrault's Tales of Mother Goose,* by Charles Perrault. New York: Pierpont Morgan Library. 13–113.

Barchilon, Jacques, and Henry Pettit. 1960. *The Authentic Mother Goose Fairy Tales and Nursery Rhymes.* Denver: Swallow.

Barnes, J. M. 1895. *Blue Beard: A Short Fairy Operetta in Five Scenes.* Manchester: Abel Heywood & Son. British Library.

Barthelme, Donald. 1987. "Bluebeard." *Forty Stories.* New York: Putnam. 92–97.

Bartók, Béla. 1912. *Duke Bluebeard's Castle.* Reprint Trans. and intro Stanley Appelbaum. Vocal score. New York: Dover, 2001.

———. 1991. *Duke Bluebeard's Castle.* Trans. John Lloyd Davies. *The Stage Works of Béla Bartók.* London: John Calder. 45–60.

Beard, Cynthia. "*Barbe Bleue* [Grétry, 1789]". Univ. of North Texas Music Library: Virtual Rare Book Room. http://www.library.unt.edu/music/special-collections/vrbr/browse/barbe-bleue-1789-andre-ernest-modeste-gretry#background-1.

Bell, Florence Eveleen Eleanore Olliffee. 1896. "Bluebeard." *Fairy Tale Plays and How to Act Them.* London: Longmans. Reprint "Bluebeard, in Two Acts." *Fairy Tale Plays and How to Act Them.* Mrs. Hugh Bell. London: Longmans, Green, & Co., 1899. 335–66.

Bellingham, Henry. 1866. *Bluebeard Re-paired: A Worn-Out Subject Done-Up Anew: An Operatic Extravaganza in One Act.* London: T. H. Lacy. Adapted from the French of Henri Meilhac and Ludovic Halévy. Music by Jacques Offenbach, arranged by J. H. Tully.

Bennett, Louisa, and Noel Vaz. 1949–1950. *Bluebeard and Brer Anancy.* Little Theatre Movement, Jamaica. LTM Pantomime. http://ltmpantomime.com/pages/detailed/Bluebeard49.html.

Benson, Anne. 2002. *Thief of Souls.* New York: Delacorte.

Bibbins, Mark. 2000, 2001. "Bluebeard." *The World in Us: Lesbian and Gay Poetry of the Next Wave.* Ed. Michael Lassell and Elena Georgiou. New York: St. Martin's. 2–3.

Bigelow, Elizabeth Gleason. 1891. *Bluebeard, or the Elixir of Life: An Operetta in Two Acts.* [n.p.: n.p.] 1894.

Black Beard, the Pirate; or the Captive Princess. 1822. [Hodgson's Juvenile Drama]. London: n.p.

Blanchard, E. L., Ferdinand Wallerstein, and Thomas Longdon Greenwood ("The Brothers Grinn [*sic*]"). 1879. *Bluebeard. (Drury Lane Pantomime)*. London: McCorquodale.

Block, Francesca Lia. 2000. "Bones." *The Rose and the Beast*. New York: Harper Collins. 153–66.

Blue Beard. [after 1861]. Typescript (unsigned). Houghton Library.

"Blue Beard." 1891. *Medleys and Songs without Music*. London: Allen. Widener Library.

Blue Beard: A Burlesque. 1889. Juvenile amateur performance in aid of Sup. Bent Old Trafford. *Manchester Athenæum*. Manchester: John Heywood.

Blue Beard: A Christmas Masque. [1884?]. James Augustus Atkinson. Manchester: John Heywood. British Library.

Blue Beard, etc. (Crystal Palace, Pantomime Season, 1894–5.) 1894. Sydenham: Crystal Palace Co.

Blue Beard; or, Female Curiosity! A Drama, in Two Acts: Adapted to Hodgson's Theatrical Characters and Scenes in the Same. 1822. London: Printed by and for Hodgson & Co. British Library.

"Blue Beard; or, Female curiosity. A sensation drama, in two acts." 1871. *Parlour Plays for Home Performance by an Experienced Amateur*. London: Dean & Son.

Bluebeard; or, The Key of the Cellar a Drama in Three Acts. 1882. London: R. Washbourne.

"Bluebeard's Castle." 1985. *Moon Knight* 2.4 (October). Michael Hobson. New York: Marvel Comics.

"The Bluebeard Murders." 1979. *Famous Murder Mysteries*. Pomfret House, Encyclopedia Britannica Educational Corporation. Chicago: Encyclopedia Britannica Educational.

Boden, Julie, and Zoë Brigley, eds. 2007. *Bluebeard's Wives*. Coventry, UK: Heaven Tree.

Booth, Michael R., ed. and intro. 1976. *English Plays of the Nineteenth Century*. 5 vols. Oxford: Clarendon.

Borrow, Antony. 1958. "v. 2. Bluebeard, A Drama in Three Acts." Reprint *The Art and Craft of Dying, a Trilogy*. Kent, England: Hand & Flower, 1963.

Bosley, Keith, and Peter Sherwood. 1991. "Annie Miller." *The Stage Works of Béla Bartók*. London: John Calder. 23–24.

Boyle, Alistair. 1998. *Bluebeard's Last Stand*. Santa Barbara, Calif.: Allen A. Knoll.

Bridgeman, J. V. 1860. *Bluebeard; or, Harlequin and Freedom in Her Island Home*. London: [Covent Garden].

Brontë, Charlotte. 1847. *Jane Eyre*. Reprint New York: Penguin, 2003.

Brophy, Brigid. 1973. "The Honest Bluebeard. [Homage to Bartók.]." *The Adventures of God in His Search for the Black Girl*. London: Macmillan.

Bundle, Jacob, pseud. 1858. *Lord Blue Beard; or, the Crim-Tartar, a Naturalised British Subject: A Dramatic Medley*. [London?]: Printed for the Author. British Library.

Burnand, Francis Cowley, Sir. 1883. *Blue Beard; or, the Hazard of the Dye. A Burlesque in Three Acts*. London: R. Wilson.

Burton, Richard, trans. 1893. "Sixth Diversion of the Fourth Day." Reprint *The Pentameron of Giambattista Basile*. London: Spring Books [195–]. 293–303.

Byatt, A. S. 1992. "The Story of the Eldest Princess." *Caught in a Story: Contemporary Fairytales and Fables*. Ed. Christine Park and Caroline Heaton. London: Vintage. 12–28.

Byron, Henry J. 1860. *Blue Beard! From a New Point of Hue; a Burlesque Extravaganza*. London: Samuel French.

Capdevila, R. 1986. *The Three Naughty Sisters Meet Bluebeard*. Trans. Marilyn Malin. London: Methuen Children's.

Carryl, Guy Wetmore. 1902. "How the Helpmate of Blue-Beard Made Free with a Door." *Grimm Tales Made Gay*. Boston: Houghton-Mifflin.

Carter, Angela. 1967. *The Magic Toyshop*. New York: Penguin, 1996.

———, trans. 1977. "Bluebeard." *The Fairy Tales of Charles Perrault*. London: Gollancz. 31–41.

———. 1979. "The Bloody Chamber." Reprint *The Bloody Chamber*. *Burning Your Boats: The Collected Short Stories*. New York: Henry Holt, 1995. 111–43.

———. 1984. *Nights at the Circus*. London: Picador.

———. 1987. "The Fall River Axe Murders." *Saints and Strangers*. New York: Penguin. 7–32.

———, ed. 1990. "Mr. Fox." *The Virago Book of Fairy Tales*. London: Virago. 8–10.

———. 1992. "Old Foster." *The Second Virago Book of Fairy Tales*. London: Virago. 10–12. Text from *Journal of American Folklore* 38 (1925): 360–61.

———. 1993a. "Alice in Prague, or The Curious Room." *American Ghosts and Old World Wonders*. London: Chatto & Windus. 121–39.

———. 1993b. "The Bloody Chamber." *The Bloody Chamber and Other Stories*. New York: Penguin.

Cave, Emma. 1995. *Bluebeard's Room*. London: Coronet.

Chapin, Anna Alice. [1910]. "Oh! Mr. Bluebeard. . . ." Words and Music by A. A. Chapin. New York: Leo Feist.

Chisholm, Louey. 1922. "Bluebeard." *In Fairyland: Tales Told Again*. New York: Putnam Sons.

Clore, Dan. 2001. "Bluebeard's Closet." *The Unspeakable and Others*. Holicong, Pa.: Wildside. 163.

Cocteau Twins. 1993. "Bluebeard." Sound recording. *Four-calendar Café*. Hollywood, Calif.: Capital Records.

Collings, Paul. 1993. "Slaughter at Bluebeard High." *Theatre Restaurant: 3 Plays*. Brisbane: Playlab.

Collins, Ted. 1950. "Was Bluebeard a Surgeon?" *Private Detective* 22.1 (February). London: Trojan Publishing.

Collognat, Annie, and Marie-Charlotte Delmas. 2007. *Les Contes de Perrault*. Paris: Omnibus.

Colman, George, the Elder. 1782. "Fatal Curiosity: A Tragedy, in Three Acts, by George Lillo." *The Select London Stage; A Collection of the Most Reputed Tragedies, Comedies, Operas, Melo-Dramas, Farces, and Interludes*. London: G. Balne, 1827.

Colman, George, the Younger. 1796. *The Iron Chest: A Play in Three Acts. First presented at the Theatre-Royal in Drury Lane, Saturday March 12, 1796*. London. Thomas Fisher Rare Book Library.

———. 1798. *Blue Beard, or Female Curiosity! A Dramatic Romance in Two Acts*. Comp. Michael Kelly. Reprint *Plays by George Colman the Younger and Thomas Morton*. Ed. and intro. Barry Sutcliffe. Cambridge: Cambridge Univ. Press, 1983. 181–210.

———. 1798a. *Blue Beard, or Female Curiosity!* Dublin: William Porter. British Library.

———. 1798b. *Blue Beard, or Female Curiosity!* 4th ed. London: Cadell & Davies. British Library.

———. 1798c. "Preface." *Blue Beard, or Female Curiosity!* 4th ed. London: Cadell & Davies. British Library.

———. 1802. *Blue Beard, or Female Curiosity!* 1798. 7th ed. As altered for the New York Theatre, with additional songs, by Wm. Dunlap. New York: D. Longworth. British Library.

———. 1811. *Blue Beard, or, Female Curiosity!* 1798. London: J. Cawthorn. British Library.

———. 1823. *Blue Beard, or Female Curiosity! . . . With prefatory remarks . . . Faithfully marked with the stage business, and stage directions, as it is performed at the Theatres Royal. By W. Oxberry, comedian*. London: Simpkin and Marshall. Harvard Theatre Collection.

Commencing Sunday Evening, Feb. 23 . . . the Ideal Extravaganza Company, Presenting Bluebeard, Jr., or, Fatima and the Fairy, in Four Acts and a Prologue by Clay M. Greene. 1890. [Program]. Chicago: W. J. Jefferson.

Cook, Méira. 1993. "Instructions for Navigating the Labyrinth." *Canadian Fiction Magazine* 79: 107–14.

Copus, Julia. 1995. "Bluebeard's Wife" and "Prosperina's Lover." *The Shuttered Eye*. Newcastle upon Tyne: Bloodaxe Books. 24, 30.

Couperus, Louis. 1947. "Bluebeard's Daughter." *A World of Great Stories*. Ed. Hiram Collins Haydn. New York: Crown Publishers.

Cross, John C. 1822. *Black Beard, the Pirate; or, the Captive Princess. A Drama, in Two Acts*. Hodgson's Juvenile Drama. London: Hodgson & Co.

Culin, Stewart. 1920. "Blue Beard's Chamber." Culin Archival Collection. Brooklyn Museum.

Cummins, Stevenson Lyle. 1922. "Bluebeard." Reprint *Plays for Children*. London: Methuen. New York: George H. Doran, 1923.

Cunningham, Robert Hays. 1889. *The Story of Blue Beard*. In *Amusing Prose Chap-books, Chiefly of Last Century*. Ed. Robert Hays Cunningham. London: Hamilton, Adams. 230–36.

Curwen, Henry. 1888. *Lady Bluebeard*. 2 vols. Edinburgh: W. Blackwood & Sons. British Library.

Dacre, Henry, W. Manning, and John Gregory. 1895. *Blue Beard the Bashaw, or Fatime the Fair, Selim the Brave and the Aesthetic Maiden, or Harlequin the Wicked, King Mammon, and the Good Fairy Hope . . . The Grand New Spectacular Christmas Pantomime*. [n.p.: Thomas Aldridge].

Davey, Peter, and Hugh Mytton. 1906. *Blue Beard.* [Kingston-on-Thames, England]: [Royal County Theatre].

de la Mare, Walter. 1927. "Bluebeard." Reprint *Told Again: Old Tales Told Again.* New York: Knopf, 1946.

de Régnier, Henri. [1892]. "Le Sixième mariage de Barbe-bleue." *Entretiens politiques et littéraires* 32[1892]: 221–32. Reprint *Les Contes de Perrault.* Ed. Annie Collognat and Marie-Charlotte Delmas. Paris: Omnibus. 2007. 537–49.

de Sade, Marquis. 1778. *Justine or the Misfortunes of Virtue.* Reprint New York: Castle Books, 1964.

Deming, Richard. 1979. "Gentle Bluebeard." *Death on Arrival.* Ed. Alfred Hitchcock. New York: Dell.

Dickens, Charles. 1860. "Nurse's Stories." Reprint *The Uncommercial Traveller and Reprinted Pieces Etc.* New York: Oxford Univ. Press, 1958, 1987. [148]–58.

Donoghue, Emma. 1997. "The Tale of the Bird." *Kissing the Witch: Old Tales in New Skins.* New York: Harper Collins.

Doyle, T. F., and Edward Saker. 1882. *Edward Saker's New and Original Grand Comic Christmas Pantomime Entitled Blue Beard.* Liverpool, England: Printed by T. J. Newman, Islington Printing Works.

Du Maurier, Daphne. 1938. *Rebecca.* New York: Avon, 1971.

Duckworth, Mary G. 1896. *The Tragedy of Blue Beard; a Greek Play.* London: J. S. Forsaith. Widener Library.

Duer, Edward Rush. 1929. *Bluebeard in Bologna, Fantasy in Two Acts.* Los Angeles: S. French.

Duffy, Carol, Tim Supple, and Melly Still. 2004. *Beasts and Beauties: Eight Tales from Europe.* London: Faber & Faber.

Dukas, Paul. 1907. *Ariane et Barbe-bleue (Ariane and Blue-Beard): A Tale in Three Acts from the Play by Maurice Maeterlinck.* Trans. Hermann Klein. New York: G. Schirmer.

———. 1910. "*Ariadne et Barbe-Bleue*: (A Story with a Moral after the Manner of Perrault's Fairy Tales)." *La revue musicale* (May–June 1936): 4–7. (Trans. by Caswell 1988, 213).

Dumont, Frank, and Alfred B. Sedgwick. 1874. *Africanus Bluebeard: A Musical Ethiopian Burlesque, in One Scene.* Reprint Ed. Michael Meckna. New York: Garland, 1994.

Dussek, O. B. [1846?]. "Blue Beard." *Fairy Songs and Ballads for the Young.* 2 vols. London: D'Almaine. Houghton Library.

Electric Light Orchestra. 1973. "Bluebeard Is Dead." Sound recording. *On the Third Day.* New York: Jet Records.

Ellis, T. E. 1930. "Bluebeard." *Five Pantomimes.* London: Elkin Mathews & Marrot.

Eno Crime Club. 1933-12-19, The Bluebeard Room. 1933a. Barry Brooks Collection. Library of Congress.

Eno Crime Club. 1933-12-20, The Bluebeard Room, part 2. 1933b. Barry Brooks Collection. Library of Congress.

Eustis, Fred J., and Clay M. Greene. 1889. *Bluebeard Jr.* [collection]: *or, Fatima and the Fairy.* n.p.:n.p. Tams-Witmark/Wisconsin Collection.

Evans, R. M. 1846. *Droll Dramas for Christmas Comedians and Parlour Performers, containing Bluebeard; and Count courtship.* London: n.p.

Ewing, Juliana Horatia. 1987. "The Ogre Courting." *Victorian Fairy Tales.* Ed. Jack Zipes. New York: Methuen. 127–33.

Ewing, Montague (Sherman Meyers.) 1932. "Old Man Bluebeard." Score. Libretto by Robert Hargreaves and Stanley Damerell. British Library.

Farnie, H. B. 1874. *Bluebeard Extravaganza.* London: [n.p.]. British Library.

The Female Bluebeard, or, The Adventures of Polyphemus Amador de Croustillac. 1845. British Library.

Fischer, Roy, and Ronald King. 1972. *Bluebeard's Castle.* Guildford: Circle. British Library.

Foster, Alice Monroe. 1924. *Blue Beard, an Operetta in One Act. Libretto by A. M. Foster, etc.* Boston: C. C. Birchart.

Fowles, John. 1963. *The Collector.* Reprint London: Pan, 1986.

France, Anatole. 1909. "Les Sept femmes de la Barbe Bleue." Reprint Trans. D. B. Stewart. "The Seven Wives of Bluebeard." *Spells of Enchantment.* Ed. Jack Zipes. New York: Viking, 1991. 566–82.

Fremlin, Celia [Celia Margaret Goller]. 1985. "Bluebeard's Key." *Ellery Queen's Mystery Magazine* (January). Reprint *John Creasey's Crime Collection 1985: An Anthology.* Ed. Herbert Harris. New York: St. Martin's, 1985. 91–103.

Frisch, Max. 1982. *Blaubart: Eine Erzählung.* Reprint *Bluebeard: A Tale.* Trans. Geoffrey Skelton. San Diego, Calif.: Harcourt Brace Jovanovich, 1983.

Frost, Gregory. 2002. *Fitcher's Brides.* New York: Tom Doherty Associates.

Frost, Sarah Annie. [1890–1899?]. *Blue Beard: A Melodramatic Travesty.* Dick's American Edition. New York: Dick & Fitzgerald. New York Public Library.

Furlan, Pierre. 2007. "Blue-beard's Work-shop." *Blue-beard's Work-shop and Other Stories.* Trans. Jean Anderson. Wellington, New Zealand: Victoria Univ. Press. 19–27.

Gaiman, Neil. 1996. "The White Road." *Ruby Slippers, Golden Tears.* Ed. and intro. Ellen Datlow and Terri Windling. New York: Avon. 359–71.

Gilbert, E. Ouseley, and Louis B. Tisdale. 1897. *Blue Beard: Operetta for Children Founded on the Well-known Legend.* London: J. Curwen & Sons.

Godwin, William. 1794. *Caleb Williams, or Things As They Are.* Reprint Ed. and intro. Maurice Hindle. London: Penguin, 1988.

Gold, Artie. 1979. "[The Bluebeard Confectionnaire...]." *Cross Country* 12. Special Postcard Issue. Montreal: Cross Country.

Goodwin, Archie, and Jerry Grandenetti. 1991. "Image of Bluebeard! (Creepy #7)." *Creepy, the Classic Years.* New York: Harris Publications.

Gower, Francis Edgerton., Earl of Ellesmere. 1841. *Bluebeard, or, Dangerous Curiosity & Justifiable Homicide. A Tragedy in Two Acts, Etc.* London: T. Brettell.

Gray, Alasdair. 2003. "No Bluebeard." *The Ends of Our Tethers: 13 Sorry Stories.* New York: Canongate U.S. 16–59.

Green, C. M. 1889. *Bluebeard, Jr.* [n.p.: n.p.]. Reproduction. Library of Congress.

Green, Clay Meredith. 1883. *The Trunk Mystery; or, Crime and Its Consequences: A Criminal Complication in 3 Tangles.* Washington, D.C.: Library of Congress.

Greene, Ward. 1930. *Life and Loves of a Modern Mister Bluebeard.* Reprint New York: Avon, 1948.

Grétry, André Ernest Modeste. [1789]. Paris: Chez l'auteur. Univ. of North Texas Music Library Virtual Rare Book Room. http://www.library.unt.edu/music/assets/vrbr/Barbebleue1789.pdf.

Grimm, Jacob and Wilhelm Grimm. 1819. *German Popular Stories, Translated from the Kinder und Haus Märchen, Collected by MM Grimm, from Oral Tradition.* 1812–1815, 1819. 2 vols. Illus. George Cruikshank. London: C Baldwyn, 1823–1826. Reprint London, J. Robins & Co., 1825–1826. Reprint London: J. Robins & Sherwood, Gilbert & Piper, 1834. Lilly Library.

Hamilton, Patrick. 1939. *Angel Street.* New York: Samuel French.

Hammett, Dashiell. 1980. *Sam Spade: Betrayal in Bumpus Hell, and The Bluebeard Caper.* Perf. Howard Duff. Sound recording. Reprint Hellertown, PA: Old Time Radio, 1989.

Hanlon, Tina L. "Appalachian Tales of Strong Women: Pretty Polly or Mister Fox." AppLit Home. http://www.ferrum.edu/applit/bibs/tales/prettypolly.htm.

Harris, Thomas. 1988. *The Silence of the Lambs.* Reprint New York: St. Martin's, 1989.

Havergal, Brian. 1913. "Bluebeard." *Doctor Merryheart: A Comedy Overture for Orchestra.* Leipzig: Breitkopf & Härtel.

Hay, Sara Henderson. 1961. "Syndicated Column." Reprint *Story Hour: A Second Look at Cinderella, Bluebeard, and Company.* Fayetteville: Univ. of Arkansas Press, 1998. 35.

Hebbel, Friedrich. 1841. *Judith: Eine tragödie in fünf acten.* Hamburg: Hoffman und Campe.

Heber, Reginald, Bishop of Calcutta. 1868. *Blue-Beard: A Serio-comic Oriental Romance. Fairy Plays for Home Performance.* No. 13. [1864, etc.]. Reprint [n.p.: n.p.], 1874. Widener Library.

Henderson, David. 1889. "Bluebeard, Jr." *Ali Baba, or, Morgiana and the Forty Thieves [Collection]: A Spectacular Extravaganza in Four Acts.* Tams-Witmark/Wisconsin Collection, 1892–1895.

Higgie, Thomas. 1847. *The Devil's Mount, or, The Female Bluebeard: A Romantic Drama in Two Acts.* London: Thomas Hailes Lacy.

———. 1850. *The Devil's Mount; or, the Female Bluebeard. A Romantic Drama, in Two Acts [and in Prose].* T. H. Lacy's acting edition of Plays etc., vol. 88. London: Thomas Hailes Lacy.

Hine, Daryl. 1968. *Bluebeard's Wife.* Illus. Virgil Burnett. Reprint Toronto: Coach House, 1975. Thomas Fisher Rare Book Library.

Hines, Kaitlin E. 2004. "Choreographing Narrative: A Movement Exploration of Bluebeard." Ph.D. diss. Hampshire College, Amherst, Mass.

Hobday, E. A. P. 1888a. *Bluebeard, or, Fickle Fatima and the Fatal Key: An Operatic Burlesque Extravaganza in 4 Acts.* Snowdon, Simla, India: Simla Fancy Repository.

———. 1888b. *Bluebeard, or, Fickle Fatima and the Fatal Key: An Operatic Burlesque Extravaganza in 4 Acts, etc.* Simla, India: "The Season" Press.

———. [n.d.]. *Bluebeard, or, Fickle Fatima and the Fatal Key: An Operatic Burlesque Extravaganza in 4 Acts, etc.* Photocopy. Reprint Chicago: Dept. of Photoduplication, Univ. of Chicago Library, 1987.

Hobson, Michael. 1985. *Moon Knight*. no. 4. New York: Marvel Comics.

Hoffman, Alice. 2001. *Blue Diary*. New York: Putnam's Sons.

Hoffman, Nina Kiriki. 2003. "Chambers of the Heart." *My Swan Sister: Fairy Tales Retold*. Ed. Ellen Datlow and Terri Windling. New York: Simon and Schuster.

Holland, J[osiah] G[ilbert]. 1858. *Bitter-Sweet*. Reprint New York: Scribner, 1881.

Holland, Sarah. 1985. *Bluebeard's Bride*. Toronto: Harlequin.

Honora, Mary, Sister. 1959. "For Bluebeard." New Haven, Conn.: Penny Poems.

Hood, Basil. C. 1888. *Bluebeard, the Second, or, The Skeleton in the Cupboard: An original burlesque*. London: Hatchards.

Hopkinson, Nalo. 2001. "The Glass Bottle Trick." *Skin Folk*. New York: Warner Aspect. 83–101.

Hopwood, Avery. 1923. *Little Miss Bluebeard: A Comedy in Three Acts (Adapted from "Der gatte des frauleins")*. Reprint New York: Samuel French, 1935.

Horrocks, G. G., and C. H. B. Jaques. 1918. *Bluebeard: A Pantomime*. London: Printed for private circulation only by C. Jaques. San Jose State University Library.

Horton, Sydney George. 1887. *A Grand Christmas Pantomime Entitled Blue Beard, or, Harlequin and the Farmer's Pet, etc.* Woolwich: F. J. Cattermole.

Huysmans, Joris Karl. 1891. *Là-Bas*. Trans. Keene Wallace. *Down There*. 1928. Reprint New York: Dover, 1972.

Igloria, Luisa A. 1999. "Blended." *Songs for the Beginning of the Millenium*. Manila: De La Salle Univ. Press. http://nycbigcitylit.com/sep2001/contents/Poetry/Feature.html#Blended.

Iles, Francis. 1932. *Before the Fact*. New York: Doubleday.

Irish, William. 1952. *Bluebeard's 7th Wife*. New York: Popular Library.

Jackson, Shirley. 1997. Introduction, "All I Can Remember," "The Honeymoon of Mrs. Smith, Version I" and "The Honeymoon of Mrs. Smith, Version II: The Mystery of the Murdered Bride." *Just an Ordinary Day*. Ed. Laurence Jackson Hyman and Sarah Hyman Stewart. New York: Bantam. vi–xii, 70–88.

Jameson, Vere. 1954. "Bluebeard." *Bluebeard*. London, Ontario: Hunter Printing. 7. Thomas Fisher Rare Book Library.

Jenkins, E. Lawrence. 1902. *Blue Beard or The Bride, the Bogie and the Blood: A Burlesque Opera in Two Acts*. New York: Hints.

Jennings, Gertrude E. 1944. *Too Much Bluebeard: A Farce in Three Scenes for Three Women*. London: S. French.

Johnson, Clifton. 1920. *Bluebeard*. Illus. Harry Smith. New York: Macaulay. Reprint Chicago: Goldsmith, 1935.

Kate, Robin. 2004. "Terror Starts at Home." *Six Feet Under*. Episode 45. (July 25). HBO.

Keating, E. H. (Eliza H.) 1860. *Blue Beard, or, Female Curiosity and Male Atrocity!!!: An Extravaganza in Two Acts. Bluebeard. Fairy Plays for Home Performance No. 2*. London: T. H. Lacy.

———. [n.d]. *Dramas for the Drawing Room; or Charades for Christmas*. London: Thomas Hailes Lacy.

Keene, Carolyn. 1986. *The Bluebeard Room*. Nancy Drew Mystery 77. Reprint New York: Minstrel, 1988.

Keller, Loren. 1999. *Four and Twenty Bluebeards*. Buffalo, N.Y.: the author.

Kelly, Michael. [1798?]. *Blue Beard; or, Female Curiosity!* Music score. Dublin: Edmund Lee. British Library.

Kelly, Tim J. 1957. *Bluebeard Had a Wife: A Comedy in One Act*. Reprint Chicago: Dramatic Pub, 1967.

Kemp, Gene. 1967. *Bluebeard's Castle*. Reprint London: Faber & Faber, 2000.

Kenney, Charles Lamb. 1870. *Blue Beard: A Comic Operetta in Three Acts and Four Tableux*. Adapted from *Barbe bleue* by Henri Meilhac and Ludovic Halévy 1866. Music by Jacques Offenbach. Harvard Theatre Collection.

Kerrigan, John. 1945. *Bluebeard*. Reprint London: Arrow, 1984.

Kilmer, Aline. 1923. "The Case of Bluebeard." *Hunting a Hair Shirt and Other Spiritual Adventures*. New York: George H. Doran. 93–98.

King, Rufus. 1945. *Museum Piece No. 13*. Reprint New York: Doubleday, 1946.

King, Stephen. 1977. *The Shining*. Reprint New York: Signet, 1978.

Knez, Dora. 2000. "One Forbidden Thing." *Five Forbidden Things*. Northampton, MA: Small Beer. 23–27.

Krohn, Herbert. [n.d.]. "Bluebeard in Love," "The Sun Rises in Her Eyes," "Bluebeard's Obsessive Fantasy," "Their Sex Life," "Bluebeard Goes to See the Gypsy," "The Dream War," "The Street of Delicious Pairs." Isabella Gardner Papers (1915–1981), Olin Library, Washington Univ., St. Louis.

Krüger, Michael. 2002. "The Bluebeard Trust." *Scenes from the Life of a Best-Selling Author*. Trans. Karen Leeder. London: Haravill.

Ladbrook, Martin. 2005. *Bluebeard: A Pantomime*. Warrington, UK: New Theatre Publications.

Lander, Randy. [n.d.]. "Fables #16 (Best of the Week!) 'Storybook Love Part Three: Duel'" *Snap Judgments*. The 4th Rail. http://www.thefourthrail.com/reviews/snapjudgments/081103/fables16.shtml.

Lane, M. Travisic. 1973. "Well, Viewed by God." *Poems 1968–1972*. Fredericton, New Brunswick: Fiddlehead Poetry Books.

Lang, Andrew, ed. and intro. 1888. *Perrault's Popular Tales*, by Charles Perrault. Oxford: Clarendon.

———. 1889. *The Blue Fairy Book*. Oxford: Clarendon.

Lardner, Ring. 1925. "Bluebeard." "Bed-time Stories." *What of It?* New York: Scribner. 70–73.

Leeds, Lucy A., Mrs. 1912. *Château Bluebeard*. London: Henry J. Drane. British Library.

Lennard, Horace. 1894. *Crystal Palace Grand Christmas Pantomime Blue Beard.* [London?: F. M. Evans].

Lewis, Matthew Gregory. 1797. *The Castle Spectre.* Theatre Rajat, Drury Lane.

Lillo, George. 1739. *Fatal Curiosity.* Reprint Ed. and intro. William H. McBurney. Lincoln: Univ. of Nebraska Press, 1966.

Lipman, Julia. 1883. *Nellie's Work-box, a Parlor Charade and Bluebeard, or, Female Curiosity: An Entertainment for the Parlor, with Full Stage Directions, and Hints for Costumes, and Decorations, Carefully Prepared by an Old Stage Manager, and Suitable for Town or Country.* New York: McLoughlin Bros.

Litt, Edward, Laman Blanchard, and Thomas Longdon Greenwood. [The Brothers Grinn.] 1879. *Bluebeard.* London: M'Corquodale.

Lochhead, Liz. 1981. "Blueshirt." *The Grimm Sisters.* London: Next Editions in association with Faber & Faber. Reprint *Dreaming Frankenstein and Collected Poems.* London: Polygon, 1984. 69–104.

Long, Karawynn. 1999. "The Shell Box." *Silver Birch, Blood Moon.* Ed. Ellen Datlow and Terri Windling. New York: Avon. 157–92.

Ludlam, Charles. 1987. *Bluebeard: A Melodrama in Three Acts.* New York: S. French.

M., G. gent., trans. 1763. *Histories, or, Tales of Past Times Told by Mother Goose: with Morals,* written in French by M. Perrault; and Englished by G. M. Gent. 3rd ed., corr. Salisbury: Printed and sold by B. Collins; [London]: also by W. Bristow, in St. Paul's Church-Yard, London, 1763. Lilly Library. Reprint Lang, *The Blue Fairy Book,* 1889. Reprint Saxon Childers, *Histories,* 1925.

MacBeth, George. 1962. "Maxims of Bluebeard." *Lecture to Trainees.* Oxford: Fantasy.

Macpherson, Jay. 1981. "Visiting," "Set-Ups." *Poems Twice Told.* Toronto: Oxford Univ. Press. 92, 93.

Madore, Nancy. 2003. "Bluebeard." *Bedtime Stories for Women.* Coral Gables, Fla.: Lumina.

Maeterlinck, Maurice. 1901. *Ariane et Barbe-bleue (Ariane and Blue-Beard): A Tale in Three Acts from the Play by Maurice Maeterlinck.* Trans. Hermann Klein. New York: G. Schirmer, 1907.

Maguire, Susie. 2000. "Bluebeard." *The Short Hello.* Edinburgh: Polygon.

Mahurin, Matt, ill. "The Inner Masculine Animus." http://www.thearchetypalconnection.com/images/Bluebeard'sSecretChamberLow.JPG.

Marriott, Charles. 1912. "Solomon Bluebeard." *The Windsor Magazine* (April).

Marshall, M. E. 1925. *Bluebeard: A Wordless Play.* London: J. Curwen & Sons.

Melville, Herman. 1876. *Clarel: A Poem and Pilgrimage in the Holy Land.* Reprint Evanston, Ill.: Northwestern Univ. Press and Newberry Library, 1991.

Merington, Marguerite. 1916. "Bluebeard." *Fairy Tale Plays.* Reprint New York: Duffield, 1925.

Millay, Edna St. Vincent. 1917. "Bluebeard." *Renascence and Other Poems.* Reprint *Collected Poems.* Ed. Norma Millay. New York: Harper, 1956. Reprint Cheryl Walker, "In Bluebeard's Closet," 1996, 16.

Miller, Webb. 1965. "Bluebeard of Paris." *Great True Stories of Crime, Mystery and Detection, from Reader's Digest.* Pleasantville, N.Y.: Reader's Digest.

Millet, Lydia. 1998. "The Wife Killer." *Mirror, Mirror on the Wall: Women Writers Explore Their Favorite Fairy Tales.* Ed. Kate Bernheimer. New York: Anchor Doubleday. 230–46.

Millward, Charles. 1869. *The Grand Christmas Comic Pantomime Entitled Bluebeard.* [n.p.]: Theatre Royal Printing Works.

Molineaux, Roland Burnham. 1903. "The Mayor of the Death Chamber." *The Room with the Little Door.* New York: G. W. Dillingham.

Montgomery, L. M. 1926. *The Blue Castle.* Reprint New York: Bantam, 1988.

Morton, John Maddison. 1854. *Harlequin Bluebeard, the Great Bashaw, or, The Good Fairy Triumphant over the Demon of Discord: A Grand Comic Christmas Pantomime.* Reprint New York: S. French, 1857.

Motley, John Lathrop, trans. 1840. *Blue Beard, a Story in Five Acts.* Ludwig Tieck. *New World I.* (Dec. 19): 449–52, 478–83.

Muller, Romeo. 1979. *Puff the Magic Dragon.* New York: Avon.

Namjoshi, Suniti. 1981. "A Room of His Own." *Feminist Fables.* London: Sheba Feminist Publishers. 64.

Nelson, Resa. 1994. "The Key to Bluebeard's Heart." *Science Fiction Age* (November): 69–72.

Novello, Sabilla. 1875. *The History of Bluebeard's Six Wives.* London: Grant and Co.

———. 1876. *Bluebeard's Widow and Her Sister Anne: Their History Evolved from Mendacious Chronicles.* London: Ward, Lock & Tyler.

Oates, Joyce Carol. 1988. "Blue-Bearded Lover." *The Assignation: Stories.* New York: Ecco. 184–86. Reprint *Caught in a Story: Contemporary Fairytales and Fables.* Ed. Christine Park and Caroline Heaton. London: Vintage, 1992. 182–84.

Oberon, Merle. 1942. "Bluebeard of Bellac." Reprint *Old-time Radio's Stars on Suspense.* Schiller Park, Ill.: Radio Spirits, 2000.

O'Donnell, Peter, and Enric Badia Romero. 2006. "The Bluebeard Affair." *Modesty Blaise: The Gallows Bird.* London: Titan.

Offenbach, Jacques. [ca. 1868]. *Barbe-bleue, (Bluebeard) Containing the French text, with an English Translation, and the Music of All the Principal Airs.* Boston: Ditson. Loeb Music Library.

Ország-Land, Thomas. 1978. *Prince Bluebeard's Castle: A Libretto, Adapted from the Hungarian of Béla Balázs.* London: Tern.

Pearson, Maggie, and Gavin Rowe. 2000. *The Headless Horseman and Other Ghoulish Tales.* New York: Crocodile Books.

Penny Pantomime of Blue Beard. [1870?]. [London]. Harvard Theatre Collection.

Perrault, Charles. 1695. *Perrault's Tales of Mother Goose. The Dedication Manuscript of 1695 Reproduced in Collotype Facsimile with Introduction and Critical Text,* vol. 1: *Text.* Reprint Ed. Jacques Barchilon. 2 vols. New York: Pierpont Morgan Library, 1956.

———. 1697. *Perrault's Popular Tales*. Reprint Ed. and intro. Andrew Lang. Oxford: Clarendon, 1888.

———. 1729. *Histories or Tales of Past Times*. Facsimile of Houghton Library copy of the London: Pote and Montagu, 1729 edition. Trans. Robert Samber. Reprint Ed. and pref. Michael Patrick Hearn. Classics of Children's Literature 1621–1932 Series. New York: Garland, 1977.

———. 1888. "La Barbe Bleue." *Popular Tales*. Ed. and intro. Andrew Lang. Oxford: Clarendon. 23–29

———. [1961]. *My First Reading Book of Little Red Riding Hood and Other Stories*. Illus. Marie-Louise Pecour. Kingfisher Colour Book. London: Ward Lock & Co. British Library.

———. 1988. "Bluebeard." *Antique Fairy Tales*. Ed. Judith Mastrangelo. Parsippany, N.J.: Unicorn.

———. 1989. "La Barbe Bleue." *Charles Perrault, Contes*. Textes établis et presentés par Marc Soriano. Paris: Flammarion. 257–62.

———. 1991. "La Barbe Bleue." *Histories ou Contes du Temps Passé*. Ed. Daniel Couty. Paris: Librarie Larousse. 44–53.

Planché, James Robinson, and Charles Dance. 1839. *Blue Beard: An Extravaganza [in One Act and in Verse]*. Reprint *T. H. Lacy's Acting Edition of Plays*, vol. 19. [1950, etc.], 1864. Widener Library.

———. 1848. *Blue Beard: An Extravaganza [in One Act and in Verse]*. Printed by S. G. Fairbrother, 31, Bow St, Covent Garden. British Library.

Plath, Sylvia. [pre-1956]. "Bluebeard." *The Collected Poems*. Ed. Ted Hughes. New York: Harper and Row, 1981. 305.

Potter, Beatrix. 1932. *Sister Anne*. Philadelphia: David McKay.

Proulx, Annie. 1999. "55 Miles to the Gas Pump." *Compact Bedford Intro to Literature*. Ed. Michael Meyer. 6th ed. Boston: Bedford. 491.

Quiller-Couch, Sir Arthur. 1910. *The Sleeping Beauty and Other Fairy Tales*. New York: George H. Doran. http://www.bartleby.com/76/.

Rayner, Shoo. 2005. *Bluebeard's Cat*. London: Orchard.

Reakes, Paul. 2003. *Bluebeard: A Pantomime*. London: Samuel French.

Reed, Jeremy. 1976. *Count Bluebeard*. Breakish, Scotland: Aquila/the Phaethon.

Reeve, William, libretto. 1791. *Blue Beard, or, The Flight of Harlequin. First produced Dec. 21, 1791, at Covent Garden Theatre, Thomas Harris, manager*. British Library.

Reeve, Wybert. [1875?]. *Pantomime of Blue Beard, the Great Bashaw, or Harlequin Stormcloud and the Fairy, Starlight Queen*. Edinburgh: J. Turner. Harvard Theatre Collection.

Rhys, Jean. 1966. *Wide Sargasso Sea*. Reprint London: Penguin, 1987.

Richards, Laura Elizabeth Howe. 1916. "Bluebeard." *Fairy Operettas*. Boston: Little Brown.

Rioux, Hélène. 1988. "Jour de Chance" ["Thirteen Chrysanthemum Avenue"]. Reprint *Three by Three*. Trans. Louise von Flotow. Montreal: Guernica, 1993.

Ritchie, Anne Thackeray. 1875. "Bluebeard's Keys." *Bluebeard's Keys and Other Stories*. New York: Harper & Brothers. 12–41.

Robinson, James. 1993. *Bluebeard*, 3 vols. Illus. Phil Elliott. San Jose, Calif.: Slave Labor Graphics.

Rohmer, Sax. 1936. "Bluebeard." *President Fu Manchu: The Oriental Edition*. New York: P. F. Collier. 110–22.

Rome, Fred. 1971. "Bluebeard." *Potted Pantos*. London: Wolfe.

Rule, Ann. 1993. *A Rose for Her Grave*. New York: Pocket.

Russell, P. Craig. 1989. "Ariane et Barbe-bleue." Reprint *Adaptations of Parisfal, Ariane & Bluebeard, I Pagliacci, and Songs by Mahler*. Comic strip. New York: Nantier, Beall, Minoustchine, 2003.

Ryan, Tracy. 1996. *Bluebeard in Drag*. South Fremantle, Australia: Fremantle Arts Center Press.

Samber, Robert. 1729. *Histories, or Tales of Past Times . . . with morals, by M. Perrault, Translated into English*. Reprint Barchilon and Pettit, *Authentic Mother Goose Tales and Nursery Rhymes*. Denver: Swallow, 1960. Reprint Opie, *The Classic Fairy Tales*, 1974. Reprint Perrault, *Histories or Tales of Past Times*, 1977.

Samuel, Kenneth Ormsby. 1948. *Bluebeard: A Pantomime in Four Acts*. London: S. French.

Sanders, Bruce. 1951. *Madame Bluebeard, a Case for Anatole Fox*. Reprint New York: Roy Publishers, 1957.

"Sanger's Hippodrome, Circus and Menagerie, Lambeth." ca. 1881. British Library.

Sansom, Clive. 1969. "The Forbidden Room." *Return to Magic*. London: Frewin. 51.

Saxon Childers, J[ames], ed. 1925. *Histories, or, Tales of Past Times Told by Mother Goose: with Morals, Written in French by M. Perrault and Englished by G. M., gent*. London: Nonesuch.

Schaeffer, Susan Fromberg. 1988. "Bluebeard's Second Wife." *Great American Love Stories*. Ed. Lucy Rosenthal. Boston: Little Brown. 566–78.

Sedgwick, Alfred B. 1875–1883. "Burlesques: Africanus Bluebeard." Reprint *The Collected Works of Alfred B. Sedgwick*. New York: Garland, 1994.

Sexton, Anne. 1979. "The Gold Key." *Transformations*. Boston: Houghton-Mifflin.

Shakespeare, William. 1600. *Much Ado About Nothing*. Reprint *William Shakespeare: The Complete Works*. Oxford: Clarendon, 1986. 611–36.

Sherman, Cindy. 1992. *Fitcher's Bird*. New York: Rizzoli.

Shute, Evan Vere [pseud. Vere Jameson]. 1954. "Bluebeard." *Bluebeard*. London, Ontario: Hunter. 7. Thomas Fisher Rare Book Library.

Solomon, Frederic. [ca. 1903]. *Mr. Bluebeard*. Adapted for the American Stage by J. J. McNally. Lyrics by J. C. Goodwin. New York: Bloom. Loeb Music Library.

Somtow, S. P. 2003. *Bluebeard's Castle*. New York: iUniverse.

Spenser, Edmund. 1590. "Book III, cantos 11–12." *The Faerie Queene*. Reprint *Poetical Works of Edmund Spenser*. Ed. J. C. Smith and E. de Selincourt. Oxford: Oxford Univ. Press, 1985.

Squier, Emma-Lindsay. 1932. "Bluebeard and the Spanish Witch." *Good Housekeeping* (December): 59+.

———. 1935. "Blackbeard vs. Blue Eyes." *Good Housekeeping* (March): 44+.

Steinbach, Meredith. 1987. "Bluebeard's Children." *Black Warrior Review* 13.2: 95–100.

Stirling, Edward. 1843. *Harlequin Bluebeard, or, The Fairy of the Silver Crescent*.n.p.:n.p.

Strauss, Gwen. 1990. "Bluebeard." *Trail of Stones*. Illus. Anthony Browne. New York: Knopf. 20–21.

Sue, Eugène [Marie-Joseph]. 1842. *Le Morne au Diable*. Reprint Trans. *The Female Bluebeard*. New York: New World, 1844.

Tatar, Maria M., ed. and trans. 2002. "'Bluebeard,' Charles Perrault." *The Annotated Classic Fairy Tales*. New York: Norton.

Tate, Allen. 2003. "The Robber Bridegroom." *The Poets' Grimm: 20th Century Poems from Grimm Fairy Tales*. Ed. Jeanne Marie Beaumont and Claudia Carlson. Ashland, OR: Story Line. 52.

Taylor, Edwin Chas. 1896. "Bluebeard's Casket: A Legend of St. Thomas, Danish West Indies." *An Island of the Sea*. [45]–58. Houghton Library.

———. [1896]. "A Remarkable Incident. A Story of Bluebeard's Castle, St. Thomas, Danish West Indies." *An Island of the Sea*. Houghton Library.

Taylor, Elizabeth. 1938. "Bluebeard." *Follies for a Fun Night: A Collection of Twelve Clever Skits for Schools, Clubs and Lodges*. San Francisco: Banner Play Bureau. 19–24.

Thackeray, William Makepeace. 1843. "Bluebeard's Ghost." *Spells of Enchantment*. Reprint Ed. Jack Zipes. New York: Viking, 1991. 337–56.

———. 1844. *The Memoirs of Barry Lyndon, Esq., of the Kingdom of Ireland*. Reprint Oxford: Oxford Univ. Press, 1992.

———. 1847. "Barbazure." *Thackeray's Miscellanies*, vol. 5: *Burlesques*. London: Smith, 1877. 49–61.

———. 1848. *Vanity Fair: A Novel without a Hero*. Reprint London: Penguin, 2001.

———. 1971. "'[Bluebeard at Breakfast]': An Unpublished Manuscript." Ed. and intro. Juliet McMaster. *Dickens Studies Annual* 8(1981): 197–230.

Thomason, Caroline Wasson. 1921. *Bluebeard/Barbe Bleue: A Play for Children in Three Scenes Arranged to Be Given in English or French*. Philadelphia: Penn Pub.

Tieck, Ludwig. 1797. *Ritter Blaubart: Blue Beard a Story in Five Acts*. Reprint Trans. John Lathrop Motley. *New World I* (Dec. 19, 1840): 449–52, 478–83.

Tilzer, Harry von. ca. 1935. "Why Did Bluebeard's Beard Turn Blue." Words by Eddie Moran. British Library.

Tong, Su. 1993. "Wives and Concubines." *Raise the Red Lantern: Three Novellas*. Trans. Michael S. Buke. New York: Penguin.

Tully, J. H. 1842. *Blue Beard; or, Hints to the Curious. A Burlesque Burletta*. Reprint London: W. W. Barth, [1850–1859?].

Tyre, Nedra. 1959. "The Gentle Miss Bluebeard." Reprint *Witches' Brew*. Ed. Alfred Hitchcock. New York: Dell, 1965. 91–103.

Uhry, Alfred. 1976. *The Robber Bridegroom*. Music by Robert Waldman. London: Josef Weinberger.

Untermeyer, Louis. 1968. *Tales from the Ballet*. New York: Golden Press.

Updike, John. 1994. "Bluebeard in Ireland," "George and Vivian." *The Afterlife and Other Stories*. New York: Knopf. 154–89.

Valentine, Mrs. L. 19–. "Bluebeard." *Home Acting for Amateurs: Seven Original Comediettas, by Nella Parker, R. L. and C.M.A. Bayliff and Mrs L. Valentine*. London: F. Warne.

Vonnegut, Kurt. 1987. *Bluebeard: A Novel*. New York: Dell.

Warner, Sylvia Townsend. 1940a. "Introduction," "Bluebeard's Daughter." *The Cat's Cradle Book*. New York: Viking. 9–40, 157–80. Reprint *Spells of Enchantment: The Wondrous Fairy Tales of Western Culture*. Ed. Jack Zipes. New York: Viking, 1991. 672–85.

———. 1940b. "Bluebeard's Daughter." Reprint *The Gender of Modernism: A Critical Anthology*. Ed. Bonnie Kime Scott. Bloomington: Indiana Univ. Press, 1990. 547–59.

———. 1940c. "Bluebeard's Daughter." Reprint *The Oxford Book of Modern Fairy Tales*. Oxford: Oxford Univ. Press, 1993

Washburn, Laura Lee. "The Devil's Pocketbook." Unpublished.

Waugh, Hillary. 1958. *The Eighth Mrs. Bluebeard*. Garden City, N.Y.: Crime Club by Doubleday. Reprint London: W. Foulsham, 1959. Reprint London: Pan Books, 1961.

Weber, Ken. 1991. "Danger at the Border." *More Five-Minute Mysteries for You to Solve*. Philadelphia, Pa.: Running. 93–98.

Weitzman, Sarah Brown. "The Forbidden." *Never Far from Flesh*. Pure Heart. http://www.mainstreetrag.com/S_Weitzman.html.

Welty, Eudora. 1942. *The Robber Bridegroom*. Reprint New York: Harcourt Brace Jovanovich, 1970.

West, Trudy. 1952. *Bluebeard: A Basic Pantomime in Three Acts*. London: S. French.

Wiggin [afterward Riggs], Kate Douglas Smith. 1914. *Bluebeard: A Musical Fantasy*. New York: Harper & Brothers. British Library.

Wood, Clement. 1926. *Bluebeard and His Eight Wives*. Girard, Kans.: Haldeman-Julius.

Wood, J. Hickory, and Arthur Collins. 1901–1902. *Grand Christmas Pantomime Blue Beard. Theatre Drury Lane*. London: J. Miles & Co. Univ. of Chicago Libraries.

Wright, Richard. 1966. *Black Boy*. New York: Harper & Row.

Yates, Margaret H. 1933. "Bluebeard: or, The Thirteenth Wife." *Easy Pantomimes by Various Authors*. New York: Fitzgerald. Reprint Boston: Baker's Plays, 1961.

Ysaye, Lisa. 1917. "The True Story of Bluebeard." *The Inn of Disenchantment*. Boston: Houghton Mill, Riverside.

Zipes, Jack, trans. and intro. 1987a. *The Complete Fairy Tales of the Brothers Grimm*. Reprint New York: Bantam, 1992.

———, trans. and intro. 1989. *Beauties, Beasts, and Enchantment: Classic French Fairy Tales*. New York: New American Library.

———, ed. 1991. *Spells of Enchantment: The Wondrous Fairy Tales of Western Culture*. New York: Viking.

BLUEBEARD FILMOGRAPHY

Barbe-bleue. 1901. Dir. Georges Méliès. *Melies the Magician*. Chicago: Facets Video, 2001.

Bluebeard. 1907. Prod. Étienne Arnaud.

Bluebeard. 1944. Dir. Edgar Ulmer. Burbank, Calif.: Hollywood's Attic, 1996.

Bluebeard. 1963. Dir. Claude Chabrol. Embassy Pictures, 1963. English dubbed version of French: *Landru*, 1962.

Bluebeard. 1972. Dir. Edward Dmytryk. Detroit: Distributed by Anchor Bay Entertainment, 2000.

Bluebeard Jr. 1922. Dir. Scott R. Dunlap.

Bluebeard's Eighth Wife. 1938. Dir. Ernst Lubitsch. Universal City, Calif.: MCA/Universal Home Video, 1995.

Bluebeard's Seven Wives. 1926. Dir. Alfred Santell.

Boom in the Moon (El Moderno Barba Azul/Bluebeard). 1946. Dir. Jaime Salvador. Madera, Calif.: Distributed by Madera CineVideo, 1990s.

"Bye, Bye Bluebeard." 1949. Dir. Arthur Davis. *Days of Swine and Roses*. Burbank, Calif.: Warner Bros., 1992.

Caught. 1949. Dir. Max Ophuls. Los Angeles, Calif.: Republic Pictures Home Video, 1988.

Dark Waters. 1944. Dir. Andre De Toth. [Chatsworth, Calif.]: Image Entertainment, 1999.

Dragonwyck. 1946. Dir. Joseph Mankiewicz. [Australia]: Umbrella Entertainment, 2004.

Experiment Perilous. 1944. Dir. Jacques Tourneur. Los Angeles, Calif.: Nostalgia Merchant: Dist. by Fox Hills Video, 1987.

Gaslight. 1944. Dir. George Cukor. Copied from Turner Classic Movies, 2004.

Hiss and Yell. 1946. Dir. Jules White. Culver City, Calif.: Columbia Pictures.

Jane Eyre. 1944. Dir. Robert Stevenson. [Beverly Hills, Calif.]: Fox Video, 1993.

Love from a Stranger. 1937. Dir. Rowland V. Lee. Medford, Ore.: Sinister Cinema. Burbank, Calif.: Hollywood's Attic, 1996.

Love from a Stranger. 1947. Dir. Richard Whorf. Eagle-Lion Films. Santa Monica, Calif.: New World Video, 1986.

The Madonna's Secret. 1946. Dir. Wilhelm Thiele. Los Anegeles, Calif.: Republic Piuctures.

Miss Bluebeard. 1925. Dir. Frank Tuttle, Hollywood, Calif.: Famous Players-Laskey, Paramount.

Monsieur Verdoux. 1947. Dir. Charles Chaplin. United Artists. New York: Fox Video, 1992.

Notorious. 1946. Dir. Alfred Hitchcock. Minneapolis: Festival Films, [n.d.].

Phantom of the Plains. 1945. Dir. Lesley Selander. Los Angeles, Calif.: Republic Pictures.

The Piano. 1993. Dir. Jane Campion. Miramax.

Rebecca. 1940. Dir. Alfred Hitchcock. Troy, Mich.: Anchor Bay Entertainment, 1998.

Secret Beyond the Door. 1948. Dir. Fritz Lang. Republic Pictures. Los Angeles, Calif.: Republic Pictures Home Video, 1990.

Shadow of a Doubt. 1943. Dir. Alfred Hitchcock. Burbank, Calif.: Warner Brothers, 1980.

The Silence of the Lambs. 1991. Dir. Jonathan Demme. Orion Pictures.

Spellbound. 1945. Dir. Alfred Hitchcock. Beverly Hills, Calif.: ABC Video, 1996.

Suspicion. 1941. Dir. Alfred Hitchcock. Turner Entertainment Co., 1988.
The Two Mrs. Carrolls. 1947. Dir. Peter Godfrey. Culver City, Calif.: MGM/UA Home Video, 1992.
Undercurrent. 1946. Dir. Vincente Minelli. Culver City, Calif.: MGM/UA Home Video, 1990.

Secondary Sources

158 Scénarios de Films Disparus de Georges Méliès. 1986. Paris: Association "Les Amis de Georges Méliès." 46–47. (Cited in Gunning 1995, 62).
A., A. Jan 20, [18]66. "Blue Beard in England." *Notes and Queries* 3rd ser. vol. 9.
Aarne, Antti, and Stith Thompson. 1961. *The Types of the Folktale: A Classification and a Bibliography, Translated and Enlarged by Stith Thompson*. Helsinki: Academia Scientarium Fennica. 101–04.
Abbott, Lynn, and Doug Seroff. 2002. *Out of Sight: The Rise of African American Popular Music, 1889–1895*. Jackson: Univ. Press of Mississippi.
Alcott, Louisa May. 1868. "Happy Women." (Cited in Showalter 1988, 205).
———. 1877b. Journal entry. (Cited in Davis 1995, vi).
Alderson, Brian, trans. 1978. *The Brothers Grimm: Popular Folk Tales*. London: Gollancz.
Apostolidès, Jean-Marie. 1991. "Des Choses Cachées dans le château de Barbe bleue." *Marvels & Tales* 5.2: 179–99.
Arnold, Marilyn. 1989. "Eudora Welty's Parody." *Critical Essays on Eudora Welty*. Ed. W. Craig Turner and Lee Emling Harding. Boston: G. K. Hall. 32–38.
Ashliman, D. L. 1987. *A Guide to Folktales in the English Language: Based on the Aarne-Thompson Classification System*. Westport, Conn.: Greenwood.
Ashman, Mike. 1991. "Around the Bluebeard Myth." *The Stage Works of Béla Bartók*. London: John Calder. 35–44.
Ashton, John. 1882. *Chapbooks of the Eighteenth Century*. London: Chatto & Windus.
Asper, Kathrin. 1991. "'Fitcher's Bird': Illustrations of the Negative Animus and Shadow in Persons with Narcissistic Disturbances." Trans. Elizabeth Burr. *Psyche's Stories: Modern Jungian Interpretations of Fairy Tales, I*. Ed. Murray Stein and Lionell Corbett. 2 vols. Wilmette, Ill.: Chiron. 1: 121–39.
Atwood, Margaret. 1977. "A Question of Metamorphosis." [Interview with Linda Sandler.] Reprint *Margaret Atwood: Conversations*. Ed. Earl Ingersoll. Willowdale, Ontario: Firefly Books, 1990. 40–57.
———. 1978a. "Defying Distinctions." [Interview with Karla Hammond.] Reprint *Margaret Atwood: Conversations*. Ed. Earl Ingersoll. Willowdale, Ontario: Firefly Books, 1990. 99–108.
———. 1978b. "My Mother Would Rather Skate Than Scrub Floors." [Interview with Joyce Carol Oates.] Reprint *Margaret Atwood: Conversations*. Ed. Earl Ingersoll. Willowdale, Ontario: Firefly Books, 1990. 69–73.

———. 1998. "Of Souls as Birds." *Mirror, Mirror on the Wall: Women Writers Explore Their Favorite Fairy Tales*. Ed. Kate Bernheimer. New York: Anchor Doubleday. 22–38.

Austen-Leigh, J. E. 1869. "A Memoir of Jane Austen." Reprint *Persuasion*. Harmondsworth: Penguin, 1985. 273–391.

Bacchilega, Cristina. 1997. *Postmodern Fairy Tales: Gender and Narrative Strategies*. Philadelphia: Univ. of Pennsylvania Press.

———. 1998a. "Folk and Literary Narrative in a Postmodern Context: The Case of the *Märchen*." *Fabula* 29: 302–15.

———. 1998b. "In the Eye of the Fairy Tale: Corinna Sargood and David Wheatley Talk about Working with Angela Carter." *Marvels & Tales* 12.1: 213–28.

Bachelard, Gaston. 1958. "The Dialectics of Outside and Inside." *The Poetics of Space*. Trans. Maria Jolas. Boston: Beacon, 1969. 211–31.

Baer, Elizabeth R. 1988. "Pilgrimage Inward: Quest and Fairy Tale Motifs in *Surfacing*." *Margaret Atwood: Vision and Forms*. Ed. Kathryn Van Spanckeren and Jan Garden Castro. Carbondale: Southern Illinois Univ. Press. 24–34.

Bal, Mieke. 1991. "Real Rape: The Importance of Telling Stories." *Reading "Rembrandt."* New York: Oxford Univ. Press.

Balázs, Béla. [ca. 1915]. *A Kékszakállú Herceg Vara: Megjegyzések a szöveghez*. (Duke Bluebeard's Castle: Notes on the Text). Reprint *Balázs Béla: Válogatott cikkek éstanulmányok*. Ed. Magda Nagy. Budapest, 1968. 35. (Trans. Leafstedt 1995, 126).

Ballaster, Ros. 2005. "Narrative Transmigrations: The Oriental Tale and the Novel in Eighteenth-Century Britain." *A Companion to the Eighteenth-Century English Novel and Culture*. Ed. Paula Backscheider and Catherine Ingrassia. Malden, MA: Blackwell. 75–96.

Banks, Paul. 1991. "Images of the Self: 'Duke Bluebeard's Castle.'" *The Stage Works of Béla Bartók*. London: John Calder. 7–12.

Barchilon, Jacques, and Peter Flinders. 1981. "Perrault in English." *Charles Perrault*. Boston: Twayne. 110–14.

Barchilon, Jacques, E. E. Flinders, and J. Anne Foreman. 1977. *A Concordance to Charles Perrault's Tales*, vol. 1: *Contes de ma mere l'oye*. 2 vols. Norwood, Pa.: Norwood Editions.

Bardens, Dennis. 1972. *The Ladykiller: The Life of Landru, The French Bluebeard*. London: P. Davies.

Barry, Florence. 1922. "Chap-Books and Ballads." *A Century of Children's Books*. London: Methuen.

Bartlett, Evan Allen. 1931. *Love Murders of Harry F. Powers: Beware Such Bluebeards*. New York: Sheftel.

Barzilai, Shuli. 2004. "The Bluebeard Barometer: Charles Dickens and Captain Murderer." *Victorian Literature and Culture* 32.2: 505–24.

———. 2005. "The Bluebeard Syndrome in Atwood's *Lady Oracle*: Fear and Femininity." *Marvels & Tales* 19.2: 249–73.

———. 2006. "A Case of Negative *Mise en Abyme*: Margaret Atwood and the Grimm Brothers." *Partial Answers* 4.2: 191–204.

———. 2009. *Tales of Bluebeard and His Wives from Late Antiquity to Postmodern Times.* New York: Routledge.

Bastide, Bernard. 2005. "Présence de Perrault dans le cinéma français des premiers temps (1897–1912)." *Contes et légendes à l'écran.* Ed. Carole Aurouet. Corlet éditions. Diffusion, France: Condé-sur-Noireau. 24–32.

Bayard, Jean-Pierre. 1955. "Les Thèmes éternels dans le conte de 'la Barbe-Bleue.'" *Mercure de France* (1 July): 456–68.

Bazin, André. 1967. "The Myth of Monsieur Verdoux." *What Is Cinema?* Trans. Hugh Gray. Berkeley: Univ. of California Press. 102–23.

Beaumont, Cyril. 1926. "Harlequin in England." Reprint *The History of Harlequin.* New York: Arno, 1976. 84–99.

Benedetti, Jean. 1971. *The Real Bluebeard.* Reprint New York: Dorset, 1988.

Bennett, Benjamin, and François Pierre Rousseau. 1934. "Bluebeard in Skirts [Mrs. Daisy de Melker]." *Up for Murder.* London: Hutchinson. 17–75.

Benson, Stephen. 2000. "'History's Bearer': The Afterlife of 'Bluebeard.'" *Marvels & Tales* 14.2: 244–67.

———. 2003. *Cycles of Influence: Fiction, Folktale, Theory.* Detroit: Wayne State Univ. Press. 167–246.

Beran, Carol L. 1992. "Intertexts of Margaret Atwood's *Life Before Man.*" *American Review of Canadian Studies* 22.2: 199–214.

Bergengren, Ralph. 1904. "Boswell's Chapbooks and Others." *The Lamp* 28: 39–44.

Bethke, Robert D. 1970. "Chapbook 'Gallows-Literature' in Nineteenth-Century Pennsylvania." *Pennsylvania Folklife* 20.1: 2–15.

Bettelheim, Bruno. 1976. "Bluebeard." *The Uses of Enchantment: The Meaning and Importance of Fairy Tales.* Reprint London: Penguin, 1988. 299–303.

Bevan, David G. 1985. "Tournier's Photographer: A Modern Bluebeard?" *Modern Language Studies* 15.3: 66–71.

Bishop, John Peale. 1942. "The Violent Country." Reprint *The Critical Response to Eudora Welty's Fiction.* Ed. Laurie Champion. Westport, Conn.: Greenwood. 1994. 53–54.

Blamires, David. 2006. "The Early Reception of the Grimms' *Kinder- und Hausmärchen* in England." *The Translation of Children's Literature.* Ed. Gillian Lathey. Clevedon, England: Multilingual Matters. 163–74.

"Bluebeard's Castle." n.d. St. Thomas, US Virgin Islands. http://www.bluebeards-castle.com.

Boaden, James. 1825. *Memoirs of the Life of John Philip Kemble.* 2 vols. London. 2:541–42. (Cited in Saxon 1968, 89).

Bodmer, George. 2003. "Arthur Hughes, Walter Crane, and Maurice Sendak: The Picture as Literary Fairy Tale." *Marvels & Tales* 17.1: 120–37.

Booth, Michael R. 1964. Introduction to *Hiss the Villain: Six English and American Melodramas.* New York: Benjamin Blom. 9–40.

———. 1973a. "Preface to [George Colman the Younger's] *John Bull.*" *English Plays of the Nineteenth Century,* vol. 3. Oxford: Clarendon. 59–62.

———. 1973b. "Preface to *The Miller and His Men*." *English Plays of the Nineteenth Century*, vol. 1. Oxford: Clarendon. 31–34.

———. 1976. Introduction to *English Plays of the Nineteenth Century*, vol. 5: *Pantomimes, Extravaganzas and Burlesques*. Oxford: Clarendon. 1–63.

Bordman, Gerald Martin. 2001. *American Musical Theatre: A Chronicle*. New York: Oxford Univ. Press.

Bossard, Abbé Eugène. 1885. *Gilles de Rais, Maréchal de France, dit Barbe-Bleue*. Reprint Grenoble: J. Millon, 1992.

Boswell. 1763. Journal entry dated July 10. (Cited in Neuburg, 1964, 43).

Bottigheimer, Ruth B. 1987. *Grimms' Bad Girls and Bold Boys: The Moral and Social Vision of the Tales*. New Haven, Conn.: Yale Univ. Press.

———. 1993. "The Publishing History of the Grimms' Tales: Reception at the Cash Register." *The Reception of the Grimms' Fairy Tales: Responses, Reactions, Revisions*. Ed. Donald Haase. Detroit: Wayne State Univ. Press. 78–101.

Bowd, W. J. 1955. "The Life of a Farm Worker." [Excerpts from the 1889 journal of James Bowd]. *The Countryman* 51.2: 293–300.

Bradbury, Steve, ed. and trans. 2002. "Translation, Bluebeard, and La Belle Infidele: A Conversation with Hung Hung." *Joseph Keene Chadwick: Interventions and Continuities in Irish and Gay Studies*. Ed. John Rieder, Joseph H. O'Mealy and Valerie Wayne. Honolulu: Univ. of Hawaii. 148–58.

Brandt, Nat. 2003. *Chicago Death Trap: The Iroquois Theatre Fire of 1903*. Carbondale: Southern Illinois Univ. Press.

Bresky, Dushan. 1969. *The Art of Anatole France*. The Hague: Mouton.

Bretèque, François de la. 2005. "Les contes de Georges Méliès." *Contes et légendes à l'écran*. Ed. Carole Aurouet. Corlet éditions. Diffusion, France: Condé-sur-Noireau. 62–71.

Briggs, Katherine M., ed. 1970. *A Dictionary of British Folk-Tale in the English Language*. London: Routledge.

Brewer, Derek. 1980. "IX." *Symbolic Stories: Traditional Narratives*. Cambri: D. S. Brewer.

The British Quarterly. 1876. Unsigned review of *History of Bluebeard's Wives*, by Sabilla Novello. *The British Quarterly* 43 (January & April). Digitized by Google.

Broadbent, R. J. 1901. *A History of Pantomime*. New York: Benjamin Blom, 1964.

Brochon, Pierre. 1954. *Le Livre de colportage en France depuis le XVI siècle; sa littérature, ses lecteurs*. Paris: Librarie Gründ.

Broer, Lawrence R. 1989. "*Bluebeard*: Redemption and the Unwavering Light." *Sanity Plea: Schizophrenia in the Novels of Kurt Vonnegut*. Rev. ed. Tuscaloosa: Univ. of Alabama Press, 1994. 161–75, 219–21.

Broughton, Simon. 1991. "Bartók and 'World Music.'" *The Stage Works of Béla Bartók*. London: John Calder. 13–20.

Brown, John. 1754. *Barbarossa*. London: Printed for T. Caslon, T. Lowndes, W. Nicole, and S. Bladen. 1777.

Brown, T. Allston. 1903. *A History of the New York Stage*, vol. 2. New York: Benjamin Blom. 353–56. Reprint "The Hippotheatron." Circus Historical Society. http://www.circushistory.org/History/Hippotheatron.htm.

Browne, Ray B., ed. 1984. *Forbidden Fruits: Taboos and Tabooism in Culture*. Bowling Green, Ohio: Bowling Green State Univ. Popular Press. 67–82.

Bunn, Alfred. 1840. *The Stage: Both Before and Behind the Curtain*. 3 vols. London. 2:216–17. (Cited in Saxon 1968, 93).

Burke, Edmund. 1786–1788. *India: The Launching of the Hastings Impeachment, 1786–1788. The Writings and Speeches of Edmund Burke*, vol. 6. Ed. Peter H. Marshall. Oxford: Clarendon, 1991. 267. (Cited in Ballaster 2005, 93).

Burke, Peter. 1978. *Popular Culture in Early Modern Europe*. New York: New York Univ. Press.

Burne, Glenn. 1986. "Andrew Lang's *The Blue Fairy Book*: Changing the Course of History." *Touchstones: Reflections on the Best in Children's Literature: Fairy Tales, Myths, Legends, and Poetry*. Ed. Perry Nodelman. West Lafayette, Ind.: Children's Literature Association. 140–50.

Burris, Patricia A. 2003. "The Evolution of Bluebeard." M.A. thesis. Wayne State College, Detroit.

Carpenter, Humphrey, and Mari Prichard. 1984. *The Oxford Companion to Children's Literature*. London: Oxford Univ. Press.

Carpenter, Lynette. 1985. "Benevolent Fantasy and the Imagination in the Popular Literature and Film of the 1940s." *The Scope of the Fantastic*. Ed. Robert Collins and Howard Pearce. Westport, Conn.: Greenwood. 51–57.

Carson, Barbara Harrell. 1988. "Eudora Welty's Dance with Darkness: The Robber Bridegroom." Reprint *The Critical Response to Eudora Welty's Fiction*. Ed. Laurie Champion. Westport, Conn.: Greenwood, 1994. 64–81.

Cashdan, Sheldon. 1999. *The Witch Must Die: How Fairy Tales Shape Our Lives*. New York: Basic.

Caswell, Austin B. 1988. "Maeterlinck's and Dukas' *Ariane et Barbe-Bleue*: A Feminist Opera?" *Studies in Romanticism* 27.2: 203–20.

Catalogue of the Lauriston Castle Chapbooks. 1963. National Library of Scotland. Boston: G. K. Hall.

Cazelles, Brigitte. 1999. "Arthur as Barbe-Bleue: The Martyrdom of Saint Tryphine (Breton Mystery)." Trans. Brett Wells. *Yale French Studies* 95: 134–51. Chadwick, Joseph Keene. 2002. *Interventions and Continuities in Irish and Gay Studies*. Honolulu: Univ. of Hawaii.

Champion, Laurie, ed. 1994. *The Critical Response to Eudora Welty's Fiction*. Westport, Conn.: Greenwood.

"Cheap Reprinting and Nursery Stories." n.d. *Children's Literature: Island 2*. Thomas Cooper Library, Univ. of South Carolina. http://www.sc.edu/library/spcoll/kidlit/kidlit/kidlit2.html.

Chew, Samuel C. 1937. "Moslems on the London Stage." *The Crescent and the Rose: Islam and England during the Renaissance*. New York: Oxford Univ. Press. 469–540.

Clemens, Valdine. 1999. *The Return of the Repressed: Gothic Horror from The Castle of Otranto to Alien*. Albany: State Univ. of New York Press.

Clement, Clara Erskine. 1882. *Charlotte Cushman*. American Actors Series. Ed. Laurence Hutton. Boston: James R. Osgood.

Cohen, Sam. 1975. *Henri Landru: L'assassin bien aimé*. Paris: Presses de la Cité.

Colman, George, the Younger. 1796. *The Iron Chest*. Facsimile ed. Oxford, 1989. xxi. (Cited in Davies 2002, 531).

———. 1798c. "Preface." *Blue Beard; or, Female Curiosity!* 4th ed. London: Cadell & Davies.

Cordingly, David. 1998. Introduction to *A General History of the Robberies and Murders of the Most Notorious Pirates*. Captain Charles Johnson. New York: Conway Maritime. vii–xiv.

Cornwell, Jason. n.d. Review of "Fables #13." *Line of Fire Reviews*. Silver Bullet Comics. http://www.silverbulletcomicbooks.com/reviews/105351145879720,print.htm.

Corson, James C. 1962. "Scott's Boyhood Collection of Chapbooks." *The Bibliotheck: A Journal of Bibliographical Notes and Queries Mainly of Scottish Interest* 3: 202–18.

Cox, Jeffrey N., and Michael Gamer. 2003. Introduction to *The Broadview Anthology of Romantic Drama*. Peterborough, Ontario: Broadview. vii–xxiv.

Cox, Philip. 2000. *Reading Adaptations: Novels and Verse Narratives on the Stage, 1790–1840*. Manchester, England: Manchester Univ. Press.

Cropper, Percy. 1892. *The Nottinghamshire Printed Chap-Books, with Notices of Their Printers and Vendors*. Nottingham: Frank Murray.

Crowther, Bosley. 1967. "Monsier Verdoux." *The Great Films: Fifty Golden Years of Motion Pictures*. New York: Putnam's. 185–88.

Cruikshank, George. 1854. *A Letter from Hop-O'-My-Thumb to Charles Dickens, Esq.* London: D. Bogue. Houghton Library.

Curran, Ronald T. 1992. "Complex, Archetype and Primal Fear: King's Use of Fairy Tales in *The Shining*." *The Dark Descent: Essays Defining Stephen King's Horrorscope*. Ed. Tony Magistrale. Westport, Conn.: Greenwood. 33–46.

Daniels, Morna. 2002. "The Tale of Charles Perrault and *Puss in Boots*." British Library electronic journals *eBLJ*. Article 5. http://www.bl.uk/eblj/2002articles/article5.html.

Darmon, Pierre. 1994. *Landru*. Paris: Plon.

Darnton, Robert. 1984. "Peasants Tell Tales: The Meaning of Mother Goose." *The Great Cat Massacre and Other Episodes in French Cultural History*. London: Allen Lane. 9–65.

Darton, Harvey. 1932. *Children's Books in England: Five Centuries of Social Life*. Reprint 3rd rev. ed. Ed. Brian Alderson. New York: Cambridge Univ. Press, 1982.

Davies, Damian Walford. 2002. "The Politics of Allusion: *Caleb Williams, The Iron Chest, Middlemarch*, and the *Armoir de fer*." *Review of English Studies* 53.212: 526–43.

Davies, Mererid Puw. 1997. "'In Blaubart's Schatten': Murder, 'Marchen' and Memory." *Gendering German Studies: New Perspectives on German Literature and Culture*. Ed. Margaret Littler. Oxford: Blackwell. 113–29.

———. 2001. *The Tale of Bluebeard in German Literature: From the Eighteenth Century to the Present*. Oxford: Clarendon.

———. 2002. "Laughing Their Heads Off: Nineteenth-Century Comic Versions of the Bluebeard Tale." *German Life and Letters* 55.4(October): 329–47.

Davis, Jim. 1984. Introduction to *Plays by H. J. Byron*. Cambridge: Cambridge Univ. Press. 1–36.

Davis, Octavia. 1995. Introduction to *A Modern Mephistopheles*. Louisa May Alcott. New York: Bantam. v–xx.

De Beauvoir, Simone. 1964. Introduction to *Bluebeard and Other Fairy Tales of Charles Perrault*. Trans. Richard Howard. Intro. and trans. Peter Green. New York: Collier-Macmillan.

Dearden, Harold. 1937. "The Original Bluebeard." *Fifty Strangest Stories Ever Told*. London: Odhams. 574–82.

Delamar, Gloria. 1987. *Mother Goose from Nursery to Literature*. Jefferson, N.C.: McFarland.

Delarue, Paul. 1952. "Les Contes Merveilleux de Perrault et la tradition populaire. II. Barbe-Bleue." *Bulletin folklorique de l'Ile de France* 14: 348–57.

Delarue, Paul, and Marie-Louise Ténèze. 1957. *Le conte populaire français: Catalogue raisonné des versions de France et des pays de langue française d'outre-mer*, vol. 1. Paris: Editions Erasme.

Dibden, Charles, Jr. 1956. *Memoirs of Charles Dibden the Younger, Dramatist and Upward of Thirty Years Manager of Minor Theatres*. Ed. George Speight. London: Society for Theatre Research. 102. (Cited in Mayer 1969, 78–79).

Dickens, Charles. 1853. "Frauds on the Fairies." Reprint *Fantastic Literature: A Critical Reader*. Ed. David Sandner. Westport, Conn.: Praeger, 2004. 56–58.

Dirks, Phyllis. 1981. "Garrick's Fail-Safe Musical Venture: A Peep Behind the Curtains, an English Burletta." *The Stage and the Page: London's "Whole Show" in the Eighteenth-Century Theatre*. Ed. George Winchester Stone. Berkeley: Univ. of California Press. 136–47.

Doane, Mary Ann. 1984. "The Woman's Film: Possession and Address." *Re-Vision: Essays in Feminist Film Criticism*. Ed. Mary Ann Doane, Patricia Mellencamp, and Linda Williams. Los Angeles, Calif.: Univ. Publications of America. 67–82.

———. 1987. *The Desire to Desire: The Woman's Film of the 1940s*. Bloomington: Indiana Univ. Press.

Doutrepont, Georges. 1926. *Les Types populaires de la littérature française*. Brussels: Lamertin. 418–23.

The Dublin University Magazine. 1878. Unsigned review of *The History of Bluebeard's Wives*, by Sabilla Novello. *The Dublin University Magazine* 1 (March): 384. Digitized by Google.

Dubois, Diane. 2001. "'Seeing the Female Body Differently': Gender Issues in *The Silence of the Lambs*." *Journal of Gender Studies* 10.3: 297–310.

Dugaw, Dianne. 1995. "Chapbook Publishing and the 'Lore' of the 'the Folks.'" *The Other Print Tradition: Essays on Chapbooks, Broadsides, and Relaxed Ephemera*. Ed. Cathy Lynn Preston and Michael J. Preston. New York: Garland. 3–18.

Duncker, Patricia. 1984. "Re-Imagining the Fairy Tales: Angela Carter's Bloody Chambers." *Literature and History*. 10: 3–12. Reprint *Popular Fictions: Essays in Literature and History*. London: Methuen, 1986. 222–36.

Durham, Weldon B., ed. 1986. *American Theatre Companies, 1749–1887*. New York: Greenwood.

Edgeworth, Maria. 1798. *Practical Education*. London: J. Johnson. 612–13. (Cited in Moore 2002, 12–13).

Ellis, John M. 1983. *One Fairy Story Too Many*. Chicago: Univ. of Chicago Press. 90–92.

Ellms, Charles. 1837. "The Life, Atrocities, and Bloody Death of Black Beard." Reprint Marine Research Society. *The Pirates Own Book: Authentic Narratives of the Most Celebrated Sea Robbers*. New York: Dover, 1993. 335–48.

Elsaesser, Thomas. 1987. "Tales of Sound and Fury: Observations on the Family Melodrama." *Home Is Where the Heart Is: Studies in Melodrama and Women's Film*. Ed. Christine Gledhill. London: British Film Institute. 43–69.

Escarpit, Denise. 1985. *Histoire d'un conte, le "Chat Botté" en France et en Angleterre*. 2 vols. Paris: Didier-Erudition.

Espy, Willard R. 1978. "Bluebeard." *O Thou Improper, Thou Uncommon Noun: A Bobtailed, Generally Chronological Listing of Proper Names That Have Become Improper and Uncommonly Common; Together with a Smattering of Proper Names Commonly Used . . . and Certain Other Diversions*. New York: Clarkson Potter. 165.

Essai de reconstitution du catalogue français de la Star-Film, suivi d'une analyse catalographique de films de Georges Méliès recensés en France. 1981. Paris: S.A.F. du C.N.C. 98. (Cited in Bretèque 2005, 63).

Estés, Clarissa Pinkola. 1992. "Stalking the Intruder: The Beginning Initiation (Bluebeard)." *Women Who Run with the Wolves: Myths and Stories of the Wild Woman Archetype*. New York: Ballantine. 39–73.

———. 1995. "Bluebeard and the Forbidden Key." *Theatre of the Imagination*, Vol. 1. Boulder, Co.: Sounds True Recordings.

Evans, Edmund. 1880. *History of Bluebeard*. London: Routledge.

Ezra, Elizabeth. 2000. *Georges Méliès: The Birth of the Auteur*. Manchester, England: Manchester Univ. Press.

"'Fables': The Comic Book Series." n.d. *Edited Guide Entry*. BBC-h2g2. http://www.bbc.co.uk/dna/h2g2/A1101448.

Fábry, Andrea. 1999. "A Comparative Analysis of Text and Music and Gender and Audience in *Duke Bluebeard's Castle*." *CLCWeb: Comparative Literature and Culture: A WWWeb Journal* 1(December): 4.

Fay, Henry Augustus. 1835. *Bluebeard, or, The Interesting Account of Charles Sterling, Who Is Now a Prisoner in the City of New York*. New York: Childs and Devoe.

Federer, Charles A., ed. 1889. *Yorkshire Chapbooks*. 1st ser. London: E. Stock.

Fiske, Roger. 1973. *English Theatre Music in the Eighteenth Century*. London: Oxford Univ. Press. 283. (Cited in Porter 1994, xxiv).

Flahault, François. 1979. "Barbe-Bleue et le désir de savoir." *Ornicer* 17–28: 70–87, 291.

Foy, Eddie, and Alvin F. Harlow. 1928. *Clowning through Life*. New York: E. P. Dutton.

Fraser, Rebecca. 1988. *The Brontës: Charlotte Brontë and Her Family*. New York: Crown. 453.

Freeman, Andrew. 1989. *The Compromising of Louis XVI: The armoire de fer and the French Revolution*. Exeter: Univ. of Exeter. (Cited in Verhoeven 1995, 527).

Freud, Sigmund. 1953–1974. "*Das Unheimliche.*" Trans. James Strachey, et al. "The Uncanny." *The Standard Edition of the Complete Psychological Works of Sigmund Freud*, vol. 17 of 24. Gen. ed. James Strachey. London: Hogarth. 217–52.

Frigon, Sylvie. 2006. "Mapping Scripts and Narrative of Women Who Kill Their Husbands in Canada, 1866–1954: Inscribing the Everyday." *Killing Women: The Visual Culture of Gender and Violence.* Ed. Annette Burfoot and Susan Lord. Waterloo, Ontario: Wilfred Laurier Univ. Press. 3–20.

G., D. "Remarks." [1837?]. *Blue Beard; or, Female Curiosity!* Colman. 7th ed. *Cumberland's British Theatre. Vol. 36. 1829, etc.* British Library.

Gabory, Emile. 1926. *La Vie et la mort de Gilles de Raiz, dit, à tort Barbebleue.* Paris: Perrin.

———. 1930. *Alias Bluebeard; The Life and Death of Gilles de Raiz.* New York: Brewer & Warner.

Gates, Philippa. 2004. "Manhunting: The Female Detective in the Serial Killer Film." *Post Script* 24.1: 42–61.

Gaudreault, André. 1987. "Theatricality, Narrativity, and Trickality: Reevaluating the Cinema of Georges Méliès." Trans. Paul Attallah. Adapted by Tom Gunning and Vivian Sobchack. *Journal of Popular Film and Television* 15.3: 111–19.

Gerring, Charles. 1900. "A Chapter on Chap Books." *Notes on Printers and Booksellers: With a Chapter on Chapbooks.* London: Simpkin, Marshall, Hamilton, Kent & Co. Ltd. 100–19.

Gill, Brendan. 1976. "Family Troubles." *New Yorker* 52(October): 61. (Cited in Hall 1992, 65).

Gillett, Sue. 1995. "Lips and Fingers: Jane Campion's *The Piano.*" *Screen* 36.3: 277–87.

Godard, Barbara. 1986. "Tales within Tales: Margaret Atwood's Folk Narratives." *Canadian Literature* 109: 54–84.

———. 1987. "Palimpsest: Margaret Atwood's *Bluebeard's Egg.*" *Recherches anglaises et nord-americaines* 20: 51–60.

Gordon, Jan B. 1983. "Narrative Enclosure as Textual Ruin: An Archaeology of Gothic Consciousness." *Dickens Studies Annual* 11: 209–38.

Gorilovics, Tivadar. 2000. "Secrets of the Forbidden Chamber: Bluebeard." Trans. Trista Selous. *Secret Spaces, Forbidden Places.* Ed. Fran Lloyd and Catherine O'Brien. New York: Berghahn Books. 17–28.

Gosse, Edmund. 1925. "Bluebeard among the Authors." *Silhouettes.* New York: Scribner. 11–20.

Grace, Sherrill E. 1982. "Articulating the 'Space Between': Atwood's Untold Stories and Fresh Beginnings." *Margaret Atwood: Language, Text and Space.* Ed. Sherrill Grace and Lorraine Weir. Vancouver: Univ. of British Columbia Press. 1–16.

———. 1984. "Courting Bluebeard with Bartók, Atwood, and Fowles: Modern Treatment of the Bluebeard Theme." *Journal of Modern Literature* 11.2: 245–62.

Graham, Marie. [ca. 1900]. *A Devout Bluebeard.* New York: Abbey. Microfilm: Wright American Fiction Series, vol. 3. 1876–1900. no. 2229.

Grant, Julian. 1991. "A Foot in Bluebeard's Door." *The Stage Works of Béla Bartók*. London: John Calder. 25–34.

Grätz, Manfred. 1988. *Das Märchen in der deutschen Aufklärung*. Stuttgart: Metzler. (Cited in Davies 2001, 6–7).

Gunning, Tom. 1995. "Phantom Images and Modern Manifestations: Spirit Photography, Magic Theater, Trick Films, and Photography's Uncanny." *Fugitive Images: From Photography to Video*. Ed. Patrice Petro. Bloomington: Indiana Univ. Press. 42–71.

Haining, Peter, ed. 1978. Introduction to *The Shilling Shockers: Stories of Terror from the Gothic Bluebooks*. New York: St. Martin's. 13–19.

Halcom, J. P. [James Peller?]. 1798. "From a review of *Santa Maria; or, The Mysterious Pregnancy*." *Gentleman's Magazine* 48(September): 446–48. [*Santa Maria*, J. Fox].

Hall, Marilee D. 1992. "Eudora Welty's *The Robber Bridegroom*: From Mississippi's Natchez Trace to the Broadway Stage." M.A. thesis. Univ. of South Florida.

Halliwell-Phillips, James Orchard. 1849. *Popular Rhymes and Nursery Tales*. Reprint Detroit: Singing Tree, 1968.

Hannon, Patricia. 2001. "*Corps cadavres*: Heroes and Heroines in the Tales of Perrault." *The Great Fairy Tale Tradition*. Ed. Jack Zipes. New York: Norton. 933–57.

Hantke, Steffen. 2003. "Monstrosity Without a Body: Representational Strategies in the Popular Serial Killer Film." *Post Script* 22.2: 34–54.

Harris, Nick, and Helene Rico. 1923. "The Modern Bluebeard." *In the Shadows: Thirty Detective Stories Showing "Why Crime Doesn't Pay": A Series of Famous Cases*. Los Angeles: Times-Mirror. 307–20.

Hartland, Edwin Sidney. 1885. "The Forbidden Chamber." *Folk-Lore Journal* 3: 193–242.

Harvey, William. 1903. *Scottish Chapbook Literature*. New York: Burt Franklin.

Haskell, Molly. 1973. "From Reverence to Rape: Female Stars of the 1940s." Reprint *Film Theory and Criticism: Introductory Readings*. 5th ed. Ed. Leo Braudy and Marshall Cohen. New York: Oxford Univ. Press, 1999. 562–75.

Hearn, Michael Patrick. 1729. Preface. Charles Perrault, *Histories or Tales of Past Times*. Reprint New York: Garland, 1977. v–xxvii.

Heckmann, Emil. 1930. "Blaubart: Ein Beitrag zur vergleischenden Märchenforschung." Ph.D. diss. Univ. of Heidelberg. (Cited in Mowshowitz 1970, 16).

Heiner, Heidi Anne. "Bluebeard." *Sur la Lune Fairy Tale Pages*. http://www.surlalunefairytales.com.

Hempen, Daniela. 1977. "Bluebeard's Female Helper: The Ambiguous Role of the Strange Old Woman in Grimms' 'Castle of Murder' and 'The Robber Bridegroom.'" *Folklore* 108: 45–48.

Heppenstall, Rayner. 1972. *Bluebeard and After: Three Decades of Murder in France*. London: Peter.

Hermansson, Casie. 2001. *Reading Feminist Intertextuality through Bluebeard Stories*. Lewiston, N.Y.: Edwin Mellen.

Herzog, Josef. 1938. *Die Märchentypen des "Ritter Blaubart" und "Fitchervogel."* Würzburg: K. Triltsh.

Higby, Chester Penn. 1939. Introduction to *John Lathrop Motley: Representative Selections, with Introduction, Bibliography and Notes*. New York: American Book Co.

Hiltbrunner, Michael. 2005a. "Hidden Debates under a Baroque Surface: *Barbe-bleue* by Georges Méliès (1901)." Unpublished paper.

———. 2005b. "Das Märchen Blaubart von 1697 bis heute." Doctoral proposal, Univ. of Zurich.

Hoile, Christopher. 1984. "The Uncanny and the Fairy Tale in Kubrick's *The Shining*." *Literature-and-Film Quarterly* 12.1: 5–12.

Holbrook, H. 1941. *Murder out Yonder: An Informal Study of Certain Classic Crimes in Back-Country America*. New York: Macmillan. (Cited in Langlois 1978, 8).

Holland, Norman N., and Leona F. Sherman. 1977. "Gothic Possibilities." *New Literary History* 8: 270–94.

Howell, George. 1995. "Anatomy of an Artist: Interview with Cindy Sherman." *Art Papers* 5(July–August): 2–7.

Hughes, Leo. 1981. "Afterpieces: Or, That's Entertainment." *The Stage and the Page: London's "Whole Show" in the Eighteenth-Century Theatre*. Ed. George Winchester Stone. Berkeley: Univ. of California Press. 55–70.

Hume, Robert D. 1981. "The Multifarious Forms of Eighteenth Century Comedy." *The Stage and the Page: London's "Whole Show" in the Eighteenth-Century Theatre*. Ed. George Winchester Stone. Berkeley: Univ. of California Press. 3–32.

Hunt, Leigh. 1817. "Theatrical Examiner No. 266," "On Pantomime, Continued from an Earlier Paper." Reprint *Selected Writings of Leigh Hunt*, vol. 2. London: Pickering and Chatto, 2003. 81–86, 94–95.

Hürlimann, Bettina. 1959, 1963. *Three Centuries of Children's Books in Europe*. [*Europäische Kinderbücher in drei Jahrhunderten*.] Reprint Trans. Brian W. Alderson. London: Oxford Univ. Press, 1967.

Hynd, Alan. 1942. *The Pinkertons and the Inscrutable Bluebeard: An Interesting Account of One of the Numerous Services of Pinkerton's National Detective Agency, Inc.* New York: Pinkerton's National Detective Agency.

———. 1948. "Chicago's Bluebeard." *The Pinkerton Case Book: Great Modern True Crimes from the Archives of the World's Leading Detective Agency*. New York: New American Library.

Index to Comic Art Collections: "Bluebeard" to "Bluey." n.d. Michigan State Univ. Library. http://www.lib.msu.edu/comics/rri/brri/bluea.htm.

Ireland, J. N. 1968. *Records of the New York Stage*, vol. 1: *1750 to 1860*. New York: Burt Franklin.

Irwin, Robert. 1994. *The Arabian Nights: A Companion*. Reprint London: I. B. Tauris, 2004.

Janer, Maria de la Pau. 2001. *Barbablava: l'heroi, el monstre*. Barcelona: La Galera.

Jenkins, Stephen. 1981. "Lang: Fear and Desire." *Fritz Lang: The Image and the Look*. London: BFI. 38–124.

Johnson, Captain Charles. 1724. *A General History of the Robberies and Murders of the Most Notorious Pirates*. Reprint New York: Conway Maritime, 1998.

Jones, Stephen. 1811. *Biographica Dramatica; or, a Companion to the Playhouse.* 3 vols. Reprint New York: AMS, 1966.

Jordan, Elaine. 1992. "The Dangers of Angela Carter." *New Feminist Discourses: Critical Essays on Theories and Texts.* Ed. Isobel Armstrong. London: Routledge. 119–31.

Kabir, Ananya Jahanara. 2006. "'Oriental Gothic': The Medieval Past in the Colonial Encounter." *Reorienting Orientalism.* Ed. Chandreyee Niyogi. New Delhi: Sage Publications. 65–88.

Kahane, Claire. 1980. "Gothic Mirrors and Feminine Identity." *The Centennial Review* 24: 43–64.

Karcz, Anthony. Review of "Fables #14" *Comic Book Reviews.* POP Comics & Games. http://www.pop-comics.com/review.php?ID=13.

Kast, Varena. 1978. "Bluebeard: On the Problem of the Destructive Animus." *Witches, Ogres, and the Devil's Daughter: Encounters with Evil in Fairy Tales.* Ed. Mario Jacoby, Varena Kast, and Ingrid Riedel. Trans. Michael H. Kohn. Boston: Shambhala, 1992. 86–104.

Keane, Marian E. 1986. "A Closer Look at Scopophilia: Mulvey, Hitchcock and *Vertigo.*" *A Hitchcock Reader.* Ames: Iowa State Univ. Press. 231–48.

Keith, W. J. 1994. "Interpreting and Misinterpreting 'Bluebeard's Egg.'" *Margaret Atwood: Writing and Subjectivity. New Critical Essays.* Ed. Colin Nicholson. New York: St. Martin's. 248–57.

Kelly, Michael. 1826. *Reminiscences of Michael Kelly of the King's Theatre and Theatre Royal Drury Lane.* 2 vols. Da Capo Press Music Reprint Series. New York: Da Capo, 1968.

Kenrick, John. 1996. "Stage Musical Chronology." Rev. 2003. http://www.musicals101.com/1860s.htm.

King, A. Hyatt. 1968. Introduction to *Reminiscences of Michael Kelly of the King's Theatre and Theatre Royal Drury Lane.* By Michael Kelly. 2 vols. Da Capo Press Music Reprint Series. New York: Da Capo. [v]–xv.

Konrad, Linn B. 1987. "Ariadne and the Labyrinth of the Creative Mind." *From the Bard to Broadway.* Ed. Karelisa V. Hartigan. Lanham, Md.: Univ. Presses of America. 147–56.

Kopper, Edward A. 1991. "Abstract Expressionism in Vonnegut's *Bluebeard.*" *Journal of Modern Literature* 17: 583–84.

Korda, Alexander, Sir. 1933. *The Private Life of Henry VIII.* London: United Artists. [Ocean City, N.J.]: Silver Screen Video, Inc.

Kretschmer, Paul. 1901. "Das Märchen von Blaubart." *Mitteilungender anthropologischen Gesellschaft* 31: 61–62.

Kreyling, Michael. 1999. *Understanding Eudora Welty.* Columbia: Univ. of South Carolina Press.

Kudszus, Winfried G. 1990. "The Bluebeard Affection." *Disease and Medicine in Modern German Cultures.* Ed. Rudolf Kaser and Vera Pohland. Ithaca, N.Y.: Cornell Univ. Press. 108–19.

Kunzle, David. 1973. *The Early Comic Strip,* vol. 1: *c. 1450–1825,* vol. 2: *The Nineteenth Century.* Berkeley: Univ. of California Press.

Lake, J. W. 1823–1824. "The Life of George Colman; the Younger, with Critical Remarks on the Drama." *The Dramatic Works of George Colman the Younger: With an Original Life of the Author.* 4 vols. Paris: Malepeyre. [i]–xxviii. Widener Library.

Lane, William Coolidge, ed. 1905. *Catalogue of English and American Chap-Books and Broadside Ballads in Harvard College Library.* Bibliographical Contributions, no. 56. Cambridge, Mass.: Library of Harvard Univ.

Lang, Andrew. 1888. "Blue Beard [notes]" and Introduction to *Perrault's Popular Tales.* Oxford: Clarendon.

———. 1889. Introduction to *The Blue Fairy Book.* Reprint Appendix. *The Blue Fairy Book.* Ed. Brian Alderson. Harmondsworth, Middlesex: Kestrel, 1975. 349–58.

———. 1890. Introduction to *The Red Fairy Book.* Reprint Appendix. *The Red Fairy Book.* Ed. Brian Alderson. Harmondsworth, Middlesex: Kestrel, 1976. 356–60.

Langlois, Janet L. 1978. "Belle Gunness, the Lady Bluebeard: Community Legend as Metaphor." *Journal of the Folklore Institute* 15.2: 147–60.

———. 1983. "Belle Guiness [*sic*], the Lady Bluebeard: Symbolic Inversion in Verbal Art and American Culture." *Signs* 8.4: 614–17.

———. 1985a. *Belle Gunness: The Lady Bluebeard.* Bloomington: Indiana Univ. Press.

———. 1985b. "Belle Gunness, the Lady Bluebeard: Narrative Use of a Deviant Woman." *Women's Folklore, Women's Culture.* Ed. Rosan A. Jordan and Susan J. Kalcik. Philadelphia: Univ. of Pennsylvania Press. 105–24.

The Last Night. Mr. Reinagle's Benefit. [1799]. [Playbill for *Lover's Vows* and *Blue-Beard.* Written by George Colman.] Chestnut Street Theatre. [Philadelphia: Printed by John Ward Fenno]. Microfilm. Early American Imprints, First Series, no. 36101. Evans Collection. Wells Library, Indiana Univ.

Le Men, Ségolène. 1992. "Mother Goose Illustrated: From Perrault to Doré." *Poetics Today* 13.1: 17–39.

Le Queux, William. 1966. *Landru, Bluebeard of France.* London: Newnes.

Leach, Maria, ed. 1972. *Standard Dictionary of Myth, Folklore, Legend.* New York: Funk.

Leafstedt, Carl. 1995. "Bluebeard as Theater: The Influence of Maeterlinck and Hebbel on Baláz's Bluebeard." *Bartók and His World.* Ed. Peter Laki. Princeton, N.J.: Princeton Univ. Press. 119–48.

———. 1999. *Inside Bluebeard's Castle: Music and Drama in Béla Bartók's Opera.* New York: Oxford Univ. Press.

Lee, Robert E. 1974. *Blackbeard the Pirate: A Reappraisal of His Life and Times.* Winston-Salem, N.C.: John F. Blair.

Leeming, David Adams, and Marion Sader, eds. 1997. *Storytelling Encyclopedia: Historical, Cultural, and Multiethnic Approaches to Oral Traditions around the World.* Phoenix: Oryx.

Leigh, Olivia [Helen Mary Elizabeth Clamp]. 1969. *The Fifth Wife of Bluebeard.* London: R. Hale.

Lemire, Marie Charles Désiré. 1886. *Un maréchal et un connetable de France: Le Barbe-Bleue de la légende et de l'histoire.* Paris: E. Leroux.

Levy, Diane Wolf. 1976. "History as Art: Ironic Parody in Anatole France's *Les Sept Femmes de la Barbe Bleue*." *Nineteenth Century French Studies* 4: 361–70.

Lewis, Philip. 1987. "Bluebeard's Magic Key." *Les Contes de Perrault: la Contestation et ses limites: Furetière*. Ed. Michel Bareau, et al. Paris: Papers on French Seventeenth-Century Literature. 41–51.

———. 1996. "Bluebeard's Secret." *Seeing through the Mother Goose Tales: Visual Turns in the Writings of Charles Perrault*. Stanford, Calif.: Stanford Univ. Press. 197–246.

Lim, Bliss Cua. 2005. "Serial Time: Bluebeard in Stepford." *Literature and Film*. Ed. Robert Stam and Alessandra Raengo. Malden, Mass.: Blackwell. 171–90.

Linder, Leslie. 1971. "Sister Anne." *A History of the Writings of Beatrix Potter: Including Unpublished Work*. London: Frederick Warne & Co. 324–26.

Lokke, Kari E. 1988. "*Bluebeard* and *The Bloody Chamber*: The Grotesque of Parody and Self-Assertion." *Frontiers: A Journal of Women's Studies* 10.1: 7–12.

Lovell-Smith, Rose. 1999. "Feminism and Bluebeard." *Estudos de Literatura Oral* 5: 43–53.

———. 2002. "Anti-Housewives and Ogres' Housekeepers: The Roles of Bluebeard's Female Helpers." *Folklore* 113: 197–214.

Maar, Michael. 2003. *Bluebeard's Chamber: Guilt and Confession in Thomas Mann*. Tran. David Fernbach. London: Verso.

MacDonald, Margaret Read, ed. 1999. *Traditional Storytelling Today: An International Sourcebook*. Chicago: Fitzroy Dearborn.

Macpherson, Don. 2005. "Critiques: *Scurvy Dogs #4*." The Fourth Rail. http://www.thefourthrail.com/reviews/critiques/050304/scurvydogs4.shtml.

Madeleva, Sister M. 1927. "Anatole France: Four Parodies on Historical Research." *Chronicle* 29.1. Jan. Berkeley: Univ. of California. 10. (Cited in Levy 1976, 370).

Madoff, Mark S. 1989. "Inside, Outside, and the Gothic Locked-Room Mystery." *Gothic Fictions: Prohibition/Transgression*. Ed. Kenneth Graham. New York: AMS. 49–62.

Maeterlinck, Maurice. 1901. *Theatre*. Ed. Eugene Fasquelle. Paris: 1: 22–23. (Cited in Caswell 1988, 203).

Maio, Kathleen L. 1983. "Had-I-But-Known: The Marriage of Gothic Terror and Detection." *The Female Gothic*. Ed. Juliann E. Fleenor. Montreal: Eden. 82–90.

Malarte-Feldman, Claire-Lise. 1999. "The Challenges of Translating Perrault's *Contes* into English." *Marvels and Tales* 13.2: 184–97.

Mank, Gregory William. 1994. "Bluebeard." Dir. Ulmer. *Hollywood Cauldron: Thirteen Horror Films from the Genre's Golden Age*. Jefferson, N.C.: McFarland & Co. 265–92.

Manley, Kathleen E. B. 1996. "Atwood's Reconstruction of Folktales: *The Handmaid's Tale* and 'Bluebeard's Egg.'" *Approaches to Teaching Atwood's Handmaid's Tale & Other Works*. New York: Modern Language Association. 135–39.

Marcellus, Juliette de. 1971. "The True Story of Bluebeard." *Soldiers, Saints and Sinners from History*. Wichita, Kans.: Learning Arts.

Marcus, Jane. 1990. "Sylvia Townsend Warner." *The Gender of Modernism: A Critical Anthology*. Ed. Bonnie Kime Scott. Bloomington: Indiana Univ. Press. 531–38.

———. 1992. "Bluebeard's Daughters: Pretexts for Pre-Texts." *Feminist Critical Negotiations*. Ed. Alice A. Parker and Elizabeth A. Meese. Amsterdam: Benjamins. 19–32.

Marrs, Suzanne. 2002. *One Writer's Imagination: The Fiction of Eudora Welty*. Baton Rouge: Louisiana State Univ.

Marx, Samuel. 1988. "A Mythical Kingdom: The Hollywood Film Industry in the 1930s and 1940s." *Film and Literature: A Comparative Approach to Adaptation*. Lubbock: Texas Tech Univ. Press. 21–32.

Mayer, David. 1969. *Harlequin in His Element: The English Pantomime, 1806–1836*. Cambridge, Mass.: Harvard Univ. Press.

———. 1975. *Annotated Bibliography of Pantomime and Guide to Study Sources*. BTI Bibliographic Series no. 4. London: British Theatre Institute.

McBurney, William H. 1966. Introduction to *Fatal Curiosity*. 1739. George Lillo. Lincoln: Univ. of Nebraska Press. ix–xxv.

McCarthy, Cliff. 1996. "*Bluebeard* and the Abstract Expressionists." *The Vonnegut Chronicles: Interviews and Essays*. Ed. and intro. Peter J. Reed and Marc Leeds. Westport, Conn.: Greenwood. 164–77.

McClary, Susan. 1991. "Introduction: A Material Girl in Bluebeard's Castle." *Feminine Endings: Music, Gender, and Sexuality*. Minneapolis: Univ. of Minnesota Press. 3–34.

McCombs, Judith. 1981. "Atwood's Haunted Sequences: *The Circle Game*, *The Journals of Susanna Moodie*, and *Power Politics*." *The Art of Margaret Atwood: Essays in Criticism*. Ed. Arnold E. and Cathy N. Davidson. Toronto: Anansi, 1981. 35–54.

———. 2000. "Searching Bluebeard's Chambers: Grimm, Gothic, and Bible Mysteries in Alice Munro's *The Love of a Good Woman*." *American Review of Canadian Studies* (Autumn): 327–48.

McGlathery, James M. 1991. *Fairy Tale Romance: The Grimms, Basile, and Perrault*. Chicago: Univ. of Illinois Press.

McLaughlin, James. 1986. "All in the Family: Alfred Hitchcock's *Shadow of Doubt*." *A Hitchcock Reader*. Ed. Marshall Deutelbaum and Leland Poague. Ames: Iowa State Univ. Press. 141–52.

McMaster, Juliet. 1976. "Bluebeard: A Tale of Matrimony." *Room of One's Own* 2.2–3: 10–19.

McMillan, Ann. 1988. "The Transforming Eye: *Lady Oracle* and Gothic Tradition." *Margaret Atwood: Vision and Forms*. Ed. Kathryn Van Spanckeren and Jan Garden Castro. Carbondale: Southern Illinois Univ. Press. 48–64.

McNaughtan, Adam. 1990. "A Century of Saltmarket Literature, 1790–1890." *Six Centuries of the Provincial Book Trade in Britain*. Ed. Peter Isaac. Winchester: St. Paul's Bibliographies. 165–80.

Menninghaus, Winfried. 1999. *In Praise of Nonsense: Kant and Bluebeard*. Trans. Henry Pickford. Stanford, Calif.: Stanford Univ. Press.

Meuss, Ruth E. K., trans. 1971. "Comorre." *Breton Folktales*. London: G. Bell & Sons. 165–74.

Modleski, Tania. 1988. *The Women Who Knew Too Much: Hitchcock and Feminist Theory*. New York: Routledge.

Monsarrat, Ann. 1980. *Thackeray: An Uneasy Victorian*. London: Cassell. 254. (Cited in Moore 2002, 97).

Moore, Emily Ruth. 2002. "Plots, Paradoxes, and Parodies: Women Writers Rewriting 'Bluebeard.'" Ph.D. diss. City Univ. of New York.

Moore, Janet C. 1991. "Art Attack: The Great Bluebeard Critic." *Ethics in Modern American Literature: Rivers to Skyscrapers*. Ed. Mark G.Newton. Saint Leo, Fla..: Saint Leo College Press.

Morricone, Ennio. 1999. *The Thriller Collection*. Sound recording. Italian soundtracks. New York: Drg Movie.

Morris, Catherine. 1999. *The Essential Cindy Sherman*. New York: Harry N. Abrams.

Mowry Roberts, Vera. 1993. "'Lady Managers' in Nineteenth-Century American Theatre." Reprint *The American Stage*. Ed. Ron Engle and Tice L. Miller. Cambridge: Cambridge Univ. Press, 1994. 30–46.

Mowshowitz, Harriet. 1970. "Bluebeard and French Literature." Ph.D. diss. Univ. of Michigan, Ann Arbor.

———. 1973. "Gilles de Rais and the Bluebeard Legend in France." *Michigan Academician* 6.1: 83–92.

———. 1979. "'Voir est un acte dangereux': An Analysis of Perrault's 'La Barbe Bleue.'" *Proceedings of the Pacific Northwest Conference on Foreign Languages* 30.1–2: 28–30.

Mr. Bluebeard. 1903. *Iroquois Theatre Chicago: Souvenir Programme. Dedicatory Performance, November 23, 1903; Opening Attraction, Klaw & Erlanger's Mr. Blue Beard.* [Chicago]: Rand, McNally. Harvard Theatre Collection.

Mr. Bluebeard: Vocal Gems [from] Klaw and Erlanger's Production of the Great Drury Lane Spectacular Entertainment, Adapted for the American Stage by J. J. McNally. Music by Frederic Solomon. Lyrics by J. Cheever Goodwin. 1903. New York: Sol Bloom. Loeb Music Library.

Muir, Percy. 1954. *English Children's Books, 1600–1900*. Reprint London: Batsford, 1985.

Mulvey, Laura. 1975. "Visual Pleasure and Narrative Cinema." Reprint *Film Theory and Criticism*. 5th ed. Ed. Leo Braudy and Marshall Cohen. New York: Oxford Univ. Press, 1999. 833–44.

———. 1991. "A Phantasmagoria of the Female Body: The Work of Cindy Sherman." *New Left Review* 188(July–Aug): 136–50.

———. 1996. *Fetishism and Curiosity*. Bloomington: Indiana Univ. Press.

Murphy, Fiona Louise Mary. 1997. "From Bluebeard's Castle to the White World of Dreams: Constrictions and Constructions in Angela Carter's Prose Fiction." Ph.D. diss. Univ. of Oxford.

Mustazza, Leonard. 1990. "The Genesis Gang: Art and Re-Creation in *Bluebeard*." Reprint *The Critical Response to Kurt Vonnegut*. Ed. Leonard Mustazza. Westport, Conn.: Greenwood, 1994. 291–300.

"Mystic Krewe of Satyricon Presents Charles Ludlam's Bluebeard." n.d. *Mystic Krewe of Satyricon*. http://www.mystickreweofsatyricon.com/bluebeard.html.

Neuburg, Victor E. 1964. *Chapbooks: A Bibliography of References to English and American Chapbook Literature of the Eighteenth and Nineteenth Centuries*. London: Vine.

———. 1968. *The Penny Histories: A Study of Chapbooks for Young Readers over Two Centuries*. London: Oxford Univ. Press.

Oates, Joyce Carol. 1998. "In Olden Times, When Wishing Was Having: Classic and Contemporary Fairy Tales." *Mirror, Mirror on the Wall: Women Writers Explore Their Favorite Fairy Tales*. Ed. Kate Bernheimer. New York: Anchor Doubleday. 247–72.

Odio, Elena Baca. 1986. "Gilles de Rais in Life, Literature and Legend: Study of an International Leitmotif and of Its Progression from Fact to Fiction." Ph.D. diss. Univ. of Arkansas, Fayetteville.

O'Donnell, Elliott. 1928. *Women Bluebeards*. London: S. Paul.

"Old Jemmy Catnach." 1867. London, Provincial, and Colonial Press News. Jan. 17. Reprint *Catalogue of Songs and Song Books Printed and Published by James Catnach 1832. A Facsimile Reprint with Indexes and Examples*. Ed. Steve Roud and Paul Smith. West Stockwith: January Books, 1985. 99–100.

Onley, Gloria. 1974. "Power Politics in Bluebeard's Castle." *Canadian Literature* 60: 21–42.

Opie, Iona, and Peter Opie, eds. and intro. 1974. *The Classic Fairy Tales*. New York: Oxford Univ. Press, 1980.

The Osborne Collection of Early Children's Books, 1566–1910: A Catalogue. 1958. 2 vols. Ed. Judith St. John. Toronto: Toronto Public Library, 1975.

P., P. 1823. Prefatory Remarks to the Oxberry edition of *Blue Beard; or, Female Curiosity!* 1798. The Harvard Theatre Collection.

Palgrave, Sir Francis. 1919–1922. *The Collected Historical Works of Sir Francis Palgrave*. Cambridge: Cambridge Univ. Press.

Pancritius, Marie. 1930. "Aus mutterrechtlicher Ziet: Blaubart." *Anthropos* 25: 879–909. (Cited in Davies 2001).

Pastoureau, Michel. 2001. *Blue: The History of a Color*. Princeton, N.J.: Princeton Univ. Press.

Patten, Robert L. 1988. "George Cruikshank's Grimm Humor." *Imagination on a Long Rein: English Literature Illustrated*. Ed. Joachim Möller. Marburg: Jonas. 13–28.

Paynter, William. 1566. *Palace of Pleasure*. Book 1. Novel 30. (Cited in Chew 1937, 481).

Pearson, Edwin. 1890. *Banbury Chap-Books and Nursery Toy Book Literature [of the XVIII and Early XIX Centuries] with Impressions from Several Hundred Original Wood-Cut Blocks by T. & J. Bewick, Blake, Cruikshank, Craig, Lee, Austin, and Others Illustrating Favourite Nursery Classics, with their Antiquarian, Historical, Literary and Artistic Associations*. London. Reprint New York: Burt Franklin, n.d.

People Play UK. n.d. "William Beaumont Model." *Theatre Museum*. http://www.peopleplayuk.org.uk.

Peterson, Nancy J. 1987. "'Bluebeard's Egg': Not Entirely a 'Grimm' Tale." *Margaret Atwood: Reflection and Reality*. Ed. Beatrice Mendez-Egle and James M. Haule. Edinburgh: Pan American Univ. 131–38.

Philip, Neil. 1993. "Translating Perrault." *The Complete Fairy Tales of Charles Perrault*. Trans. Neil Philip and Nicoletta Simborowski. New York: Clarion. 128–29.

Philip, Neil, and Nicoletta Simborowski, trans. 1993. *The Complete Fairy Tales of Charles Perrault*. New York: Clarion.

Pichérit, Jean-Louis. 1988. "Qui était Barbe Bleue?" *Neophilologische Mitteilungen* 89.3: 374–77.

Planché, J. R. 1858. "Appendix: Blue Beard." *Four and Twenty Fairy Tales: Selected from Those of Perrault and Other Popular Writers*. London: G. Routledge. 515–17.

———. 1872. *Recollections and Reflections: A Professional Autobiography*. Reprint New York: Da Capo, 1978.

Plowright, Frank, ed. 1997. *The Slings and Arrows Comic Guide*. Reprint London: Slings & Arrows, 2003.

Pope, Christopher D. 2002. "From Breakfast to Bluebeard: Vonnegut after Experimentalism." Ph.D. diss. Mississippi State Univ., Starkville.

Porter, Susan L. 1990. "The Locked Room; or, *Blue Beard* [1798] as Barometer." *American Music* Spring: 54–70.

———. 1994. "Musical Theater at the Turn of the Nineteenth Century." *British Opera in America: Children in the Wood (1795) and Blue Beard (1811)*. Ed. Susan L. Porter. New York: Garland. xiii–xxx.

Propp, Vladimir. 1958. *Morphology of the Folktale*. Trans. Laurence Scott. Bloomington: Research Center, Indiana Univ.

Pyrhönen, Heta. 2007. "Imagining the Impossible: The Erotic Poetics of Angela Carter's 'Bluebeard' Stories." *Textual Practice* 21.1(March): 93–111.

Rampton, David. 1993. "Into the Secret Chamber: Art and the Artist in Kurt Vonnegut's *Bluebeard*." *Critique: Studies in Contemporary Fiction* 35: 16–26.

Raphoz, Fabienne. 1995. *Les femmes de Barbe-Bleue: une histoire de curieuses*. Genève: Les Editions Metropolis.

Reitz Mullenix, Elizabeth. 2000. "Acting between the Spheres: Charlotte Cushman as Androgyne." *Wearing the Breeches: Gender on the Antebellum Stage*. New York: St. Martin's. 185–230.

Renfroe, Cheryl. 1998. "Initiation and Disobedience: Liminal Experience in Angela Carter's 'The Bloody Chamber.'" *Marvels & Tales* 12.1: 82–94.

Reynolds, Frederick. 1826. *The Life and Times of Frederick Reynolds*. 2 vols. London. 2, 403–04. (Cited in Saxon 1968, 89).

Rice, Craig. 1952. "Bluebeard's Buried Treasure." *14 Murderers: A Collection of True Crime Stories*. New York: Simon & Schuster. 206–11.

Rich, B. Ruby. 1991. "Never a Victim: Jodie Foster, a New Kind of Female Hero." Reprint *Women and Film: A Sight and Sound Reader*. Ed. Pam Cook and Philip Dodd. Philadelphia: Temple Univ. Press, 1993. 50–61.

Rigby, Elizabeth. 1848. *The Quarterly Review* December. (Cited in Fraser 1988, 453; Moore 2002, 97).

Rigney, Barbara Hill. 1987. "'The Escape Artist': *Lady Oracle*." *Margaret Atwood*. Totowa, N.J.: Barnes. 62–81.

Roberts, Nancy. 1924. *Blackbeard and Other Pirates of the Atlantic Coast*. Winston-Salem, N.C.: John F. Blair, 1993.

Roberts, Paul. n.d. "Paul Roberts Lecture." The Village Music Project Lecture: Sidmouth Festival, 10th August 2000. http://www.village-music-project.org.uk/robert.htm.

Rockett, Will H. 1983. "Landscape and Manscape: Reflection and Distortion in Horror Films." *Post-Script: Essays in Film and the Humanities* 3.1: 19–34.

Roe, Steven C. 1992. "Opening Bluebeard's Closet: Writing and Aggression in Hemingway's *The Garden of Eden* Manuscript." *The Hemingway Review* 12.1: 52–66.

———. 1994. "The Artist as Bluebeard: Hemingway Critiques Hemingway in the *Garden of Eden* Manuscript." Ph.D. diss. Univ. of British Columbia. Ottawa: National Library of Canada.

Roscoe, S., and R. A. Brimmell. 1981. *James Lumsden & Son of Glasgow: Their Juvenile Books and Chapbooks.* Pinner, Middlesex: Private Libraries Association.

Roud, Steve, and Paul Smith. 1985. *Catalogue of Songs and Song Books Printed and Published by James Catnach 1832. A Facsimile Reprint with Indexes and Examples.* West Stockwith & Addiscombe: January Books.

Rowe, Karen E. 1983. "'Fairy-born and human-bred': Jane Eyre's Education in Romance." *The Voyage In: Fictions of Female Development.* Ed. Elizabeth Abel, Marianne Hirsch, and Elizabeth Langland. Hanover, N.H.: Univ. Press of New England. 69–89.

Roy, G. Ross. 1974. "Some Notes on Scottish Chapbooks." *Scottish Literary Journal* 1: 50–60.

Russ, Joanna. 1973. "Somebody's Trying to Kill Me, and I Think It's My Husband: The Modern Gothic." *Journal of Popular Culture* 6: 666–91.

Saintyves, P. 1923. *Les Contes de Perrault et les récits parallèles: leurs origines (coutumes primitives et liturgies populaires).* Paris: E. Nourry.

Saltus, Edgar. [1890–1899]. "Bluebeard [Gilles de Rais]." *Love throughout the Ages.* London: Sisley's.

Saxon, A. H. 1968. *Enter Foot and Horse: A History of Hippodrama in England and France.* New Haven, Conn.: Yale Univ. Press.

Schechter, Harold. 1984. "The Bloody Chamber: Terror Films, Fairy Tales, and Taboo." *Forbidden Fruits: Taboos and Tabooism in Culture.* Ed. Ray B. Browne. Bowling Green, Ohio: Bowling Green State Univ. Popular Press. 67–82.

———. 1994. *Depraved: The Shocking True Story of America's First Serial Killer.* New York: Pocket Books.

Schlobin, Roger. 1989. "The Femivore: An Unnamed Archetype." *Journal of the Fantastic in the Arts* 2.1: 89–96.

Schwenger, Peter. 1995. "Uncanny Reading." *English Studies in Canada* 21.3: 333–45.

Shattuck, Roger. 1996. *Forbidden Knowledge: A Landmark Exploration of the Dark Side of Human Ingenuity and Imagination.* San Diego, Calif.: Harcourt Brace.

Sheets, Robin Ann. 1991. "Pornography, Fairy Tales, and Feminism: Angela Carter's 'The Bloody Chamber.'" *Journal of the History of Sexuality* 1: 633–57.

Shepard, Leslie. 1969. *John Pitts: Ballad Printer of Seven Dials, London 1765–1844, with a Short Account of His Predecessors in the Ballad and Chapbook Trade.* London: Priv. Lib. Assn. Singing Tree.

———. 1973. *The History of Street Literature.* Newton Abbot: David and Charles.

Showalter, Elaine. 1988. Introduction to *Alternative Alcott.* Reprint New Brunswick, N.J.: Rutgers Univ. Press, 1989. ix–xliii.

Simms, Karl N. 1987. "Caleb Williams' Godwin: Things as They Are Written." *Studies in Romanticism* 26.3: 343–63.

Simons, John, ed. 1992. "Romance in the Eighteenth-Century Chapbook." *From Medieval to Medievalism*. Ed. John Simons. New York: St. Martin's. 122–43.

Simpson, Philip L. 1999. "The Politics of Apocalypse in the Cinema of Serial Murder." *Mythologies of Violence in Postmodern Media*. Ed. Christopher Sharrett. Detroit: Wayne State Univ. 119–44.

———. 2000. *Psycho Paths: Tracking the Serial Killer through Contemporary American Film and Fiction*. Carbondale: Univ. of Southern Illinois Press, 2000.

Sims, George Robert. 1915. *The Bluebeard of the Bath [George Joseph Smith]: A Story of Marriage and Murder*. London: C. A. Pearson.

Sine, Nadine. 1988. "Cases of Mistaken Identity: Salomé and Judith at the Turn of the Century." *German Studies Review* 11: 9–29.

Skaggs, Merrill Maguire. 1976. "The Uses of Enchantment in Frontier Humor and *The Robber Bridegroom*." Reprint *The Critical Response to Eudora Welty's Fiction*. Ed. Laurie Champion. Westport, Conn.: Greenwood, 1994. 57–63.

Skenazy, Paul. 1990. "Poking Holes in the Social Fabric." *Critical Essays on Kurt Vonnegut*. Ed. Robert Merrill. Boston: G. K. Hall. 64–66.

Smith, Allan Lloyd. 1984. "On the Other Side: The Uncanny." *ESQ: A Journal of the American Renaissance* 30.4: 260–72.

Smith, Edward H. 1926. "The Wives of Dr. Bowers," "The Stockyards Bluebeard." *Famous American Poison Mysteries*. London: Hurst & Blackett. 78–91, 92–106.

Somogyi, Peter J. 1985. "A Comparison of the Bluebeard Legend in Operatic Settings by Béla Bartók and Paul Dukas." Ph.D. diss. Univ. of Southern California, Los Angeles.

Soriano, Marc, ed. 1989. *Charles Perrault: Contes*. Paris: Flammarion.

Spufford, Margaret. 1981. *Small Books and Pleasant Histories: Popular Fiction and Its Readership in Seventeenth-Century England*. Athens: Univ. of Georgia Press.

St. Andrews, Bonnie. 1986. *Forbidden Fruit: On the Relationship between Women and Knowledge in Doris Lessing, Selma Lagerlöf, Kate Chopin, and Margaret Atwood*. Troy, N.Y.: Whitson.

The Stage Works of Béla Bartók. 1991. Ed. Nicholas John. London: John Calder.

Stalleybrass, Peter, and Allon White. 1986. *The Politics and Poetics of Transgression*. Ithaca, N.Y.: Cornell Univ. Press.

States, Janel A. 1996. "Confronting the Forbidden: Reshaping Cultural Identity with Bluebeard." M.A. thesis. Utah State Univ., Logan.

Stebbins, Emma. 1878. *Charlotte Cushman: Her Letters and Memories of Her Life*. Boston: Houghton, Osgood.

Stein, Karen. 2003. "Talking Back to Bluebeard: Atwood's Fictional Storytellers." *Margaret Atwood's Textual Assassinations: Recent Poetry and Fiction*. Ed. and intro. Sharon Wilson. Columbus: Ohio State Univ. Press. 154–71.

Steiner, George. 1971. *In Bluebeard's Castle: Some Notes towards a Redefinition of Culture*. London: Faber.

Stewart, Mary E. 1988. "Max Frisch's *Blaubart*: A Trivial Pursuit?" *Forum for Modern Language Studies* 24.3: 248–55.

Stocker, Margarita. 1998. *Judith, Sexual Warrior: Women and Power in Western Culture.* New Haven, Conn.: Yale Univ. Press.

Stone, Harry. 1979. *Dickens and the Invisible World.* Bloomington: Indiana Univ. Press. (Cited in Barzilai 2004, 521 n.).

Stone, Kay F. 1975. "Things Walt Disney Never Told Us." *Women and Folklore.* Ed. Claire R. Farrer. Austin: Univ. of Texas Press. 42–50.

———. 1986. "Feminist Approaches to the Interpretation of Fairy Tales." *Fairy Tales and Society: Illusion, Allusion, and Paradigm.* Ed. Ruth B. Bottigheimer. Philadelphia: Univ. of Pennsylvania Press. 229–36.

———. 1993. "Burning Brightly: New Light from an Old Tale." *Feminist Messages: Coding in Women's Folk Culture.* Ed. Joan Newlon Radner. Urbana: Univ. of Illinois Press. 289–305.

Storch, Robert. 1982. "Introduction: Persistence and Change in Nineteenth-Century Popular Culture." *Popular Culture and Custom in Nineteenth-Century England.* Ed. Robert Storch. London: Croom Helm. 1–19.

Suschitzky, Anja. 1997. "*Ariane et Barbe-Bleue*: Dukas, the Light and the Well." *Cambridge Opera Journal* 9: 133–61.

Sutherland, John. 1997. *Can Jane Eyre Be Happy? More Puzzles in Classic Fiction.* Oxford: Oxford Univ. Press. (Cited in Lovell-Smith 2000, 201).

Tatar, Maria M. 1981. "The Houses of Fiction: Towards a Definition of the Uncanny." *Comparative Literature* 33.2: 167–82.

———. 1987. "Taming the Beast: Bluebeard and Other Monsters." *The Hard Facts of the Grimm's Fairy Tales.* Princeton, N.J.: Princeton Univ. Press. 156–79.

———. 1988. "Beauties vs. Beasts in the Grimm's *Nursery and Household Tales. The Brothers Grimm and Folktale.* Ed. James M. McGlathery, et al. Urbana: Univ. of Illinois Press. 133–45.

———. 1992. "Daughters of Eve: Fairy-Tale Heroines and Their Seven Sins." *Off with Their Heads! Fairy Tales and the Culture of Childhood.* Reprint Princeton, N.J.: Princeton Univ. Press, 1993. 94–119.

———. 1999. "Introduction: Bluebeard." *The Classic Fairy Tales: Texts, Criticism.* New York: Norton. 138–44.

———. 2002. "Bluebeard." *The Annotated Classic Fairy Tales.* New York: Norton.

———. 2004. *Secrets Beyond the Door.* Princeton, N.J.: Princeton Univ. Press.

Taubin, Amy. 1991. "Grabbing the Knife: *The Silence of the Lambs* and the History of the Serial Killer Movie." *Women and Film: A Sight and Sound Reader.* Ed. Pam Cook and Philip Dodd. London: Scarlet. 123–31.

Taylor, Edgar. 1823–1826. Preface. *German Popular Stories.* 2 vols. Bodleian Library. Opie Collection.

Taylor, Troy. 2006. "Chicago's 'Bluebeard': The Serial Murders of Johann Otto Hoch." *Bloody Chicago: The History and Mystery of Chicago Crime.* Decatur, Ill.: Whitechapel Press.

Taylor, W. C. 1848. "Origin of the Story of Blue Beard." *Bentley's Miscellany* 23: 136–42. (Cited in Tuthill 1999, 70).

Thackeray, William Makepeace. 1859. *The Selected Letters of William Makepeace Thackeray*. Ed. Edgar F. Harden. New York: New York Univ. Press. 346. (Cited in Moore 2002, 156).

Thiselton-Dyer, T. 1906. "Woman's Curiosity." Folk-Lore of Women. Chicago: A. C. McClurg. http://www.sacred-texts.com/wmn/fow/fowoo.htm.

Thody, Philip Malcolm Waller. 1997. *Don't Do It!:A Dictionary of the Forbidden*. New York: St. Martin's.

Thompson, James. 1989. "Surveillance in William Godwin's *Caleb Williams*." *Gothic Fictions: Prohibition/Transgression*. Ed. Kenneth Graham. New York: AMS Press. 173–98.

Thompson, Stith. 1946. "The Folktale from Ireland to India." *The Folktale*. Reprint Berkeley: Univ. of California Press, 1978.

Thomson, Peter. 2006. *The Cambridge Introduction to English Theatre, 1660–1900*. Cambridge: Cambridge Univ. Press.

Todorov, Tzvetan. 1973. "*L'Etrange et le merveilleux*." "The Uncanny and the Marvelous." Trans. Richard Howard. *The Fantastic: A Structural Approach to a Literary Genre*. London: Press of Case Western Reserve Univ. 41–57.

Tolkien, J. R. R. 1986. "On Fairy-Stories." *The Tolkien Reader*. New York: Ballantine. 3–84.

Traubner, Richard. 1983. *Operetta: A Theatrical History*. New York: Doubleday.

Trilling, Lionel. 1942. "American Fairy Tale." Reprint *The Critical Response to Eudora Welty's Fiction*. Ed. Laurie Champion. Westport, Conn.: Greenwood, 1994. 55–56.

Trimmer, Sarah Kirby. 1803. *Guardian of Education*. (Cited in Moore 2002, 13).

Trozzi, Adriana. 1992. *Fairy-Tale Criticism within Fiction: The Feminist Elements*. Memoria e interpretazione 4. Marina di Patti: Pungitopo.

Tuthill, Allison Hope. 1999. "Forbidden Curiosity: Episodic Repetition in 'Bluebeard' Tales from France, Germany, and the West Indies." M.A. thesis. Univ. of Virginia, Charlottesville.

Uhry, Alfred. 1998. Album notes for *The Robber Bridegroom*. Georgetown, Conn.: Original Cast.

Ulanov, Ann, and Barry Ulanov. 1994. "Borderlines, Bluebeard and Death." *Transforming Sexuality: The Archetypal World of Anima and Animus*. Boston: Shambhala.

Untermeyer, Louis. 1968. "Bluebeard." *Tales from the Ballet*. New York: Golden. 42–46.

Uphaus, Robert W. 1977. "*Caleb Williams*: Godwin's Epoch of Mind." *Studies in the Novel* 9.3: 279–96.

Van Raamsdonk, Renée. 1976. "The Bluebeard Legend in French Literature." M.A. thesis. Univ. of Calgary.

Varadan, Savitha. n.d. "Walk Back in Time in Historic Charlotte Amalie." *Hampton Roads Travel*. Atevo Travel.

Velay-Vallantin, Catherine. 1987. "Le Miroir des contes. Perrault dans les bibliothèques bleues." *Les Usages de l'imprimé*. Ed. R. Chartier. Paris: Fayard. 129–85.

———. 1992. "Barbe-Bleue." *L'histoire des contes*." Paris: Fayard. 43–93.

Verhoeven, W. M. 1995. "Opening the Text: The Locked-Trunk Motif in Late Eighteenth-Century British and American Gothic Fiction." *Exhibited by Candlelight: Sources and Developments in the Gothic Tradition*. Ed. Valeria Tinkler-Villani, Peter Davidson, Jane Stevenson. Amsterdam: Rodopi. 205–19.

Verrill, A. Hyatt. 1924. *Love Stories of Some Famous Pirates*. London: W. Collins Sons.

Viellieries, Fouille, trans. 1870. "Preliminary Discourse." *Bluebeard, or, Dangerous Curiosity and Justifiable Homicide, A Tragedy in Three Acts*. As Acted at Oatland. Paris: T. Brettell.

Vincent, David. 1982. "The Decline of the Oral Tradition in Popular Culture." *Popular Culture and Custom in Nineteenth-Century England*. Ed. Robert Storch. London: Croom Helm. 20–47.

Vincent, Lewis. 1926. *Gilles de Rais: The Original Bluebeard*. London: A. M. Philpot.

Vincent, Sybil Korff. 1983. "The Mirror and the Cameo: Margaret Atwood's Comic/Gothic Novel, *Lady Oracle*." *The Female Gothic*. Ed. Juliann E. Fleenor. Montreal: Eden. 153–63.

Vitkus, Daniel. 2003. "Othello Turns Turk." *Turning Turk: English Theater and the Multicultural Mediterranean, 1570–1630*. New York: Palgrave Macmillan. 77–106.

Vizetelly, Ernest Alfred. 1900. *Bluebeard: An Account of Comorre the Cursed and Gilles de Rais, with summaries of various tales and traditions*. London: Chatto & Windus, 1983.

Von Franz, Marie-Louise. 1974. *Shadow and Evil in Fairy Tales*. Rev. and ed. Boston: Shambhala, 1995.

———. 1996. *The Interpretation of Fairy Tales*. Boston: Shambhala.

Waite, John. 1993. "Exposing Bluebeard! Angela Carter Gets Delirious in *The Magic Toyshop, Heroes and Villains*, 'The Bloody Chamber,' and 'The Fall River Axe Murders.'" M.A. thesis. Eastern Illinois Univ., Charleston.

Wakefield, H. Russell. 1936. *Landru: The French Bluebeard*. London: Duckworth.

Waldman, Diane. 1983. "'At Last I Can Tell It to Someone!' Feminine Point of View and Subjectivity in the Gothic Romance Film of the 1940s." *Cinema Journal* 23: 29–40.

Walker, Cheryl. 1996. "In Bluebeard's Closet: Women Who Write with the Wolves." *Literature Interpretation Theory* 7.1: 13–25.

Walsh, W. S. 1915. *Heroes and Heroines of Fiction-Classical, Medieval, Legendary*. Reprint Detroit: Gale, 1966.

Walton, James H. 1975. *"Mad Feary Father": Caleb Williams and the Novel Form*. Salzburg: Institut für Englische Sprache und Literatur, Univ. Salzburg.

Walz, Robin. 2000. "Murder, Mirth and Misogyny: The Dark Humor of Henri Desiré Landru, the Bluebeard of Gambais." *Pulp Surrealism: Insolent Popular Culture in Early Twentieth-Century Paris*. Berkeley: Univ. of California Press. 76–113.

Warner, Marina. 1989. "Bluebeard's Brides: The Dream of the Blue Chamber." *Grand Street* 9: 121–30.

———. 1994. "Demon Lovers: Bluebeard I," "The Ogre's Appetite: Bluebeard II." Reprint *From the Beast to the Blonde: On Fairy Tales and Their Tellers*. London: Vintage, 1995. 241–58, 259–71.

Warren, Leland E. 1987. "*Caleb Williams* and the 'Fall' into Writing." *Mosaic* 20.1: 57–69.

Wearing, J. P. 1976. *The London Stage 1890–1899: A Calendar of Play and Players.* 2 vols. Metuchen, N.J: Scarecrow.

Weber, Samuel. 1973. "The Sideshow, Or: Remarks on a Canny Moment." *Modern Language Notes* 88: 1102–33.

Wehrs, Donald R. 1988. "Rhetoric, History, Rebellion: *Caleb Williams* and the Subversion of Eighteenth-Century Fiction." *Studies in English Literature* 28.3: 497–511.

Weigel, Marta I. 1986. "I Have No Language for My Reality: The Ineffable as Tension in the 'Tale' of *Bluebeard*." *World Literature Today* 60.4: 588–92.

Weiss, Harry B. 1935. *A Catalogue of the Chapbooks in the New York Public Library.* New York: New York Public Library.

———. 1938. *American Chapbooks.* Trenton, N.J.: privately printed.

———. 1942. *A Book about Chapbooks: The People's Literature of Bygone Times.* Reprint Hatboro, Pa.: Folklore Associates, 1969.

———. 1945. *American Chapbooks, 1722–1842.* New York: New York Public Library.

Welch, Jennifer. 1994. "Revisioning Traditional Magic Tales: Another Look at Cinderella, Bluebeard, and Sinbad." M.A. thesis. Univ. of Louisiana, Lafayette.

"Welcome to Bluebeard's Castle." St. Thomas, US Virgin Islands. http://www.bluebeards.net/Castle.html.

Weldon, Fay. 1998. "The Journey to Mr. Fox." *Mirror, Mirror on the Wall: Women Writers Explore Their Favorite Fairy Tales.* Ed. Kate Bernheimer. New York: Anchor Doubleday. 318–41.

Welty, Eudora. 1948. Letter written to John F. Robinson, December, Eduora Welty Papers. Louisiana and Lower Mississippi Valley Collections. Louisiana State University Libraries, Baton Rouge. (Cited in Marrs 2002, 57).

———. 1975. *Fairy Tale of the Natchez Trace.* Jackson: Mississippi Historical Society.

Westall, William. 1890. "A French Bluebeard." *Strange Crimes.* London: Ward & Downey.

Wheeler, William A. 1866. "Blue-beard." *A Dictionary of the Noted Names of Fiction.* London: Bell & Daldy. 49.

Whipple, B. C. Addison. 1957. *Pirate Rascals of the Spanish Main.* New York: Doubleday. (Cited in Lee 1974, 48).

White, Alfred D. 1986. "Max Frisch Revisited: *Blaubart*." *Monatschefte fur Deutschen Unterricht-Deutsche Sprache und Literatur* 78.4: 456–67.

Williams, Anne. 1995. *Art of Darkness: A Poetics of Gothic.* Chicago: Univ. of Chicago Press.

Williams, Linda. 1984. "When the Woman Looks." *Re-vision: Essays in Feminist Film Criticism.* Ed. Mary Ann Doane, Patricia Mellencamp, and Linda Williams. Frederick, Md.: Univ. Press of America and the American Film Institute. 83–99.

Wilson, Colin, and Patricia Pitman, eds. 1961. *Encyclopaedia of Murder.* Reprint London: Pan, 1984.

Wilson, Robert Rawdon. 1982. "Godgames and Labyrinths: The Logic of Entrapment." *Mosaic* 15.4: 1–22.

Wilson, Sharon Rose. 1986. "Bluebeard's Forbidden Room: Gender Images in Margaret Atwood's Visual and Literary Art." *American Review of Canadian Studies* 16.4: 385–97.
———. 1988. "Sexual Politics in Margaret Atwood's Visual Art." *Margaret Atwood: Vision and Forms*. Ed. Kathryn Van Spanckeren and Jan Garden Castro. Carbondale: Southern Illinois Univ. Press. 205–14.
———. 1993. *Margaret Atwood's Fairy-Tale Sexual Politics*. Jackson: Univ. Press of Mississippi.
Wilson, Thomas. 1899. *Blue Beard: A Contribution to History and Folk-lore, Being the History of Gilles de Retz of Brittany, France, Who Was Executed at Nantes in 1440 AD and Who Was the Original of Blue-Beard in the Tales of Mother Goose*. New York: Bloom, 1971.
Wilt, Judith. 1980. "Jane Austen: The Anxieties of Common Life." *Ghosts of the Gothic: Austen, Eliot and Lawrence*. Princeton, N.J.: Princeton Univ. Press. 121–72.
Windling, Terri. 2002. "Bluebeard and the Bloody Chamber." *Realms of Fantasy Magazine* (October): 32–39. Reprint Gregory Frost, *Fitcher's Brides*, 2002, [11]–29.
Wolf, Leonard. 1980. *Bluebeard: The Life and Crimes of Gilles de Rais*. New York: Crown Publishers.
Wolstonholme, Susan. 1993. *Gothic (Re)visions: Writing Women as Readers*. Albany: State Univ. of New York Press.
Wright, Richardson. 1927. *Hawkers and Walkers in Early America*. New York: Frederick Ungar, 1965.
Yearsley, MacLeod. 1924. "Bluebeard and the Forbidden Chamber." *The Folklore of the Fairy-Tale*. Reprint Detroit: Singing Tree, 1968. 121–37.
York, Lorraine M., ed. and intro. 1995. *Various Atwoods: Essays on the Later Poems, Short Fiction, and Novels*. Concord, Ontario: Anansi.
Ziolkowski, Theodore. 2000. *The Sin of Knowledge: Ancient Themes and Modern Variations*. Princeton, N.J.: Princeton Univ. Press.
Zipes, Jack. 1987b. "Once There Were Two Brothers Named Grimm." *The Complete Fairy Tales of the Brothers Grimm*. Reprint New York: Bantam, 1992. xvii–xxxi.
———. 1987c. Introduction to *Victorian Fairy Tales: The Revolt of the Fairies and Elves*. New York: Methuen. xiii–xxix.
———. 1988. *Fairy Tales and the Art of Subversion: The Classical Genre for Children and the Process of Civilization*. New York: Methuen.
———, ed. 2001. "Cross-Cultural Connections and the Contamination of the Classical Fairy Tale." *The Great Fairy Tale Tradition*. New York: Norton. 845–69.
———. 2006. "The Male Key to Bluebeard's Secret." *Why Fairy Tales Stick: The Evolution and Relevance of a Genre*. New York: Routledge. 155–93.

Index

A kékszakállú herceg vára. See *Duke Bluebeard's Castle*
Aarne, Anthi, xiv, xv. *See also* Aarne-Thompson
Aarne-Thompson, xiv; AT 311, xiii, 4; AT 312, xiii, 4, 181n2; AT 312B, xiii, 181n2; AT 955, 4, 7; classification, xiii, 4, 181n2; as Eurocentric, xiii, xiv–xv, 181n2
Abomelique, xi, 51, 57, 60–64, 74–75, 96, 98–100, 192n4, 195n22, 198n40, 208n28, 212n3
Adams, Marion, 212n3
Adventures of Philip, 209–10n12
Alcott, Louisa May, 122–23, 211n26
Alderson, Brian, 209n6
"Alien Territory," 175
amateur and parlor plays, 104–7, 130, 132, 145, 221n18
amateur theatre, 208n28
American Musical Theatre, 207n26
ancien régime, xiii, 59. *See also* Bluebeard: historical interpretation
Andersen, Hans Christian, 113
animal grooms. *See* Bluebeard: archetypes
Anton, Gregory, 157
Apostolidès, Jean-Marie, xiii. *See also* Bluebeard: historical interpretation
Apuleius, 15. *See also* myth
Arabian Nights. See *Thousand and One Arabian Nights, The*
Arabian Nights' Entertainment, The, 109, 113, 192n5. See also *Thousand and One Arabian Nights, The*
Ariadne and Bluebeard, 133, 138–40, 213n8, 214nn17–20
Ariane et Barbe-bleue. See *Ariadne and Bluebeard*
Armoire de Fer, 196n25
armoire de fer, 52, 58–59. See also *Caleb Williams*
Arnaud, Étienne, 213n8
Arnold, Marilyn, 149, 218n8
Ashliman, D. L., 209n4, 209n8
Ashton, John, 199n1
Asper, Katherin, xvi, xvii. *See also* psychology: Jung, Carl
AT. *See* Aarne-Thompson
Atwood, Margaret, xi, 160–61, 171, 173–75, 178, 221n4, 221n19, 222n23
Austen, Jane, 175, 184–85n29, 210nn20–21
Awful History of Blue Beard, The, 114

Bacchilega, Cristina, 220n1, 222n20
Balanchine, George, 179n4
Balázs, Béla, 16, 133, 134, 138, 141–42, 144–45, 151, 156, 177, 212n5, 215n28, 216n30, 216–17n32, 217n2. *See also* Bartók, Béla; *Duke Bluebeard's Castle*
ballad, 12
Ballad of Anne Molinár, 141, 215–16n29
Ballantyne, John, 156. *See also* Edwardes, Anthony
Ballaster, Ros, 192–93n6
Banbury Chap-books, 192–93n6
Barbarossa, 54, 194n13
"Barbazure," 107, 114, 115–16
Barbe Bleue (Perrault). *See* "La Barbe Bleue"
Barbe Bleue (1869), 207n26
Barbe bleue (1897), 213n8
Barbe-Bleue (1746), 60, 91, 197n33
Barbe-bleue (1901), 133, 134–35, 158, 171
Barbe-Bleue ou la Sorcière du Danube, 186n16
Barbe-Bleue ou les Enchantements d'Alcine: Tableaux en Trois Actions, 198–99n45
Barchilon, Jacques, xiii, 42, 46, 49, 187nn1–2, 187n4, 188n10, 189n12, 190n14, 191n20, 191n25. *See also* Bluebeard: historical interpretation
Barnaby Rudge, 117

Barnard, A. M. *See* Alcott, Louisa May
Barry Lyndon. See *Memoirs of Barry Lyndon, The*
Barthelme, Donald, 160
Bartók, Béla, xi, 16, 133, 138, 141–42, 144–45, 151, 156, 159, 177, 212nn5–6, 215–16nn28–29, 216n30, 216–17n32, 217n2. *See also* Balázs, Béla; *Duke Bluebeard's Castle*
Barzilai, Shuli, xvi, 180n14, 210n18, 222n23. *See also* psychology: Freud, Sigmund
Bashaw, 51, 53, 54, 60, 61, 63, 74, 89, 98, 99, 104, 107, 119 185n31, 197n35, 210n21, 211n29
Basile, Giambattista, 14. *See also* Pentamerone, The
Bayard, Jean-Pierre, 180n11
Bayley, F. W. N., 85, 124
Beaumont, William, 204–5n10, 205–6nn14–15
Beauties, Beasts and Enchantment: Classic French Fairy Tales, 112, 188n10
Bechstein, Ludwig, 110, 182n8, 208–9n3
Bedtime Stories for Women, 221n10
Before the Fact, 156
"Belle Gunness," 186nn19–20
Bellingham, Henry, 89, 97, 101–3
Benson, Ann, 18
Benson, Stephen, 222n22
Bergengren, Ralph, 70, 199n1
Bettelheim, Bruno, xv, xvi, 180n8. *See also* Bluebeard: feminist interpretation
Bible, 14–15, 16–17, 79, 189n12
Bishop, Jean Peale, 149
Bittersweet, 108
Black Beard, the Pirate; or, the Captive Princess, 26
Blackbeard, 19, 21–26, 27, 28, 29, 176, 185nn3–4, 186n8; beard, 21, 22, 185n2. *See also* Teach, Captain Edward
"Blackbeard vs. Blue Eyes," 28
Blackbeard's Castle, 27
Blamires, David, 209n8
"Blaubart," xiii–xiv, 5, 110, 208–9n3. *See also* Grimm, Jacob and Wilhelm
Bleak House, 117
Block, Francesca Lia, 170
Bloody Chamber, The, 222n20
"Bloody Chamber, The," 174
"Bloudie Jacke," 161–62
Blue Beard (1821), 77
Blue Beard (1839), 93, 104
Blue Beard (1854–1856), 71–82
Blue Beard (1916), 215n26
"Blue Beard" (1922), 132
"Blue Beard" (1925), 132, 145
Blue Beard (Pott & Amery), 202n18
Blue Beard (S. Marks & Sons), 75
Blue Beard (toy book), 76
Blue Beard: A Grand Musical, Comi-Tragical, Melo-Dramatic, Burlesque Burletta, in One Act, 98. *See also* Dance, Charles; Planché, James Robinson
Blue Beard: A Melodramatic Travesty, 104
Blue Beard: Adorned with Cuts, 81–82
Blue Beard: An Extravaganza, 97, 206n19
Blue Beard, an Operetta in One Act, 213–14n14
Blue Beard; or, Female Curiosity! (1798), ix, 37, 51, 52, 55, 56, 57, 58, 60–66, 74, 78, 87, 89, 91, 94, 97, 98, 99, 101, 106–7, 109, 116, 119, 136, 195n22, 197–98nn39–40, 201n11, 206n19, 209–10n12, 210n15, 212n3. *See also* Bluebeard: Turk/oriental
Blue Beard; or, Female Curiosity! (1811), 66, 198–99nn44–45, 204–5n10
Blue Beard, or Female Curiosity, A Sensation Drama in Two Acts and Two Scenes, 105
Blue Beard, or, The Fatal Effects of Curiosity and Disobedience, 79, 87
Blue Beard, or, The Flight of Harlequin, 37, 52, 56–57, 91, 93
Blue Beard, or Tommy in Fairyland, 132
Blue Beard and Puss in Boots, 87
Blue Beard Re-Paired; a Worn-Out Subject Done Up Anew, 89, 97, 101–3, 207–8n27
"Blue Beard's March." *See* "Grand March"
Blue Chamber, 61–63, 71, 78, 86, 106, 129, 197n37, 202n21, 202n24
Blue Fairy Book, 41, 112–13, 188–89nn9–10, 209n11
Bluebeard: archetypes, x, xi, xiv–xviii, 3–4, 12–13, 14–17, 176, 180nn8–11, 180n15, 181n5; censorship of, x, 73, 79–81, 87–88, 108, 122, 131, 132, 178, 179nn1–2, 182n9, 197n32, 203n36, 214n15; chapbooks (*see* chapbooks); cross-dressed casting, xi, 56, 94–96, 129–30, 177, 208n28; disappearance of, 79–81, 179nn1–2; *fée* (fairy/enchanted) elements, 4, 7, 46, 57, 65, 100, 112, 137–38 (*see also* Bluebeard: folkloric elements; "La Barbe Bleue": plot); feminist interpretation, xiii, xiv, xv, xvi, xvii, xviii–xix, 131, 134, 135, 139, 155–58, 180n8, 180–81n16, 181n2, 214n23, 219–20nn11–18; feminist treatment of, 118–23, 168–76, 177–78, 211n23, 214n16, 221nn4–5, 221n16; folkloric elements, 5, 6, 7, 9–10, 11, 20, 180n8, 181n1, 182n8, 182n15, 209n4; historical

interpretation, xii–xiv, 59; international variants, xiii–xiv, 3–4, 179n6; interpretation, xii–xix; morals, 49–50, 75–77, 81, 82, 105, 108, 161, 188n8, 190n13, 191–92n27, 201nn13–14, 202n16, 202–3n30, 209–10n12; narratological, 161–68, 175–76, 177, 181n17; nationalist interpretation, xi, xii–xiv, 7, 179nn5–6, 178n8, 181nn3–5, 182n10, 183–84n24, 204n4, 208–9n3, 211n28, 220n3; as pirate, ix, 19, 26–29, 176, 178; scopic elements, 6–7, 49, 180–81n16, 182n7 (*see also* gothic); topical allusions in (drama), 74, 96–97, 101, 103, 107, 206n17, 206–7n20; Turk/oriental, ix, xi–xii, xiv, 13–14, 51–66, 70, 73, 74, 75, 88, 89, 98–99, 105–7, 113, 120–21, 159, 176, 201n12, 204n3, 207n23, 208n28, 210n20, 211n29 (*see also* Fatima; Selim); as werewolf, xiii, 180n8. *See also specific works*; "La Barbe Bleue"

Blue-Beard (1864–1875), 84

Bluebeard (1944), 155, 156, 157, 161, 219n13, 220n16

Bluebeard (1963), 30. See also *Landru*

Bluebeard (1972), 162–65

Bluebeard (1987 novel), 160, 165–67, 179n1

Bluebeard (1987 play), 159

"Bluebeard" (1987), 160

Bluebeard (1993), 168

Bluebeard (*Grand Christmas Pantomime Blue Beard*), 129

"Bluebeard" (Perrault), 12, 13, 110–13, 174, 186n17, 209n9, 213n8

Bluebeard: A Tale, 160

Bluebeard: The Life and Crimes of Gilles de Rais, 184n27

Bluebeard, Jr., 151

Bluebeard; or, Dangerous Curiosity and Justifiable Homicide, 104

"Bluebeard Affair, The," 179n1

Bluebeard and After: Three Decades of Murder in France, 30. *See also* Landru, Henri Désiré

"Bluebeard and French Literature," 214n15

Bluebeard and His Eight Wives, 183–84n24

"Bluebeard and the Spanish Witch," 28–29

"[Bluebeard at Breakfast]," 114, 115, 117, 209–10n12, 210n14

Bluebeard Caper, A, 217n1

Bluebeard Had a Wife, 159

Bluebeard in Bologna, 212n3

Bluebeard in Drag, 221n12

"Bluebeard in Ireland," 222n22

Bluebeard Picture Book, The, 125

Bluebeard's Bride, 168

Bluebeard's Castle (amusement park), 27

Bluebeard's Castle (Charlotte Amalie), 27. *See also* Blackbeard's Castle; Bluebeard: as pirate

Bluebeard's Castle, 177

"Bluebeard's Daughter," 134, 145, 146–48, 217–18nn2–4

Bluebeard's Egg, 175, 178

Bluebeard's Eighth Wife (film), 151, 152–54

Bluebeard's Eighth Wife (play), 151, 152–54

"Bluebeard's Ghost," 114, 115–17, 121

"Bluebeard's Key," 170

"Bluebeard's Keys," 119–21, 184–85n29

Bluebeard's Keys and Other Stories, 211n22

Bluebeard's Last Stand, 217n1

Bluebeard's Picture Book, 125

Bluebeard's Room, 184–85n29

Bluebeard's Second Wife, 160, 169

"Bluebeard's Seven Wives," 59

Bluebeard's Seven Wives, 151

Bluebeard's Widow and Her Sister Anne: Their History Evolved from Mendacious Chronicles, 121

Bluebeard's Wives, 177

Blue-beard's Work-shop, 178

Boccaccio, Giovanni, 14. *See also* Pentamerone, The

Boden, Julie, 177

Bodily Harm, 175

Bodmer, George, 222n21

Bogart, Humphrey, 162

Boileau, Nicholas. *See* Perrault, Charles: debate with Nicholas Boileau

Bonny, Anne, 25. *See also* Teach, Captain Edward

Boom in the Moon, 151

Booth, Michael, 94, 205–6n14, 206n16

Bordman, Gerald, 207n26

Bossard, Eugene, 133, 183–84nn24–25

Bostwick, Barry, 218n5

Boswell, James, x, 70, 200n4. *See also* chapbooks

Bottigheimer, Ruth B., 180n8

Boulotte, 103, 207–8n27

Boulotte, 207n26

Bowd, W. J., 201n8

Boyles, Alistair, 217n1

Brandt, Nat, 212n2

Brewer, Derek, 180n11

Bretèque, François de la, 213n8, 213n13

Bridgeman, J. V., 96

Brigley, Zoë, 177

British Opera in America, 195n22

"Britomart," 113

Broadbent, R. J., 91, 93, 94, 184–85n29, 197n33, 205n11
Brochon, Pierre, 187n4, 200n5
Brontë, Anne, 210n20
Brontë, Charlotte, 109, 210n21
Brophy, Brigid, 212n6
Broughton, Simon, 216n30
Buffy the Vampire Slayer, 177
Burke, Edmund, 54, 194n14
burlesque, 54, 60, 89–90, 91, 97–101, 129–31, 204n8, 204–5nn9–10, 206–7nn19–20. *See also* extravaganza
burletta. *See* burlesque; extravaganza
Burne, Glenn, 113
Burris, Patricia, xix. *See also* Bluebeard: feminist interpretation
Burton, Sir Richard, 109, 162, 182n18, 186n16
Busha Bluebeard, 177, 222n3
Byatt, A. S., 169

Caleb Williams, 37, 52, 57–59, 192–93n6, 196n25. See also *armoire de fer*
"Calico Jack." *See* Rackham, Jack
Campion, Jane, x, 171, 173
cannibalism, 9, 161, 171, 180n8, 182n11, 209n8
Capdevila, R., 159–60
"Captain Murderer," 9, 117–18, 119, 210n19. *See also* cannibalism; Dickens, Charles
Carlell, Lodowick, 193–94n10
Carlyle, Thomas, x
Carradine, John, xii, 156, 220n16
Carson, Barbara Harrell, 219n10
Carter, Angela, 160–61, 173–74, 221–22n19–20, 222n22
"Case of Bluebeard, The," 222n4
Cashdan, Sheldon, xiii. *See also* Bluebeard: historical interpretation
"Castle of Death, The," 181n2
"Castle of Murder, The," 110, 181n2
Castle Spectre, 52
Cat's Cradle-Book, The, 146–48
Caught, 155, 157, 219–20n13–14
Cave, Emma, 184–85n29
Cazelles, Brigitte, 183n21, 183n24
"Cellar of Blood," 182n10
Chabrol, Claude, 30, 186n16. *See also* Landru, Henri Désiré
"Cham" (Amédée de Noé), 109
chapbooks, x, xxi, 4, 37, 39, 47, 51, 53, 60, 66, 69–88, 89, 108, 109, 119, 131–32, 136, 184n29, 187n4, 192n5, 195n22, 198n41, 199n1, 199n3, 200n4, 200n6, 201nn8–11, 203n31, 203n33; decline of, 70; illustration of, x, 4, 53, 72–73, 83–88, 202n17, 202–3nn30–31, 203nn33–34, 203n36; pirating of, 69, 199n2, 202n18; publication and distribution of, 69, 72, 199n1, 199–200n3; readership of, 70, 71, 78, 199n1, 200n4, 201n8; role in preserving fairy tales, 70, 200nn6–7
Chap-Books of the Eighteenth Century: With Facsimiles, Notes, and Introduction, 70
Chapin, Anna Alice, 161, 215n26
Chaplin, Charlie, 156
Charles Town blockade. *See* Teach, Captain Edward: Charles Town blockade
Charlotte Amalie, St. Thomas, 27, 28. *See also* Bluebeard: as pirate; Blubeard's Castle (Charlotte Amalie)
Château Bluebeard, 183n20
Chaucer, Geoffrey, 192n4
Chew, Samuel C., 193–94nn10–13
Chicago Death Trap: The Iroquois Theatre Fire of 1903, 212n2
Child, Francis, 182n14
Child Ballad, 182n14
Chisholm, Louey, 132
"Cinderella," 174
circus, 204–5n10
Clarel, x
Clarke, Harry, 131
Clown, 92, 94, 129, 204–5n10, 205–6n14
Cocteau Twins, x
Colbert, Claudette, 152
Collins, Arthur, 129
Colman, George (elder), 55, 58, 194–95n15
Colman, George (younger), xi, 37, 51, 53–54, 55, 57–59, 60–66, 97, 104, 192n4, 194n13, 195–96nn24–26, 197nn32–33, 197nn–35–37, 197n39, 198nn40–41, 204–5n10; collaboration with Michael Kelly (*see* Colman-Kelly); as Examiner of Plays, 196n25, 206n19; his libretto, 98; "Preface," 65. *See also* Kelly, Michael
Colman-Kelly, 51, 52, 53–54, 55, 56, 57, 66, 74, 78, 89, 90, 91, 94, 95, 97, 98, 99, 102, 106–7, 109, 111, 116, 119, 136, 198–99n45, 201n11, 203n3, 209–10n12, 212n3. See also *Bluebeard, or, Female Curiosity!*
Columbine, 92, 204–5nn10–11
Colven, May, 215–16n29
Comedie Italiene, 205n11
commedia dell'arte. *See* harlequinade

Comôr the Accursed, xiii, 17–18, 183n20, 183n23. *See also* Bluebeard: historical interpretation
Complete Fairy Tales of Charles Perrault, The, 188n10
Complete Fairy Tales of the Brothers Grimm, The, 110
Contes de Ma Mère l'Oye. See *Mother Goose*
Cook, Méira, 160
Cooper, Gary, 152
Corneille, Jean, 42, 190n14
Corson, James C., 70
Couperus, Louis, 145
Couragious Turke, or Amurath the First, 193–94n10
Cowper, William, 191n21
Cox, Philip, 195n23
Crane, Walter, 109, 122, 124–26, 211n29
Cruikshank, George, 5, 109, 110, 117, 123, 124, 192–93n6, 210n17, 211n25. See also *German Popular Stories*: illustration
Cruikshank, George, Jr., 121, 211n25
Cruikshank, R., 61, 66, 89
Cummins, Stevenson Lyle, 131, 212n3
Cunningham, Robert Hays, 83
Cupid. *See* Psyche and Cupid
Cushman, Charlotte, xi, 104, 208n28
cutlass, 27, 42, 49, 51, 112, 191n24, 203n33, 211n29

Dance, Charles, 53, 97–101, 104. *See also* Planché, James Robinson
Dandru, Desire, 31. *See also* Landru, Henri Désiré
Dark Waters, 155, 157
Darnton, Robert, 179n5
Darton, Harvey, 5, 19, 38, 66, 69, 110, 192n5, 199n1, 200n6, 202n29
"Das Mordschloss." *See* "Castle of Murder, The"
"Das Waldhaus." *See* "House in the Forest, The"
d'Aulnoy, Marie-Catherine, 188–89n9
David Copperfield, 210n18
Davies, Damian Walford, 58–59, 195–96nn24–25, 196n27
Davies, Meredid Puw, xiv, xvii–xviii, 131, 179n6, 180n8, 181n1, 190n15, 204n4, 208n3, 221n4. *See also* psychology: Lacan, Jacques
de la Mare, Walter, 214n18
de Melker, Daisy, 186n18
de Rais, Gilles, xiii, 17, 18, 30, 60, 98, 112, 133, 144, 183–84nn22–27, 184–85n29, 197n34, 213n7. *See also* Bluebeard: historical interpretation; serial killer
de Régnier, Henri, 215n26
Dean & Son, 75, 76, 79, 81, 105, 201n13
Deardon, Harold, 183–84n24
Debussy, Claude, 216n130
Decameron, 14. *See also* Pentamerone, The
Defoe, Daniel, 21, 185n1. *See also* Johnson, Captain Charles
Delamar, Gloria, 200n7
Demme, Jonathan, 171–73, 221nn16–17
"Der Treue Johannes." *See* "Faithful John"
Desire to Desire: The Woman's Film of the 1940s, The, 155, 219–20nn11–18
"Devil Gets Tricked, The," 7. *See also* Bluebeard: folkloric elements
Devil's Mount, or, the Female Bluebeard, The, 91. See also *Female Bluebeard, or, The Adventures of Polyphemus Amador de Croustillac, The*
Dibden, Charles, 204–5n10
Dickens, Charles, 9, 39, 88, 109, 117–18, 159, 161, 210n18; on Bluebeard, x. *See also* chapbook: illustration
Dickens and the Invisible World, 39
Die Kinder- und Hausmärchen. *See* Grimm, Jacob and Wilhelm: *Die Kinder- und Hausmärchen; Kinder- und Hausmärchen*
Die Märchentypen des "Ritter Blaubart" und "Fitchervogel," 179n6
"Discreet Princess, The," 38
Dmytryk, Edward, 162–65, 186n16
Doane, Mary Ann, 155, 219nn11–12, 220nn17–18. See also *Desire to Desire: The Woman's Film of the 1940s, The*
Döblin, Alfred, 216n30
"Doctor Forster," 182n10
"Don Firriuleiddu," 5. *See also* Bluebeard: folkloric elements
Don Juan, 180n9
Dooley-McHaffie-Lewis-Meyer-Southard-Whitlock-Shaw, Lyda, 32. *See also* lady Bluebeard
Doré, Gustave, 109
Doutrepont, Georges, 60, 197n33
Down There, 133
Dragonwyck, 155
Dramas for the Drawing Room; or Charades for Christmas, 106
Dreyfus Affair, 133, 144, 213n7, 215n24
Dubois, Diane, 171, 221n16
Duer, Edward Rush, 212n3
Dugaw, Diane, ix

Dukas, Paul, 133, 138–40, 144, 151, 212n5, 213n8, 215n24
Duke Bluebeard's Castle, 16–17, 133, 141–43, 147, 159, 177, 215–16nn28–31, 217n33
Dulac, Edmund, 131, 203n36
Dussek, O. B., 211n29

Eden, Governor Charles, 22, 23, 25, 185n4. *See also* Teach, Captain Edward
Edgworth, Maria, 108
Edwardes, Anthony, 156. *See also* Ballantyne, John
Elliott, Phil, 168
Ellis, T. E., 212n3
Ellms, Charles, 22. *See also* Teach, Captain Edward
Elsaesser, Thomas, 219n11
English Fairy and Other Folk Tales, 114
English Fairy Tales, 114
Enter Foot and Horse, 198–99n45
Estés, Clarissa Pinkola, 180n15
Eulenberg, Herbert, 216n30
Eve (biblical), xv, 15, 16, 79, 105, 125
Ewing, Juliana Horatia, 118–19
Ewing, Montague, xvi, 180n13
Experiment Perilous, 155, 156–57, 219n13
extravaganza, 91, 93, 97–101, 206–7n20

Fables, x
Faerie Queene, The, xi, 10, 113
"Fair Young Bride, The," 7. *See also* Bluebeard: folkloric elements
Fairy Songs and Ballads for the Young, 211n29
"Fairy Tale of the Natchez Trace," 218n8
"Faithful John," 110, 181n2
Fatal Curiosity, 55, 194–95n15, 196n17. See also *Guilt Its Own Punishment; or, Fatal Curiosity*; Lillo, George
Fatima, ix, xiv, 50, 51, 52, 53–54, 60–64, 70, 71, 74, 75, 76–77, 79–80, 81, 85–86, 88, 89, 95, 96, 97, 99, 100, 102, 104, 105–8, 115–17, 121, 122–23, 129, 131–32, 145, 146, 147, 195n22, 198n40, 201n9, 201n11, 202n16, 202n22, 204–5n10, 206n18, 208n28, 210n15, 211–12n29, 212n3, 219–20n13, 220n2, 222n4. *See also* Bluebeard: Turk/oriental
fée. *See* Bluebeard: *fée* (fairy/enchanted) elements
Female Bluebeard, or, The Adventures of Polyphemus Amador de Croustillac, The, 91. See also *Devil's Mount, or, the Female Bluebeard, The*
female curiosity. *See* Bluebeard: archetypes
"Fichters [sic] Vogel." *See* "Fitcher's Bird"
Fielding, Henry, 194–95n15
Fifth Wife of Bluebeard, The, 184–85n29
"55 Miles to the Gas Pump," 169–70
Fiske, Roger, 195n22
Fitcher's Bird, 162, 167–68
"Fitcher's Bird," xi, 3, 5–7, 12, 13, 110, 167–68, 170, 174, 175, 178, 181–82n6, 182n8, 186n17, 208–9nn3–4, 209nn7–8, 221n19; plot, 5–6
"Fitcher's Feathered Bird," 222n21
"Fitcher's Vogel." *See* "Fitcher's Bird"
Five Forbidden Things, 169
Flahault, François, 180–81n16
Flinders, Peter, xiii, 46, 188–89n9, 190n14, 191n25. *See also* Bluebeard: historical interpretation
Folk-Lore Society, 114
Folktale, The, 37, 181n5
Forrester, Alfred Henry, 109, 124
Forty Thieves, The, 194n13
Foster, Alice Monro, 212n3
Foster, Jodie, 172–73
Four and Twenty Blubeards, 159
Four and Twenty Tales, 111–12
Foy, Eddie, xii, 130, 212n2
France, Anatole, 133, 136–38, 148, 213–14n13–14
"Frauds on the Fairies," 117
Fremlin, Celia, 170
French feminism, 135
Freud, Sigmund. *See* psychology: Freud, Sigmund
Frigon, Sylvie, 155
Frisch, Max, 160
Frost, Gregory, xi
Furlan, Pierre, 178

G. M., 32–42, 43, 44, 46, 47–49, 50, 51, 70, 81, 112–13, 182–83n19, 187–88nn4–6, 188–90nn9–12, 191n20, 191–92n27, 192n2, 209n9. *See also* Miège, Guy
"Gaffer Blackbeard," 27, 201n11. *See also* Bluebeard: as pirate; *New History of Blue Beard, written by Gaffer Blackbeard, for the Amusement of Little Lack Beard and His Pretty Sisters, A*
Gaiman, Neil, 170
Galland, Antoine, 14, 192n5
Garrick, David, 54, 91, 205n12
Gaslight, 155, 157, 219–20nn13–14
Gaudreault, André, 213n11
Gein, Ed, 32, 221n15. *See also* serial killer

General History of Pirates, A, 21. *See also* Blackbeard; Bluebeard: as pirate
"Gentle Miss Bluebeard, The," 220n15
"George and Vivian," 222n22
German Popular Stories, 5, 110, 113, 123, 182n9
Gerring, Charles, 200n5
Gilbert-Holland, Josiah, 108
Gill, Brendan, 150
Gillet, Sue, 173
"Girl Who Got up a Tree, The," 182nn12–13
Godwin, William, 52, 57–59, 196nn25–26
Goffe, Thomas, 193–94n10
Golden Ass, The, 15. *See also* myth
Good Housekeeping, 27–28. *See also* Bluebeard: as pirate
Goring, Charles, 54
gothic, 6–7, 57–59, 75, 87, 120, 133, 146, 154–58, 195n22, 196n26, 198n40, 203n31, 204n3, 210n20, 219–20nn11–18. See also *Blue Beard; or, Female Curiosity!*
Gower, Francis, 104
Grace, Sherrill E., 222n23
"Grand March" (Michael Kelly), 61, 95–96, 99, 101, 106, 198n40, 198n42, 208n30, 209–10n12
Grand Opera House and Cirque, The (Belfast), xii
"Grand Pantomime of Blue Beard," 204–5n10
Grant, Cary, 156
Grant, Julian, 216–17n32
Gravenhurst, x
Green, Ward, 162, 163
Grétry, André Ernest Modeste, 51, 55–56, 60, 195n20, 198–99n45
Grimaldi, Joseph, 204–5n10, 205–6n14
Grimm, Jacob and Wilhelm, xi, xiii–xiv, xvi, 3, 5, 13, 37, 38, 107, 113, 149, 150, 161, 170, 174, 180n8, 181n2, 209n4; *Die Kinder- und Hausmärchen*, 109–11
Gufler, Max, 31. *See also* serial killer
Guilt Its Own Punishment; or, Fatal Curiosity, 55, 195n17. See also *Fatal Curiosity*
Gunness, Belle, 32. *See also* lady Bluebeard
Gunning, Tom, 213n12

Hailes. *See* N. Hailes
Halliwell-Phillipps, James Orchard, 113
Halvéy, Ludovic, 89, 101–3
Hamlet, 156
Handmaid's Tale, The, 222n23
Hannon, Patricia, xiii, 191n24. *See also* Bluebeard: historical interpretation
Hard Times, 117
"Hare's Bride, The," 7, 12, 110. *See also* Bluebeard: folkloric elements
Harlequin, 27, 92, 94, 204–5nn10–12
Harlequin and Blue Beard, 92, 93, 204–5n10
Harlequin and Bluebeard, 204n8
Harlequin Blue Beard, the great bashaw, or The good fairy triumphant over the demon of discord! A Grand Comic Christmas Pantomime, 94–96
Harlequin Bluebeard (1840), 204–5n10
Harlequin Bluebeard (1864), 204–5n10
Harlequin Fat and Harlequin Bat, or, The Giant's Causeway, 206n15
harlequinade, 91–97, 177, 204n7, 204–5n10, 205nn11–12, 206n15, 206–7n10. *See also* pantomime
Harris, Thomas, 171
Hartland, Edwin Sidney, 114, 186n17
"Häsichenbraut." *See* "Hare's Bride, The"
Haskell, Molly, 219n11
Hastings, Warren, 54, 194n14
Hay, Sara Henderson, 168, 169
Headless Horseman and Other Ghoulish Tales, The, x. *See also* Bluebeard: censorship
Hearn, Michael Patrick, 188–89n9
Heatherton, Joey, 164
Hebbel, Friedrich, 142, 216–17n32, 217n34
Hempen, Daniela, xviii. *See also* Bluebeard: feminist interpretation
"Hen Is Tripping in the Mountain," 7. *See also* Bluebeard: folkloric elements
Henry VIII, xi, xiv, 17, 18–19, 98, 106, 184–85nn29–31, 207n23, 209–10n12
Henvey, Lt. Col. R., 212n3
Hermansson, Casie E., xviii, 210n16, 210n20, 221n5, 222n23. *See also* Bluebeard: feminist interpretation
Herzog, Josef, 179n6
Hesiod, 15
"Hesitations Outside the Door," 175–76
Higgie, Thomas, 91
Hiltbrunner, Michael, 213n10
Hippotheatron, xii, 179n3
Hiss and Yell, 155
History of Blue Beard (1852), 79–81
History of Blue Beard (W. Davison), 77, 86
History of Blue Beard (J. L. Marks), 201n12
History of Blue Beard, The (W. S. Johnson), 199n2
History of Bluebeard (E. Billing), 83

History of Bluebeard: An Entertaining Story for Children, The, 78
History of Bluebeard's Six Wives, The, 121–22
History of the Cruel Monster Blue-beard, 74
Hitchcock, Alfred, 155, 220n15
Hoch, Johann Otto, 31. *See also* serial killer
HoHo and HaHa: Adventures Narrated and Illustrated, 122
Holland, Sarah, 168
Holmes, H. H., 29–30
Home Acting for Amateurs, 212n4, 221n18
"Honeymoon of Mrs. Smith, Version I, The," 169
"Honeymoon of Mrs. Smith, Version II: The Mystery of the Murdered Bride, The," 169
Hood, G. P. Jacomb, 113
"Hop o' My Thumb," 117, 210n17
Hopwood, Avery, 151
Horrocks, G. G., 212n3
"House in the Forest, The," 110
Household Stories, 110
Household Words, 117
"How the Devil Married Three Sisters," 7. *See also* Bluebeard: folkloric elements
Howell, George, 221n8
Howitt, Mary, 113
Hughes, Leo, 204n8
Hunt, Leigh, 93, 109
Hürlimann, Bettina, 192n5
"Hut in the Forest, The," 181n2
Hutcheon, Linda, 220n1
Huysmans, Joris Karl, 133

Iles, Frances, 156
image. *See* chapbook: illustration
"Ímarasugssauq, Who Ate His Wives," 7. *See also* Bluebeard: folkloric elements
In Bluebeard's Castle, 217n33
Inn of Disenchantment, The, 144–45
"Instructions for Navigating the Labyrinth," 160
Irene, 54
Irene, 52, 53–54, 56, 60–61, 63, 195n22
Irene, a Tragedy, 54
Irene, or the Fair Greek, 54
Iron Chest, The, 52, 55, 57–59, 195–96n24–25. See also *armoire de fer*
Iroquois Theatre, fire, xii, 130, 212n2. See *Mr. Bluebeard*
Isaure, 55–56

"Jack and Old Bluebeard," 182n15
"Jack and the Devil," 182n11
"Jack Tale," 12. *See also* "Mr. Fox"
Jackson, Shirley, 169
Jacobs, Joseph, 114
Jacques, C. H. B., 212n3
James, George Payne Rainsford, 107, 115–16
Jane Eyre (1847), 109, 119, 210n20, 211n26, 222n3
Jane Eyre (1944), 155, 219n13
Jenkins, E. Lawrence, 130–31
Jennings, Gertrude, 220n2
Joan of Arc, 18, 133, 213n7
John Adams 1804, 201n11
John Babcock 1800, 201n11
John M'Culloch 1797, 82
Johnson, Captain Charles, 21, 22, 23, 25, 26, 185n4. *See also* Teach, Captain Edward
Johnson, Clifton, 200n4
Johnson, Dr. Samuel, 54
Jones, Stephen, 197n35
Judith, 142–43, 216–17n32, 217n34
Judith: Sexual Warrior, 216n31, 217n34
"Judith: The Significance of the Name," 216n31
Judith of Holofernes, 15, 16–17, 141–43, 167, 211n26, 216–17nn31–32, 217n34
Jung, Carl. *See* psychology: Jung, Carl
"Jurma," 7. *See also* Bluebeard: folkloric elements

Karloff, Boris, xii, 220n16
Kast, Verena, xvi. *See also* Bluebeard: feminist interpretation; psychology: Jung, Carl
Kean, Edmund, xi, 64, 195–96n24
Keating, E. H. (Eliza H.), 106
Keaton, Buster, 155
Keene, Laura, 204n8
"Keepsake for Children, A," 78
Keller, Loren, 159
Kelly, Michael, xi, 37, 51, 55–56, 57, 58, 60–66, 99, 106, 194n13, 208n30; collaboration with George Colman (*see* Colman-Kelly; Colman, George [younger]); inspiration for melodrama (see *Raoul Barbe Bleue*); memoirs of, 56, 60, 64–65, 195n20, 197n39, 198n44. See also *Blue Beard, or, Female Curiosity!*
Kelly, Tim J., 159
Kemble, John Philip, 58, 65, 198–99n45
Kenrick, John, 204–5n10
Kerrigan, John, 217n1
key (fairy/enchanted), 137. *See also* Bluebeard: *fée* (fairy/enchanted) elements
"Key to Bluebeard's Heart, The," 221n11
KHM. See *Kinder- und Hausmärchen*
Kilmer, Aline, 222n4

Kinder- und Hausmärchen, 208–9n3; editions, 5 (see also *German Popular Stories*; Taylor, Edgar); English translations, 5, 37; illustration of, 5; as nationalist, xiii–xiv
King, Rufus, 176
King Arthur, 183n21, 193n9
King Lear, 154
Klein, Kevin, 218n5
Knez, Dora, 169
Kodály, Zoltán, 215–16n29
Kudszus, Winfried, xvi. *See also* psychology: Freud, Sigmund

"La Barbe Bleue," 3–5, 12, 13, 24, 37–50, 113; dedication of manuscript, 84–85, 190n16, 190n18, 203n32; illustration, 38; morals, 49–50; plot, ix–x, 4–5. *See also* Bluebeard; Perrault, Charles: *Mother Goose*
Là-Bas. See *Down There*
Lacan, Jacques. *See* psychology: Lacan, Jacques
lady Bluebeard, 29, 31, 32–33, 186n20. *See also* serial killer
"Lady Bluebeard, The," 32
Lady Bluebeard: The True Story of Love and Marriage, Death and Flypaper, 32
Lady Isabel, 12, 215–16n29. *See also* ballad
"Lady Isabel and the Elf Knight," 182n14
Lady Oracle, 175
Landru, 30
Landru, Henri Désiré, 30, 31, 186n13, 186n16
Lane, Edward, 109
Lang, Andrew, 14–15, 41, 109, 112–13, 182–83n19, 186n4, 188–89nn9–10, 209n11
Lang, Fritz, 157
Lardner, Ring, 132, 145
"Lass 'At Seed Her Awn Graave Dug," 182n12
Le Men, Ségolène, 84, 202–3n30, 203nn32–33
Leafstedt, Carl, 213n7, 214n17, 215n29, 216–17nn30–32
Lee, Robert, 22, 23, 24, 25, 185nn3–4. *See also* Teach, Captain Edward
Leeds, Mrs. Lucy A., 183n20
Leigh, Olivia, 184–85n29
Leno, Dan, 129
"Les Sept Femmes de la Barbe Bleue." *See* "Seven Wives of Bluebeard, The"
Les Usages de l'imprimé, 203n33
Lewis, Matthew Gregory, 52, 192n4
Lewis, Philip, xiii, 180–81n16. *See also* Bluebeard: historical interpretation; psychology: Lacan, Jacques
L'Héritier de Villandon, Marie Jeanne, 38, 187n4
Licensing Act, 97, 205–6nn14–15, 206n19
"Life of a Farm Worker, The," 201n8
Lillo, George, 55, 194–95n15, 195nn17–18
"Lillo's Fatal Curiosity," 195n16
Lim, Bliss, 221n13
Little Women, 123
Lives and Loves of a Modern Bluebeard, 162, 163
Lo Cunto deli Cunti overo Lo Trattenemiento de' Peccerille. *See* Pentamerone, The
"Lonton Lass," 182n12
Lot's wife, 15, 16
Louis XVI, 52, 58. See also *armoire de fer*
Love from a Stranger, 151, 219n13
Love Murders of Harry F. Powers: Beware Such Bluebeards, 31. *See also* serial killer
Love Stories of Some Famous Pirates, 185n5. *See also* Teach, Captain Edward
Lovell-Smith, Rose, xviii. *See also* Bluebeard: feminist interpretation
Lubitsch, Ernst, 151
Ludlam, Charles, 159

Macbeth, 55
MacKenzie, Henry, 194
MacPherson, Jay, 170
Madame Vestris, 97
Madeleva, Sister M.,138
Madonna's Secret, The, 155
Madore, Nancy, 221n10
Maeterlinck, Maurice, 133, 134, 138–39, 144, 151, 212n5, 213n8, 214n17, 214n21, 215n24, 215n27
Malarte-Feldman, Claire-Lise, 188–89n9, 190n13, 190–91nn15–19
Mank, Gregory, 220n16
Manley, Kathleen, 222n23
Märchen, xiii–xiv. *See also* Grimm, Jacob and Wilhelm
Marcus, Jane, 217n33, 217n2 (chap. 9)
"Marienkind." *See* "Mary's Child"
Marriott, Charles, 212n6
Marrs, Suzanne, 149, 218–19n9
Marvel Comic Book, 27
"Mary, the Maid of the Inn," 9. *See also* "Mr. Fox"
"Marya Morévna," xv, 181n2
"Mary's Child," xv, 3, 110, 181n2, 182n7, 209n8
May Colven, 12. *See also* ballad
Mayer, David, 204–5n10, 206n19
Maynard, Lt., 25. *See also* Teach, Captain Edward
McBurney, William, 194–95nn15–18

McLoughlin Bros., 76, 77, 81, 202n19
McMaster, Juliet, xiv, 209–10nn12–14, 210n17, 222n23
McPherson, Don, 27. *See also* Bluebeard: as pirate
Meilhac, Henri, 89, 101–3
Méliès, Georges, 133, 134–35, 136, 158, 171, 213nn8–9, 213nn12–13
melodrama, 94, 195n23, 196n25, 198n40, 206n16
Melville, Herman, x
Memoirs of Barry Lyndon, The, 114, 117, 209–10n12, 210n20
Menninghaus, Winfried, 196–97n30
Mercedita, 27, 28. *See also* Bluebeard: as pirate
Merington, Marguerite, 145, 212n3, 215n26
Merry, James, 172
Miège, Guy, 40, 191n20. *See also* G. M.
Millay, Edna St. Vincent, 138, 177, 222n4
Mille et une Nuits. See *Thousand and One Arabian Nights, The*
Miller, Annie, 12, 215–16n29. *See also* ballad
Miller, Lydia, 170
Millward, Charles, 51, 96–97, 206n18
Millward's pantomime, 96–97; cross-dressed casting in, 96. *See also* Bluebeard: cross-dressed casting
Miss Bluebeard (1925), 151
Miss Bluebeard (silent film), 151
Mme L'Heritier. See *Mother Goose*
Modern Mephistopheles, A, 123
Monsarrat, Ann, 119
Monsieur Verdoux, 155, 156
Moon Knight, 27
Moore, Emily Ruth, xix, 211nn23–24, 222n23. *See also* Bluebeard: feminist interpretation
Morton, John, 94, 95–96
Morton's pantomime, 95–96; cross-dressed casting in, 96. *See also* Bluebeard: cross-dressed casting
Mother Goose (Charles Perrault), 38, 41–42, 50, 108, 131, 188n7, 189n10; chapbooks (*see* chapbooks); dedication manuscript of, 38; first publication, 84–85; original contents, 38, 187nn1–2; pirated editions, 39; translations into English, 14, 37, 53 (*see also* Samber, Robert; G. M.). *See also* "La Barbe Bleue"
Mother Goose Tales, 38, 113
Motley, John Lathrop, 59, 90–91
Mowshowitz, Harriet, 180–81n16, 181n3, 183n23, 197nn33–34, 214n15
Mr. Bluebeard, xii, 129–30, 212n2
"Mr. Bluebeard," 5. *See also* Bluebeard: folkloric elements
"Mr. Foster," 9. *See also* Bluebeard: folkloric elements; "Mr. Fox"
"Mr. Fox," xi, 3, 9–12, 112, 113–14, 121, 145, 161, 170, 174, 177, 178, 182nn12–13, 186n17
Mrs. Inchbald's *British Theatre*, 58
Much Ado About Nothing, xi, 10
Mudgett, Herman. *See* Holmes, H. H.; serial killer
Muir, Percy, 53, 192n5
Muller, Romeo, 27. *See also* Bluebeard: as pirate
Mulvey, Laura, 219n11, 221n9
"Murder Castle, The." *See* "Castle of Murder, The"
Museum Piece No. 13, 157, 176
Mystery of Edwin Drood, The, 117
myth, 14–16, 138

Namjoshi, Suniti, 170
Napoleon Bonaparte, 192n4
Nelson, Resa, 221n11
Neuburg, Victor, 199n1, 200n6
New History of Blue Beard, Written by Gaffer Blackbeard, for the Amusement of Little Lack Beard and his Pretty Sisters, A, 199–200n3
New York Ballet, xii, 179n4
New York World, The, 30. *See also* Holmes, H. H.
Newcomes, The, 209–10n12
Nicholson, Watson, 206n19
Nietzsche, Friedrich, 133, 144
Nights at the Circus, 221n19
noir films, 145, 155
Northanger Abbey, 175, 210n20
Notorious, 155, 220n14
Novello, Sabilla, 121–22
"Nurse's Stories." *See* "Captain Murderer"

Odio, Elena Baca, xiii, 183n23. *See also* Bluebeard: historical interpretation
O'Donnell, Peter, 179n1
Offenbach, Jacques, 207–8nn26–27, 213n13
"Ogre Courting, The," 118–19
"Oh! Mr. Bluebeard," 161, 215n26
"Old Bluebeard," 12, 174. *See also* "Mr. Fox"
Old Curiosity Shop, The, 210n18
"Old Foster." *See* "Mr. Foster"
"Old Rinkrank," 110
Old Story Teller: Popular German Tales, The, 110

"Oll Rinkrank." *See* "Old Rinkrank"
"On Pantomime," 93
opera bouffe, 91, 97, 101–3, 207n26
operetta, 207n24, 208n28, 213n13
Opie and Opie, 188n10, 201n9
oriental. *See* Bluebeard: Turk/oriental
Ormond, Mary, 22, 25–26, 185n3. *See also* Teach, Captain Edward
Orpheus, 15–16
Osmond the Great Turk, 193–94n10
Othello, 46, 47–48, 52, 53, 55, 89, 99–100, 104, 106, 107, 112, 182–83n19, 193nn7–8, 193–94n10, 195n18
"Our Lady's Child." *See* "Mary's Child"
Our Mutual Friend, 117
"Oxford Student, The," 9, 113, 182n12. *See also* "Mr. Fox"

Pandora, 15, 16. *See also* myth
Pantaloon, 66, 92, 94, 129, 204–5n10
pantomime, 91–97, 129, 130, 173, 176, 177, 204n3, 204–5nn8–10, 205n12, 206n15, 206–7n20, 212n3, 222n3. *See also* harlequinade
parlor plays. *See* amateur and parlor plays
Payne, John, 109
Paynter, William, 194n11
Peele, George, 193–94n10
Pendennis, 209–10n12
Penny Histories, The, 199n1, 200n6
Pentamerone, The, 14
"Perifool," 13, 179n5, 182n12. *See also* "Mr. Fox"
Perrault, Charles, xi, 3, 21, 24, 26, 28, 29, 37–50, 53, 60, 71, 73, 82, 89, 90, 102, 108, 110, 112, 113, 131, 136, 148, 161, 166, 170, 174, 178, 180n8, 182–83n19, 184n27, 188–89nn9–10, 190n13, 213n10, 213–14n14, 214n18, 215n27; authorship of *Mother Goose*, 38–39, 187n1, 187n4; debate with Nicholas Boileau, xiii; difficulty in translating, 42–49, 77–78, 82, 112, 187n3, 189n10, 190n15, 190–91n19, 191nn22–23; as lawyer, xiii, 79, 191n25; manuscript of *Contes*, 84–85. *See also* "La Barbe Bleue"
Perrault, Pierre. *See* Perrault, Charles
Perrault's Popular Tales, 14–15, 112
Phantom of the Plains, 155
Philip, Neil, 42, 189n10, 190–91n19, 191–92n27
Piano, The, x, 160, 171, 173, 221n18
Pichérit, Jean-Louis, xiii. *See also* Bluebeard: historical interpretation
Pickwick Papers, The, 117
pirate. *See* Bluebeard: as pirate; Teach, Captain Edward
Pirate Rascals of the Spanish Main, 24. *See also* Teach, Captain Edward
Pirates Own Book, 22
Pitt, William, 192n4
Planché, James Robinson, 18, 53, 93, 97–101, 104, 111–12, 183n22, 191n23, 206n15, 206n19, 207n22; memoirs of, 98; style of extravaganza, 206–7n20. *See also* Dance, Charles
Plath, Sylvia, 170
Poets Grimm, The, 170
Popular Rhymes and Nursery Tales: A Sequel to the Nursery Rhymes of England, 113
Popular Story of Blue Beard, or, Female Curiosity, The, 199n2
Popular Story of Blue Beard, or, the Effects of Female Curiosity, The, 199n2
Porter, Susan L., 195n20, 195n22, 198nn41–44
Potter, Beatrix, xii, 146
Powers, Harry F., 31. *See also* serial killer
"Pretty Molly," 9. *See also* ballad
Pretty Polly, 11
"Pretty Polly," 9. *See also* ballad; cannibalism
Propp, Vladimir, xiv, xv. *See also* Bluebeard: archetypes
Proulx, Annie, 169–70
Psyche, xviii, 15, 16. *See also* myth; Psyche and Cupid
Psyche and Cupid, 215–16n29
Psycho, 32, 221n15. *See also* serial killer
psychology, 180n8; Freud, Sigmund xv, xvi, 133, 142, 144, 180n14; Jung, Carl, xvi, 180n8; Lacan, Jacques, xvii, 180n14
Puff the Magic Dragon, 27. *See also* Bluebeard: as pirate
"Puss in Boots," 39

Quiller-Couch, Sir Arthur, 131, 213–14n14

Racine, Pierre, 42, 190n14
Rackham, Arthur, 215–16n29
Rackham, Jack, 25. *See also* Teach, Captain Edward
Raoul Barbe Bleue, 51, 55–56
Raphoz, Fabienne, xiv. *See also* Bluebeard: archetypes
Reakes, Paul, 177
Rebecca, 155, 219n13
Reeve, William, 37, 56

Reminisances. *See* Kelly, Michael: memoirs of
Reward of Disobedience and Imprudent Curiosity, The, 79
Rhys, Jean, 222n3
Rich, John, 91, 204n8, 205n12
"Riddle Me, Riddle Me Right," 182n12
Rigby, Elizabeth, 119
Ritchie, Anne Thackeray, 119–21, 184–85n29, 211n23
Ritter Blaubart (1759), 52, 59, 90–91, 198–99n45
Ritter Blaubart (1905), 216n30
"Ritter Blaubart," 216n30
Robber Bride, The, 175, 222n23
Robber Bridegroom, The, 134, 146, 148–50, 218–19nn5–10
"Robber Bridegroom, The," xi, 3, 7–9, 110, 123, 170, 177, 178, 186n17, 209n4; plot, 7–8
"Robber Bridegroom, The" (1984), 175
"Robber's Bride, The," 7, 9. *See also* Bluebeard: folkloric elements; cannibalism
Roberts, Nancy, 21, 26. *See also* Blackbeard
Robinson, Corinne. *See* Roosevelt, Corinne
Robinson, James, 168
Robinson Crusoe, 205n12
Roosevelt, Corinne, 104, 208n29
Rose and the Ring, The, 209–10n12
Rose for Her Grave, A, 31. *See also* serial killer
Roth, Randy, 31. *See also* serial killer
Russell, Craig, 214n19
Russell, Diarmuid, 149
Ryan, Tracy, 221n12

Saint Tryphine et le roi Arthur. Mystère Breton en deux journées et huit actes, 183n21
Saintyves, P., xv, 180n10. *See also* Bluebeard: archetypes
Salomé, 217n34
Salome (biblical), 142
Samber, Robert, 4, 14, 37, 38, 39, 41–42, 43, 44, 46, 47–49, 50, 51, 52, 70, 77, 82, 89, 112, 187nn2–4, 188–90nn8–13, 191n20, 191–92n27, 209n9, 213–14n14
Samuel, Kenneth Ormsby, 121n3
Sanders, Bruce, 217n1
Sargood, Corinna, 174, 222n20
Saxon, A. H., 198–99n45
Saxon Childers, James, 182–83n19
Scaramouche. *See* Clown
Schaeffer, Susan Fromberg, 160, 169
Schechter, Harold, 30, 186nn10–11, 186n17, 221n15. *See also* Holmes, H. H.
Scheherezade, 13–14, 53, 148, 168, 192–93n6. *See also* Bluebeard: Turk/oriental; *Thousand and One Arabian Nights, The*
Schlobin, Roger, 180n9
Scott, Sir Walter, 70
Scurvy Dogs, 27
Secret Beyond the Door, 155, 157, 219–20nn13–14
"Secret Room, The," 12, 13. *See also* "Mr. Fox"
Secrets Beyond the Door: The Story of Bluebeard and His Wives, 212n6
Sedaine, Paul, 52, 55
Selim, xi–xii, xvi, 50, 51, 54, 60–64, 74, 89, 95, 96, 100, 101–2, 104, 105, 106–7, 129, 147, 194n13, 201n11, 204–5n10, 208n28, 212n3
Selim the Grim, 194n13
Sendak, Maurice, 222n21
serial killer, 29–33, 178, 221n6
"Seven Wives of Bluebeard, The," 133, 136, 148
Shadow of a Doubt, 155
Shakespeare, William, xi, 11, 47, 89, 90, 104, 137, 153–54, 195n18
Shakespeare *Varorium*, 114
Shaw, George Bernard, 159
Sheridan, Richard Brimsley, 65, 194n13, 205n12
Sherman, Cindy, xi, 162, 167–68, 171, 221nn8–9
Showalter, Elaine, 211nn26–27
Silence of the Lambs, The (film), 160, 171–73, 221nn16–17
Silence of the Lambs, The (novel), 172, 221n14
"Silvernose," 7. *See also* Bluebeard: folkloric elements
Simborowski, Nicoletta, 188n10, 191–92n27
Sine, Nadine, 217n34
Sister Anne, xii, 146, 219n13. *See also* Potter, Beatrix
Six Feet Under, x
Sleeping Beauty and Other Fairy Tales, The, 131
Smith, George, xiv
Smith, George Joseph, 31. *See also* serial killer
Solomon, Frederic, 129
"Solomon Bluebeard," 212n6
Somogyi, Peter J., 214n20
Somtow, S. P., 177
Spellbound, 155, 156, 219n13
Spenser, Edmund, xi, 10, 113
Spufford, Margaret, 39, 200n4
Squier, Emma Lindsey, 27–29. *See also* Bluebeard: as pirate
Squire King Caley, 182n10
St. Joan, 159
States, Janel, 180–81n16

Stein, Karen, 222n23
Steinbach, Meredith, 222n23
Steiner, George, 217n33
Stepford Wives, The, 221n13
Sterling, Charles, 31. *See also* serial killer
Stone, Kay, xv
Storace, Stephen, 58, 169
"Story about OhMy, The," 182n11
Story of Blue Beard, The (Thomas Nelson), 77, 81
"Story of the Eldest Princess, The," 169
"Story of the Third Calendar, The," xv, 13–14, 53, 182n7
Struggle for a Free Stage in London, The, 206n19
Sue, Eugène, 204n5
"Sultan and the Greek Slave Girl, The," 54
"Sultan and the Slave Girl (Irene), The," 52, 194n11
Suspicion, 155, 156
Swinhoe, Gilbert, 54, 193–94n10
"Syndicated Column," 168, 169

Tabart, Benjamin, 66, 208n1
Tale of Bluebeard in German Literature, The, 181n1, 190n15
Tales from the Ballet, 193n9
Tales Told Again. See *Told Again: Old Tales Told Again*
Taming of the Shrew, The, 153
Tatar, Maria, xiv, 155, 181n2, 209n8, 212n6, 220n14, 221n5, 222n23
Tate, Allen, 171
Taylor, Edgar, 5, 110, 113, 182n9, 209n8
Teach, Captain Edward, 21–26, 28, 186n8; Charles Town blockade, 23, 24; dealings with Governor Eden, 22, 23, 185n4; death of, 25; marriage to Mary Ormond, 22, 25, 185n3, 185n6; relationships with women, 23–24, 25, 185nn5–6. *See also* Blackbeard
[Ten] Favourite Stories for the Nursery, with Numerous Illustrations, 87
Tenant of Wildfell Hall, The, 210n20
Texas Chainsaw Massacre, The, 32, 221n15. *See also* serial killer
Thackeray, William Makepeace, 107, 109, 114–17, 120, 121, 123, 161, 209–10nn12–14, 210n20
Theater Regulation Act of 1843, 97, 205–6n14
Thief of Souls, 18
Third Calendar. *See* "Story of the Third Calendar, The"
Thiselton-Dyer, T., 194–95n15
Thomason, Caroline, 212n3, 221n18
Thomson, Peter, 206–7n20
Thomson, Peter G., 201n10
Thompson, Stith, xiv, xv, 37, 181n5. *See also* Aarne-Thompson
Thousand and One Arabian Nights, The, xv, 13–14, 53, 182n7, 182nn17–18, 184–85n29, 192–93nn5–6
Three Naughty Sisters Meet Bluebeard, The, 159–60
Tieck, Ludwig, xvi, 52, 59, 90–91, 196–97nn30–31. *See also* Motley, John Lathrop
Timour the Tartar, 198–99n45
Told Again: Old Tales Told Again, 214n18
Too Much Bluebeard, 220n2
Torrens, Henry, 109
Tragedy of the Unhappy Fair Irene, The, 54, 193–94nn10–11
Trilling, Lionel, 149
Troubadours of Divine Bliss, x
Trueblood, Anna Eliza. *See* Dooley-McHaffie-Lewis-Meyer-Southard-Whitlock-Shaw, Lyda
Tully, J. H., 97, 101–3
Turk. *See* Bluebeard: Turk/oriental
Turkish Mahomet and Hyrin the Fair Greek, 193–94n10
Tuthill, Allison, xv. *See also* Bluebeard: archetypes
Two Mrs. Carrolls, The, 151, 157, 162, 220n17
Tyre, Nedra, 220n15

Uhry, Alfred, 150, 218–19nn5–9
Ulmer, Edgar, xii, 155–56, 157, 162, 220n16
Uncommercial Traveller, The, 117
Under the Lilacs, 122–23
Undercurrent, 155, 219n13
"Underworld Adventure, The," 182n15
Unhappy Fair Irene. See *Tragedy of the Unhappy Fair Irene, The*
Untermeyer, Louis, 193n9
Updike, John, 222n22
Uses of Enchantment, The, xv–xvi

Valentine, Mrs. L., 212n4, 221n18
Van Raamsdonk, Renée, xiii. *See also* Bluebeard: historical interpretation
Vanity Fair, 209–10n12
variants. *See* Bluebeard: international variants; Bluebeard: nationalistic interpretation
Velay-Vallantin, Catherine, xiii, 203n33. *See also* Bluebeard: historical interpretation

Verhoeven, W. M., 196n26, 196n28
Verill, A. Hyatt, 185n5
"Visiting," 170
"Visual Pleasure and Narrative Cinema," 219n11
Vitkus, Daniel, 53, 193–94n10
Vonnegut, Kurt, 160, 179n1

W. Walker & Sons, 74, 79, 201n10, 201n14
Wagner, Richard, 215n24, 216n30
Waldman, Robert, 218n5
Walker, Cheryl, xviii, 222n23
Wallace and Gromit, 177
Warner, Marina, xiii, 171
Warner, Sylvia Townsend, 134, 146–48, 217–18nn2–4
Watson, James "Bluebeard," 31. *See also* serial killer
Weiss, Harry, 69, 83, 199–200n3
Weldon, Fay, 168–69
Welty, Eudora, xi, 134, 146, 148–50, 218–19nn5–9
"White Dove, The," 181n3
"White Road, The," 170
Wide Sargasso Sea, 222n23
"Widow and Her Daughters, The," 13, 182n15. *See also* "Mr. Fox"
"Wife Killer, The," 170
Wiggin, Kate, 144
Wilde, Oscar, 142, 217n34
Williams, Linda, 221n17
Wilson, Sharon Rose, 222n23
Witches Brew, 220n15
Wolf, Leonard, 184n27
Wollstonecraft (Shelley), Mary, 192n4
Woman's Film of the 1940s. See *Desire to Desire: The Woman's Film of the 1940s, The*
Women Bluebeards, 32. *See also* lady Bluebeard
Women Who Run with the Wolves, 180n15
Wood, J. Hickory, 129
Works and Days, 15
Wynne, Wish, 131, 132

Ysaye, Lisa, 145

Zipes, Jack, xiii, 108, 110, 112, 180–81n16, 181–82n6, 188n10, 190n13, 190–91n19, 209n8, 211n24